LAWRENCE

τὰ περὶ τὸ σῶμα μέχρι τῆς χρείας ψιλῆς παραλάμβανε, οἷον τροφάς, πόμα, ἀμπεχόνην, οἰκίαν, οἰκετίαν· τὸ δὲ πρὸς δόξαν ἢ τρυφὴν ἄπαν περίγραφε.

In things that pertain to the body take only as much as your bare need requires, I mean such things as food, drink, clothing, shelter, and household slaves; but cut down everything that is for outward show or luxury.

EPICTETUS, *The Encheiridion*

∽⚭∾

TATTERED
FLAG

Tattered Flag Press · East Sussex

LAWRENCE

WARRIOR AND SCHOLAR

BRUCE LEIGH

To:
Amoghavajri Leigh
Ronald S. Pickersgill
Graham Chainey
Anthony Lines

The Author

Bruce Leigh has held a deep interest in T.E. Lawrence since the age of fourteen. He has spent many subsequent years studying the literature and historiography of Lawrence, and reflecting upon the 'enigma' of the man, his extraordinary life and activities. He holds a degree in Politics and Philosophy and has persistent interests in music, philosophy and the Classical World. He also shares Lawrence's passion for churches and castles and was a Church Custodian for the Churches Conservation Trust as well as a member of the T.E.Lawrence Society.

He lives in Brighton with his wife, where he spends his time teaching violin, reading philosophy, occasionally writing poetry, and studying Classical Greek and Buddhism. He has also, on occasion, played amplified electric violin with an improvisational fusion band. This is his first book.

Published in Great Britain in 2014 by
Tattered Flag Press
11 Church Street
Ticehurst
East Sussex TN5 7AH
England

office@thetatteredflag.com
www.thetatteredflag.com

Tattered Flag Press is an imprint of Chevron Publishing Ltd.

Lawrence
© Bruce Leigh

Jacket Design and Typeset: Mark Nelson, NSW

Cover photograph: Getty Images
British Library Cataloguing in Publication Data

A Catalogue Record for this book is available from the British Library

ISBN 978-0-9543115-7-5

Printed and bound in Great Britain

For more information on books published by Tattered Flag Press visit
www.thetatteredflag.com

CONTENTS

ACKNOWLEDGEMENTS

FIRSTLY, I would like to elaborate here on the debts of gratitude I owe to my dedicatees and others. To my wife Linda/Amoghavajri Leigh who has shown great patience over the years with my preoccupations, and she has been an unfailing help with the computer. To Ron Pickersgill who gave me my first book on Lawrence when I was fourteen. To my friend Graham Chainey, a Lawrence scholar with a deep knowledge of the subject, and a copious memory. Also to Anthony Lines for support and help in the fraught early days of writing and also in the search for a publisher.

Secondly, I would like to register my debt to the many scholars and translators whose books I have read with interest and profit. Their books feature in the bibliography: and without their expertise on Chivalry, Classical Greek Stoicism and Cynicism in particular, and Ancient philosophy in general, I would not have been able to write this book.

Thirdly, I register here my gratitude to my editor, Robert Forsyth of Chevron Publishing and Tattered Flag Press. His careful editing has greatly improved my original manuscript. He is the only publisher with the bottle to publish this book, which is *sui generis*.

Finally, any errors of fact or interpretation are entirely mine.

Bruce Leigh
Sussex 2013

INTRODUCTION

Why Lawrence?

Another book on Lawrence? Who was he anyway?

MOST people have either seen the film of his exploits in Arabia, or come across, if not read, one of the many books about him. Even so, there is something elusive about this small but charismatic fellow. In one sense he is an intellectual Victorian – born in 1888—who seems to mutate into many different figures as he enters the 20th Century – only to die suddenly in a motorcycle crash in 1935. His wandering parents finally settle in Oxford, where he and his four brothers – all illegitimate – proceed successfully through the classical and Christian education, which the city had offered for so long. He shows from the earliest days an unusual character, combining practical skills, a strong antiquarian bent and an interest in archaeology, with a cult of self-hardening; an urge to explore the limits of the physical and mental self beyond the complacencies of his class and time. His later fame, resting on his extraordinary achievements in helping to foment and lead the revolt of the nomadic and feuding Arabs in the First World War, is only one facet of his life. Equally, he could live on as a brilliant letter-writer, a diplomat, archaeologist, historian, or as a practitioner and theorist of guerrilla warfare, and developer of speedboats for the RAF. Critics still argue about the merits and demerits of his account of the Arab Revolt, the *Seven Pillars of Wisdom* and his book about the beginnings of the RAF, *The Mint*, written from the inside as a nobody with another name. Whatever may be the case, along with the letters, they will ensure his place in English writing.

The general account of his life has been rehearsed by many authors. In a broad sense the writing about him may be divided between two main types: the historical overviews (for or against), and the 'anoraks'—the latter perhaps more interested in photographing the factory which made the spark plugs for his motorcycles. Although they are both useful, they are not what interest me. In my view, Lawrence is nothing if he is not a Mind. Accordingly, I go in search of this Mind, trying to understand and to begin to delineate it via his formation and experience. It is because he mixed with all classes, and certainly knew the powerful and influential people of his time, that I begin with his judgement of Ronald Storrs, who was military Governor of Jerusalem and Oriental Secretary in Cairo. Storrs was of a similar intellectual calibre and formation; therefore, I believe their mutual appraisal is instructive.

Finally, I do believe that there is something to be learnt from Lawrence's life and writings, and that there is a message in them which our times need, even though we are very unlikely to hear it or believe it. By trying to delineate his mind and personality, my hope is that some, however few, will hear this message and even transmit it to the future.

'His shadow would have covered our work and British policy in the East like a cloak, had he been able to deny himself the world, and to prepare his mind and body with the sternness of an athlete for a great fight.'

Seven Pillars of Wisdom, page 57, Penguin Edn. T.E.Lawrence's judgement of Ronald Storrs, Oriental Secretary, and page 37, 1922 Oxford Text.

As a youth of 14, interested in Lawrence, I was given a Penguin book, edited by David Garnett, called *The Essential T.E. Lawrence*. One passage, in which Garnett quotes Eric Kennington, has stayed with me ever since:

'I had long wished to get a statement from him, which would throw light on the spiritual difference I knew there was between us. What was his God? He answered without hesitation, and once more I missed his words, so beautiful was his face. He had a glory and a light shone in his eyes, but more of sunset, than sunrise or midday. What I think I heard in the flow of eloquence, was a record of process without aim or end, creation followed by dissolution, rebirth, and then decay to wonder at and to love. But not a hint of a god and certainly none of the Christian God.' [page 22]

Garnett adds: *'In other words T.E. Lawrence was a rationalist.'* I did not believe that he was a 'rationalist' then or now. What remained was the enigma of the missing words, and the question of how to understand what Kennington had recalled. In a sense the hunt was on, and only many years, and hundreds of books, later, did I understand what Lawrence was talking about.

In the following years, like many others, I read the various biographies, and the four main texts which Lawrence left us – *Crusader Castles*, the *Seven Pillars of Wisdom*, *The Mint*, and the *Collected Letters*.

It is not necessary to go very far into these books, or the surrounding literature, before coming across the critics and detractors. Lawrence could be evasive, posey, annoying, and apparently inconsistent. Our times are deeply impatient with the heroic, and lost in an automatic ironical treatment of all serious values. Ready to hand lie psychology, politics, sociology, and theories of ideology. More recently, the diffusion of a glib deconstruction has given relativism new instruments, and armed a generation of New Sophists. The '*Traison des Clercs*', at least of most public intellectuals, is evident in the strident confusion of the public culture, the loss of conviction in most judgements of evaluation, and a preoccupation with, what earlier times would have called, the trivial.

Easily, it seems, that Lawrence, and any 'god' he may have had, can be dismissed; masochist, homosexual, poseur, imperialist, militarist, elitist, liar. If I was convinced that any of these strictures were importantly true, I would not have begun this book, and gone in search of his philosophy of life. I shall return later to the arrangements Lawrence made to encounter more pain. So far as most psychology is concerned, like Sartre criticizing standard left views of Flaubert or Valery, I find little explained—certainly Flaubert was a petit bourgeois, but why was this particular petit bourgeois Flaubert?

If masochist and/or homosexual was the whole story, then Lawrence could have stayed in Oxford collegiate life, like Maurice Bowra and Dadie, or searched for rough trade in Soho. For those interested in the factual record, I refer them to Jeremy Wilson's magisterial study, and John E. Mack's compassionate *Prince of our Disorder*.

For myself, I am interested in something more complex and elusive, and I put aside as much as possible, any ready-to-hand explanatory devices and systems, and go in search of answers to the following questions which animate this book, as ways to discover the sources of his extraordinary energy and variety of achievement; his philosophy and practice during a life of such multiple activity.

1. Apart from ambition, what was it that got him to Damascus by the age of 30?

2. What motivated him, and gave him the strength to walk 1,100 miles through Syria, alone, at the age of 21, for his thesis about Crusader Castles?

3. To begin again, in 1922 in the RAF?

4. To turn away from food, sex, comfort, luxury, money, fame, much of the 20th century, and from most of the so-called necessities which sustain many other lives?

5. To change name, identity, career and milieux more than once?

Indeed, what was his god or his philosophy? Beginning the search for some answers, I did not, of course, expect a systematic belief system, or philosophy; perhaps a working ethic and practice, a particular comportment towards life, maybe something like the Regimen which Foucault begins to explore in his studies of the Stoics and early Christians.[1] Perhaps even a simpler version of the Regimen as it was formulated by Kant in *The Conflict of Faculties* (with a strikingly stoic flavour).[2] Reflecting more, and reading more deeply, I came to the realization that if there was any sense in the very idea of 'T.E. Lawrence's Philosophy', I was more likely to find it in the pre-Cartesian, pre-Modern, Ancient World sense: Philosophy as a way of life.[3] In any case, I resolved to look for it in the following:

1. What he read and wrote. After all, a primary part of his self definition was as a writer. In his books and judgements I would look for the Perspective, the valuations.

2. What he did.

3. What those who knew him said, such as Colonel W.F. Stirling: '*On one occasion he rode his camel 300 miles in three consecutive days (no one ever seems to comment on the camel's endurance). I once rode with mine 50 miles at a stretch, and that was enough for me... his spiritual equipment overrode the ordinary needs*

of flesh and blood.' (Quoted by J.E. Mack, page 201)[4] Of course, my question is, what is this 'spiritual equipment'?

4. Lawrence had an intense and enduring relationship to books, and those remaining at Clouds Hill at his death were the results of complex and revelatory choices. As Marguerite Yourcenar writes in the endnotes of *Memoirs of Hadrian*, '… *one of the best ways to reconstruct a man's thinking is to rebuild his library.'* [*Memoirs of Hadrian*, page 260, 1983][5] Accordingly, I examine this library, and read some of it with the foregoing questions in mind.

5. In the beliefs of his youth and his formation (what Hegel and Nietzsche call *Bildung*). I look for the connection between the extraordinary number of transitions he made in job, role, persona, status, and identity. A trajectory which passes from Classically-educated Christian archaeologist, via guerrilla warfare theorist and practioner, to marine racing engine specialist, voicing a near-Stoic version of materialism. Necessarily there will be quotation from what he sardonically dubbed his Collected Works; the things everybody knows. I will also dwell on aspects of his life and writings which have either been ignored or misread.

6. I examine the several matrices of influence: Biblical, archaeological, medieval, Crusader, military, and strategic; looking for the principles of action which pass through and beyond even his undoubted, and declared, ambition.

7. I happily admit my many debts, particularly to the books which led me into a better understanding of Chivalry, and the world of Classical Greek literature.[6] Without them I would never have been able to work out the sources of Lawrence's extraordinary power and mobility.

Endnotes

[1] See Foucault, *History of Sexuality*, 3 vols.

[2] See Kant, *The Conflict of Faculties*: 'A regimen for prolonging man's life must not aim at a life of ease; for by such indulgence towards his powers and feelings he would spoil himself.' [page 181].

[3] See Pierre Hadot, *Philosophy as a Way of Life*.

[4] Also in Stirling's *Safety Last*, page 83, and in *Friends*, page 155.

[5] See 'Books at Clouds Hill' in *T.E. Lawrence by His Friends*.

[6] As M.D. Allen rightly remarks in *The Medievalism of Lawrence of Arabia*, there is a book to be written on The Classicism of Lawrence of Arabia (page 204). After dealing with the literature of Chivalry, I make a beginning of the larger issue of this Classicism.

Lawrence ca. 1934. A photograph by his friend, Flight Lieutenant R.G. Sims.
They had first met in Iraq, and shared an interest in photography and classical music.
Lawrence spent weekends with the Sims family at their cottage.

CHAPTER ONE

Ethics and the Culture of War

༄

TWO absolute forms of struggle – War and Ethics – meet in Lawrence, a rare instance of a warrior and a scholar, who also happened to be a writer, who records the Agon of these two realms as they meet in his experience. These two elements, or forms, emerge very early in Lawrence's life, and can be traced throughout his formative years, and indeed thereafter. The *locus classicus* for their medieval combination, which Lawrence studied so closely, is Chivalry. And within Chivalry can be discerned two of the paths which lead to personal perfection – the Monk and the Knight. And these two paths can be studied in 'real' history, or in literature. This combination inevitably generates its tensions and instabilities either within an individual's lived experience, or between the two paths.

In any case, Lawrence's early immersion in medieval history, particularly military architecture, the subject of his Degree thesis, armour, Archaeology, the military theorists, and above all, the Crusades, would have inevitably brought him to the literature of Chivalry. And it is in this literature, at least in Europe, and in the Crusader kingdoms of Latin Syria and the Middle East, where warfare first tries on its religious masks, whether Christian or Islamic, and militant spiritualities first encounter each other across Europe and the Middle East.

It seems indisputable that Lawrence began his studies as a Christian, although his education was also classically oriented in the Victorian culture of late 19th century Oxford. His mother and elder brother, Dr. M.R. Lawrence, were sufficiently dedicated to their faith to go to China as missionaries. And Lawrence himself taught at St. Aldgate's Sunday School, and was an officer in the Church Lads' Brigade. When the Reverend Alfred M.W. Christopher, a leader of the 19th century Evangelical Movement retired in 1905 from St. Aldgate's, Lawrence and his brothers continued Bible study classes at his home. The impact of this early Christian study clearly mark the letters he wrote home on his first explorations of Palestine. In confirmation of the intensity of this early Christian formation, Mack notes, 'I have seen the well-thumbed and extensively annotated and underlined Bibles from which the parents read to their children.'[1]

It is from within this Christian culture that Lawrence conducted his first explorations of the military strategists and Chivalry through extensive readings, and bicycle journeys to castles and significant battlefields. The *Letters to his Biographers* (Robert Graves and Liddell Hart) are particularly instructive.[2]

Liddell Hart: *When did you begin to read books on the theory of war as distinct from history?*

Lawrence: *In my 16th year, when at school in Oxford – about 1903(?).*

Liddell Hart: *What books did you begin with?*

Lawrence: *The usual schoolboy stuff – Creasey,[3] Henderson,[4] Mahan,[5] Napier,[6] Coxe,[7] – then technical treatises on castle-building and destruction: Procopius,[8] Demetrius Poliorcetes,[9] and others which I have forgotten. I also read nearly every manual of chivalry. Remember that my 'period' was the Middle Ages, always.*

Emphasising this preoccupation with Chivalry, Lawrence also writes to Robert Graves, [pg 48]: '*At Jesus read history, officially: actually spent nearly three years reading Provencal poetry, and medieval French chansons de geste.*'[10]

This relatively arcane branch of literature may seem remote from the literature of War, and even History, but Maurice Keen in his authoritative study of Chivalry demonstrates that the *chansons de geste* are '… the earliest sources that can fully and properly be called "Chivalrous"… and in them the wars against the heathen in the Carolingian age… hold the centre of the stage again.'[11]

However much credence we may give to the time Lawrence devoted to medieval poetry, it seems clear that from his 16th year to at least his 23rd, initially, he devoted much of this approximate seven-year period to Chivalry and Christianity, and then the literature, history, architecture, and materiality [e.g. armour], of warfare. In fact, glancing ahead for a moment, we can see this interest continuing: for example, his Thesis on Crusader Castles, his later references to Xenophon, the continuing interest in Malory, and his praise of Caesar's Gallic Wars. And this does not even begin to engage with the flurries of reference to military strategists in the *Seven Pillars*.

Returning to Chivalry and its literature: it is not that we have here first Christianity, then War, as two separate domains, but that medieval literature and history, particularly of the Crusades, ('the epitome of chivalrous activity'– Keen) show us religious faith with sword in hand, and at the same time, warfare itself as a culture of spiritual values with complex and unstable relations with Christianity. Celebrated organisational forms for this amalgam were, of course, the military religious orders: the Templars, the Hospitallers, the Teutonic Knights. And not for nothing is a well-known study of these orders appropriately entitled *The Monks of War*.[12] In passing, we can also see another layer of meaning in Lawrence's description of his entry into the RAF, as like a monastery, and his quasi-religious/vocational view of the 'conquest of the Air.'

However, the development of a Warrior Ethos, or code, can also be discerned in the systematically elitist literature and practices of Chivalry, whether it wears the Crusader Cross or not. And this aspect of Chivalry connects less directly to the 'spiritual', and more to the ancient cultures of 'Honour', which can be traced back at least as far as Homer. For example, just as in Homer, Geoffroi de Charny, a 14th century warrior and writer on Chivalry, advises knights to 'Love and serve your friends, [and] hate and harm your enemies.'[13] In fact, as late as 1928, Lawrence made the connection between Homer and the *chanson de geste* in a letter to Emery Walker. Speaking of the *Odyssey*, Lawrence remarks that, 'The author writes in metre, as that was the consecrated form of the early novel or *chanson de geste..*'[14] Even in connection with Krak des Chevaliers, Lawrence locates its entrance as '… a long way after' Rum Kalaat, and then, parenthetically, adds, '[Hromgl of Walter von der Vogelweider]' – thus casually connecting major Crusader Castles with the greatest of the early German *Minnesinger*.[15]

Lawrence had multiple routes of access to the world of Chivalry, castles, and warfare, from boyhood onwards. Along with the interest in the medieval world, and a 'passionate absorption in the past',[16] went deep involvements in heraldry, monumental brasses, church architecture, old coins, and pottery. And these interests led to friendships with archaeologists including Leonard Woolley and D.G. Hogarth, as well as other staff at the Ashmolean Museum. Gradually the exploration of castles expanded – from England in 1905 (to Colchester, Norwich and King's Lynn), by bicycle with his father, to Wales, and then to France in 1906, 1907 and 1908. The latter tour was the longest of this period; Lawrence's authorised biographer remarks that this 2,400-mile journey was 'not exceptional.'[17] In passing, the letters home of this period also register an almost Spartan austerity. By preference perhaps, or as a test, living on one or two Francs per day, and eating a diet of fruit, bread, and milk, whilst cycling long distances (up to 100 miles per day). In the summer of his 21st birthday, Lawrence walked 1,100 miles through Palestine and Syria visiting every Crusader Castle of importance. The overt official project was that he could establish his Thesis considering the influence of Levantine military architecture on that of the West. Liddell Hart opines that, 'His basic intention in exploring Syria was a strategic study of the Crusades.'[18] Lawrence obtained first class honours in History, but his letters of the period also exhibit a profound grasp of the strategic problems of waging war in Palestine and Syria. He asserts, finally, that the 'whole history of the Crusades was a struggle for the possession of [certain] castles',[19] thus demonstrating his feel for territory and the siting of fortresses but, even more presciently, the importance of sea power to support the Crusaders: 'Latin Syria lived on its fleets.'[20] This was to be exactly the strategy of support in the Arab Revolt 6-7 years later.

Meanwhile, in the Chivalrous literature which Lawrence was studying at the time, the pressures of war-making in the Holy Land were registering themselves in certain cultural developments. Some historians of war, for example John Keegan, argue plausibly that the principal response to these pressures was 'an ever closer assimilation of the code of warriordom by which they lived, with the appeal to Christian service that drew them across the Mediterranean in the first place. It was no longer sufficient to have a horse, a coat of mail and a Lord to follow, the basis of fealty itself was changing from certain material considerations to ceremonial and religious relations. The oath/vow of fealty which bound a knight in personal service to his lord—swore not merely to obey but also to behave in knightly fashion, which meant to lead an honourable and even virtuous life.'[21] In short, both Christianisation and the introduction of a culture of Honour had begun. It is clear that Lawrence was profoundly immersed in this world, and by giving it due weight many of his later views and reactions become understandable and even admirable.

Endnotes

[1] J.E. Mack, *Prince of Our Disorder,* pp. 13, 14. Also Wilson, p. 44.
[2] *Letters to His Biographers,* pp. 50-51.
[3] Sir E.S. Creasey, author of *Fifteen Decisive Battles of the World.*

[4] George Francis Henderson, 1852-1903. Colonel in British Army. Active service in India and Egypt; taught military history at Sandhurst and at Staff College. Intelligence Officer to the British Commander–in–Chief during Boer War. Held a particular interest in the American Civil War; his biography of Stonewall Jackson became a military classic. 'It is the leader who reckons with the human nature of his troops and the enemy, rather than with their mere physical attributes, numbers, armaments and the like, who can hope to follow in Napoleon's footsteps.' Quoted in Tsouras, pp. 205, 507.

[5] Either – Alfred Thayer Mahan (1840-1914). Rear Admiral U.S. Navy, author of the *Influence of Sea Power in History*, which revolutionised naval strategy. 'The love of glory, the ardent desire for honourable distinction, by honourable deeds, is amongst the most potent and honourable of military motives.' Tsouras, pp. 193, 515.

Or – Dennis Hart Mahan (1802-1871). Engineer and Educator. Dean of the Faculty at West Point. Nearly all the great Civil War Generals were his students. 'It is in military history that we are to look for the source of all military science.' 'To do the greatest damage to our enemy with the least exposure to ourselves, is a military axiom lost sight of only by ignorance of the true ends of victory.' Tsouras, pp. 199, 286, 515.

[6] Sir William Napier (1785-1860). Lieutenant General, British Army. Served in Portugal 1809-11. Became Governor of Guernsey. Wrote *History of The War in the Peninsular [1828-40]*, and *History of the Conquest of Scinde [1844-46]*. 'An ignorant officer is a murderer.' Tsouras, pp. 254, 518.

[7] William Coxe, author/editor of the *Memoirs of Marlborough* (1847).

[8] Born between 490-507 B.C. Byzantine Historian. From 527-531 he was advisor to the military commander Belisaurus, about whom Robert Graves wrote a novel. His *Secret History* is a later supplement to his more extensive writings on The Persian Wars, the Vandal Wars in Africa, and the Gothic Wars in Sicily and Italy. Several references in *Crusader Castles*. See Oxford Edn.

[9] Demetrius I Poliorcetes (336-283 B.C.). Son of Alexander's general, Antigonus I. Macedonian General and Ruler. Involved in the Wars of the Diadochi. Captured by Seleusis 1.

[10] *Chansons de geste*: a genre of poetry. *Geste* = an exploit, a tale of adventure, a romance. From the old French/Latin *Gesta* = things done.

[11] Maurice Keen, *Chivalry*, p. 51.

[12] Desmond Seward, *The Monks Of War – The Military Religious Orders*.

[13] Geoffroi de Charny, *Book of Chivalry*, p. 129.

[14] Quoted in Wilson, p. 842.

[15] See Keen, *Chivalry*, p. 36.

[16] See Garnett, *Letters*, p. 39.

[17] Jeremy Wilson, *Lawrence of Arabia*, p. 45.

[18] T.E. Lawrence to his Biographers, p. 49.

[19] See 'Letter to Leonard Green', *Letters of T.E. Lawrence*, pp. 36-39 (1911).

[20] *Letters*, Edited by Garnett, p. 38.

[21] Keegan, *A History of Warfare*, p. 294.

CHAPTER TWO

'As I lie here out of sight'

BRASS RUBBINGS

ᴄᴠᴐ

NY close reading, not only of the *Letters*, but also of the recollections of those who knew him, especially in *T.E. Lawrence By His Friends*, demonstrates conclusively that Lawrence began the study of these medieval things very early. At the age of nine and a half, he began what was to become an extensive collection of brass rubbings of knights in armour. One of his childhood friends, C.F.C. Beeson, who knew him at the age of fifteen, recalls:

'Cut out and pasted on the walls of his bedroom were life-size figures of knights and priests, with Sir John d'Abernon and Roger de Trumpington, a crusader, in pride of place.'[1]

These striking brass rubbings are not merely objects of aesthetic appreciation, but depict a certain heroic ideal as well as a technical appeal; produced around 1326 in the Cemoys style, they show the use of plate armour for extra protection of the joints.[2] Beeson remarks that this interest was no collector's hobby, but was backed up by 'much searching in libraries for the history of these priests and knights and ladies', and included visits to the Wallace Collection and the Tower Armouries, and the permanent acquisition of a Herald's jargon. This, together with his attachment to Sir Thomas Malory, author of *Le Morte D'Arthur*, enriched the vocabulary and range of reference of the *Seven Pillars*, and even leaves traces in *The Mint*.[3] The fact that Chivalry and the technicalities of armour can still provide sources of metaphor within the engineers' milieux of the RAF in 1925, suggests that the medieval world of these early studies had provided Lawrence with some enduring vocabulary and values.

In view of Lawrence's later remarks about, and attitude to the body, some attention should be given to another unusual brass in his room. In interviews with other boyhood friends, E.F. Hall and Janet Louise Hall Smith, it emerges that along with the Crusaders, Lawrence's room also had a brass rubbing of a corpse being eaten by worms, and that his mother complained that he was sleeping in a coffin-shaped box six feet long, two feet high and two feet wide. Hall remarks, '… he'd think of this chap dying, eaten by worms every night when he went to bed.'[4] The most probable candidate for this rare and unusual brass is the monumental brass commemorating Ralph Hamsterley, from Oddington, Oxfordshire. The Monumental Brass Society takes the view that Lawrence '… undoubtedly rubbed the skeleton in a shroud at Oddington.'[5] Hamsterley, as Rector of Oddington Church, laid down this memorial in his own church years before his death.

Lawrence was an enthusiastic maker of brass rubbings, usually of medieval knights.
This gruesome shroud brass of Ralph Hamsterley (1450-1518), a Fellow of Merton College, Oxford,
was probably made in 1510. Lawrence's childhood friend, Janet Laurie Hallsmith, remarked that
his room was 'hideous with them'. Hamsterley was probably pasted on the ceiling. (Brass rubbing by
Bruce Leigh - permission kindly given by The Reverend Andrew Rycraft and the Churchwardens of
St. Andrew's, Oddington.)

In his paper for the *Transactions of the Monumental Brass Society*, V.J.B. Torr describes the brass as a 'unique and most terrifying type of the shrouded and decomposing corpse, already partly a skeleton, and being consumed by worms the very skull is cracked with age, yet the stomach, though putrescent, is still relatively fleshly! [*Transactions*, page 227.] Torr counts 13 worms in all '… carefully drawn little creatures, all save one being ringed naturistically', and translates the curving mouth scroll:

'*I, here to worms become a prey*
Try by this picture thus to say,
That as I lie here out of sight
So must pass all earthly might.'

In passing, it is worth noting that this 'message from the skeleton' strikingly echoes the medieval Christian austerity of the classic Chivalrous text *L'ordene de Chevalrie*:[6]

'*Death and earth where you will rest*
Whence you came and wither you will return
This is what you must keep before your eyes.'

To make a rubbing of such a brass would involve a close acquaintance with all its details, even more, to sleep under it would ensure that, whatever one's thoughts about 'earthly might', the ultimate fate of the body would be difficult, if not impossible, to ignore and forget. Less seriously, this brass may also explain the origin of Lawrence's curious greeting at the end of some of his youthful letters to his family: '*My worms to …*' – a possibly obscure, perhaps childish family in-joke. More generally, a certain attitude to the body, sometimes instrumental, at others contemptuous, along with odd-sounding pleonasms, for example, '*I resolved while I lived,*' [*Seven Pillars*]; all these are consistent with the values expressed in both the English and the French poems on Chivalrous subjects.

The classicist in Lawrence would have known, of course, that Christianity does not have a monopoly on the asceticism expressed in these poems. It can be found in the texts and practices across the entire Graeco-Roman world; in the tradition inaugurated by Socrates – in Plato, Aristotle, the Stoics (both Greek and Roman), the Cynics, Plotinus and the Neoplatonists, amongst others. In all these thinkers and schools, the Body is variously problematised, disciplined, or repudiated in the name of 'higher' intellectual or spiritual goals. To some extent, the traces of this tradition can be found in Lawrence's writings and practices. However, it is rarely overtly theorised in the manner of later modern thinkers such as Nietzsche, Foucault, or Ernst Jünger, perhaps because Lawrence's writing projects were powered by different motives with other goals. The most explicit views Lawrence articulated on the subject are directed more at Food, and Habits per se, than at Sex. This itself seems to be engagingly pre-modern, and I shall return to it subsequently.

The record of those who knew Lawrence at university demonstrates the level of self-discipline which he embraced. Initially, perhaps, these austerities could be misread as personal eccentricity, or mere undergraduate affectation. Even his brother, A. W. Lawrence, writes that, 'At college he made *fun* for himself by eccentricity, riding his bicycle up hills and walking it down.'[7] If we understand such eccentricities more charitably as personal choices informed by the traditions of austerity in the Christian and Graeco-Roman

*Brass rubbings of medieval knights made by T.E. Lawrence in his youth.
Left: Sir John D'Aubernoun, 1277; right: Sir Roger de Trumpington, 1289.*

worlds, which he knew, they are part of the *regimen of askesis*[8] which Lawrence clearly followed throughout his life.

> '*Lawrence sat cross-legged on the floor quietly explaining that he never sat on chairs if he could help it, that he never indulged in the meals known as breakfast, lunch, tea and dinner, nor smoked nor took drinks, in fact he did nothing which qualified him as an ordinary member of society. But he added drolly that he had no objection to my doing any of these things.*'

> [A.G. Pryce-Jones, a Jesus College contemporary. Quoted in Wilson, page 43]

> '*At University never played or looked on at any game or sport. Lived only one term in College. Read all night, and slept in the mornings. Vegetarian, non-smoker, T.T. Never dined in Hall. Took no part in College life.*'

> [Lawrence to Robert Graves in Graves, Robert, and B.H. Liddell Hart in *T.E. Lawrence to His Biographers*, pages 48-49]

> '*... one glance at his eyes left no doubt at all that he told the truth when he said that he had been working for 45 hours at a stretch without food, to test his powers of endurance. I did not realize that he was, in his own later words "hardening for a great endeavour." I thought it was that other side of him – the consuming power of the desire to know – in this case, how much the human frame could stand.*'

> [E.F. Hall, who was at Oxford High School and Jesus College with Lawrence. Quoted in *Friends*, page 47]

C.F.C. Beeson, another school friend who knew him for about five years, and accompanied him on his 1906 trip to France, recalls how his friend 'had to prove himself... was always making himself tough, always climbing, always testing to the limits of his powers.' Once, in Brittany, they visited a castle ruin with a moat that was crossed by a bridge. According to Beeson, Lawrence had to jump the moat instead of using the bridge. Lawrence seemed to take unusual, even reckless, chances when climbing about old walls with loose stones.[9] 'An image has stayed in Beeson's mind of Lawrence atop some rocks in France with a foot trembling as he tried to find a footing. Beeson warned him, "You'll fall", and offered to help. But Lawrence would not let him'. [quoted in *Prince of Our Disorder*, interview with the author, John E. Mack, page 49].[10]

'He came to visit me one breakfast time on his racing motor bicycle: he had come about 200 miles [in five hours]. He would eat no breakfast... "When did you last have a meal?" I asked. "On Wednesday." Since then he had had some chocolate, an orange and a cup of tea. This was Saturday. [Lawrence] "It's my occasional habit to knock off proper feeding for 3 days [rarely five] just to make sure I can do it without feeling worried or strained. One's sense of things gets very keen, and it's good practice for hard times. My life has been full of hard times."' [T.E.L. to Robert Graves in *Letters to his Biographers*, page 72.] Graves also recalls: 'Lawrence, (when his own master) avoids regular hours of sleep. He has found that his brain works better if he sleeps as irregularly as he eats.'

How far this ambitious asceticism is informed by, or consistent with, Medieval Chivalry, is questionable. But Lawrence claims that he read '... nearly every manual of chivalry.' Therefore, to test the hypothesis that Lawrence lived by this warrior code, I propose to examine some aspects of Chivalrous literature, both 'handbooks' and *'chansons de geste'*, and to look at his writings, manifest practice, judgements, and library, with the Chivalry question in mind.

Endnotes

[1] *T.E. Lawrence by His Friends,* p. 53.

[2] See Peter Coss, *The Knight in Medieval England*, p. 92.

[3] Chivalry references '… the mail and plate of our personality', *The Mint*, p. 232.

[4] Quoted in John E. Mack, *A Prince of Our Disorder*, p. 24.

[5] Correspondence with the Society.

[6] See Maurice Keen, *Chivalry*, p. 6 *et passim*.

[7] Italics added. As a fifteen-year old cyclist, I was personally struck by this, and only later came to see it as a manifestation of Lawrence's strange 'counter-Will', a kind of wit of the Deed.

[8] Ascesis – the practice of disciplining oneself: asceticism. From the Greek 'askesis' = exercise, training. See Chambers Dictionary and Liddell and Scott Greek *Lexicon*, p. 208. And, for example, *Cynics* by William Desmond. Also Richard Finn, *Asceticism in the Graeco-Roman World*. Op. cit.

[9] Climbing the walls of castles was also one of the risks he took for his thesis on Crusader Castles. Sometimes it was the only way to establish facts, for example wall thickness, or to read inscriptions, or to obtain good angles for photographs. 'He had climbed the old walls barefoot', a don remembered later. [See Michael Haag, Preface to *Crusader Castles*, p. 12.]

[10] Lawrence continued dangerous climbs. See *Crusader Castles*, pp. 97, 141, 154, etc: '… very difficult to make notes… because of the darkness and because I was clinging with teeth and eyelids on a ledge about 4 inches wide, halfway up the tower.' And after the war putting a Hejaz flag on top of an Oxford college.

CHAPTER THREE

Chivalry

❧

VARIOUS gross obstacles lie in the way of any modern understanding of Chivalry. Somewhat analogous to the difference between Ancient (Classical) Cynicism and modern cynicism, any possible understanding of Chivalry as a way of life must disperse the modern conception of it as being merely a trivial preoccupation with manners and correct comportment between the sexes, or as theatrical Round Table Camelotian posturing. To understand Chivalry is to think and imagine against the grain of modern irony and cynicism. Firstly, because Chivalry promotes lists of virtues that are almost embarrassing to the modern nihilist eye, i.e. Honour, Prowess, Loyalty, Truth, Generosity, and Courtesy.

Maurice Keen notes that 'from a very early stage... the romantic authors habitually associated together certain qualities which they regarded as the classic virtues of good knighthood... [and] to the end of the Middle Ages their combination remains the stereotype of chivalrous distinction.'[1] That Lawrence took this literature of Chivalry seriously is evident from his *Crusader Castles* onwards. After all, the 'world view' of Chivalry was the cultural high ground and reference point for the knights who lived in, and sallied forth from, the many castles Lawrence had studied. He wrote in *Crusader Castles*:

'*Obviously, in Europe, France is the country chiefly to be considered. In the Middle Ages, she produced all that was best in Gothic art. Italy flowered later, after the downfall of medieval culture, and in the 12th and 13th centuries, Germany also was barbarous in art, and had Chivalry by no means equal to that of the Western Kingdoms. From France and England come all medieval masterpieces in literature and architecture...*'[2]

And, considering the relative advantages of the Military Orders, i.e. the Templars and the Hospitallers, in castle building under Syrian conditions, Lawrence remarks:

'*The military orders were ideally suited for such conditions. The members were celibate, and so, easy to control, and without private interests: they had no heirs to search after, and no domain to preserve intact. Then the Orders were everlasting, with an inexhaustible supply of the finest Chivalry in Europe to draw upon in case of need. The military ability of the commanders, and of the simple members of either order is again and again brought out in striking contrast with the inefficiency of the laymen of the kingdom. There was a tradition, after a little, among the knights, of the conduct of warfare against the Infidel, and each newcomer of repute vivified this tradition with the fruits of his own talent and experience.*'[3]

In reading *Crusader Castles* one often has the uncanny feeling of lived experience – as if he was really there – as Lawrence describes the strengths and weaknesses of the castles he examines. He tests the construction – for example, at Crac (or Krac) des Chevaliers he climbs a thick sloping wall (a Glacis): '… it had the drawback of making easy escalade. I was able barefoot to climb more than halfway, c. 40 feet…' He could have merely described it.[4]

Just as Lawrence engaged closely with the architecture of the castles and churches he studied, so it seems he did so with the literature of the times in which they were built. A college friend recollected '… a rare occasion when he came to a meeting of the College Literary Society: a paper was read on the *Chanson de Roland*. When it was over Lawrence spoke for about 20 minutes in his clear quiet voice, ranging serenely about the epic poetry of several languages: *'It was all first hand: you felt he had been there.'*[5]

Taking Lawrence's assertion that he had read 'nearly every manual of chivalry' seriously, the question is immediately generated: What is a manual of Chivalry? Or at least, what could count as such? Maurice Keen in his study of Chivalry, usefully distinguishes the Romances of Chivalry from those books which are like treatises, are systematic, and 'attempt to treat chivalry as a way of life and offer instruction to that end.'[6]

Keen suggests three candidates:
1. *The Ordene de Chevalrie* (Anon).
2. *The Book of the Order of Chivalry*, Ramon Lull.
3. *The Book of Chivalry*, Geoffroi de Charny.

All of these were available from libraries 'within the general circulation of the time', i.e. between 1900 and 1914[7] and Lawrence was familiar enough with the other European languages into which these books were translated not to be obstructed by the absence of an English text. Furthermore, Lawrence's youth overlapped with a period in which many Chivalrous texts were being published or republished; for example, Sir Walter Scott, and Tennyson's first Arthurian poems had been published in 1832. An English version of the *Mabinogion* was published in 1837 by Lady Charlotte Guest, while Thomas Wright's new edition of Malory's *Morte d'Arthur* appeared in 1857, although curiously this book, which Lawrence rated so highly, figures in his library at Cloud's Hill in the humble two-volume *Everyman* edition of 1908. Also, dating from 1822, and in Lawrence's library, marked 'T.E.S.' – and thus post-dating his Arabian period – is Kenelm Henry Digby's *The Broadstone of Honour or the true sense and practice of chivalry*, an 1844 edition. The Oxford Union itself was decorated in 1857 with Arthurian paintings by Rossetti, William Morris and Burne-Jones. Taken together with his William Morris and Crusader interests, it is evident that Lawrence had multiple access to the literature of Chivalry.

1. The *Ordene de Chevalrie*

This anonymous text, variously described as '… a late 12th century didactic poem',[8] and dated by Keen as 'probably composed before 1250',[9] pre-dates the considerably more famous and influential exposition of knighthood by Ramon Lull, but is the source of some of Lull's material, and was widely accepted amongst practising knights.

In the *Ordene*, the process and meaning of the ritual of becoming a knight are described and explained in detail by the Frankish knight, Hugh, Count of Tiberias,[10] to Saladin, who has captured him in battle. Hugh has been given the choice of either paying an enormous ransom, or of initiating Saladin into the Order of Knighthood to obtain his release.

The ritual, and its symbolic meaning, are profoundly Christian, but the idea of inauguration into an Order, like the Church and other Estates of the medieval world, but separate from them, is also present, as is the emphasis on certain specifically knightly virtue; for example, prowess, hardiness, loyalty and courtesy.[11]

Thus, while the ritual seems to carry the ethical values, the Prowess, which had encouraged Saladin to seek 'ordination' from Hugh in the first place, had to be achieved by Hugh by a systematic disciplining and toughening of the body. And this demonstrates a certain distance from the 'militant crusading zeal' of St. Bernard's version of Chivalry. Although he had captured him in battle, if Saladin had not respected Hugh's valour and prowess, he would not have agreed to release him in return for Ordination into a basically Christian organisation. The implausibility of a Muslim entering into such an agreement will strike the modern reader. Perhaps one should recall this is an imaginary setting for the explication of knighthood to a medieval audience, and it is the ethical and ascetic dimension, as well as the notion of Prowess, which can cross religious affiliations, and indeed the centuries, to reach a sensibility like Lawrence's.

The representations of the ritual are:
1. The dressing of beard and hair.
2. The bath of baptism, meaning the washing away of sins and which also signifies courtesy and bounty.
3. A fair bed to signify the repose of paradise (to be won by Chivalry).
4. White robe for cleanness of body.[12]
5. Scarlet cloak which is to remind the knight of his duty to shed his blood in defence of the Church.
6 Brown stockings for the earth in which he must eventually lie; prepare for death.
7. White belt for virginity.
8. Gold spurs – i.e. be quick to follow God's Commandments.
9. The sword – two edged – 'Justice and Loyalty' must go together and the knight must defend the poor from the strong and rich.[13]

The Commandments are:
1. Not to consent to false Judgement.[14]
2. Not to be a party to treason.
3. Honour and help all women and damsels to the limit of his power.
4. Hear Mass every day if possible.
5. Fast every Friday in remembrance of Christ's passion.[15]

It is perhaps worth remarking that the overlapping of prowess and Christian ethics, the combination of spiritual and bodily discipline, particularly in the practice of fasting (done by Lawrence almost casually), is in the name of, and for the sake of, a practical and active asceticism. Without the sword and the cult of prowess, it would be merely monkish or contemplative, and not the channelled and devoted violence of Chivalry. This path to an ideal of personal perfection and honour was therefore immensely demanding, entailing a kind of endless effort. As Keen writes, 'No order of religion imposes heavier rigours than Chivalry does, and the regular observance of the points of religion is as needful to the knight as it is to any religious, for there is no order in which soul and body alike must be so continually prepared against the hour of death.'[16]

Partly due to the pressure of the Crusades and the politics which accompanied them in Europe, it is evident that the spiritual dimension of Chivalry increased over time, e.g. from the pre-Christian warrior as exemplified in the *Kalevela*. For the present, it is significant for our understanding of Lawrence to note that the cover of *Seven Pillars* has, in Lawrence's handwriting, the words:

> *The*
> *Sword*
> *Also means*
> *Clean-ness*
> *&*
> *death*

2. *Book of the Order of Chivalry*, **Ramon Lull**

Translated from the French, edited and printed by William Caxton in 1484 as *The Book of the Ordere of Chyvalry of Knighthode*, this handbook was widely influential and was not only translated into French and English, but also Latin, Middle Scots, and Castilian, from the original Catalan.

Lull's book is one of the foremost candidates for a manual or handbook of Chivalry and Christian Knighthood. It is not only one of the most famous and widely disseminated of the genre, but also contains practical and ethical recommendations by which a Christian knight could have lived. This advice of a disciplinary and ascetic nature, whilst clearly consistent with Christian doctrine, is not necessarily reducible to it.

The editor of the current English edition, A. T. Byles, notes that since 1781, 'All the chief writers on Chivalry have recognised Caxton's '*Ordere of Chyvalry*' as the most compendious medieval treatise on the obligations of knighthood, and have quoted it freely.' Indeed it is difficult to find a serious survey of Chivalrous literature which omits it, and the picture of the encounter between the aspirant knight and the hermit recurs as an almost standard trope in much other Chivalrous literature. It could even be argued that Lawrence's encounter with the wanderer whilst having a swim in the springs at Rumm, is a distant echo of this tradition. [Chapter LXIII, *Seven Pillars*.][17] It certainly provoked some reflections on the difference between 'Semitic' and Christian beliefs which challenged some of Lawrence's Evangelical Anglican beliefs.

Byles provides an interesting short biography of Ramon Lull which, in places, has curious resonances with Lawrence's career: the Chivalrous dedication to a great task, the theme of 'preaching', the study of Arabic, the semi vagabondage and prodigious activity:

'... the apostle to the Saracens and indefatigable author, who was born at Palma in Majorca about 1235. His extraordinary career – "*cette vie etrange, partagee entre l'apostolat, la vagabondage, l'hallucinatio et une activité prodigieuse.*"'

As described by E. Littre and B. Haureau in '*L'Histoire Litteraire de la France,* Vol XXIX, which also contains a detailed description of his works. Lull was the son of a wealthy and distinguished Majorcan soldier, and after marrying at an early age he was made seneschal at the court of James II of Aragon. Here he lived the life of a gay worldling, but was probably no more profligate than the average courtier of his day. The gift of poetry appeared in him in his youth, and the collection of Catalan poems, edited by M. Rossello, is of more value today than the mass of his scholastic philosophy. His poetry was devoted to amorous and other secular themes until 1266, when the whole course of his life was changed by a vision of the crucified Christ, seen on five successive nights. He determined to devote himself to some great Christian service, and accordingly he essayed the task of converting the Saracens, chiefly in the north of Africa. The idea of overcoming the Saracens by love and persuasion was quite new at a time when the Crusades were not yet over. Not the less remarkable is the fact that it was as a layman that Lull undertook this mighty task. He learnt Arabic from a Saracen slave and commenced the long series of treatises in Arabic, or in vulgar Catalan, which only terminated with his death. Most of his works are extant in Latin translation, but there is good reason for the belief that he wrote little in Latin and that his command of the language was slight. The three objects of his life, besides his missions to the Saracens, were the establishment of colleges and professorships, by means of which men could learn Arabic and obtain missionary training; the organisation of a Crusade which should have love and spiritual instruction rather than armed force as its basis; and the overthrow of the doctrines of the Moslem philosopher, Averroes, by demonstrating the place of reason in religion. In 1276 he founded the College of the Holy Trinity at Miramar in Majorca, where thirteen monks were enabled to learn Arabic. He lived there for ten years, during which he produced many works, including probably *The Order Of Chivalry*. Towards the end of his life, in 1311, he placed his favourite projects before the great Council of Vienne, and to his satisfaction it passed a decree establishing professorships in Oriental languages at Oxford, Paris and other universities.

Lull's first journey to Africa took place in 1291, the year of the fall of Acre and the end of the Crusades. At the last moment his heart failed him and he delayed his departure, but after his first venture, not banishment, nor privation, nor imprisonment, nor threats of death, could keep him from the little colony of converts that he had established in Tunis and Bugia. In his last years he was obsessed with yearning for martyrdom and in 1315, when he was eighty years old, he came into the open to preach at Bugia after living twelve months in secret with his disciples. The enraged Saracens stoned him to death on the seashore. His memory is deeply venerated to the present day by Majorcans, who gave him the title of '*Doctor illume et martyr*'.[18]

Because Lull had moved away from his active and successful worldly life, following his powerful visions of Christ, by the time he wrote his Order of Chivalry, he had therefore acquired a certain distance on the unspiritual aspects of Chivalry. In short, his view of Chivalry is dominated by his Christian faith, and accordingly structured by it. The original text was written about 1275, but the book known in the English- speaking world was translated, printed and augmented by Caxton in 1484. It was very popular, and there are still at least ten extant manuscripts of French translations, and printed editions dating back to 1504 and 1505.

The Chivalrous instruction is transmitted by a hermit, mystic, and ex-knight; a figure familiar to readers of the Grail Quest, Chretien de Troyes, and other Romance authors. The book begins by praising God and describing a feudal cosmology with 'Kynges, prynces and grete lordes' having a secondary sovereignty, after God, over the knights, who in turn govern the people.

A flavour of the book can be gained from its beginning:

> 'For to shewe that to the sygnifyaunce of god the prynce almyghty which seygnoryth aboue the seuen planettes… And the knygtes by symylytude oghten to have power and dominacion ouer the moyen people. And this booke conteyneth VIII chapitres.'

Strikingly, at this relatively early stage in the history of Chivalry, Lull already sounds a note suggesting that there has been a falling away from an earlier ideal: perhaps because his own trajectory has been towards the ecclesiastical.

> 'All the knights now injurious and proud, full of wickedness be not worthy to chivalry, but ought to repute for nought.'

The knight should return to his destiny, to his truth, his lord and to the people. The 'people' include women, widows, orphans and the sick and those not 'puissant nor strong'.

> 'For like as custom and reason it that the greatest and most mighty help the feeble and less, and that they have recourse to the grat. Right so is chivalry, by course She is great, honourable and mighty, be in surrow and in aid to them that be under him and less mighty and less honoured than his is.' (Lull)[19]

This lost excellence could only be regained by following the strenuous and endlessly demanding path of the Christian knight.

The laws and practices of this path are passed on from a virtuous hermit and ex-knight to a young squire on his way to a great king's court, hoping to be knighted. This custodian of the inner meaning of knighthood has chosen to become a hermit because,

> '… brave though he was, he realized that he could no longer live as he had done in the past and was approaching his end… for his natural virtues were undermined by old age, and he no longer had the strength or will to use weapons as he had been accustomed to.' (Lull)[20]

Along with the Christian ethics and symbolism, there is also more than a nod towards the physical hardiness and prowess, together with expertise in handling weapons, as celebrated in the prose Romances of Chretien de Troyes, and in the French Arthurian Romance *Lancelot du Lac*:

> 'A knight should ride warhorses, joust, go to tournaments, hold Round Tables, hunt stags and rabbits, bears, lions and similar creatures: these things are a knight's duty because to do them exercises a knight in the practice of arms and enables him to maintain the order of knighthood. To despise and to neglect the things by which a knight is made more fit for his duties is to despise and neglect knighthood itself.' (Lull)[21]

Compare this with a fairly standard passage from Chretien De Troyes' *Story of the Grail* (Perceval) in 'Arthurian Romances':

> 'My good friend, every profession requires effort and devotion and practice: with these three one can learn everything.'[22]

Thus, here, Lull is developing his description of the path of Christian Chivalry by combining elements from the Romance ideal of knighthood as found in Chretien De Troyes, with the Christian ethics and symbolism of the *Ordene de Chevalrie*. Courage itself is to be found in the cultivation of Christian and Chivalrous values: '… seek noble courage in faith, hope, charity, justice, strength, moderation and loyalty.'[23]

The motivation of the young squire will also be called into question:

'*Thou knight that examyest the squyer arte bounden more strongly to enserche noblesse and valoyre in a squyer than any other persone… thou oughtest to knowe for what entwncion the squyer hath wil to soiourne or for to be honoured.*'[24]

In other words, just as simony vitiates the calling of 'clerks' (monks), so wrong motivation should be looked for in a would-be knight. Keen remarks that these questions are eminently sensible and, with a change here and there of vocabulary, would do no discredit to a selection board for commissions in an armoured regiment today. And Lull's wish that there be schools for instruction in Chivalry – schools of prowess – is '… a first glimpse of the potential of military colleges as the forcing grounds of the military ethos.' A potential which was not to be realised until the early Renaissance, in another two-and-a-half centuries.[25]

In the Sixth Chapter Lull returns to the customs (practices) of a knight, and again enumerates the Seven Virtues emphasising their practical usefulness:

'*… fayth / hope / charyte, justice / prudence / strength and attemperaunce… Hope maketh knyghts to susteyne and suffer trauailles and for to be auenturous in perls / in whiche thay puute them self ofte / Also hope maketh thenm to syuffre hongre and thurst in casrtels cytees and fortresses.*'

Similarly, prudence is most necessary to a knight:

'*For no men put their bodyes in so many peryls as done the knyghts. For many bat018ylles ben many times vaynsquysshed more by maystrte / by wytte and Industrye / than by multitude of people of hors ne good armours.*'[26]

Of the Seven Deadly Sins, which are all contrary to Chivalry, Gluttony is particularly singled out:

'*Gloutonye engendreth feblesse of body / by ouer oultragyous drynkynge and etynge / For in ouermoche drynkyng gloutonye chargeth alle the body with metes / and engendreth slouthge and lachenes of body which greueth the soul.*'[27]

It is not until quite late in his text that Lull finally deploys his first 'historical' figure, Alexander the Great, dwelling on his liberality as an example of Chivalrous largesse:

'*… in desprysyng auarice & couetyse [he] had alwey the hands stratched forth for to gyue vnto his knyghts.*'[28]

In passing, it is striking that Lawrence is quite content to use an anachronistic Chivalrous vocabulary when discussing Alexander the Great with Liddell Hart. In his *Decisive Wars of History*, Liddell Hart had concluded his analysis of Alexander's campaigns by remarking that '… there was more of the Homeric hero than in the other great captains of history… His lessons for posterity lie at the two poles – war policy and tactics.'

Lawrence's reply, in 1929, was '*Alexander was part knight-errant, and part experimenter with life. He is so above rules that ordinary people daren't follow him.*'[29]

Having finally dealt with an historical figure cited by Lull, this is probably an apposite place to deal with the circularity of Chivalrous texts across genre, not only in Lull, but also in Caxton's epilogue and other writers. What this means, amongst other things, is that the genre 'manual, or handbook of Chivalry' cannot be watertight and self-founding. At the textual level, scholars have found that a close reading of the *Ordene de Chevalrie* will reveal unmistakable echoes of, for example, Chretien de Troyes' *Perceval*. Similarly, traces of both the *Ordene de Chevalrie* and the *Lady of the Lake's* advice in the Vulgate Lancelot, can be found in Lull's book.[30]

In Caxton's epilogue, the references range beyond the handbook genre to both real historical figures and the heroes of the Romances. Firstly, Caxton, as often in Chivalrous literature, laments the contemporary decline:

> '… *the exersytees of chivalry/not used/ honoured/ne exercised/ as hit hath been in auncyent tyme/ at whiche tyme the noble actes of the knyghtes of England that vsed chyualry were renomed thurgh the vnyuersal world…*' for example, before Christ, '… *where were there euer ony lyke to brenius and belynus?*'[31]

Brennius and Belinus are to be found in Geoffrey of Monmouth's *History of the Kings of Britain* (*Historia Regum Britanniae*), completed in 1136. This Romance history, which was given widespread credence for the next 600 years, is the book in which King Arthur makes one of his earliest appearances; and it is, of course, King Arthur and his Knights, particularly in the hands of French authors, who became the central Chivalric myth; that Rome was never sacked by Belinus as Monmouth's epic history maintains does not vitiate the book's influence. Without Geoffrey's history there would have been no *Morte d'Arthur*, and no *Idylls of the King* either.[32]

It is easy to demonstrate that Lawrence was very familiar with Geoffrey's *History*, as well as Malory, and Tennyson. He had received a prize at school for an essay on him, and there are many references in the letters, e.g. 'lotos eating' at Carchemish, and even as late as 1925 references in a letter to Lionel Curtis.[33] In fact, traces of even the minor texts of the Chivalry canon can be detected in Lawrence's letters from an early stage: references to (e.g. Aucassin et Nicolette), an early 13th century *chant fable* or song-story, in a letter dated 1908 to Beeson,[34] and in a letter to his mother dated 1908, also printed in *Crusader Castles*.[35]

That Lawrence was very familiar with both Geoffrey's *History* and the Grail Legend is clear from his letter to Mrs. Rieder of 26 September 1911, in which he tries to convey the scope of Doughty's book *Dawn in Briton*:

> '*Behold an epic in 6 volumes; a stage from Greece to the North Pole:- a period of 500 years, from the sack of Rome by Brennus [sic] to the siege of Jerusalem, and the departing this life of Joseph of Arimathea.*'[36]

Joseph of Arimathea, a key figure in the Grail Legend (first keeper of the Holy Grail) derives ultimately from the New Testament Apocrypha via Robert de Boron's Romance of that name, written about 1200.[37] It is Joseph who obtains the body of Christ and the cup used at the Last Supper, from which Christ had drunk, and it is Joseph who has caught the last drops of blood as the body is brought down from the Cross. As Keen remarks, a link is thus made between the story of the Round Table and its highest quest, and the climax of the Gospel story.[38]

We can therefore see that Lawrence, in his description of the historical scale of Doughty's book, uses as his reference points two of the key episodes from the Romance fictional 'histories' in Chivalry literature (a sort of Literary genre) – one rooted in the British, the other in the French tradition.

Caxton's epilogue continues, (pg 122):

'*And syth the Incarrnacion of oure lord/ behold that noble king of Brytayne Kyng Arthur with al the noble knyztes of the roud table/ whos noble actes & noble chyualry of his knyghts/ occupy so many large volumes/ that is a world/ or as a thing incredible to byleue/ O ye knyghtes of England where is the custom and vsage of noble chyualry that was vsed in tho days/ what do ye now/ but go to the baynes & playe att dyse And some not well aduysed use not honest and good rule ageyn alle ordre of knyghthode/ leue this/ leuse it and rede the noble volumes of saynt graal of lancelot/ of galaad/ of Trtstram/ of perseforest/ of percyual/ of gawayn/ & many mo/ Ther shalle ye see manhode/ curtosye and gentylnesse/ And loke in latter dayes of the noble actes syth the coquest/ as in king Rychard dayes cuer du lyon / Edward the fyrste /and the third/ and his noble sones/ Syre Robert knolles/ syr Iohan Hawkwode/ Sye Iohan chandos/ & Syre gaulties Manny/ rede Froissart/ And also behold that vyctoryous and noble kynge Harry the fyfthe/ and the captayns vnder hym his noble brethren/ Therle of Salysbury Montagu/ and many other whoos names shyne gloriously by their virtuous noblesse & actes that they did in thonour of chyualry/ Allas what doo ye/ but slepe & take ease/...*'[39]

'*Thenne late euery man that is come of noble blood and entedeth to come to the noble ordre of chyualry/ rede this lytl book/ and doo therafter/ in kepyng the lore and commaundments therin comprised...*'

We can see, in Caxton's envoi to Lull's text, the same double feature of reliance noted in the examination of the 'Handbook' genre. That is, in this instance, firstly the injunction to read the Romance literature (the Graal of Lancelot, etc) and, implicitly, to take it seriously as a guide to 'custom and usage'. Secondly, '... loke in latter days...' that is, study the 'noble actes' (*Gestes*) of real history, e.g. Richard Coeur De Lyon, onwards. Also to study Kings and Knights, most of whom continue to figure in Chivalrous texts in the future, and who function as role models, and even as warrior heroes – perfect instances of the combination of Prowess, liberality or largesse, courtesy, loyalty, hardiness, and franchise (the free and frank bearing that is visible testimony to good birth with virtue). The sheer range of plausible candidates from Lancelot and Richard the Lionheart forward to Geoffroi de Charny give a clue to the liveliness and vitality of this ideal, and its potency as a way of life.

Lastly, a telling detail from the end of Caxton's translation, where an incomplete account of the *Making of a Knyghte of the Bathe* is included. Recalling Lawrence's well-known and unaccountable practice of turning up for college meals and not eating, we read that after the knighting ceremony described in the Appendix of the *Book of the Ordre* [sic] *of Chivalry*, page 127:

'*He then sits with the knights at dinner, but he must neither eat nor drink at the table, nor look about him more than a bride.*'[40]

The Book of Chivalry, Geoffroi de Charny

The son of a Crusader, a life-long warrior and bearer of the Oriflame, the French King's royal standard, who died at the Battle of Poitiers in 1356, de Charny is in many ways the perfect instance of the practising, worldly knight: pious, but intensely involved in the military and political struggles of his violent times. In Froissart's *Chronicles* de Charny is simply 'the wisest and bravest knight of them all.'[41] His *Book of Chivalry*, the most pragmatic of all surviving Chivalry manuals was written at the height of the Hundred Years War. Less spiritual than Lull, and much more engaged in the practical, in the conduct and evaluation of knightly existence, de Charny was concerned with the ranking of worthiness in local tourneys or foreign wars, as well as the reform of Chivalry in France. In fact, de Charny announces a clear principle, variously formulated as, 'he who achieves more, is the more worthy';[42] and 'he who does more is of greater worth';[43] and 'he who does best is most worthy'. An explicit announcement of the competitive elitism which operated within the ranks of knighthood, even as knights struggled to serve their leaders and institutions during the Hundred Years War.

De Charny draws upon the literary tradition of Chivalry, as well as his own experience, to formulate a text which is almost coach-like in the practicality of his advice. In the backgound, of course, is Lull's book, which he almost certainly knew, and via that text, *Lancelot du Lac*. The influential Arthurian prose Romances were, of course, just beginning to appear about the time de Charny was born. The definitive textual link between de Charny's *Book of Chivalry* and Arthurian Romance is established when de Charny refers to Guinevere.[44] The idea in the Romance literature is that love is a major source of inspiration to the young knight. In de Charny this is finessed to the extent that he argues that the Lady's honour will be increased if she inspires a knight to great deeds.

Considering the dedication of the *Seven Pillars* to 'S.A.', it may be that there the Chivalrous inspiration was one that, in those times, could not quite speak itself aloud. What is indisputable is that Lawrence certainly knew about the *Lady of the Lake*, and explicitly refers to her in one of his letters.

Where de Charny seems closest to Lawrence is where he emphasises the physical suffering to which Chivalry exposes its devotees, and the advisability of cultivating a certain austerity in bodily appetites. That knights suffer more than clergy:

> '*The good order of knighthood… should be considered the most rigorous order of all, especially for those who uphold it well and conduct themselves in a way in keeping with the purpose for which the order was established… considering the hardships, pains, discomforts, fears, perils, broken bones, and wounds which the good knights… have to suffer frequently, there is no religious order in which as much is suffered.*'[45]

The practical advice which de Charny offers comes from:

> '*… good knights and men-at-arms whose great achievements and honourable deeds of prowess and valour… [they] have accomplished through suffering great hardship, making strenuous efforts, and enduring fearful physical perils and the loss of friends whose deaths they have witnessed… the above-mentioned good men-at-arms teach that those who want to achieve this honour should not set their minds on the pleasures of the palate, neither on very good wine nor on delicious food, for these delights are very out of place at a time when they are not to be had nor found at will… and desire for such things makes it more difficult for them to endure, and their hearts and bodies find it less easy to bear the lean fare in food and drink*

which the quest for such honour requires. A man will be reluctant to risk death who has not learnt this, and also a man is reluctant to abstain from such pleasures of eating and drinking who has become accustomed to them. One should take no pleasure in such delights; do not concern yourself with being knowledgeable about good dishes and fine sauces nor spend too much time deciding which wines are the best, and you will live more at ease… for men of worth say that one should not live in order to eat, but one should eat in order to live, for no one should eat so much that he is too full, nor drink so much that he is drunk… one should do all these things in moderation… and not grow sluggish in this way.'[46]

It seems that de Charny is as firm in his strictures against Gluttony as Lull, but that his argument is more practically based, and less ecclesiastical/moral. It is clear that de Charny is very aware of the softening effects on '… the young men who are maintained in the great courts of powerful men… [and having] dipped their fingers in the sauce of the court… may be reluctant to give this up.'

Lawrence's own version of this austerity is consistent with it, but somehow raised to another level; symptomatically occurring on a page entitled Artemis Orthia.[47] In the *Seven Pillars*, when discussing his own endurance, he writes:

'For years before the war I had made myself trim by constant carelessness. I had learned to eat much one time; then to go two, three, or four days without food; and after to overeat. I made it a rule to avoid rules in food; and by a course of exceptions accustomed myself to no custom at all. So, organically, I was efficient in the desert, felt neither hunger nor surfeit, and was not distracted by thought of food.'

And similarly with sleep: '*Such liberties came from years of control (contempt of use might well be the lesson of our manhood), and they fitted me peculiarly for our work…*'[48] And should this level of austerity seem distant from the aristocratic warrior ethos of 14th century Chivalry, it is noteworthy that de Charny devotes two sections to '*A good Man-at-Arms Should not Pamper his Body*', and '*Have No Fear of Discomfort*':

'… you must in no way indulge in too great fondness for pampering your body, for love of that is the worst kind of love there is. But instead direct your love toward the preservation of your soul and your honour, which last longer than does the body.'[49]

And:

'The pampering of these wretched bodies also requires white sheets and soft beds, and if these are sometimes lacking, such men's backs and ribs ache so much that they can do nothing all day… The contrary is true of those who seek honour, for more often than not they have poor beds and many a time sleep without beds at all and with their clothes on; and this rest and repose is quite enough for them, for they would not want it otherwise for the great profit and honour they expect to have from it.' Similarly also with heat and cold,'… those wretched men have to be sustained and pampered so that in winter they are wrapped in furs and warmly clad and live in warm houses, and in summer are lightly clad and live in cool houses or in the coldest vaults, otherwise they cannot survive because of their decadent habits.'[50] Those who want to win honour 'adapt to the seasons,' 'endure the cold,' and 'put up with the heat.' In general, 'good knights may have to undergo hard trials and adventures, for it can be truly said to them that when they want to sleep, they must keep vigil, when they want to eat, they must fast, and when they are thirsty, there is often nothing to drink, and when they would rest, they have to exert themselves all through the night, and when they would be secure from danger, they will be beset by great terrors…' Nevertheless, deeds of arms performed for the right motives will provide a path to redemption, '… for those who perform deeds of arms

more to gain God's grace and for the salvation of the soul than for glory in this world, their noble souls will be set in paradise to all eternity and their persons will be for ever honoured and well remembered.'[51]

★ ★ ★

Besides the 'Manual of Chivalry' genre, other areas of the canon were available to Lawrence, and it can be proved, in some instances, that he not only read them closely, but that they also left traces in his writing, and even in the person he was becoming. Unsurprisingly, considering Lawrence's preoccupation with the *Crusader Castles*, and his one-time project of a 'monumental book on the Crusades' (letter of 24 January, 1911), his knowledge of the literature seems extensive. However, he advised his brother Will Lawrence to 'always read something that throws a side-light on the set authorities'. That is, Lawrence had not read the set authorities until he had read the more obscure Armenian Chroniclers. Lawrence advised his brother that he himself '… didn't touch them till he had read the Armenian Chroniclers,[52] William of Tyre,[53] and the gestes'.

Perhaps less arcane, and nearer to the central literature of Chivalry, were the books Lawrence carried with him on his arduous journey on foot through Northern Syria in the summer of 1911. The diary he kept, later published in *Oriental Assembly*, records how, along with Rabelais, he packed his *Holy Grail* and *Song of Roland/Chanson de Roland*. The next day the text is registered in the diary in Oriental Assembly by Lawrence as the *Holy Graal* thus indicating the old French text. A year earlier during his cycle tour of France, Lawrence was similarly carrying 'Montaigne [2 vols], *Tristan and Iseult, Jehan de Saintre* and *xiii the cent fabliaux*.'[54]

Lawrence was particularly pleased to have found a good copy of *L'Histoire du Petit Jehan de Saintre*, which deals, amongst other things with the transition from castle to court. His copy is marked '*T.E.L. Beauvois 1910*', and in a letter to his mother dated September, 1910 from Le Petit Andelys where he had read some of it in the castle sitting 'below the keep', as he relates:

> '*The book I had was Petit Jehan De Saintre, a XV cent. novel of knightly manners – very good – I had wanted to read it for a long time but the Oxford Union copy was so badly printed that I had not the heart for it. Now I have found (for 1 f.25) a series quite nicely typed on fairly good paper. So far I have only got 4 volumes, because they are rather much to carry (as for expense I saved that on food – only 6 francs, and I reckoned to spend 3 frs a day on it).*'[55]

The flavour of the book can be had from a brief excerpt, where it appears to be consistent with Lull and de Charny:

> 'Be loyal of hands and mouth, and serve every man as best you may. Seek the fellowship of good men; hearken to their words and remember them. Be humble and courteous wherever you go, boasting not nor talking overmuch, neither be dumb altogether…'[56]

Le Petit Jehan de Saintre deals, amongst other things, with the transition at the onset of adolescence from the world of childhood, where any Chivalric education has been by precept and example, to the larger world. The aspiring knight is sent to a noble household to become a page or squire as, for example, William Marshal, a knight errant and Baron, and a Regent for Henry III in 1216, would be. The hero in La Sale's book is a page at the French court, already 'skilful and hardy' at riding an unbridled horse, singing, dancing, playing tennis, running and leaping.'[57] Rather like Lancelot in *Lancelot of the Lake*, a young lady befriends him and undertakes to teach him manoeuvres and morals: 'If he were to study, his best guide was history… and to find in the real or fictional past the exemplars for the good life. By thus reading, hearkening to and remembering noble histories, examples and teaching, you may acquire the everlasting Joys of Paradise, honour in arms, honour in wisdom and honour in riches, and live worshipfully and cheerfully.' This advice to study a certain kind of history ('noble histories') with a particular motivation – to take them as exempla – is consistent with the earlier Chivalry texts such as Lull and de Charny, as well as Caxton's envoi to Lull. Curiously, the only modern to offer remotely similar advice is the 'wild' classicist Nietzsche. In *The Uses and Disadvantages of History for Life* Nietzsche writes, 'Satiate your soul with Plutarch and when you believe in his heroes dare at the same time to believe in yourself.'[58] In so doing, Nietzsche's readers would have entered the world of the Greek and Latin classics just as Lawrence was so assiduously entering the world of Medieval Chivalry, and perhaps similarly beginning to believe in himself. After all, in a letter to Dick Knowles in 1927, Lawrence writes that it was when he was 17 that he began his 'own, independent, voluntary, travels.' It was 'the age at which I suddenly found myself.'[59]

So far as *Jehan de Saintre* is concerned, one way to read it is to see it as a courtly development of the late Middle Ages, a novel not too distant from the real knightly careers of such persons as Chevalier Bayard, Du Gueslin, William Marshal, Richard I, and Edward III.

Finding in 'the real or fictional past the exemplars of the good life' seems to have been precisely one of Lawrence's activities, and along with his close and vigorous engagement with military architecture (the towers climbed at night), his reading strategies helped to sustain this search. His brother, A.W. Lawrence, remarks that 'His medieval researches were… a dream way of escape from bourgeois England as well as a detached study of another civilisation.'[60] If this is so, then Lawrence not only dreamed, but also read his way out of bourgeois England with particular intensity and unusual reading practices. And not only 'escape from', but 'entry into'. All readers of a particularly romantic or heroic temperament, or those just plain unhappy in the mediocre nightmare of modern consumer culture (say from Baudelaire onwards), will know and understand the joy with which one can enter other worlds by sufficiently intense reading. And the mysterious alchemy by which one returns changed. And how by such methods – including, as with Lawrence, reading the book at a particular site (for example with De Sale's *Jehan de Saintre* another Self is chosen and developed.) The appetite and drive with which Lawrence pursued his reading strategy is perfectly illustrated in a minor, not to say late and humble, piece of Chivalrous text – Maurice Hewlett's *Richard Yea and Nay*. John E. Mack in *A Prince of Our Disorder* describes it, brutally, if fairly justly, as '… a turn of the century novel which tells how Richard I's indecisiveness cost him the love of his sweetheart.'[61] Lawrence describes how he read the novel in Egypt for the *ninth time*. Examined a little more closely, one sees that it is dedicated to '*His friend Edmund Gosse [always benevolent to his invention] This Chronicle of Anjou and a Noble Lady.*'

Why would Lawrence read this nine times? Perhaps one can say that in general, whatever the book's merits or faults, it evokes the medieval world and mindset.

That it also evokes the personality (true or false) of Richard I, a hero of Lawrence's, not least as a castle-builder, but also as celebrated in *Crusader Castles*, may explain some of its appeal.[62] By reading it so many times he could inhabit it. [Curiously, John Pendlebury, who fought with the Greeks in the Second World War, and who was known as 'the Cretan Lawrence', was also very fond of *Richard Yea and Nay*.][63]

This view or philosophy of reading is lyrically espoused in the letter to his mother of August 1910 from Le Petit Andelys,[64] where he has already discussed *Petit Jehan de Saintre*:

> '*You know, I think, the joy of getting into a strange country in a book: at home when I have shut my door and the town is in bed – and I know that nothing, not even the dawn – can disturb me in my curtains: only the slow crumbling of the coals in the fire: they get so red and throw such splendid glimmerings on the Hypnos and the brasswork. And it is lovely too, after you have been wandering for hours in the forest with Percivale or Sagramors le desirous, to open the door, and from over the Cherwell to look at the Sun glowering through the valley mists. Why does one not like things if there are other people about? Why cannot one make one's books live except in the night, after hours of straining? And you know they have to be your own books too, and you have to read them more than once. I think they take in something of your personality, and your environment also – you know a second hand book sometimes is so much more flesh and blood than a new one – and it is almost terrible to think that your ideas, yourself in your books, may be giving life to generations of readers after you are forgotten. It is that specially which makes one need good books: books that will be worthy of what you are going to put into them. What would you think of a great sculptor who flung away his gifts on modelling clay or sand? Imagination should be put into the most precious caskets, and that is why one can only live in the future or the past, in Utopia or the Wood beyond the World. Father won't know all this – but if you can get the right book at the right time you taste joys – not only bodily, physical, but spiritual also, which pass one out above and beyond one's miserable self, as it were through a huge air, following the light of another man's thought. And you can never be quite the old self again. You have forgotten a little bit: or rather pushed it out with a little of the inspiration of what is immortal in someone who has gone before you.*'[65]

We can infer from the references to *Percivale* and *Sagramors* that Lawrence had been reading either Chretien de Troyes or Malory. The first story of Perceval occurs in de Troyes, where he emerges as the second most holy knight after Galahad, involved with the other Knights of the Round Table in the Grail Quest. The other source would be Malory's *Morte d'Arthur*, although Wolfram von Eschenbach's *Parzival* is also possible. Malory seems more probable, given that he was a favourite of Lawrence's and he carried *Morte d'Arthur* with him in Arabia along with Aristophanes and the *Oxford Book of English Verse*. Lawrence mentions having *Morte d'Arthur* in his saddlebags as late as January 1918, and again in August in his effort to describe Auda, so this text at least survived the rigours of desert warfare.[66] In fact, whilst snow-bound in Tafileh, Lawrence evidently found Malory sustaining:

> 'In my saddle bags was a Morte d'Arthur. It relieved my disgust. The men had *only* physical resources; and in the confined misery their tempers roughened.'[67]

Oddly, in the Oxford edition, the passage reads '… which *should* have relieved my disgust.' [Oxford Edn., page 549], thereby ascribing an almost therapeutic or soteriological power to the book.[68] Whatever may be the case, perhaps the book functioned as a reminder of core Chivalry values, and thereby sustained Lawrence's sense of self and morale. Recalling that the warrior ethic of Chivalry can be summed up as the aspiration to achieve Honour (if not Salvation) in Arms, this aspiration can at times look very fragile – as at Tafileh – and needs sustaining, perhaps by those values which are ancillary to Honour, such as strength and self-reliance, or basic to military strategy itself, such as initiative and mobility. Malory's equivalent for Honour is 'Worship', and it occurs in many places in the *Morte d'Arthur* and is, indeed, picked up and used by Lawrence, more sparingly, in the *Seven Pillars*. In a way, reflecting the inner tensions of Chivalry between unreconstructed warrior and Christianity, it is only at the end of the book, with the renunciation of the worldly warrior path, that Malory begins to speak of 'perfection,' as the surviving protagonists enter monastic institutions (one is almost irresistibly reminded of Lawrence's entry into the RAF and his intense valorisation of 'the conquest of the air', and his perception of that vocation as the 'meaning of his generation'). Where the Christianisation of Chivalry is most explicit, we see that it has become much more sophisticated and its aspirations, whilst still partly based on the original warrior values, have become transcendental. This is clear in the *Quest of the Holy Grail*:

'*Beloved son, now canst thou range over all the world and soar above the ranks of chivalry.*'[69]

And, conversely, the holy man's interpretation of Gawain's dream of the future, where, amongst other things, he explains why the Grail hid itself:

'*For in the presence of the sacred vessel his eyes will lose their sight because he sullied them gazing on the midden of this world, and his body will be sapped of strength for the years in which he used it in the enemy's service.*'[70, 71]

Returning finally to a consideration of the five basic Chivalrous values – *Prouesse* (Prowess), *Loyaute* (Loyalty), *Largesse* (Generosity), *Courtosie* (Manners), *Franchise* (free and frank bearing), and their relationships, it can be seen that they support each other and form a kind of organic totality. Considering each one in isolation, the logic of their relations becomes evident, that is:

Loyalty without Prowess has no power, effectivity, or unity.
Prowess without Loyalty risks mere brigandage and violence.
Prowess without Courtesy is vulgar, offensive and vain.
Prowess without Generosity is rabid and narrow.
Generosity without the other virtues has no basis in achievement.

Franchise can be seen as the outward mark, if not necessarily of good birth, then at least of the good conscience flowing from the sincere pursuit or achievement of the other virtues. The literature of Chivalry does provide an image of this totality in the Pentangle, or endless knot, which Sir Gawain carries on his shield and coat; and it is Simone Weil who notices this unity of the virtues, and is probably also aware that such unity is a Stoic doctrine.[72]

A person living by this elaborated code would necessarily judge their activities and achievements by it, as well as their perceived failures. So, along with the explicit Chivalry values, one might expect to hear of values which are ancillary, or supportive of the 'classical' five or so virtues. In other words, one would be unsurprised to meet a cult of effort, expertise, will, honour, endurance, rank, duty, and power. And the negative of these, e.g. renunciation, abstention, cleanliness, purity etc. Whilst the upper reaches of these scales of values inevitably generate an idea of perfection, all the degrees of relative success and failure also have a rank and place. So, suffering pain and death find their place and meaning as well. Perhaps it is here that we can better understand the strange line (2524) in the *Song of Roland*, which we have seen Lawrence knew so well:

> 'He who knows true pain has learnt a great deal.'

Roland's suffering and death are consequences of his profound sense of his duty and personal honour.

> 'For his Lord a vassal must suffer great hardship
> And endure great heat and great cold,
> And he must lose both hair and hide'[73]

That Lawrence had indeed 'adventured' his own body, is well attested by many witnesses, not least by his commanding officer at Mountbatten, Wing Commander Sydney Smith, and his wife Clare Sydney Smith:

> 'Sydney, who wasn't well enough to swim, pointed out to me all the scars and bullet wounds on TES's skin. There was hardly a place on his body that wasn't marked in this way. I shuddered to think of the close shaves he has come through.'[74]

Endnotes

[1] See Maurice Keen, *Chivalry*, pp. 2, 11, 37, 52, etc.

[2] T.E.L., *Crusader Castles*, p. 27.

[3] T.E.L., *Crusader Castles*, p. 83.

[4] T.E.L., *Crusader Castles*, p. 97.

[5] Quoted In Mack, p. 12.

[6] Keen, *Chivalry*, p. 6.

[7] Information from the Bodleian Library.

[8] Gies, *The Knight in History*, p. 97.

[9] Keen, p. 6.

[10] Lawrence added a marginal note to the typescript of *Crusader Castles*. 'Cp. Tiberias', p. 83 where he was considering death rates in Palestine, and transferability of fiefs.

[11] See Keen, pp. 6-8.

[12] One is inevitably reminded here of Lawrence's cult of white robes in the desert. And of his use of the word 'cleanness' in other contexts. e.g. the cover of *Seven Pillars*.

[13] Again, note the cover of *Seven Pillars*: 'The sword also means…'

[14] 'I do well remember him saying to me, "There are two things I am afraid of – an untruth, and injustice."' Lieutenant Colonel Archibald Donald Strange-Boston. Quoted in '*Lawrence of Arabia in Dorset*', p. 16.

[15] See Keen, p. 7. And Gies, pp. 97, 103.

[16] The medieval source for this is the prose Livre de Chevalrie printed in *Oeuvres de Froissart*, see p. 256. See also Keen, p. 14.

[17] See Penguin Edn, pp. 362-366. Also quoted in *Essential T.E.L.*, p. 142.

[18] *Book of the Order of Chivalry*, Byles' Introduction, p. XII.

[19] Michael Foss, *Chivalry*, Transcription, p. 174.

20 R. Barber, *Reign of Chivalry*, p. 109.
21 R. Barber, *Reign of Chivalry*, p. 110.
22 Arthurian Romances, p. 399.
23 Barber transcription, p. 110.
24 Lull, *Book of the Order of Chivalry*, p. 60.
25 Maurice Keen, *Chivalry*, p. 10.
26 Lull, pp. 92-96.
27 Lull, p. 97.
28 Lull, p. 101.
29 T.E.L. *To his Biographers*, p. 8.
30 Gies, *The Knight in History*, p. 97.
31 Lull, p. 121.
32 See Lewis Thorpe's translation and introduction. And *Aspects of Malory*. Edited by Takamiya and Brewer.
33 Wilson, p. 38. Mack, p. 24. *Letters*, Ed. Garnett, p. 487.
34 *Letters of T.E. Lawrence*, Ed. Garnett, p. 57.
35 *Crusader Castles*, Haag Edn., p. 196.
36 *Essential T.E.L.*, p. 55. *Letters*, Ed. Garnett, p. 122.
37 Another reference occurs in the letters of 1908, where a gateway 'is supposed to be B. de Bornish.' Garnett, p. 61.
38 Keen, *Chivalry*, pp. 60, 62, 118.
39 It is notable that every individual named here except Syre Robert Knolles figures in Maurice Keen's study of Chivalry.
40 A.T. Byles' notes to Lull, p. 127.
41 Froissart, *Chronicles*, p. 129.
42 Keen, p. 12.
43 Geoffroi de Charny, *The Book of Chivalry*, pp. 87, 93, 95, 97, etc.
44 De Charny, p. 119. 'And there are many who say they would not want to love Queen Guinevere if they did not declare it openly or if it were not known.
45 De Charny, pp. 175-177.
46 De Charny, p. 111.
47 Worshipped in Sparta where youths were whipped during certain ceremonies in her temple. Recorded in Plutarch.
48 *Seven Pillars*, Penguin Edn., pp. 476-477.
49 De Charny, pp. 123, 125.
50 De Charny, p. 125.
51 De Charny, p. 177.
52 Probably Matthew of Edessa. Cited by Gies, pp. 51, 234.
53 Lawrence refers to Prof. Oman's quotation of William of Tyre in *Crusader Castles*, p. 68. Oxford Edn.
54 Letter to V.W. Richards, 29 Aug., 1910. *Letters of T.E. Lawrence*, Ed. Garnett, p. 87.
55 *Letters of T.E.L.*, Ed. Malcolm Brown, p. 23.
56 Chivalry. *The Path of Love*, pp. 54, 55.
57 See Foss, *Chivalry*, pp. 221-226.
58 See Friedrich Nietzsche, *'Untimely Meditations'*, p. 95.
59 *Selected Letters of T.E. Lawrence*, Ed. Garnett, p. 255.
60 *T.E. Lawrence by His Friends*, p. 586.
61 John E. Mack, *Prince of our Disorder*, p. 101. The source in Lawrence is *Home Letters*, p. 193.
62 *Crusader Castles*, Oxford Edn., p. 116.

[63] Imogen Grunden, *The Rash Adventurer: A Life of John Pendlebury*, pp. 18, 26.

[64] *Letters*, Ed. Garnett, pp. 84–85.

[65] Ibid.

[66] *Seven Pillars of Wisdom*, 'Oxford' 1922 text, pp. 99, 549, 658.

[67] *Seven Pillars*, Penguin Edn., p. 495.

[68] Italics added.

[69] *Quest of the Holy Grail*, p. 148.

[70] Lawrence's Preface to *Seven Pillars*. Penguin Edn. 'It does not pretend to be impartial. I was fighting for my hand, upon my own midden.'

[71] *Quest*, p. 173.

[72] *Sir Gawain and the Green Knight*, p. 45.

[73] *Song of Roland*, Line 1010.

[74] Clare Sydney Smith, *The Golden Reign*, p. 80.

CHAPTER FOUR

Clouds Hill Books

✧

ALL his life Lawrence was a voracious and intense reader, working his way through everything that interested him in the Oxford libraries, sometimes at the rate of two or three books in a night. Some of this must have been highly selective, and as any experienced reader knows, there are strategies for getting to the essence of a book very fast if need be. Just so, Lawrence maintained that he could tear the heart out of a book in half an hour, and that he,

> '... read every book which interested me in the library of the Oxford Union [best part of 50,000 vols I expect] in 6 years. My father used to get me books while I was at school: afterwards I borrowed always 6 vols a day, in his name and my own. For three years I read day and night, on a hearth rug which was mattress, so that I could fall asleep as I read. Often 18 hours reading in a day, and so good at the job, by practice, that I could tear the heart out of the soberest book in half an hour.'[1]

Lawrence was also very interested in the technicalities and aesthetics of book production; partly due to his admiration for William Morris. If the First World War had not occurred, his plans to print and bind rare books with Leonard Green or Vyvyan Richards might well have flowered. He had got as far as buying land at Pole Hill, had acquired old beams for a roof, and bought jars of crushed Murex in Syria to stain the vellum they planned to use for binding.

Even in later life, Lawrence was prepared to put serious efforts into his reading practice. In a letter to F.N. Doubleday in 1929, he remarked, 'One can't read in odd half hours: reading is to soak oneself hour after hour all day in a single real book, until the book is realer than one's chair or world.'[2] Similarly, with his review of Men of Letters by Philip Guedalla, Lawrence wrote, 'The whole body of his writing seemed better on a second acquaintance. Therefore I tried it a third time. That's hard on a new book, to be read three times straight off.'[3] In passing, it may be that Lawrence was aware of the Cistercian practice of Lectio Divino (divine reading) whereby sacred books were as much meditated upon as read; until the author's mind was one with the readers. Of course, Lawrence had great ambitions as a writer, and accumulated, judged, and analysed books with this in mind, closely examining technique and style. As Jeremy Wilson notes, 'In the event there was to be no period in Lawrence's life after 1908 when he was not planning or working on a literary project of some kind.' After the war, he prepared himself for a writing career by intensive study.'[4] The enormous difference between the impacted and highly-wrought prose style of the

Seven Pillars, with its wealth of allusion and reference, and the almost laconic economy and clarity of *The Mint*, may be one of the effects of these studies, as well as Lawrence's restless dissatisfaction with the *Seven Pillars*, despite his best efforts.

The books left at Clouds Hill after Lawrence's death had therefore met various criteria, and were the results of complex choices and long-term interests. Even allowing for time, chance, and theft, they tell us something about the mind of their owner. We also know that Lawrence could be quite ruthless in getting rid of unwanted books. He simply posted them through random letter boxes at night.

An initial glance through the list of titles which was published by his brother after his death shows an enormous range of books, mostly in English, but also in French, Latin, and Greek.[5] There are also many novels and much poetry, along with non-fiction that includes music scores and motor boat manuals. The list ranges from Henry Adams and Aeschylus (in vellum) to Zinner's study of Typhus, *Rats, Lice, and History*.

Collecting together the books which are about Chivalry, or of Chivalrous provenance, produces the following list:

1. Antioch. *La Conquête de Jérusalem: faisant suite à la chanson d'Antioche composée par le pèlerin Richard et ren. par Graindor de Douai au XIII siècle pub.* par C. Hippeau. Paris, A. Aubry, 1868, 8in. Half calf. 'T.E.L.'
   La chanson d'Antioche, composée au commencement du XII siècle par le pèlerin Richard. 2 vols. [Both vols uncut].

2. Arrian. *History of the expedition of Alexander the Great, and conquest of Persia*, trans. by Mr. Rooke, corrected and enlarged. London, J. Davis, 1812.

3. *Aucassin et Nicolete.* Edited and revised by F.W. Bourdillon. Frontispiece by L. Pissarro. [Last book printed in Vale type by E. and L. Pissarro at the Eragny Press, 1903]. 'T.E.L.'

4. Baerlein, H. *On the Forgotten Road: a chronicle of the crusade of children, 1212.* London, J. Murray, 1909.

5. Bayard. *The Right Joyous and Pleasant History of the Chevalier Bayard, by the Loyal Servant.* Trans. S. Coleridge [Newnes' Pocket Classics]. London. 'T.E.L. Beyrout. 1911'.

6. Caesar. *Commentarii cum supplementis Auli Hirtii et aliorum* [Oxford Pocket Classics]. Oxonii, J. Parker 1880. 'T.E.S.'
   Gai Iuli Caesaris commentarii rerum in Gallia gestarum VII accedit Auli Hirti commentarius ex rec. T. Rice Holmes. London, Medici Soc., 1914. Limp vellum 'T.E.L. 1919'.

7. Castiglione, B. *The Courtyer of Count Baldessar Castilio very necessary and profitable for younge gentilmen done into Englyshe by Thomas Hoby*, ed. by J.E. Ashbee: Essex House Press [lim. ed. no. 65]. London, E. Arnold, 1900. Vellum. 'T.E.L. Pole Hill, Chingford, E.4.'

8. Cervantes. *El Ingenioso hidalgo Don Quijote de la Mancha.* Paris, Garnier Hermanos, 1886.

9. Clausewitz, C. von. *On War*, trans. by Col. J.J. Graham. New and revised ed. with intro. by F.N. Maude. 3 vols. London, Kegan Paul, 1911. 'T.E.L.'

10. Comines, P. De. *The History of Comines,* Englished by T. Danett; intro. by C. Whibley. 2 vols. [Tudor Translations, ed. by W.E. Henley, vols. 17 and 18]. London, D. Nutt, 1897. 'T.E.L.'

11. Digby, K.H. *The Broadstone of Honour, or the true sense and practice of chivalry.* Godefridus. London, E. Lumley, 1844. [Bookplate of William Hopetown, Earl of Northesk, inside front cover]. 6 vols. On flyleaf 'T.E.S.' (Therefore after 1923).

12. Edward the Confessor. *La Estoire de Seint Aedward le rei.* Reproduced in facsimile from the unique MS. Intro. by M.R. James [Roxburghe Club]. Oxford, O.U.P., 1920.

13. Elmer, R.P. and Smart, C.A. *The Book of the Longbow*, ed. by Robert P . Elmer and Charles Allen Smart, with illus. by Will Crawford [lim. ed., no. 135]. New York, Doubleday Doran, 1929. Uncut.

14. Fabliaux. *Recueil de Fabliaux.* Paris, J. Gillequin. Half-calf, red, tooled back. 'T.E.L. Caen 1910.'

15. Ffoulkes, C. *Armour and Weapons.* Pref. by Viscount Dillon. Oxford, Clarendon Press, 1909. 'With kind regards from the author, Charles ffoulkes. Nov. 1909'.

16. Fitz-Warine, F. *The History of Fulk Fitz-Warine*, trans. A. Kemp-Welch [King's Classics]. London, A. Moring Ltd, 1904. 'T.E.L.'

17. Froissart. *Chronicle*, trans. by Sir John Bourchier, Lord Berners. Intro. by William Paton Ker. 6 vols. [Tudor Translations]. London, D. Nutt, 1901-3.

18. Gaya, L. De. *Gaya's Traité des Armes*, 1678, ed. by C. ffoulkes [Tudor and Stuart Library]. Oxford, Clarendon Press, 1911.

19. Godefrey of Boloyne. *The History of Godefrey of Boloyne and of the conquest of Jherusalem* [from Caxton's ed.]. Hammersmith, Kelmscott Press, 1893. 'T.E.L.'

20. Homer. *Ilias*, ed. Walter Leaf [Parnassus Library]. London, Macmillan, 1895. Suède.
    – *Ilias*, the first twelve staves, trans. by Maurice Hewlett. London, Cresset Press, 1928. Pages uncut.
    – Introduction by James M. Paton, 2 vols. [Chiswick ed.] [lim. ed. no. 11] London, Pickering and Chatto, n.d. Vellum. 'T.E.L. Oxford 1911'.

21. – *The Odyssey of Homer*, done into English verse by W. Morris. London, Longmans, Green, 1897.
    – *Odyssey*, trans. by T.E. Lawrence. [lim. ed.] London, Emery Walker, 1932. Black calf.
    – *The Odyssey of Homer*, newly trans. into English prose by T.E. Lawrence [lim. ed. copy *extra seriem*]. New York, Oxford University Press, 1932. 'T.E.S.'
    – text of 1896 ed. By D.B. Monro: designed by R. Proctor [lim. ed.]. Oxford, University Press, 1909. Pages uncut. 'To T.E. Lawrence from Sydney C. Cockerell Mar. 27, 1922'.

22. La Sale, A. de. *Le petit Jehan de Saintré*. Paris, J. Gillequin et Cie, n.d. 'T.E.L. Beauvais 1910'.

23. Machiavelli, N. vol I. *The Art of War,* trans. by P. Whitethorne, 1560; *The Prince,* trans. by E. Dacres, 1640. Vol II. *The Florentine History*, trans. by T. Bedingfeld, 1595 [Tudor Translations, ed. by W.E. Henley, vol. v 39 and 40]. London, D. Nutt, 1905.

24. Malory, Sir T. *Le Morte d'Arthur*, 2 vols. [Everyman's Library]. London, Dent, 1908.

25. Marie De France. *Poésies*, publiées par B. de Roquefort, 2 vols. Paris, Chasserian, 1820. Half calf.

26. Morris. W. *The Story of Sigurd the Volsung and the Fall of the Niblungs*, with two pictures designed by E. Burne-Jones and engraved by W.H. Hooper. Hammersmith, Kelmscott Press, 1898. Limp Vellum. 'T.E.L.'

27. Plutarch. *Plutarch's Lives of the noble Grecians and Romans*, Englished by Sir Thomas North anno 1579, with an introduction by George Wyndham, 6 vols. [Tudor Translations, ed. by W.E. Henley, nos. 7-12]. London, D. Nutt, 1895-6. 'T.E.L.'

28. Roland. *La Chanson de Roland* [Bibl. Romanica]. No imprint. Vellum. 'T.E.L. Oxford 1909'.

29. *Romance of the Rose*, by W. Lorris and J. Clopinel, Englished by F.S. Ellis, vols I and III [Temple Classics]. London, Dent, n.d. 'T.E.L.'

30. Sturlason, S. *Heimskringla: the Olaf Sagas*, trans. S. Laing [Everyman's Library]. London, Dent, n.d.

31. Tristan. *Le Roman de Tristan et Iseut*, ed. J. Bedier [Lim. ed., no. 280]. Paris, H. Piazza, 1918. 'T.E.L.'
    – *The Romance of Tristan and Iseult*, re-told by J. Bédier, trans. by H. Belloc. London, G. Allen, 1913.

32. Troy, *The recuyell of the historyes of Troye*. 2 vols. Hammersmith, Kelmscott Press, 1892. Limp Vellum. Uncut. 'T.E.L.'

33. Usamah. *An Arab-Syrian gentleman and warrior in the period of the crusades: memoirs of Usamah Ibn-Munqidh*, trans. by Philip K. Hitti [Records of Civilisation]. New York, Columbia University Press, 1929.

(Author Note: Lawrence tended to mark his books 'T.E.L.' until 1923 when he adopted 'T.E.S.' Details in J.M. Wilson, *Authorised Biography of T.E. Lawrence*.)

There are, naturally, marginal cases where categorisation is awkward, for example Caesar's *Gallic War*, Churchill's *Life of Marlborough*, and various Scandinavian sagas, such as the *Olaf Sagas*, *Lagerlof*, and Gosta Berling's saga. Also books which A.W. Lawrence mentions, for example *The Kalevela*, and *Huon of Bordeaux*, which are no longer present. Nevertheless, an initial survey of the rest of the Clouds Hill library (over 1000 volumes), shows that there are about 40 titles on war and military subjects, over thirty of which are broadly 'Chivalrous'. There are approximately seventeen titles on Christianity and adjacent spiritual subjects, such as those by Blake and Dante, as well as the *Chronicle of Jocelin of Brakeland* (whom Richard I had visited), and Sir Thomas Brown's *Religio Medici*.

The adoption of a further group of categories, for the purposes of broad classification, besides 'Warfare', 'Chivalry' and 'Christianity', such as 'Novels', 'Poetry', 'Plays', 'Non-fiction', and 'Philosophy', yields the following, approximate, totals of titles per category:

Novels 348
Poetry 334
Plays 61
Non-fiction (including history) 166
Philosophy 10

Even allowing for argument about classification and category ascription, it is obvious that there is about three times more imaginative literature than non-fiction. Furthermore, the quantity of overt philosophy is strikingly small: Epicurus, Epictetus, Lucretius, Montesquieu. Montaigne, Nietzsche, Schiller, Swedenborg, Voltaire, and Spinoza are present, but virtually no modern, post-Cartesians.

Another story emerges, however, if the library is examined for classical, canonical texts. Apart from the extensive set of Loeb classics presented by Lord Riddell,[6] single classics are dotted throughout the library in English, Latin, and Classical Greek, e.g.

1. Aeschylus. *Tragoediae* and *Oresteia*, both marked 'T.E.L.'
2. Anacreon. *The Odes with the fragments of Sappho and Alcaeus*, trans. T. Orger. London, R. Hunter, 1825. [Inside front cover: *Bookplate of John Morgan*. Flyleaf: *Bookplate of Maurice Baring*. '*Maurice Baring: 1914*'. '*T. Shaw from Maurice Baring, 1929*. A gift from Maurice Baring in 1929.]
3. What appears to be a Greek Anthology with a Latin commentary, viz: *Anthologia Florilegium diversorum epigrammatum in septem libros distinctum. Venetiis, apud Aldifilios*, 1550. Leather. 'T.E.L. Aleppo 1912'.
4. Anthology. 1 vol. [Selections from vols. I and II of Firmin-Didot, with Latin translation, Anthologia Platina]. 'Arab Bureau Cairo' in rubber stamp. 'T.E.L. 1914'.
5. Apuleius. *The Golden Asse of Apuleius, done into English*. See also '*Asse*' [sic]. by William Adlington, with an introduction by Thomas Seccombe [lim. ed.]. London, Grant Richards, 1913. 'T.E.L.'
    – *The Golden Ass*, trans. out of Latin by William Adlington, *anno* 1566, intro. by Charles Whibley, [Tudor Translations IV]. London, D. Nutt, 1893.
6. Aristophanes, *Comoediae accedunt perditarum fabularum fragmenta ex rec. G. Dindorfii*, vol I. Oxonii, Typ. Academ, 1835. MS. list of contents on flyleaf. 'T.E.L. Oxford 1914. This copy went with me through the Arab war. T.E.L.'
7. Arrian. *History of the expedition of Alexander the Great, and conquest of Persia*, trans. by Mr. Rooke, corrected and enlarged. London, J. Davis, 1812. (Listed with Chivalry texts.)
8. Caesar's Commentaries: previously listed with Chivalrous texts.
9. Epictetus. *The Book of Epictetus, being the Enchiridion together with chapters from the Discourses and Selections from the Fragments of Epictetus*. Trans. E. Carter [Harrap Library]. London, Harrap, n.d. 'T.E.L., Paris'.
10. Epicurus, *Epicurus's Morals*: collected, and faithfully Englished, by W. Charlton. With an introductory Essay by F. Manning [lim. ed.]. London, P. Davies, 1926. 'To T.E. Shaw for the purpose of comparison, from Frederic Manning. 3.iii.1930'.
11. Herodotus, *Historiarum libri IX. Textus Wesselingianus passim refictus opera Frid. Volg. Reizii*. 2 vols. Oxon, J. Cooke & J. Parker, 1808. Vellum.
    – *The Famous Hystory of Herodotus* trans. By B.R. 1584, intro. By Leonard Whibley [Tudor Trans. 2nd series]. London, Constable, 1924.
12. Homer. Seven Homer texts, as listed under Chivalry, in English, Latin, and Greek.
13. Horace, *Horati carminum libri IV*, [lim. ed.). Londini. Peter Davies, 1926. Uncut.

— *Quintus Horatius Flaccus. Londini*, G. Pickering, 1824. Leather. ['T.E.L. Shaw from Ronald Storrs'].

— *Opera*, ed. F.W. Cornish. London, Kegan Paul, Trench et Soc. 1888. 'T.E.L.'

— *Quinti Horati Flacci carmina Sapphica*. Chelsea, in aed. St. J. Hornby, Ashendene Press, 1903. On Japanese vellum.

— *Carminum librum quintum a R. Kipling et C. Graves Anglice redditum* ed. A.D. Godley. Oxonii, B. Blackwell, 1920.

14. Lucian. *Lucian's True History*, trans. by F. Hickes, illus. by W. Strang, J.B. Clark and A. Beardsley, [lim. ed.]. A.H. Bullen, 1902. Suède.

15. Lucretius, *T. Lucreti Cari de rerum natura libri sex. Chelsea*, in aed. St. J. Hornby, 1913. 'T.E.L.'

— *De rerum natura libri sex recogn.* C. Bailey. ed. altera, [Scrip. class. bibl. Oxon). Oxonii, Typ. Clarend., 1921.

16. Thucydides. *Eight bookes of the Peloponnesian warre written by Thucydides the sonne of Olorus. Interpreted with faith and diligence immediately out of the Greeke by Thomas Hobbes, the author of the book De Cive, Secretary to the late Earle of Devonshire.* London, Charles Harper, 1676. Leather. Rebacked.

17. Xenophon. *Complete Works*, trans. by Ashley, Spelman Smith, Fielding [new ed.]. London, W.P. Nimmo, 1877.

Before considering these Greek and Latin texts, it is worth recalling Arnold Lawrence's remark about T.E.'s 'quick reading… and almost faultless memory [that] had set him mentally at home in Biblical Palestine, in Medieval France and Ancient Greece, and to a lesser extent in ancient Egypt and Mesopotamia, before his submergence in Arab nationality.'[7]

Whereas Lawrence's Biblical knowledge shows clearly in his letters to his mother from Palestine, and in the letters written around the time of the *Wilderness of Zin*, his inhabitance of the culture of Medieval France has been sufficiently demonstrated in the matter of his Chivalry and Crusader and military architecture interests. The 'submergence' or 'mental at-homeness' within ancient Greek culture is a more subtle affair. Lawrence seems to have preferred Greek to Latin. Whilst still at school, he had taken papers on Xenophon's *Anabasis*, and Caesar's *De Bello Gallico*, although his marks were not particularly high. However, he does not appear to have been put off, because when he had some leisure time in 1927, he wrote to Charlotte Shaw to say that he had returned to Xenophon, although he expected that reading him would take him many weeks. He proposed to go on to Herodotus after that, and then the Odyssey: 'Greek literature is so good that it is almost the best second language for a reader.'[8] This is a view that Lawrence seems to have maintained, because in 1934 he wrote to C. Day-Lewis, *'My Latin wasn't ever much good, so that I never enjoyed Catullus. I suppose that means that I have never justified the time I spent trying to learn the beastly language? There seem to me to be ten good Greek books to every Latin one.'*[9]

Ronald Storrs records his friendship with Lawrence during the First World War having met him in the winter of 1914: 'I would come upon him in my flat, reading always Latin or Greek, with corresponding gaps in my shelves… We had no literary differences, except that he preferred Homer to Dante and disliked my placing Theocritus before Aristophanes.'

Lawrence was fluent enough to write a fragment of a Greek Epigram to Storrs, as a postscript to his letter announcing the end of his RAF career, in which he expressed both his mastery of the language and his unhappiness in three allusive words.

The complete epigram is as follows:

'*Here Lie I of Tarsus*
Never having married, and would that my father had not.'[10]

Lawrence's p.s. reads:

'*I leave here tomorrow a.m. … and the R.A.F. that same moment.*'

Apart from the Aristophanes that he carried with him in Arabia, and his later translation of Homer, Lawrence showed an enduring interest in three Classical Greek authors: Xenophon, Lucian, and Philostratus (the source for the *Life of Apollonius of Tyana*). These I will examine in more detail in the following chapters.

Endnotes

[1] *Letters to Biographers*, p. 64.
[2] *Letters,* Garnett Edn., p. 661.
[3] Reprinted in the *T.E. Lawrence Society Journal*, Vol I, No.2.
[4] *Journal*, Vol III, No.2, p. 36.
[5] See *T.E. Lawrence By His Friends*, Books at Clouds Hill, pp. 476–510 and Appendix 1.
[6] *Friends*, Books at Clouds Hill, p. 496.
[7] *Friends*, p. 591.
[8] Quoted in Wilson, p. 1137.
[9] *Letters*, Ed. Garnett, p. 839.
[10] See Ronald Storrs, *Orientations*, p. 468. Quotation from Mackail. *Selected Epigrams,* p. 172, 1911.

CHAPTER FIVE

Xenophon

ↄ∿ↄ

WHEN Lawrence returned to his study of Greek during a period of enforced leisure at Karachi, he took up Xenophon's *Anabasis* again, writing to Charlotte Shaw, '*I find it charming: so cunningly full of writing tricks, by an amateur soldier who had (like a recent fellow of my experience) obviously studied better men's books and copied them carefully. It is alive and pretentiously simple.*'[1]

Xenophon, c. 428 B.C.-354 B.C. Soldier, historian, and writer on various subjects, Xenophon is one of the sources for our knowledge of Socrates. Xenophon was an admirer and fellow traveller of the Spartans. He was widely read by elites through antiquity and subsequently.

A Greek historian, soldier, Spartan sympathiser, and follower of Socrates, Xenophon wrote on a wide variety of subjects from hunting to leadership. He is one of the contemporary sources for our knowledge of Socrates, other than Plato, Aristotle, and Aristophanes, but as a famous, if not notorious, Spartan sympathiser, his friendship with the Spartan king Agesilaus, and his admiration for the Spartan regime, colour his representation of Socrates, so that a much tougher and more straightforward figure emerges than the subtle dialectician that Plato evokes. Also, Xenophon has much to say about leadership, having led the Greek mercenaries back home after the defeat of the Persian governor's insurrection against the Persian King, near Babylon.

We know also that Lawrence had turned to Xenophon in the *Seven Pillars* for the word diathetics 'which had been the art of Cyrus before he struck',[2] to explain the psychological element in his own war. Lawrence also casually reveals his familiarity with Xenophon over a minor episode where the Zaagi had shot a buzzard; he remarks that '… their white meat was still as good as Xenophon had found it.'[3] Lest this seem affected or precious, it is as well to recall that another traveller with a Classics background, who was also very familiar with Xenophon – Gertrude Bell – several times refers to him in her writings. In her account of *A Journey Along the Banks of the Euphrates, 'Amurath to Amurath'* (published in 1911 as an account of her 1909 visit), she describes how she spent the evening with the books which had served as guides down the Euphrates: *'the best of all guide-books to Mesopotamia, the Anabasis (of Xenophon) and Ammianus Marcellinus.'*[4]

For Bell, these writers provide a vivid account of the *geography* as much as cultural insights – prescient as these may be: 'With Xenophon, with Julian, with all the armies captained by a dream of empire that dashed and broke against the Ancient East, the thoughts go marching down to the river which was the most famous of all frontier lines.'

There may be several reasons why Lawrence had a certain affinity with Xenophon. One of them could have been that Xenophon's allegiances were in transition from Athens to Sparta via the professions of arms and politics, and it is certain that the loyalties that Lawrence felt to both Britain and its empire on the one hand, and to his Arab friends and colleagues on the other, created great distress in his mind during the peace processes after the war – and indeed before the end when he became aware of the Sykes-Picot Agreement.

As a Victorian, Lawrence was raised in a culture of some esteem for Xenophon, the kind of ethos expressed in the Matthew Arnold idea of education, and summed up in the well-known phrase from Juvenal, *'mens sana in corpore sano'* ('a healthy mind in a healthy body'). With his turn-of-the-century Oxford education, Lawrence would have been familiar with the sources of our knowledge of the Spartans, of Plutarch and the great classical historians, Herodotus and Thucydides. He had their books on his shelves at Clouds Hill. It is also possible that Lawrence sidestepped the nascent Historicism criticised by Nietzsche; as much by luck as by personal predilection and his reading strategies. That is to say, Historicism has a certain 'distancing' or ironising effect. Another conservative thinker, Leo Strauss, has remarked that, 'The historicist assumes that all human thought is "historical" and is therefore compelled to attempt to understand the thought better than it understood itself before he has understood it exactly as it understood itself.'[5] To see past this Historicism so that we can begin to understand how Xenophon, like the literature of Chivalry, was a lasting resource for Lawrence, requires a closer acquaintance with this problematic writer. And the acceptance of the fact that Lawrence was not an Historicist, not subject to its ironising distance, and practised the reverse strategy of immersion.

Throughout Antiquity, and up to and including Machiavelli, Xenophon was highly esteemed. The weight accorded his writings can be judged by the fact that during the last centuries of the Roman Republic, they were part of the education of every future statesman and military leader. As Strauss remarks, 'Until the end of the 18th century he was generally considered a wise man and a classic in the precise sense.' However, a curious feature of Xenophon's reputation is that since the 19th century, it has been in decline. He has been compared with Plato, and found wanting (as a philosopher), and compared with Thucydides, and similarly found wanting (as a historian). Strauss suggests, reasonably, that Xenophon may not have wished to be understood in such ways, and advances the idea that Xenophon is misunderstood because he deploys a Socratic rhetoric, and that 'great thinkers... have used a kind of caution or thrift in communicating their thought to posterity.' Both of these ideas suggest a certain care and humility in approaching this currently underrated writer – and a return to Lawrence's provocative oxymoron, 'pretentiously simple', perhaps one sense of which is 'misleadingly simple'.

Whatever may be the case, Xenophon is a major source for our knowledge of Sparta and Socrates, and even, to a lesser extent, of the Cynics. His writings, (seven volumes in the Loeb edition), range across Hunting, Horses, Command of Cavalry, Household Management, History, and studies of his heroes, Agesilaus, the Spartan king, and Cyrus the Younger. But perhaps he is known most famously for his account of the military adventure which he joined, its defeat, and the struggle to lead the return of thousands of stranded Greeks back to their homes – *The Anabasis*. Interestingly, not only is Xenophon's Socrates a tougher, more soldierly figure than Plato's, but he also extends the list of classical virtues to include Patriotism, along with Piety, Justice, Self-Control, and Wisdom – a list not so dissimilar to the Chivalry virtues, and perhaps so because Xenophon also sought Honour through Arms. The Spartans, who had turned Warfare and training for it into a way of life, were particularly admired by Xenophon, and they were known in the ancient world as 'Artists of War', or simply 'Professionals'. Notoriously, they lived off a semi-slave class called Helots who did all the menial work so that the Spartans could devote themselves undistractedly to Warfare. The Helots were bound to the land, and kept down by terror, psychological oppression, and legalised manslaughter. Over this Helot class, the Spartans maintained their rigid educational and communal institutions which made extraordinary demands on their inhabitants in turn. Not for nothing was the educational system which formed their youth known as *The Agon* – cognate with agony, from the Greek meaning 'contest'. The training was savage. Spartan superiority in Warfare, and features of their intensely conservative culture, attracted the attention and admiration of some Athenian intellectuals, amongst them Plato and Socrates, as well as Xenophon. It should be recalled that internecine warfare was a feature of the ancient world from the Hittites, whom Lawrence studied, onwards. It certainly marked the Mediterranean city state cultures of which Athens was one of the most prominent instances. After all, the Peloponnesian War, in Thucydides' renowned account, is the greatest example of these endless struggles. Xenophon's association with those in Socrates' circle who were pro-Oligarchic, and critical of democracy, eventually led to his formal exile from Athens and a practical alliance with the Spartans. It may be noted in passing, that the great 19th century historian, Jacob Burckhardt, defined the whole of ancient Greek culture as essentially Agonistic, i.e. marked by competitiveness and struggle, and this is certainly in accord with the ethos which pervades the writings of Greece's greatest poet, Homer: 'Always be the best.'

Xenophon, who was a part of this tradition, was highly esteemed throughout antiquity, particularly by the Romans. For the most part he was valued as a wise man, a writer of clarity, and a source of advice and inspiration, particularly on Leadership, until the end of the 18th century. In Machiavelli, amongst the classical sources referred to, only Livy has more citations.

Perhaps because, as Leo Strauss has argued, Xenophon's version of the Socratic rhetoric is no longer understood, we no longer know how to read him. And because of his anti-democratic ethos, and ruling class, officer tone, and understatement, he is found dissonant to the modern ear, and unsympathetic to its values and assumptions. Whatever may be the case, in general, his reputation has plummeted for the first time in centuries, and it is instructive to reflect on why this is so. Amongst classicists, Xenophon is now dismissed for the most part as 'beef-witted',[6] and even Peter Levi describes him as a 'buffoon'. According to Levi, 'The most bone-headed kind of conservative, anti-democratic, anti-Athenian, and violent against slaves and the poor.'[7]

Apparently almost alone amongst 20th century intellectuals, only Leo Strauss, and his pupil Alan Bloom, have the patience to read and defend Xenophon. Aware that Plato and Thucydides overshadow him, and that we need to understand how to read him, they argue that the Historicist mindset and its reflexes must be understood and suspended; if we are no longer busily situating a writer in his time and culture, (or only doing that), we may understand the text in hand in its own terms: 'When Averroes and Thomas Aquinas read Aristotle they did not think of him as a Greek and put him into his historical context. They had no interest in Greek Civ but treated him as a wise man, *hence a contemporary at all times.*'[8]

It may be that Lawrence was free of this Historicist reflex, and read, in effect, trans-historically. Recalling the description of him as 'a one man monastery', his immersal in Chivalrous literature, and his ascetic practices, suggest that Lawrence also read 'ancient' literature as a contemporary, as a guide, out of a kind of need or necessity. Consider again Bloom's view of Nietzsche reading Socrates, and Machiavelli reading Xenophon. Nietzsche did not seek out Socrates because Socrates was part of the classical canon that German boys learned in school. Nietzsche did so in spite of that fact. Socrates was necessary to him as the profoundest statement of what philosophy is and as the worthiest of rivals. Machiavelli, comparatively, was impelled by real need when he sought out Xenophon, not by conformism.[9] The language in which Lawrence describes his recourse to Xenophon is revelatory in this perspective:

> 'I went to Xenophon, a temporary soldier like myself, and stole his word diathetics which had been the art of Cyrus before he struck.'[10]

From this we can infer that Lawrence regarded Xenophon, at least, as a useful and reliable source and guide, and that the word 'diathetics' had the resonances he needed. The fact is that Liddell and Scott's Greek-English Lexicon defines diathesis as '*a disposing in order, arrangement, a state, disposition, condition.*'[11] Not only does *diathesis* have these resonances, but according to the founders of Stoicism, Zeno and Chrysippus, virtue itself is a fixed disposition of the ruling part of the soul, (according to Plutarch's report). So Lawrence used this word, which had all the right resonances, to evoke Cyrus's strategic/psychological arrangements and ruses, which the Persian used in his military struggle with his brother, Artaxerses, who was at that time on the Persian throne. All this latter aspect is recounted in Xenophon's *Anabasis*. In the background may well have been a reading, also, of the *Cyropaedia* – the education of Cyrus, which is usually described as a historical romance-cum-encomium of Cyrus the Great. After all, Lawrence had the *Complete Works* of Xenophon in translation in his library, and may have had access to the Loeb Greek text via the library of his friend Ronald Storrs in Jerusalem.

By using the word 'diathetics' Lawrence was reaching beyond what is sometimes now called 'psy-ops', and beyond psychology and propaganda, even though he begins to discuss it characteristically, on a self-deprecating note: '*Our propaganda* [refers to Lawrence's persuading or 'preaching' of the Arabs to fight the Turks] *was its stained and ignoble offspring. It was the pathic* [that is felt] *in war.*'

Tacitly following the logic and definition of the word, i.e. its sense of 'arrangement', Lawrence goes on to speak of the 'adjustment of the crowds', of 'pre-arrangement'. The '… arrangement of minds, not only of "our men", but also the enemy… and the nation supporting us behind the firing line, since more than half the battle passed there in the back… There were many humiliating material limits, but *no moral impossibilities*: so that the scope of our diathetical activities was unbounded… for us the diathetic would be more than half command.'[12]

Lawrence adds that, 'In Asia the regular elements were so physically weak that the irregulars could not let the metaphysical weapon rust unused.' Even though he could say that, 'Feisal's creed of nationality made every Arab ours', it is evident that Lawrence is not thinking only within the conventional circle of ideas about 'propaganda'. His focus on 'minds', 'spirit', and 'metaphysics', and the manner of his deployment of these terms, the way he thinks within them, is an effect of the rhetoric of another time, (maybe Xenophon's), and one that was particularly apposite for the conditions he faced.

Xenophon's works portray precisely the strategies of leadership and the efforts to control morale in very inhospitable circumstances, the kinds of problems which were very similar to Lawrence's. Completely unlike the Western Front, with its industrialisation of warfare and its European combatants, the war in the desert, with its mobility, nomad fighters, and general lack of materiel, must have strengthened the appeal and relevance of Xenophon to Lawrence, and re-validated his pre-Historicist view of the texts.

Deeper affinities are also discoverable. The much tougher, more soldierly Socrates who emerges from Xenophon's *Memoirs of Socrates* has already been mentioned, but the appeal to an ambitious young intelligence officer who intended to be a General by the age of 30 is worth further examination, not least in the light of Lawrence's earlier formation by, and immersion in, the values of Chivalry.

Xenophon's Socrates emphasises discipline, and especially self-discipline, as the foundation not only of the other virtues, i.e. Justice, Piety, Wisdom, but indeed of all worthwhile achievement, and especially so for would-be leaders. Since lack of self-discipline is often described as 'slavish' in Xenophon, and particularly in the *Memoirs*, we are led to see that freedom itself depends on self-discipline:

> '*Surely every man ought to regard self-discipline as the foundation of moral goodness, and to cultivate it in his character before anything else. Without it, who could learn anything good or practise it to a degree worth mentioning? Or who could escape degradation of both mind and body if he is a slave to his appetites.*'[13]

Xenophon connects this to the education of young men precisely so that they will '… be capable of governing, and those who haven't "not even to aspire" to governing.' Here, similarly to the Chivalry texts, especially that of Geoffroi de Charny, Xenophon specifies the practice of self-control with regard to food, sex, sleep, heat and cold, and physical exertion.[14] Xenophon drives home his view of the necessity of physical fitness by asserting:

> '… the fact that our country does not conduct military training at public expense is no reason for individuals to neglect it… Many people's minds are often so invaded by forgetfulness, despondency, irritability, and insanity because of their poor physical condition that their knowledge is driven out of them.'[15]

Xenophon reminds us that Socrates rescued a wounded man in battle, that he would walk barefoot in snow, wore the same cloak all year round, and ate and drank only when hungry or thirsty. In effect, he combined ascetic lifestyle with military values, a combination that can be found not only with the Spartans, but later with the Military Orders in Syria and Palestine, the Templars and Hospitallers, for example, and indeed guerilla fighters such as Lawrence's nomads. The Spartans may have established their legend as the hardest warriors, but Lawrence knew there were others, and by predilection in youth and fatality in adulthood – the war – followed their paths.

Lawrence even admired the German troops he encountered in the desert, retreating amidst the chaos around Deraa, in 1918; they were very much in a situation analogous to Xenophon's Greeks centuries before:

> '… for the first time I grew proud of the enemy who had killed my brothers. They were marching for their homes 2,000 miles away, without hope and without guides, in conditions mad enough to break the bravest nerves. Yet each section of them held together, marching in firm rank, sheering through the wrack of Turk and Arab like an armoured ship, dark, high-set, and silent. When attacked they halted, faced about, took position, fired to order. There was no haste, no crying, no hesitation. They were glorious.'[16]

Strikingly, such appraisals were mirrored by at least one German officer's view of the English. Ernst Jünger, who was fighting as a Storm Trooper on the Western Front wrote, 'Of all the troops who were opposed to the Germans on the great battlefields, the English were not only the most formidable, but the manliest and the most chivalrous.'[17]

The hidden affinity which connects the evaluations of both Lawrence and Jünger, despite the latter's Nietzschean sympathies, is their shared Classical education, such that either's judgement could have been voiced by Xenophon himself. After all, Jünger had claimed explicitly, as his own problem, the one first voiced by Marx, i.e. 'Is Achilles possible with gunpowder and lead?' This reference to Homer's *Iliad*, the founding text of every elite warrior in the Western world, to which Jünger could answer 'yes', demonstrates that even warriors fighting on such disparate battlefields shared worlds of cultural formation. And where Lawrence reached for Xenophon, Jünger reached for Homer.

When Lawrence came to articulating his own qualifications for translating Homer's *Odyssey*, he made some very strong claims, as always, even with a text as remote from us as Homer, standing outside the Historicist reading, almost encountering the text in situ as with certain Chivalry texts:

> 'I'm in a strong position vis-a-vis Homer as most of his translators. For years we were digging up a city of roughly the Odysseus period. I have handled the weapons, armour, utensils of those times, explored their houses, planned their cities. I have hunted wild boars and watched wild lions, sailed the Aegean (and sailed ships), bent bows, lived with pastoral peoples, woven textiles, built boats and killed many men. So I have odd knowledges that qualify me to understand the Odyssey, and certain experiences that interpret it to me.'[18]

One could perhaps say that whereas with Chivalrous texts, Lawrence worked hard to inhabit them, reading them in situ and 'at first hand', until they came alive for him, similarly with his first explorations of Palestine, the landscape opened up to him through his prior deep knowledge of the Bible and Classical history. Lawrence's landscapes, external and internal, perhaps even more so than Gertrude Bell's, were already informed, felt, and imagined by intensely experienced reading as well as imagination. On the other hand, with Xenophon, and even reaching back to Homer, the experiences of life, whether as archaeologist or military leader, would have re-illuminated texts already known and studied since boyhood. Thereby, they perhaps created a uniquely enriching circularity between texts, life lived, and the understanding of both.

Endnotes

[1] Letter to C. Shaw, 28.1.1927. Quoted in *T.E.L. Soc. Journal,* Vol III, No.2, Spring 1994.
[2] *Seven Pillars*, Penguin Edn., p. 200.
[3] *Seven Pillars*, Oxford Edn., p. 591. See also Xenophon, *The Persian Expedition*, p. 75. Penguin. 1946/72: 'Their flesh was delicious.'
[4] See also Gertrude Lowthian Bell, *Amurath to Amurath*, pp. 16, 18, 24, 200. Ammianus Marcellinus. Like Xenophon, an army officer before he was an historian. Comparable with Livy and Tacitus, wrote on the Later Roman Empire. A.D. 354–378.
[5] *On Tyranny*. Leo Strauss. A reading of Xenophon's Dialogue Hiero, or Tyrannicus, pp. 25, 26.
[6] A Plato insult usually applied to Athletes.
[7] *History of Greek Literature*, Peter Levi, p. 307.
[8] *Giants and Dwarfs*, Allan Bloom, p. 27.
[9] Ibid., p. 29.
[10] *Seven Pillars*, Oxford Edn., p. 198.
[11] Liddell and Scott, p. 161.
[12] *Seven Pillars*, Oxford Edn., p. 199.
[13] Xenophon, *Memoirs of Socrates*, in *Conversations of Socrates*, Penguin, pp. 94, 95, 96, 100, etc.
[14] Xenophon, *Memoirs*, p. 100.
[15] Ibid., p. 172.
[16] *Seven Pillars*, Oxford Edn., p. 779.
[17] Ernst Jünger, *The Storm Of Steel*, Chatto and Windus Edn., 1941, p. xiii. See also *Ernst Jünger and Germany: Into the Abyss, 1914-1945*, Thomas Nevin.
[18] *Letters*, Ed. Garnett, pp. 326/7.

CHAPTER SIX

Lucian

∾

L UCIAN was a late writer in the Greek classical canon (c. A.D. 120-180). He may appear a tangential figure in Lawrence's formation and, at first glance, particularly after the soldierly/Spartan earnestness of Xenophon, an unlikely source of guidance in the search for Lawrence's philosophy, least of all his actual practice and worldly comportment. However, Lawrence's brother, A.W. Lawrence, records that along with the Chivalrous texts his brother possessed, such as the Romances of Huon of Bordeaux,[1] the *Kalevala*,[2] and tales by William Morris, he frequently read Lucian's *True History*, a parody of improbable travel stories. Part of the attraction of this author, it is suggested, stems from the fact that Lucian was born at Samsat, on the Euphrates, near Carchemish, where Lawrence was excavating. According to A.W. Lawrence's recollection, Lawrence had apparently bought a complete set of Lucian in Greek and Latin on one of his last home visits before the war (eight volumes in the current Loeb edition which provides the Greek text with an English translation). However, it seems that Lawrence's brother may have been mistaken about the 'sets' of Lucian. According to the publishers, only one volume of Lucian had been published by the Loeb Classical Library in 1913 – Volume One which contains the following essays: *Lucian 1. Phalaris. Hippias or the Bath. Dionysus. Heracles. Amber or the Swans. The Fly. Nigrinus. Demonax. The Hall. My Native Land. Octogenarians. A True Story. Slander. The Consonants at Law. The Carousal (Symposium or The Lapiths)*. Lucian was translated into Latin during the Renaissance by Erasmus and Thomas More. These foregoing texts include information about the Cynics, particularly Nigrinus and Demonax.[3] For scholars of Classical Cynicism, Lucian has proved a valuable resource.

In his entry to the book *T.E. Lawrence by his Friends*, A.W. Lawrence states:

> *'I fancy that his philosophy of life may have owed something to Lucian's interpretation of the doctrines of the Cynics – abstention from honour and power with their attendant temptations, and satisfaction with the simple life of the righteous poor.'*[4]

Lucian's appeal to Lawrence may have operated in several ways. As one of the greatest satirists of the ancient world, like many others who mocked pretension and hypocrisy, there is a serious message which can be inferred from his writings, even though it may be difficult to say exactly what it is.

Perhaps some of the appeal to Lawrence of Lucian is the outsider's perspective, which the latter had, despite his mastery of the official Canon. Born of non-Greek stock in

Lucian, c. 120 A.D.-180 A.D: 'I am eager that the noblest young men, whose bent is toward philosophy, should not only have the ancient role models to emulate, they should also have an exemplar from our own lifetimes before their eyes. Demonax is the best philosopher I am acquainted with and a fine example for them to follow.' Demonax was like Diogenes in his frugality and practised the Cynic creed of self-sufficiency, training, and freedom of speech.

Syria, where the native language was Syriac, the language of culture Greek, and the official language Latin, Lucian must have begun his extensive travels with a certain distance on the Greek culture and literature which he nevertheless mastered. As a satirist and a parodist, he used the profound knowledge of Greek literature which he acquired in order to pursue his own serio-comic intentions of mocking pretension, hypocrisy, folly, and superstition. He is the master of many genres, even turning the previously serious *Dialogue*, famously deployed by Plato, to humorous ends, using his rhetorical fluency not only to adopt many 'voices' and to entertain his audiences, but also to lead them to infer the critique he was making. It has been suggested that Lucian had 'the complex of a metic' – the resident outsider,[5] and this epithet seems curiously apposite for Lawrence, who, after all, had cutting things to say about serving other cultures and had, indeed, been a resident outsider at more than one time in his career. The educated audience Lucian addressed would have savoured the vast range of Greek literature to which he referred: he was one of the voices of what became known to scholars as the Second Sophistic – a relatively late phase which consciously looked back to the standards of a Golden Age, a flowering which had occurred before the coming of the Romans. However, even as he looked back and united the traditions of Aristophanes, Menander, Plato, and Menippus the Cynic, Lucian produced his own quasi-hybrid, the Lucianic Dialogue, combining these traditions for new purposes. Perhaps this apparently frivolous but, in fact, highly learned humour, appealed to Lawrence, whose own education and mixed heritage uniquely qualified him to appreciate it. Perhaps also, he had an affinity with the criticism Lucian was mounting against imposture and conceit. After all, some scholars have argued that the common characteristic of all Lucian's various authorial stances and voices is precisely 'the purposeful application of wit, verbal play, ridicule, detachment, and self-deprecating humour, and skepticism', in an attack on deception and self-deception.[6] And the figures who were the targets for these various attacks, whether by mockery, parody, or satire, are ubiquitous in any literate culture: religious figures, sophists, philosophers, wealthy aristocrats, and representatives of officialdom.

Where Lucian is philosophically interesting is as a source for our knowledge of Classical Cynicism.[7] He is close enough to the apogee of Cynic philosophy in the 2nd century to be scathingly satirical towards some Cynics, such as in *The Death of Peregrinus*, but discerning enough to see what might be praiseworthy in others, for example his eulogy of Demonax, and Menippus of Gadara, Cynics famous for certain views, attitudes, and practices.

The Cynicism of the historical Demonax (c. A.D. 70-170) which is primarily known through Lucian, was gentler than some versions of the school, but nevertheless an unmistakable and intransigent instance of this ancient philosophy and the practice(s) that flowed from it. Demonax' intellectual genealogy is impeccable. He had been a student of the great Stoic Epictetus, and he venerated Socrates, the Cynic Diogenes, and Aristippus, another pupil of Socrates who had, however, adopted other views and founded the Cyrenaic school himself. Whatever Lucian's humorous agenda may have been in most other contexts, he appears to have presented Demonax as a Classic Cynic, although a cheerful one. Lucian's Demonax spent his life wandering around Athens telling people to be happy in the present, and reminding them that, 'Nothing – neither wealth, poverty, health, nor sickness – will last long and so one should live free from hope and fear.'[8] Perhaps Lucian suspended his mockery in Demonax's instance because Demonax was, himself, always cheerful, not above 'poking fun', and a great reconciler whose highest ideals were friendship and philanthropia. Like the early Cynic, Crates, in old age he would go uninvited to people's houses and always be welcomed as a 'good daimon', as if his visit were the 'manifestation of a god'.[9] Thus it is that Lucian's Demonax is apparently the unembarrassed promotion of the hero. Lucian writes that he wants to commemorate Demonax, and spells out his reasons without equivocation:

'… *so that he may be retained by men of culture… and that young men of good instincts who aspire to philosophy may not have to shape themselves by ancient precedents alone, but may be able to set themselves a pattern from our modern world and to copy that man, the best of all philosophers whom I know about.*'[10]

In short, Lucian puts Demonax forward unambiguously as an exemplar of how to live. In the event, this is not so far from the Spartan ideals found scattered across the Greek historians, including Xenophon, nor from the more demanding ideals of endless effort found in some Chivalry texts.

Thus: '… *he had trained his body and hardened it for endurance and in general he had made it his aim to require nothing from anyone else.*'[11]

Demonax devoted himself completely to freedom and the unfettered expression of his views, and he continued living a life which was 'upright, healthy and impeccable.'[12] From his boyhood, his impetus to philosophy drove him to scorn all worldly goods. When Demonax was no longer able to be self-sufficient in old age, he refused to eat or drink and 'left life cheerfully'. When asked about his funeral preferences, having lived to almost 100, without illness or pain, he responded, 'Don't borrow trouble. The stench will get me buried.' When his interlocutor said that it was disgraceful that the body of such a man should be exposed for birds and dogs to devour, Demonax replied that he saw nothing unusual in 'trying to be useful to the living even in death'. In fact he was sufficiently revered to receive a magnificent public funeral.[13] Even the stone seat where he used to rest was an object of respect.

The Cynic philosophy espoused by Demonax, although less harsh and confrontatory than that of many other Cynics, shared the Classical Cynic critique of worldly values, the cult of freedom and self-sufficiency, and the cultivation of physical toughness and endurance. Demonax emerges as a kinder and more affable figure than Diogenes, in fact almost a rival to the burgeoning Christianity of the times, in his Socratic piety and personal austerity. In these respects he was closer to the more unworldly Apollonius of Tyana, another figure from the ancient world to interest Lawrence, than to Xenophon, the Spartan sympathiser.

Endnotes

[1] Another *Chanson de Geste*. Huon of Bordeaux: the title character of a 13th century French epic. Lawrence may have had Lord Berners' translation.

[2] Epic poem of Finland, compiled from ancient sources, in the 19th century. 'It suggests to our minds the proto-twilight of Homeric Greece. Its historic background is the misty age of feud and foray.' Intro. In Everyman Edn.

[3] Information received by the author from Harvard University Press.

[4] *Friends*, p. 585.

[5] Bakhtin, quoted in Banham *Unruly Eloquence*, p. 229.

[6] See Banham, *Unruly Eloquence*, pp. 57-65.

[7] There are extant some fragments of 'true' Cynics such as Diogenes and Crates, but in general Cynicism is mainly known through its more 'literary' adherents and inheritors. The most important sources are: Diogenes Laertius *Lives of the Philosophers*, Book 6; Epictetus *Discourses*, 3.22 and 4.8, various dialogues of Lucian. See '*Cynics*', William Desmond, p. 5. And *The Cynics: The Cynic Movement in Antiquity and its Legacy*, R. Bracht Branham and Marie-Odile Goulet-Caze.

[8] See *Cynics*, William Desmond, pp. 67-69, etc.

[9] See Desmond.

[10] Lucian, Loeb Edn., p. 143, Vol I.

[11] Lucian, Loeb Edn., p. 145.

[12] Lucian, Penguin translation, '*Chattering Courtesans and Other Sardonic Sketches*' [*Demonax the Philosopher*], p. 36.

[13] Lucian, Loeb Edn., p. 173.

CHAPTER SEVEN

Apollonius of Tyana

꼭

A FIRST century A.D. Neopythagorean philosopher, wandering holy man and apparent miracle-worker, all that is known about Apollonius, a contemporary of Jesus Christ, comes from *The Life* written by Flavius Philostratus, a philosopher himself, in the third century A.D. at the request of the empress Julia Domna.

Apollonius of Tyana, 15 A.D.-100 A.D. A Greek Neopythagorean philosopher and traveller; a vegetarian miracle-worker and clairvoyant, advanced by some as a pagan rival to Christ, he opposed animal sacrifices and believed in the transmigration of souls. He was also known to the medieval Islamic world. Apollonius maintained a silence for five years.

A.W. Lawrence records how Lawrence became interested in Apollonius after the First World War, and suggests an interesting connection between Lucian and Apollonius which, in turn, begins to make the affinity Lawrence had for these figures clearer:

'After the War, his interest in Hellenised Syria led him to study the Philosophy of Apollonius of Tyana, and to plan an edition of the Gadarene poets and a book on the society into which Christ was born. These men had belonged, as he himself now did, to a two-fold civilization, European and Asiatic. Lucian and Apollonius especially combine with their western education, a trace of the oriental carelessness about the trappings of life. I have no doubt that the young T.E. Lawrence greeted it at his first sight of the East, not with the usual western revulsion, but as a disciple. He would recognize the similarity to medieval Europe, in which he was learned. The similarity goes deeper than the mere surface of life; the definitive structure of our feudal society can be paralleled in the tribes…'[1]

The 'carelessness about the trappings of life' is widely attested in Lawrence's life and writings, and flows, I suggest, from his fundamental judgements and philosophy. For the present, a couple of instances may suffice, as evidence. Ronald Storrs records that Lawrence, when in Jerusalem, always stayed at his house, saying that he liked it,

'… because it contained the necessities and not the tiresomenesses of life; that is to say there were a few Greek marbles, a good piano and a great many books – but (I fear) not enough towel-horses, no huckabacks, and a very irregular supply of cruets and dinner-napkins. Not all my guests agreed with Lawrence.'

Storrs added that, 'My servant Said once observed, "When your Excellency has none other than Urenz in the house, the cook prepared *ala kaifu* – without bothering himself…"'[2] – the point being that the chef knew that Lawrence did not care about fussy food and would therefore not make any special effort. Lawrence himself, in a letter to his university friend, V.W. Richards, in July 1918, wrote that,

*'You guessed rightly that the Arab appealed to my imagination. It is the old, old civilization, which has refined itself clear of household gods, and half the trappings which ours hastens to assume. **The gospel of Bareness in materials is a good one**, and it involves apparently a sort of moral bareness too.'*[3]
[emphasis added]

This note of material austerity is a feature of Lawrence's life and thought, early and late. It is also shared by the Military Orders like the Templars, the Spartans, and Xenophon; and Lucian, at least in his commemorations of the Classical Cynics, such as Demonax and Negrinus, and Apollonius of Tyana, also commends it. Lawrence himself explicitly reflected the teaching shared by the foregoing to Ernest Thurtle, M.P. in his own version of the gospel of 'Bareness' in materials. Lawrence had contacted Thurtle in 1929 after the latter had asked a question in Parliament about Lawrence's use of a false name. In the event they developed a lasting friendship. Thurtle's view of Lawrence emerges in both his contribution to *Friends* and his article for the Rationalist Annual for 1938 entitled '*A Secular Saint*'. In this article, the M.P. describes Arnold Lawrence's views about his brother's liking for Lucian's interpretations of the doctrines of the Cynics as 'discerning'. He goes on to write that Lawrence's fervour for the freeing from oppression of an alien race, whilst genuine, did not endure, and did not have the same fundamental grip upon the man as the craving for personal freedom. According to Thurtle:

'The path to freedom, as he saw it, lay in the rigid restriction of needs. Hence it was a weakness, a sign of surrender, to hanker after anything but the bare essentials of existence. He resembled an Eastern ascetic in the way he strove to rid himself of wants calculated to fetter his freedom… Deliberately… he schooled himself to be satisfied with barest minimum in the form of shelter, clothes, and food. He intended, when

he settled in his cottage at Clouds Hill, where he had planned to live after leaving the Air Force, to keep bread, butter, and cheese under glass bells, and to go out occasionally to spend a few pence on bacon and eggs, or fish and chips. This much he could enjoy and still be free. A more comfortable and luxurious life meant bondage in some form or other, and the price was too high. For him, in a choice between comfort and freedom, comfort went to the wall every time.'[4]

As a Pythagorean, Apollonius was a strict vegetarian, and would not even wear animal products. Philostratus, his biographer, records that, like Socrates, Apollonius was another minimalist where material wants were concerned, and offered to the gods the prayer: 'O ye gods, grant me to have little and to want nothing.'[5]

Also, like Lawrence, Apollonius was a teetotaller and praised the drinking of water; those who did drink it saw 'things as they really are... and are never found to be giddy, nor full of drowsiness or of silliness, nor unduly elated.' Furthermore, the faculty of divination by means of dreams, which Apollonius holds to be the divinest and most god-like of human faculties, is muddied and stained by wine.[6]

Lastly, and perhaps surprisingly, he is recorded as expressing great admiration for the Spartan King Leonidas, who had held the pass at Thermopylae for two days against the invading Persian army in 480 BC. Philostratus wrote, 'As for the monument of Leonidas the Spartan, he almost clasped it in his arms.'[7]

Apollonius was familiar enough to Lawrence for him to come to mind during an episode in the *Seven Pillars* (Ch. 97), during which he reflects on the reasons for the failure of an expedition to Mudowwara.[1] Lawrence ascribes the failure to a variety of causes: the 'old problem' of cooperation between regulars and irregulars, the stupidity of old Sherif Mohammed Ali el Beidawi who, when he came to water, declared a 'Noon halt'...

'... and then sat there for two months, pandering to Bedouin laziness, and to his own physical and mental weakness of good intention: but still more to that hedonistic streak among the Arabs which made them helpless slaves of carnal indulgences; and in Arabia where life was so simple and life so hard, luxuries might be as plain as running water or a shady tree, whose rareness and misuse often turned them into lusts. Their story reminded me of Apollonius of Tyana: "Come off it you men of Tarsus, sitting on your river like geese, drunken with its white water!" Even where superfluities lacked, the temptation of necessary food lay always on men. Each morsel which passed their lips might, if they were not watchful, become pleasant to them.'[9]

It is almost as if Lawrence is describing a ladder of increasingly demanding and rarefied standards of explanation and existence, ranging from the most material – mixtures of troops – to ordinary stupidity, and 'Bedouin laziness' (they sat there for two months); then physical and mental weakness stemming from good, but unquestioned intentions, on to hedonism and carnal indulgence. Next, Lawrence moves on to a level of explanation and a standard of judgement which implies a moral and physical austerity only found, rarely, in some Classical Greek philosophers such as the Stoics and Cynics, (for example, Antisthenes: 'I'd rather be mad than feel pleasure.'[10]), and the early Christian traditions, such as those of the Desert Fathers. It is a philosophy or religion deeply suspicious of pleasure as such, but it would have been alien to Xenophon and Lucien, and certainly alien to Geoffroi de Charny. One feature of this meditation on what is, at first glance, 'only' a question of leadership and surface discipline, is that it implies that the 'rarity and misuse' and lack of watchfulness which can generate pleasure and lusts, can arise from the plainness of even running water, or the necessity of food. And this last quasi-trap is not even ascribed to 'Arabs' or 'Bedouin', but simply 'was always on men'. So, the problem does not lie in any intrinsic property of things, but in the level of our watchfulness or awareness, in the midst of our shared human condition. And only a philosophy or religion which provides a path or comportment towards such issues, can protect or guide any but the rarest individual. The need for such a philosophy or religion can perhaps be inferred from the foregoing.

The episode in Philostratus where Lawrence recalls Philostratus saying 'come off it you men of Tarsus, sitting on your river like geese' [*Seven Pillars* (Ch. 97)] occurs when Apollonius has been taken to Tarsus, at the age of 14 to study with Euthydemus:

> *'Now Euthydemus was a good rhetor, and began his education; but, though he was attached to his teacher, he found the atmosphere of the city harsh and strange and little conducive to the philosophic life, for nowhere are men more addicted to luxury: jesters and full of insolence are they all; and they attend more to their fine linen than the Athenians did to wisdom; and a stream called the Cydnus runs through their city, along the banks of which they sit like so many water fowl. Hence the words which Apollonius addresses to them in his letter; "Be done with getting drunk upon your water."'*[11]

And even on the same page, we find that Apollonius' next teacher was himself deficient in that '… he was not a very serious person, nor one who practised in his conduct the philosophy he taught; for he was the slave of his belly and appetites, and modelled himself on Epicurus.'

A prominent feature of Apollonius' reputation in the ancient world, was that some writers of the 3rd century promoted him as pagan rival to Christ. After all, he also was alleged to have raised the dead, healed the sick, purified temples, and appeared to his disciples after death. Lawrence's interest in the period of time around the birth of Christ, and indeed the surrounding culture, is attested in his letters. Robert Graves gives more details of this interest, and Lawrence's knowledge of the subject, in his autobiographical *Goodbye to All That*, where he recalls a meeting with Lawrence at All Souls in 1920:

> *'Lawrence talking to the Regius Professor of Divinity about the influence of the Syrian philosophers on early Christianity, and especially about the importance of the University of Gadara close to lake Galilee, mentioned that St. James had quoted one of the Gadarene philosophers (I think Mnasalcus) in his Epistle. He went on to speak of Meleager and the other Syrian-Greek contributors to the Greek Anthology whose poems he intended to publish in English translation.'*[12]

The fact that Lawrence was well-read enough to discuss the intellectual background to early Christianity should not lead us to infer that he was similarly distanced on the ideals of personal integrity, in short, morality, in which he had been raised. Nor, indeed, that the standards of Honour and Truth that Chivalry teaches, and which he had studied so closely, were some remote posture, which could be shrugged off easily. Just so, also, with the writings of Xenophon, and Lucian, and Philostratus. As his meditation in the *Seven Pillars* on the deeper reasons for Sherif Beidawi's failure of leadership demonstrates, Lawrence's moral sensibility was closer to the Nitrean desert (to which he refers later) and certain Stoics, than to the instrumentalism which might have been expected from an Oxford-educated guerilla leader. He espouses unflinchingly the moral austerity of the early Desert Fathers. Of course, at the same time, there is the uncharted trajectory of the loss of his orthodox Christian faith. ('hungry time has taken from me the articles of the creed except the first …'[13]). The belief in the Doctrine and creedal formulation had gone, but not the basic ethical stance, buttressed as it was by Chivalry and the Classics. So Lawrence's entry into the post-war world was inevitably problematic.

Endnotes

[1]   *Friends*, A.W. Lawrence, p. 586.

[2]   *Orientations*, Ronald Storrs, p. 460.

[3]   *Letters*, Ed. Garnett, p. 244.

[4]   Reprinted in *The Journal of the T.E. Lawrence Society*, Vol IV, No.2, Spring 1995.

[5]   Philostratus: *The Life of Apollonius of Tyana*, Vol I. p. 95.

[6]   Ibid., p. 215.

[7]   Ibid., p. 399.

[8]   *Seven Pillars*, Oxford Edn., p. 555.

[9]   Ibid.

[10] *Lives and Opinions of Eminent Philosophers*, Diogenes Laertius, Vol II, VI. 2-4. p. 5.

[11] Philostratus, *Life of Apollonius of Tyana*, Vol I. p. 17.

[12] Robert Graves, *Goodbye to All That*, p. 143.

[13] T.E. Lawrence, *The Mint*, p. 171.

CHAPTER EIGHT

After Arabia

сⱱɔ

L AWRENCE ended his Arabian campaigns in Syria in early October 1918 with
military victory, moral defeat, and a doubtful political situation. Public honour and
fame, partly as a result of Lowell Thomas, the American journalist's show, were
freely accorded him but these, as well as any material benefit, he was convinced must be
disowned and repudiated. Damascus had been taken from the Turks at the beginning of
October 1918, he had marched into Jerusalem with Allenby, and his fame was established,
and the myth about him began to grow; but he had known since at least 1916 about the
Sykes-Picot Agreement. This deal, which by secretly conceding to French claims in Syria,
gave the lie to the Nationalist aspirations which Lawrence had so actively helped to
foment and organise. The war in the Middle East had to be continued by other means –
through politics and writing, especially of the *Seven Pillars of Wisdom*, which can be seen
not only as an account of the Arabian Campaign and writerly ambition, but also as an
attempt to recoup and redeem his moral position and influence upon the politics of the
future: the continuation of war and politics by other means. Perhaps this may explain the
ubiquity of the geopolitics of religion and ethical considerations in much of Lawrence's
public commentary after the war.

Having achieved military honour and prestige in the public realm, Lawrence felt
morally horrified as a private individual; he felt deeply fraudulent. He had, by great efforts,
become successful in the art of guerrilla warfare by his personal austerities and practices,
which actually pre-dated the war, and by a close study of military thinkers and strategists
dating back at least to Caesar's *Gallic War* and Xenophon. However, as the First World War
progressed he had found himself enmeshed in an essentially tragic situation in which he
necessarily had to serve two masters whose interests increasingly diverged, similar to the
dual allegiance described in Lancelot of the Lake and Malory's *Morte d'Arthur*. Perhaps
inevitably, this structure of developing conflicts of interest was initially addressed by
Lawrence within a Christian moral universe, and with a Christian moral language, even
though the experience of the war had shaken the form of Christianity in which he had
been raised. Scattered throughout the *Seven Pillars*, his letters and *The Mint*, are many
traces of this Christianity, as well as references to, and meditations upon, its deeper roots.
These went beyond the Oxford Evangelism of his youth, back to the desert mystics of
Nicea, and indeed the philosophical and spiritual influences of Hebrew, Greek, and Latin
thinkers, which had formed the minds of the Church's early intellectuals and mystics.

The inner necessity for these developments, of course, partly stemmed from the need to reach the gentiles if Christianity was to become more than a Jewish heresy.

To the extent that Lawrence's early Christian formation, along with his personal integrity, were now in question, he was forced back on this tradition, or outside it, to further asceticism, or nihilism, or suicide. Even as his traditional faith was fading, one should bear in mind that Lawrence had also had his moment of profound temptation – the fundamental temptation of power itself, as if he had 'been taken up into a high place'. He refers explicitly to his fear of the 'liberty of power', that his 'empty soul would be 'blown away'. Less spiritual, but equally revelatory of crisis and trauma, were the nightmares which were bad enough to disturb his fellow airmen to the extent that they instituted an unofficial court martial. The trajectory of Lawrence's declared positions on Christianity can be followed through his writings: we can see how his thorough knowledge of the Bible gives depth to his explorations of Palestine, providing not only an introduction to the geography of the Middle East, but background to the mores of nomadic peoples. In his long letter to his mother from Beyrout dated 2 August 1909, amongst many other matters he describes Banias (Caesarea Philippi) as being:

> '… on a hill above the plain of Huleh, the swampy lake North of Galilee… Banias mother will remember from Matthew XVI or Mark VIII and other places. To read such extracts on the spot is certainly much the best way [we have seen this practice before with Le Petit Jehan]; it may be that the Transfiguration took place on one of the neighbouring spurs of Mt. Hermon: of course that is not known, but it would be a very pleasantly appropriate place.'[1]

The Christianity which Lawrence is discussing had, at least in its higher manifestations, both early and medieval, preached renunciations, and these renunciations were empowering in the sense that they withdrew energy from worldly concerns which can then be devoted to other purposes. Where this renunciation is genuine religious asceticism, it tirelessly preaches the abnegation of the self. Classic instances of this can be found in, for example, Thomas à Kempis' *The Imitation of Christ*:

> 'My son, complete self-denial is the only road to perfect liberty. Those who are obsessed by self-interest and self-love are slaves of their own desires; they are greedy, inquisitive, and discontented.

> 'Very many people have been harmed by publicity and by lightly bestowed praise for their virtues. But grace is most powerful when preserved in silence in this transitory life, which consists wholly of temptation and warfare.'[2]

Where this renunciation is in a military context, as in Chivalry, or with the Templars, and Hospitallers, for example, it is at least partly aimed at physical and practical excellence. These renunciations, whether for spiritual or military purposes, necessarily involve a redistribution of the perceptions and values which are usually found on the axes between pleasure and pain/guilt and innocence/honour and dishonour. Such redistributions do not accord with the conventional 'worldly' evaluations. Anyone subject to these disciplines, whether spiritual or military, must re-describe themselves according to the institution they inhabit. In either case there is a struggle involved to perfect the self in the light of new criteria. Latent in these struggles is the question which Chivalry formulates as *its* primordial question: 'Who do you serve?'

Seen in these perspectives, Chivalry, especially in its highly Christianised form, can be read as an ethos of struggle (agon), both physical and spiritual and, like any ethos, it generates meanings, but uniquely entails discomfort, pain, and death because of its objectives – military victory and spiritual redemption. One should not forget that the Crusades, whatever other motives may be ascribed to them, were also penitential and redemptive ('to pray in our Lord's Sepulchre'). One could say that Chivalry, in both its Military and Spiritual aspects, is a 'technology of the self'; a form of continuous training with its own style of self-realisation and self-judgement; a combination of path and ultimate goal, structured by a teleology of deeds.[3]

In passing, a late attempt to recoup asceticism outside of a religious context can be found in Nietzsche:

> 'I also want to make asceticism natural again: in place of denial, the aim of strengthening; a gymnastics of the will; abstinence and periods of fasting of all kinds, in the most spiritual realms too; *a casuistry of deeds* in regard to the opinions we have regarding our strengths; an experiment with adventures and arbitrary dangers… asceticism, one hardly has courage so far to display its natural utility, its indispensability in the service of the education of the Will.'[4]

There are here various other links to Lawrence, although there is no known evidence that he had read this particular Nietzsche text (see Appendix 2 for Nietzsche texts at Clouds Hill). Lawrence does, of course, speak of the Will, as do others when assessing and describing him, but the contexts in which he deployed his well-known willpower and his various capacities were problematic for him until he was finally settled into the RAF.

One result of Lawrence's war experiences and the political struggles which followed them, was that he experienced Perspectivism – particularly in the sense that the contingency of the culture in which he had grown up became apparent to him. One of the formulations which he used to express this, and the attendant discomfort, was 'the lack of an Absolute'. This tended to emerge when discussing literature and the possibility of criticism, but the issue also had larger metaphysical dimensions:

> '… *there's no absolute in the imaginative world, and so journeymen like myself are confused and miserable in it.*[5]

> '*In my case, the efforts for these years to live in the dress of Arabs, and to imitate their mental foundation, quitted me of my English self, and let me look at the West and its conventions with new eyes: they destroyed it all for me. At the same time I could not sincerely take on the Arab skin: it was an affectation only. Easily was a man made an infidel, but hardly might he be converted to another faith. I had dropped one form and not taken on the other, and was become like Mohammed's coffin in our legend, with a resultant feeling of intense loneliness in life, and a contempt, not for other men, but for all they do. Such detachment came at times to man exhausted by prolonged physical effort and isolation. His body plodded on mechanically, while his reasonable mind left him, and from without looked down critically on him, wondering what that futile lumber did and why. Sometimes these selves would converse in the void; and then madness was very near, as I believe it would be near the man who could see things through the veils at once of two customs, two educations, two environments.*'[6]

The distanciation and loneliness described here seem to emerge after the war, and these experiences had to be understood with concepts which his original Christian and

Classical education had provided. One of the main practical solutions was, of course, the RAF, which not only provided new, meaningful work, and the interest of machines, the early days of flight, and the development of fast motor boats; but also, more subtly, an arena for the secularisation and updating of Chivalry. The RAF also provided 'the group of Aspiration', replacing the monastery as the site of a shared faith in a future hope towards which work could be done in the present. It provided this work as a deed-to-be-accomplished, namely, 'The Conquest of the Air'. One can add the companionship Lawrence also found in the RAF. This may account for his intense valorisation of the RAF and his denigration of the Army, and the Tank Corps in particular:

> 'We do regard flying as a sort of ritual: more an art than science, it is. Unreasonable to expect other people to feel like that, of course; but it is not an unpresentable Crusade: compared with the Lord's Sepulchre.'[7]

Returning to Chivalrous literature for a moment, in works by writers such as Malory, where the austere Cistercian influence is largely absent, there is nevertheless an aspiration to an ideal, expressed in a group – i.e. the band of knights around King Arthur – as having a kind of corporate spirituality, somewhere between the regiment or corps spirit, and the solidarity of the monastic community. Christian or military, it can be a transcendental orientation in that it refuses the present in the name of a possible future. From the point of view of worldly concerns, it is a counter-ethic; it chooses its duty within the world, without being of it. An early intimation of this sense of aspiration – not exactly duty– can be seen in a letter of Lawrence's from Jerablus, on the west bank of the Euphrates, near Carchemish, where he had excavated a Hittite site before the war in 1911:

> '… still, the product of fairly healthy brains and tolerable bodies will not be all useless in this world. One of us must surely get something of the unattainable we are all feeling after.'[8]

Even at this early age, there is the suggestion of 'service' to the world, at the same time accompanied by the sense of unreachable aspiration. The distance Lawrence's mind had travelled from orthodox Christianity, and some of the metaphysics associated with it, by the time he wrote *The Mint* in 1922, is evident in the following reflections, as is his affiliation to the group of other servicemen. The tone and vocabulary are almost Nietzschean, and the complex solidarity with his fellow servicemen is accompanied by an uncomfortable awareness of his own capacity for reflection:

> 'Another monotonous failure of a church, in the grey cold rain which rusted our bayonets and made uncomfortable our clothes. This apparatus of a parade service prejudices into blasphemy what thin chance organized religion ever had over vigorous men. Our blood distrusts and despises that something emasculate on the Padre's ascetic face. He aims so crooked too, when he tries to convict our party of sin. They are yet happy, being innocent of the reflection which creates a sense of sin.

> 'Contact with natural man leads me to deplore the vanity in which we thinking people sub-infeudate ourselves. I watch, detachedly… judging myself now carried away by instinct, now ruling a course by reason, now deciding intuitively: always restlessly cataloguing each aspect of my unity. Like the foolish early Christians, with their Father, Son, and Holy Ghost, three sides of God, in that Creed for whose performance we just now had to stand up.

> 'Hungry time has taken from me year by year more of the Creed's clauses till now only the first four words remain. Them I say defiantly, hoping that reason may be stung into new activity when it hears there's yet

a part of me which escapes its rule: though it's as hard, by thinking, to take an inch off our complexity as to add an ell.

'There it goes again: that conflict of mind and spirit. Whereas here are men so healthy that they don't chop up their meat into mince for easy digestion by the mind: and who are therefore intact as we are thereby diseased. Man, who was born as one, breaks into little prisms when he thinks: but if he passes through thought into despair, or comprehension, he again achieves some momentary onenesses with himself. And not only that. He can achieve a oneness of himself with his fellows: and of them with the stocks and stones of his universe: and of all the universes with the illusory everything (if he be positive) or with the illusory nothing (if he be nihilist) according as the digestive complexion of his soul be dark or fair. Saint and sinner touch – as great saints and great sinners.'[9]

Elsewhere in *The Mint* Lawrence expresses this view even more trenchantly:

'… the padre read a lesson from St. Paul, prating of the clash of flesh and spirit and of our duty to fight the body's manifold sins… Our ranks were too healthy to catch this diseased Greek antithesis of flesh and spirit. Unquestioned life is a harmony, though then not in the least Christian.'[10]

It may be that these reflections not only register Lawrence's growing distance from Christianity – at least in its creedal form – but also his personal struggle to become more like his fellows; to escape the 'unicorn in a stable' feeling, to become more ordinary and less lonely. Yet even at the philosophical level the 'oneness' he speaks of is simply the perceptual side of Monism, and there is a respectable antecedent for it in the Greek tradition he mentions – classical Stoicism. Perhaps the differences in tone and philosophy between the *Seven Pillars* and *The Mint* can also be ascribed to the profound differences in the books as Projects, as well as the mind states in which they were written. In his letter to Frederic Manning in 1930, Lawrence describes how he wrote as a novice with 'hanging over me the political uncertainty of the future of the Arab Movement. We had promised them so much, and at the end wanted to give them so little… I wrote it in some stress and misery of mind… *The Mint* describes how the Air Force rounds off its pegs to fit into their holes.'[11]

Of course, the fact is that the political motivation was only one of the many forces behind the *Seven Pillars*, and Lawrence himself endlessly pronounced on the subject, variously describing it as an 'autobiography epic', 'a summary of what I had thought and done and made of myself in these first thirty years', and 'carrying a superstructure of ideas', depending on who he was writing to, and when. What does seem to carry through both the *Seven Pillars* and *The Mint* is the inner self-reflexive voice with its restless clarity, certain attitudes to the body, a bedrock austerity of practice and evaluation, and a tireless ranging over Western thought from Homer onwards. All of these seem to colour and inform his judgements. It may be that there is a Cistercian influence, although this would be trickier to prove. Considering Lawrence's deep study of the Crusades and Crusader Castles it is obviously highly plausible that he would have been aware of the influence of St. Bernard of Clairvaux, not only as one of the major preachers of the First Crusade, and the author of *De Laude Novae Militae*, but also as the writer of *The Rule* which the Templars followed, and by which they achieved a workable synthesis of their military and spiritual duties. As might be expected, the deployment of the two codes of virtue – the military and the religious or spiritual – can be seen as Lawrence makes his assessments and judgements of the Bedouin in the *Arab Bulletin* of 18 November 1916:

> '*As for their physical condition, I doubt whether men were ever harder. Feisal rode twelve days journey in six with 800 of them, along the Eastern road, and I have had them running and walking with me in the sun through sand and over rocks for hour after hour without turning a hair. Those I saw were in wild spirits, as quick as hawks, keen and intelligent, shouting that the war may last ten years.*'[12]

Yet, in the *Bulletin* of 23 May 1917, Lawrence writes:

> '*The Bedu are odd people. Travelling with them is unsatisfactory for an Englishman unless he has patience deep and wide as the sea. They are absolute slaves of their appetites, with no stamina of mind, drunkards for coffee, milk or water, gluttons for stewed meat, shameless beggars for tobacco… Had the circumstances of their life given them greater resources or opportunity, the Bedouin would have been mere sensualists. It is poverty which makes them simple, continent and enduring.*'[13]

The severity of these judgements is somewhat moderated by a notebook jotting, probably of the same month, complaining about the succession of feasts: '*I had been twenty-eight years well fed and had no right to despise these fellows for loving their mutton… But I wish to God I was quit of it.*'[14] Even so, in August the same year, he wrote the famous *Twenty-Seven Articles*, of which number 16 includes, '*Do not let them ask you for things, since their greed will then make them look upon you as a cow to milk.*'[15]

The problem which emerges is the apparent contradiction between the foregoing and the evocation of the 'gospel of bareness in materials', and the 'refounding clear of household gods' which Lawrence describes in his letter of 1918 to Vyvyan Richards. In the *Seven Pillars*, a distinction is made between the pleasure-loving soft townsmen and the austere desert-dweller in the phrase 'We abstinents of the desert' – a phrase which summarises his own philosophy, and what he finds admirable and useful in the Bedouin. That is, the self-reliance, mobility, and lack of material dependence of the nomadic Arabs which Lawrence used to advantage in his guerrilla war against the orthodoxy and relative inertia, not to mention, predictability of the Turks.

However, there is a striking anticipation of the 'bareness/simplicity gospel' in an article published in the Jesus College Magazine in January 1913, three or four years before the above quotations, entitled *The Kasr of Ibn Wardani*. In it Lawrence describes a visit to the scented halls of Ibn Wardani, where each of the rooms had '… strange, indefinable scents, memories of myrtle and oleander, musk, cinnamon and ambergris.'

> 'At last we came into a great hall, whose walls, pierced with many narrow windows, still stood to more than half their height. "This," said he, "is the *liwan of silence*: it has no taste", and by some crowning art it was as he had said. The mingled scents of all the palace here combined to slay each other, and all that one felt was the desert sharpness of the air as it swept off the huge uncontaminated plains. "Among us," said Dahoum, "we call this the sweetest of them all", therein half-consciously sounding the ideal of the Arab creed, for generations stripping itself of all furniture in the working out of a gospel of simplicity.

> 'And the secret of the place? Old Khalil told us that night over his hearth-fire, that Ibn Wardani was as a king among the Arabs, and bricks of his palace were kneaded not with common water, but with those precious oils and essences of flowers which of old the Arab druggists could so well compound.'[16]

Firstly, this visit could not have been later than the Carchemish period of Lawrence's life. Wilson remarks that the truth about the palace '… was probably more prosaic, for Lawrence told his parents that the palace of Ibn Wardani has many strange scents about it.' Lawrence wrote, 'as I wrote: it is famous all over north Syria, and my description is more like the rumour than the reality.'[17] However, even if this deprecatory note is true, Lawrence's promotion of a (supposed?) Arab asceticism which Wilson remarks 'appealed to some fundamental element in his own nature', gives us a marker for the substance of his own views. And, taken together with such examples as his letter to Vyvyan Richards of 1918, which praises Arab austerity and, for example, his lifestyle in the Forces and at Clouds Hill (where there were no cooking facilities, no toilet, sleeping bags, and the bread and cheese were under glass covers etc.) give us not only Lawrence's views, but also his practice. If this celebration of Arab asceticism is considered along with Lawrence's lifestyle, i.e., at Clouds Hill, we can see his philosophy and practice more clearly. It seems to be as the M.P., Ernest Thurtle, says that everywhere there was a reduction of material needs and, where comfort and freedom were in the balance, always was comfort sacrificed. In short, from Lawrence's article in the Jesus College Magazine in 1913, to his letter to Vyvyan Richards in 1918, and subsequently while in the RAF and Tank Corps, and for the rest of his life, Lawrence chose austerity and simplicity.

Comparison between the Richards letter of July 1918 and the College Magazine article of January 1913 shows a consistency of view despite minor changes in formulation. Whereas in the 1913 article we have the transitions from 'silence' to 'no taste' to ' stripping… of all furniture in the working out of a gospel of simplicity', five years later we have 'refined itself clear of household gods, and half the trappings which ours [civilisation] hastens to assume. The gospel of bareness in materials is a good one…' In both instances there is a series of negations, of 'furniture' or 'household gods' as the case may be; in any case, by implication, the trivial, the petty, material things – mere 'stuff'. In both cases the positive is the announcement of a gospel, either of simplicity, or of bareness in materials. Both point away from the usual measures of worldly success, and the valuation of things. Nothing could be further from the culture of accumulation.

Corroboration of the simplicity/'bareness in materials gospel' can be found in a surprising source – from Lawrence's dentist, W. Warwick James, who met him in 1922:

'He was not understood by those who did not realize how little the ambitions of the majority of people appealed to him. He appeared to be an ascetic – perhaps hardly true, for his exclusion of things was effected by positive actions, rather than by mere self-denial. He had achieved an extreme simplicity, had an acute mind and an unusual capacity for assimilating any subject presented to him. These attributes and his great capacity to utilize time distinguish him from the ordinary individual.'[18]

Naturally enough it would be easy to point out where Lawrence does not live up to these austere views: simply, the accumulation of so many books – 2,000 in Clouds Hill according to a letter of 1932.[19] The large, expensive motorcycles and the cult of speed. It would be tedious to attempt the 'justification' of these things, and I will not do so, being convinced that they do not vitiate Lawrence's philosophy and basic comportment, nor that it was his duty to be a saint or follow a 'foolish consistency'. The possible roots for these views about simplicity and material bareness may have lain in Lawrence himself, but I consider it more plausible that they can be found in Christianity and the Classics; and propose to return to them after considering in more depth the struggles depicted in the *Seven Pillars*.

Endnotes

[1] *Selected Letters*, Ed. Garnett, pp. 23-24.

[2] Thomas à Kempis, *The Imitation of Christ*, p. 137. Biblical Ref. to 1. 2 Tim.iii,2.

[3] See both Foucault, *History of Sexuality*, Vols 2 and 3, and Peter Brown, *The Body and Society*.

[4] Italics added. Nietzsche, *The Will to Power*, pp. 483-484.

[5] *Selected Letters*, Ed. Garnett, p. 147.

[6] *Seven Pillars*, Penguin Edn., p. 30. Oxford Edn., pp. 11-12.

[7] *Letters*, Ed. Garnett, p. 646. 1929.

[8] *Letters*, Ed. Malcolm Brown, p. 34.

[9] T.E. Lawrence, *The Mint*, Penguin Edn., pp. 171-172.

[10] *The Mint*, p. 77.

[11] *Letters*, Ed. Garnett, pp. 691-692.

[12] *Arab Bulletin* 18/11/16. Published in *Secret Despatches from Arabia*, p. 53.

[13] *Arab Bulletin* 23/5/17. Published in *Secret Despatches*, pp. 136-137.

[14] See J. Wilson, *Authorised Biography*, pp. 409, 1069.

[15] *Secret Despatches*, p. 157. Article 16.

[16] From T.E. Lawrence, *Seven Essays*. Originally published in *Jesus College Magazine*, Vol I, No.2, January 1913. Republished in *The Journal of the T.E. Lawrence Society*, Vol III, No.1, Summer 1993.

[17] See J. Wilson, pp. 112, 996 for reference to Home Letters, p. 239.

[18] *T.E. Lawrence By His Friends*, p. 514.

[19] *Letters*, Ed. Garnett, p. 753.

CHAPTER NINE

Seven Pillars of Wisdom

༄

L AWRENCE'S systematised views on military and psychological leadership and, by implication, his philosophical/ethical positions, are laid out with great clarity in the 27 Articles (see Appendix 1) published originally in the *Arab Bulletin* of 20 August 1917. The level and variety of skills discussed is extraordinary, as is the essential self-demand on which it is all predicated. This exacting self-demand is summed up in *Seven Pillars* as '… no man can lead Arabs unless he lives level with them, eats the same food, and yet appears a better man in himself.' *Seven Pillars*, amongst other things, unpacks and describes the detailed experience of living up to such an agenda, where the background personal view is the 'simplicity/bareness' gospel discussed previously. Curiously, a hard-edged version of these high standards can be found ten years later in a letter to Lionel Curtis from Karachi:

> '*I notice an incredible shabbiness and second-rating in all our effort here. We talk so much of climate. A gowk in a paper of this week said that the climate of Karachi was like a taste of Hell in summer… Well, this year it has not once been uncomfortably warm. It has never been hot, in the sense that Baghdad and Cairo are hot… Yet they burble of hardship, and sleep at midday, and wear sun-helmets, and cut the work hours to half the hours of England, and excuse themselves any laxity or indulgences of temper or disposition… It is laziness, pure or impure, and simple or complicated. We could work exactly as men do in England, and be all the better for it, for we would not then have the time to remember and cultivate all these fancies of fever and disease. Believe me, I am ashamed of my race, here. They deserve to lose ground in the world, for their frivolous ineptitude.*'[1]

If the foregoing can be taken as an example of the level of physical demand which Lawrence thought reasonable, and in *peacetime*, the following instance demonstrates his ethical stance during the war; particularly around the moral problem generated by the Sykes-Picot Agreement of May 1916, which basically gave the lie to the promises which Lawrence was making to the Arabs on behalf of the British Government. The document was never actually sent from Lawrence to Captain Gilbert Clayton, principal intelligence officer in Cairo. It was in a notebook he was to leave behind, which was subsequently found among his wartime notes, heavily pencilled over, and finally read under special lighting and magnification. Lawrence was in Wadi Sirham at the time, a place he described as 'hopeless and sad… putrid smelling… salt and snakes of evil doing.' [cf. Wilson page 410.] Although unsent, it spells out Lawrence's moral distress.

'Clayton, I've decided to go off alone to Damascus, hoping to get killed on the way: for all sakes try and clear this show up before it goes further. We are calling them to fight for us on a lie, and I can't stand it.'[2]

A similar line of thought is discernible in *Seven Pillars*:

'A man might clearly destroy himself: but it was repugnant that the innocence and the ideals of the Arabs should enlist in my sordid service for me to destroy… but we the masters had promised them results in our false contract, and that was bargaining with life, a bluff in which we had nothing wherewith to meet our stake. Inevitably we would reap bitterness, a sorry fruit of heroic endeavour… Accordingly, on this march I took risks with the set hope of proving myself unworthy to be the Arab assurance of final victory. A bodily wound would have been a grateful vent for my internal perplexities, a mouth through which my troubles might have found relief.'[3]

[Author's note: a reminiscence of Chretian de Troyes, the wound which becomes a mouth.]

Nowhere in his writings does Lawrence take refuge from these moral pressures in *real politik* or instrumentalism; the dilemmas remain personal, intense, and expressed in a language perfectly consistent with the braced conscience of his Christian youth, or indeed the honour so dear to Chivalry. At the same time the strategic and geopolitical considerations which were to serve his own country's interests were studied and pursued with equal drive and honesty. Not for nothing did Lawrence want the portraits of both Allenby and Feisal on his walls in Clouds Hill.[4]

In Lawrence, the tension and conflict between mind and body, or soul and body, which he had inherited from his Christian background, was allied in him with an additional attitude of instrumentality towards the body, an attitude summed up in his remark, *'If my body fails me now I will break it.'* Perfectly consistent with this was the cult of the Will: a combination (instrumentality and willpower) perfectly designed to serve an Ideal. The emerging problem, one which seeps through the pages of *Seven Pillars* and gives biting irony to its sub-title *'A Triumph'*, is what happens in the failure – absence or pollution of the Ideal? In a sense this is Lawrence's defining problem, and the search for solutions to it, the drive which powers some of his post-war activities. Some French commentators have formulated this problem in terms of the search for the Absolute, and Lawrence does indeed use this term, but mostly in literary contexts, already noticed, for example, 'there's no absolute in the imaginative world, so journeymen like myself are confused and miserable in it.'[5] Nevertheless, for one who lived by a militant asceticism, the dangers were real. In the light, not only of his experiences in the war, but also of his emerging judgement of his fame, coupled with the lost transcendence of his waning Christian faith, where does an ex-Crusader go, and what can replace the Ideal?

Lawrence's solutions were various. Already mentioned is his joining of the RAF and high valorisation of 'the conquest of the air'. As always, he had various writing projects, although always with a strong undertow of self-doubt. Especially in question was the production, value, and reception of *Seven Pillars*. It is unsurprising that the book is so variously filed in bookshops and libraries under 'Military History', 'Biography', 'Literature', 'Gay Interest', 'Fiction', 'Middle Eastern Politics' and elsewhere. The reason is its production served so many purposes. If ever the production and intent of a text was over-determined, this was. Lawrence, of course, provided dozens of explanations and remarks about his war and the writing of *Seven Pillars*, all more or less tailored to their recipients. Arranging some of these in an order beginning with the most external, yields the following:

> 'After peace came I found myself the sole person who knew what had happened in Arabia during the war, and the only literate person in the Arab army. So it became a professional duty to record what happened.'[6]

In 1919, Lawrence responded by letter to a question about his motives during the war from G.J. Kidston, a Foreign Office official:

> 'You asked me "why" today, and I'm going to tell you exactly what my motives in the Arab affair were, in order of strength:
>
> (i) Personal. I liked a particular Arab very much, and thought that freedom for the race would be an acceptable present. [Author's note: Probably a reference to Dahoum.]
>
> (ii) Patriotic. I wanted to help win the war, and Arab help reduced Allenby's losses by thousands.
>
> (iii) Intellectual curiosity. I wanted to feel what it was like to be the mainspring of a national movement, and to have some millions of people expressing themselves through me: and being a half-poet, *I don't value material things much. Sensation and mind seem to me to be much greater, and the ideal, such a thing as the impulse that took us into Damascus, the only thing worth doing.* [Italics added.]
>
> (iv) Ambition. You know Lionel Curtis has made his conception of the Empire – a Commonwealth of free peoples – generally accepted. I wanted to widen that beyond the Anglo-Saxon shape, and form a new nation of thinking people, all acclaiming our freedom, and demanding admittance to our Empire. There is, to my eyes, no other road for Egypt and India in the end, and I would have made their path easier, by creating an Arab Dominion in the Empire.
>
> I don't think there are any other reasons. You are sufficiently Scotch to understand my analyzing my own mind so formally. The process intended was to take Damascus and run it (as anyone knowing the East and West could run it), as an independent ally of G[reat] B[ritain]. Then to turn on Hejaz and conquer it: then to project the semi-educated Syrians on Yemen, and build that up quickly (without Yemen there is no re-birth for the Arabs) and finally receive Mesopotamia into the block so made: all this could be done in thirty years of directed effort, and without impairing British holdings. It is only the substitution of a 999 years' lease for a complete sale.
>
> Now look what happened when we took Damascus:
>
> Motive (i): I found had died some weeks before; so my gift was wasted, and my future doings indifferent on that count.
>
> Motive (ii): This was achieved, for Turkey was broken, and the central powers were so united that to break one was to break all.
>
> Motive (iii): This was romantic mainly, and one never repeats a sensation. When I rode into Damascus the whole country was on fire with enthusiasm, and in the town a hundred thousand people shouted my name. Success always kills by surfeit.

Motive (iv): This remained, but was not strong enough to make me stay. I asked Allenby for leave, and when he gave it me, came straight home. It's the dying remains of this weakest of all my reasons, which made me put up a half-fight for Feisal in Paris and elsewhere, and occasionally drives me into your room to jest about what might be done.

If you want to make me work again you would have to recreate motives (ii) and (iii). As you are not God, Motive (i) is beyond your power.

I'm not conscious of having done a crooked thing to anyone since I began to push the Arab Movement, though I prostituted myself in Arab service. For an Englishman to put himself at the disposal of a red race is to sell himself to a brute, like Swift's Houyhnhnms. However, my body and soul were my own, and no one can reproach me for what I do to them: and to all the rest of you I'm clean. When you have got as far as this, please burn it all. I've never told anyone before, and may not again, because it isn't nice to open oneself out. I laugh at myself because giving up has made me look so futile.'[7]

A letter to Edward Garnett in 1922:

'I can't write poetry: so in prose I aimed at providing a meal for *the fellow-seekers with myself.* [Italics added.] For this the whole experience, and emanations and surroundings (background and foreground) of a man are necessary. Whence the many facets of the book, its wild mop of side-scenes and side-issues, the prodigality and profuseness: and the indigestibility of the dish. They were, when done, deliberate: and the book is a summary of what I have thought and done and made of myself in these first thirty years. Primarily it's that, and not a work of art: and when the book was finished and I read it, the fact that it wasn't a work of art rose up and hit me in the face, and I hated it, because artist is the proudest profession. I never hoped to be nearly one, and the chance allures me.'[8]

A letter to Edward Garnett in 1922:

'The personal revelations should be the key to the thing: and the personal chapter actually is the key, I fancy, only it's written in cipher.'[9]

A letter to E.M. Forster in 1928:

'The Seven Pillars is a sort of introspection epic, you know: and it would have taken a big writer to bring it off.'[10]

A letter to E.M. Forster in 1928:

'Of course The Seven Pillars is bigger than The Mint. I let myself go in the S.P. and gave away all the entrails I had in me. It was an orgy of exhibitionism. Never again... I've done my very best with every line of both books. Overdone it, rather than underdone it. Edgar Wallace does not take half my pains, I think.'[11]

A letter to Robert Graves in 1935:

'What I was trying to do, I suppose, was to carry a superstructure of ideas upon or above anything I made.'[12]

Endnotes

[1] *Letters,* Ed. Garnett, pp. 558–560.

[2] See Wilson, *Introduction to Lawrence's Minorities,* pp. 32–33.

[3] *Seven Pillars,* Oxford Edn., pp. 295–296.

[4] 'In the flesh that double allegiance was difficult: but the two quiet heads on the wall will let me do what I please. I shall grow philosophical, at finding that problem solve itself.' (1933). *Letters,* Ed. Garnett, p. 774. Letter to Edward Garnett.

[5] *Letters.* To E. Garnett, Ed. Garnett, p. 358.

[6] Letter to Bernard Shaw in 1922. *Letters,* Ed. Garnett, pp. 356–357.

[7] *Letters,* Ed. Malcolm Brown, pp. 168–170.

[8] *Letters,* Ed. Garnett, p. 371.

[9] *Letters,* Ed. Garnett, p. 366.

[10] *Letters,* Ed. Garnett, p. 621.

[11] *Letters,* Ed. Garnett, pp. 622, 624.

[12] *Letters.* Ibid., p. 853.

CHAPTER TEN

The Personal Chapter in Seven Pillars

∽

THE 'personal' chapter of *Seven Pillars* – a chapter of only six pages in the Penguin edition – is written in some of Lawrence's most impacted prose: so layered with a logic of disavowal, negation and allusion, as to be indeed 'in cipher'.[1]

It begins with Lawrence describing how he helped the Camel Corps 'lazily and mildly' in the watering of their camels; it proceeds with an acutely self-aware appraisal of himself, 'taking stock of where I stood, mentally, on this my thirtieth birthday', and ends with self-repudiation.

Lawrence recounts how, four years before, he had meant to be a general by thirty, and knighted, but that now his 'sense of the falsity of the Arab position' had cured him of 'crude ambition', although it had left him his 'craving for good repute among men'. So he was aware that even though the foregoing 'temporal dignities' would be within his grasp, as he wrote (if, indeed, he survived the next four weeks), 'nothing in this war was honourable to me'.

Externally, so far as the war was concerned, the primary Chivalrous value of honour via arms was therefore impossible and polluted because Lawrence was aware of the secret Sykes-Picot deal and therefore of his duplicity vis-à-vis the Arabs, and the emptiness of British promises to them (which contradicted Chivalric values). Internally, in his self-appraisal, Lawrence's awareness of his craving for 'good repute' and honour amongst his peers, led him to be suspicious of his truthfulness to himself: 'Only too good an actor could so impress – or wish to impress – men, with his favourable opinion.'[2] Perhaps an aggravating factor in this self-critique, apart from Lawrence's Puritan background, was the necessarily performative – almost actorly aspect – of his role and function in the Revolt. To carry on his duties both to Allenby and to Feisal required an acceptance of what Lawrence describes as 'praise wages', which he found so dubious. Lawrence's self-perception was that he was neither a soldier nor a man of action. Hence, in his view, his war and activity were 'overwrought and overthought.' A certain contempt for his own 'passion for distinction', the 'craving for being known and famous, and a horror of being known to like being known' led him to refuse the honours offered. The self that Lawrence describes is, unsurprisingly, abnormally shy, awkward, over self-aware, yet unable to let go: ' I... could see happiness in the supremacy of the material, and could not surrender to it.'

Perhaps the most 'encyphered' passages are those where Lawrence discusses the 'will' in two paragraphs on the same page. Firstly, 'True there lurked always that will, uneasily waiting to burst out. My brain was sudden and silent as a panther, my senses like mud clogging its feet, and my self... telling the panther that it was bad form to spring, and vulgar to feed upon the kill.' Here, 'will' seems to be much more like 'desire,' 'impulse', or even 'ambition'. Curiously, Ronald Storrs had described Lawrence as 'A pardlike spirit beautiful and swift.'[3] Secondly, Lawrence uses 'Will', this time capitalised, in a much more orthodox sense '... many roads leading from purpose to achievement, with Will a sure guide through matter in the end. There was no flesh.'[4] Here his use of the word seems much more of a piece with his near-Platonic conception of 'our intellectual nature' (page 680) as radically [different] other than 'matter'. Also it fits with the idea of 'willpower', a conception ascribed to him by others, not least his brother, A.W. Lawrence, and the 'no flesh' phrase tacked on as an afterthought, again emphasising intellectuality vis-à-vis the body, and its 'mud-like' senses.

Following this, Lawrence next describes his views of his political and military 'Chiefs' – Brigadier General Clayton and General Allenby – in terms of almost embarrassing subservience. 'Always in working I had tried to serve, for the scrutiny of leading was too prominent for me... It was part of my failure never to have found a chief to use me. All of them were weak, and through incapacity or fear or liking, allowed me too free a hand. I was always hoping for a master whom I could have fought till I dropped at his feet to worship: for with respect man could only worship the gods which had proved stronger than himself, and a tragedy of the world had been their fewness.

'I used myself as I would have let no man use another; but needed over me one yet harder and more ruthless, who would have worn me to the last fibre of my strength. To him I would have given such service as few masters have had, and would have given it zealously, for voluntary slavery was a deep pride of a morbid spirit and vicarious pain its gladdest decoration. Instead of this they were all nice to me and valued me aloud, and gave me licence, which I abused to raise their anger – but I always reached insipid indulgence. An orchard fit to rob must have a guardian, dogs, a high wall, barbed wire. I broke rules with joyless impunity.'[5]

The only 'Chief' who came near to Lawrence's needs was Allenby, who had the quality of 'greatness', an epithet sometimes used by Lawrence, also in literary contexts, but never, perhaps inevitably, defined. Lawrence's praise for Allenby is so fulsome that he wrote that he 'reconciled him to the sanity of the vision of a super-man, or the mystical conception of God, including vice and virtue.'[6] But even with Allenby, Lawrence avoided him and kept out of sight '... for fear lest he show feet of clay with that friendly word that must shatter my allegiance.' Aware, perhaps, of how all this would read, Lawrence partly qualifies it by adding, 'So extravagant an estimate of my Chief was partly a refuge against the meanness of our enemy. The Turks were too-poor creatures for me to fight.'

Part of these masochistic declarations may have been caused by Lawrence's awareness of several factors in his apparent success which were not always evident to admirers, such that his Puritan conscience was bad; an over-nuanced conscience, over-braced by circumstances, not least 'the cross-strains of hunger, fatigue, heat, or cold, and the beastliness of living among Arabs.'[7] His acute awareness of his own opportunism rankled against the background of the knowledge of his own capacities: 'I was a standing court-martial on myself, inevitably, because to me the inner springs of action were bare, with the knowledge of how much was just exploited chance.' As a trained historian Lawrence was aware of the contingency of fame and repute.

Privately, Lawrence suggests a near Cynic abstemiousness as his basic orientation: 'When a thing was in my reach I no longer wanted it. My delight lay in the desire, and not in the desired. I believed that everything which my mind could wish for was attainable, and used to strive until I just had to open my hand and take it. Then I would turn away.'[8]

Externally, there was a kind of hunger to know himself, '... an everlasting endeavour to free my personality from its accretions, and to project it unencumbered on a fresh medium, that my curiosity to see its naked shadow might be fed. The hidden self was reflected clearest in the still water of another man's incurious mind.' At the same time, Lawrence's anti-physicality seems to have provided an insuperable barrier and distancing effect since '... they ('other men') were interested in so much of which my self-consciousness was ashamed. They talked of food and illness, games and pleasures: with me, who felt that to recognise our possession of bodies was degradation enough, let alone to enlarge upon their needs and attributes.[9] These others were outwardly so like me that I would feel shame for myself seeing them wallow in what I judged shame: since the physical could be only a glorification of man's cross. Indeed the truth was always that I did not like myself.'[10]

Whilst the asceticism evoked here is expressed in a language which is partly Christian, more seems to be signalled than is contained in most forms of that religion. So much so that perhaps we may be correct in thinking that Lawrence may have been reaching further back into Antiquity, to the Greek and Roman civilisations, and the spiritual exercises and philosophical schools which are known to have influenced early Christianity and made it accessible to 'the Gentiles'. These spiritual exercises, which sometimes included fasting,[11] as well as other renunciations and disciplines, can be found throughout the ancient world, from Plato to Plotinus onwards, and variously elaborated in the schools of the Cynics, Stoics, Eliatics, and Socrates himself.

We can recall Lawrence's devotion to Classical Greek; not only in his carrying Aristophanes during the war, but also in his translation of *The Odyssey*, and in Ronald Storrs' recollection of him always reading Greek or Latin in Storrs' flat in Jerusalem during his visits in 1914. So, given Lawrence's education, and enjoyment of Classical literature, we may assume that he had assimilated some of the practices and values contained in it, being aware that not all of them were confined to Christianity. Indeed, we now know that this Classical culture, and some of its values and practices, have a way of resurfacing – and not necessarily always under the pressure of war – in such disparate figures as Montaigne, Goethe, Ernst Jünger, Wilfred Thesiger, E.M. Cioran, Simone Weil, and John Pendlebury in Crete.

One conceptual link between early Christianity and the antecedent world of Greek philosophy where, in particular, Lawrence's recoil from the body, as such, may have its roots, can be found in Plato, even though later in *The Mint* Lawrence had stigmatised it as 'diseased'. And this conceptual link is the distinction between body and mind. A good example can be found in Plato's dialogue *The Phaedo*, where philosophy itself is conceived to be a kind of training for death (and the next life):

'Separating the Soul as much as possible from the body, and accustoming it to gather itself together from each part of the body and concentrate itself until it is completely independent, and to have its dwelling, so far as it can, both now and in the future, alone and by itself, freed from the shackles of the body.'
[Phaedo 67C]

The word 'accustoming' here indicates a practice or exercise, so as to be able to achieve a liberation from the tyranny of the body, the senses in particular ('like mud' – Lawrence), since the knowledge dependent upon them was regarded as unreliable. The ultimate object of all this was to achieve the freedom to rise to the contemplation of universal and eternal truths. Or, as the Christian philosopher of our own times remarked, '… the asceticism and everything to do with it is just a beginning, the condition of being able to become witness to the truth.'[12] When, therefore, we come across such sentences in Lawrence as, 'The lower creation I avoided, as a reflection upon our failure to attain real intellectuality' (Penguin Edn., page 580), or, more savagely, 'The lower creation I avoided as an insult to our intellectual nature' (Oxford Edn., page 680), we are seeing the result of a certain reading of the Classical tradition, perhaps heightened by a personal asceticism which had been reinforced and informed by both Christianity and Chivalry. The Plato references are also evident in Lawrence's references to 'doxa' (δόξᾰ), and 'episteme' (ἐπιστήμη). These are standard in Plato and are a feature of the epistemology of *The Republic*, marking the difference between opinion and knowledge.[13]

Lawrence links his consideration of the age-old movement of the tribes of Arabia between the desert and the more fertile land, with the genesis of the three great monotheistic religions. The desert itself which surrounded the groups of oases called Kasim and Aridh wherein, in Lawrence's view, lay the true centre of Arabia: 'In this group of oases lay the true centre of Arabia, the preserve of its native spirit, and its most conscious individuality. The desert lapped it round and kept it pure of contact.' Lawrence argues that the founders of the 'three great creeds' had all followed the same pattern: 'Their birth set them in crowded places. An unintelligible, passionate yearning drove them out into the desert. There they lived a greater or lesser time in meditation and physical abandonment…' Those who failed to establish lasting religions because 'time and a disillusioned world had not heaped up dry souls ready to be set on fire…' 'The fringes of the deserts[14] were strewn with the broken pieces of faiths which had suffered shipwreck.'[15]

The philosophically telling point in Lawrence's picture of the genesis of the three monotheisms of Judaism, Christianity and Islam (which all preach against the value of the world, and take flight away from 'crowded places' into the desert), is that: 'The base of all these Semitic creeds, the winners and the losers, was common in the one great idea of world-worthlessness. Their profound reaction against matter led them to preach bareness, renunciation, poverty: and the atmosphere of this invention stifled the minds of the desert pitilessly.'

Whether the devotees of the three great monotheisms will recognise their faith in these descriptions, or be content with them, is, of course, another question. The fact is that this is how Lawrence saw them at the time of the writing of *Seven Pillars*, and indeed earlier, i.e., in his 1918 letter to Vyvyan Richards lauding the 'gospel of bareness in materials', and in his 1913 article for the College Magazine which speaks of a 'gospel of simplicity', where very similar formulations occur. In any case, the visit to the Kasr of Ibn

Wardani was an early articulation of the 'gospel of simplicity' and recurs later in *Seven Pillars*.[16]

> '*A first knowledge of their sense of the purity of rarefaction was given me in early years, when we had ridden out over the rolling plains of North Syria to a far ruin of the late Roman period which the Arabs believed was made by a prince of the border as a desert palace for his queen.*'

Similarly to the 1913 article, Lawrence describes how he is led from room to room, his guides saying:

> '*This is Jessamine, this ambergris, this rose,*' [until Dahoum leads him] '*into the main lodging, to the gaping window sockets of its eastern face, and there drank with open mouths of the effortless, empty, eddyless wind of the desert, throbbing past… "This", they told me, "is the best: it has no taste." My Arabs were turning their backs on perfumes and luxuries, and looking out towards the wilderness, choosing the things in which mankind had had no share or part.*

> '*The Beduin of the desert had been born and had grown up in it, and had embraced this nakedness too harsh for volunteers with all his soul, for the reason, felt but inarticulate, that there he found himself undubitably free. He lost all material ties, all comforts, all superfluities or complications to achieve the personal liberty which haunted starvation and death. He saw no virtue in poverty herself: he enjoyed the little vices and luxuries – coffee, fresh water, women – which he could still preserve. In his life he had air and winds, sun and light, open spaces and great emptiness. There was no human effort, no fecundity in nature: just the heaven above and the unspotted earth beneath. There he came near to God.*'[17]

As always, where Lawrence is elaborating on the asceticism which he ascribes to the Bedouin it is not always entirely clear how much it is really theirs, how much it is a feature of the form of Islam they followed, and to what extent it is also something he shared and approved himself. Going back to the 1918 letter to Vyvyan Richards, it is clear at least that there he writes that '… the gospel of bareness in materials is a good one'. In the above passage from *Seven Pillars*, it seems plausible to read approval into it, not only in its tone, but also in the description of the 'little vices and luxuries' with its distant echo of Apollonius of Tyana. Also it is consistent, not only with the undergraduate Lawrence, but also the water-drinking Lawrence who told Lowell Thomas that he never drank tea or coffee at home. Consistent also with the personal philosophy described by Ernest Thurtle. That Lawrence was still human is attested by Lowell Thomas's description of the contents of Lawrence's tent:

> '*Lawrence neither drank nor smoked, but was inordinately fond of chocolate, and there were dozens of empty tins piled in the corner of his tent together with books, bits of theodolites, a camel saddle, cartridge drums, and odds and ends of machine guns. In one of the empty chocolate tins was the French decoration which Pisani had presented.*'[18]

To be sure, Lowell Thomas is not always esteemed as the most reliable witness, but the suggestion of this simple pleasure, together with the other details, somehow makes the evocation of a philosophy and practice of such austerity, more believable. It is, of course, a very characteristic Lawrencian touch to list 'coffee, fresh water, women' as 'little vices and luxuries', and in that order; doubtless shocking to the modern eye. However, such a view is consistent with Lawrence's anti-materialism/anti-physicality stance. Perhaps it can be said that Lawrence felt a particular affinity for the asceticism found amongst some of the Bedouin from 1913 onwards.

Having reached the purity of the palace room with no perfume, and enlarged upon the philosophy of the freedom of the absence of material ties, Lawrence moves easily into the consideration of the notion of God for such a philosophy, a conception marked also by negations, where he again deploys classical Greek terms:[19]

'God was to him (the Bedouin) not anthropomorphic, not tangible, not moral or ethical, not concerned with the world or with him, not natural, but the being thus qualified not by divestiture, but by investiture,[20] a comprehending being, ἀχρώματος, ἀσχημάτισστος, ἀναφής, the egg of all activity, with nature and matter just a glass reflecting him.'[21]

These three alpha-negatives from the classical Greek basically mean 'uncoloured, shapeless, untouched, not to be touched'. All these words signal a transcendence beyond the scope of the senses, a transcendence like the 'Plotinian One', above being and time – of which all predicates are finally inappropriate. Perhaps these negatives in Lawrence's writing are an echo of the mysticism of the Desert Fathers which he almost certainly knew about from his later reference to Nitria, the area of Northern Egypt where Christians retired to the desert to practise austerities and found monasteries in about AD 4,[22] or emerged from his own struggles to articulate a vision of God removed from the more familiar anthropomorphism of some Western Christianity. It seems to be the case that this mysticism of negations, resembling the *Via Negativa* of the Middle Ages, is consistent with the way of life characterised by Lawrence as 'bareness/simplicity/no ties' in the name of a certain freedom and mobility, even though it 'haunted death and starvation'.

Lawrence is evidently aware of the dangers which seem inherent in these views of the 'emptiness of the world and the fullness of God.'[23] That is, inherent in the sense that this world-denial could lead to a certain harshness in the absence of ameliorating factors. Lawrence goes on to enlarge upon this further in his chapter on monotheism:

'The desert-dweller arrived at this intense condensation of himself in God by shutting his eye to the world, and to all the complex possibilities latent in him which only contact with wealth and temptations could bring forth... His sterile experience robbed him of compassion and perverted his human kindness to the image of the waste in which he hid. Accordingly he hurt himself, not merely to be free, but to please himself. There followed a delight in pain, a cruelty which was more to him than goods. The desert Arab found no joy like the joy of voluntarily holding back. He found luxury in abnegation, renunciation, self-restraint. He made nakedness of the mind as sensuous as nakedness of the body.'[24]

Lawrence goes on to end the monotheism chapter with some large and general assertions about the 'Semitic Mind' and people, which are also consonant with both his own asceticism, and with the austerities he finds in some Bedouin. He manages to combine these, somehow, into the 'power' that reaches as far as Damascus (possibly the power of the idea that galvanised the tribes). Lawrence writes, 'One such wave [and not the least] I raised and rolled before the breath of an idea, till it reached its crest, and toppled over and fell on Damascus.' [*Seven Pillars*, Oxford edition, page 23.]

'They were a people of starts, for whom the abstract was the strongest motive, the process of infinite courage and variety, and the end nothing… Since the dawn of life in successive waves they had been dashing themselves against the coasts of the flesh. Each wave was broken but, like the sea, wore away ever so little of the granite on which it failed, and some day, ages yet, might roll unchecked over the place where the material world had been, and God would move upon the face of those waters. One such wave (and not the least) I raised and rolled before the breath of an idea, till it reached its crest, and toppled over and fell at Damascus.'

One thing at least is clear from the foregoing; and that it is difficult, if not impossible, to disentangle what is Lawrence and what is the Bedouin in all this. Perhaps the wisest strategy is to assume that some of the austerities can be ascribed to some of the Bedouin; and that the near mysticism of 'the coasts of the flesh' passages describe Lawrence's mindset and attitudes, a kind of idealism of abstention which helped him to inspire and lead, and almost certainly helped to motivate him, so that he could motivate others.

If this is so, then it is likely to be reflected in the process of the selection of his personal bodyguard: the ones who would have been closest to him and in the greatest personal danger. After all they had prices on their heads, and were vulnerable to many hazards, as well as betrayal. In fact, turning to the description of the interactions of Lawrence with his bodyguard, there is evidently a kind of dialectic of excellence, so far as endurance and austerity are concerned:

'With quaint justice, events forced me to live up to my bodyguard, to become as hard, as sudden, as heedless. The strain so put upon me was great, especially when the climate cogged the die. In winter I outdid them, with my allies of the frost and snow: but in the heat they could outdo me. In endurance there was less disparity. For years before the war, and during it, I had kept myself trim by constant training in carelessness. I had learnt to eat much one time, and then to go two, three or even four days quite without food: and after to overeat. I made it a rule to avoid rules in food, not to regulate my life by hours or bells, never to have fixed meals, or a fixed number of meals. Such a course of exceptions accustomed me to no custom at all.

'So physically I was every whit as efficient in the desert as my companions, felt neither hunger nor surfeit however great the feast or long the fast, and was never distracted by thought of food during my work. I had followed the same habit of avoiding habit in drink and sleep and rest, and on the march could go dry between wells (since to carry a water-bottle was rightly thought effeminate among the Arabs) and like the Arabs could drink greatly at wells both for the thirst of yesterday and against the thirst of tomorrow. No quality of water or food – and we met odd varieties of either – disturbed me… Such liberties came from years of past control (contempt of use might well be the lesson of our manhood) and they fitted me peculiarly for my men and our conditions: but of course in me they were only the effect of training and trying, half from choice, half from poverty, and I was never able to assume them effortlessly like the Arabs. Yet in compensation they had not my energy of motive, and their less-taut wills flagged before mine, and made me seem to them tough and active.

'Together we often saw men push themselves, or be driven, to what some might have thought a cruel extreme of endurance: and yet never was there an intimation of physical break. The collapse of men from overstrain always rose from a moral weakness eating into the body, which itself, without traitors from within, had no power over the will. To men whose spirits were filled with desire there was no flesh. While we rode we were disembodied, all-unconscious of physical needs or feelings: and when at an interval this excitement faded and we did see our bodies it was with hostility, with a contemptuous sense that they reached their *highest purpose, not as instruments of the spirit, but when, dissolved, their elements served to manure a field.'*[25]

One odd feature of these pages is that whereas the Oxford text is almost invariably longer, as a rule, here a paragraph is added to the (usually) shorter Penguin version. Here, on page 477 of the Penguin edition, Lawrence has a brief excursus on the kind of monism which is usually associated with *The Mint*:

> 'The conception of antithetical mind and matter, which was basic in the Arab self-surrender, helped me not at all. I achieved surrender [so far as I did achieve it] by the very opposite road, through my notion that mental and physical were inseparably one: that our bodies, the universe, our thoughts and tactilities were conceived in and of the molecular sludge of matter, the universal element through which form drifted as clots and patterns of varying density. It seemed to me unthinkable that assemblages of atoms should cogitate except in atomic terms. My perverse sense of values constrained me to assume that abstract and concrete, as badges, did not denote oppositions more serious than Liberal and Conservative.'

It seems that where Lawrence is considering his personal practice, by 'keeping himself trim by constant training in carelessness', by having 'no rules about food, sleep and drink', and by 'a habit of no habits', he is cultivating a personal freedom, mobility and toughness of an extraordinary degree. In fact, similar to his views about Clouds Hill in later years, a place where, 'While I have it there shall be nothing exquisite or unique in it. Nothing to anchor me.'[26] On the other hand, where, for example, he is enlarging upon the dynamics of his bodyguard, or 'the Semitic mind', he uses terms like 'the will', 'the spirit', 'moral weakness', 'the body'. These terms seem far more voluntaristic, and on a different plane compared with his more materialistic monism which is couched in a language of atoms, and 'molecular sludge' (although this phrase sufficiently signals his attitude to matter). Similarly, there appears to be a disjunction in the level of discourse where he occasionally speaks of 'nihilism', a term which has various significations in Lawrence. Again, a term not present in the Oxford edition, but where it is present in the shorter version: perhaps just added 'on reflection'.

Reading the chapters of the *Seven Pillars* where Lawrence discusses pain, (particularly in connection with the discipline of his bodyguard, but generally as a characteristic of some Bedouin), can be shocking to our soft psychological minds, especially when joined to Lawrence's frequently dismissive attitude to the body. It is, indeed, difficult to evaluate the apparent masochism and apparent hatred of the body; or to decide whether there has been a drift towards sadism or masochism in an environment of war in a savage climate, with no Christian or post-Christian moderating ambience. On the one hand:

> 'In half an hour they [the bodyguard] would make ready for a ride of six weeks.'

And:

> 'They would travel day and night, at my whim, and made it a point of honour never to mention fatigue.'

While on the other hand:

> 'Abdulla and the Zaagi ruled them, by my authority, with an unalloyed savagery which could only be excused by the power of each man to quit the service if he wished.'

And:

'Servants were afraid of the sword of justice, and of the whip, not because the one might put an arbitrary term to their existence, and the other print red rivers of pain about their sides, but because these were the symbols and the means to which their obedience was vowed. They had a gladness of abasement, a freedom of consent to yield to their master the last service and degree of flesh and blood, because their spirits were equal with his and the contract voluntary.'[27]

There are some clues as to how to assess these pages in the headings to each page in the shorter edition: *'Picked Recruits'*, *'Esprit De Corps'*, *'Artemis Orthia'*. By comparison, the Oxford edition has just 'My Bodyguard'. The most telling is *Artemis* Orthia:[28] in Ancient Greece, Artemis was the twin sister of Apollo, and associated, amongst other things, with uncultivated places and wild animals. In Sparta, where she was merged with the Dorian Goddess, Orthia, there was a whipping ceremony in which boys had to try to steal cheeses from an altar at the risk of being struck by whips. The ancient sources for our knowledge of this ceremony are primarily Xenophon's *Spartan Society*, and Plutarch's life of Lycurgus.[29] Although in later years the spectacle became the object of a dubious tourism, no records remain of the meaning of it for the Spartans of the time; whether it was a rite of passage, or part of the often brutal Spartan training, as a result of which they remained militarily superior for centuries, is not known. Some scholars argue that the blood on the altar pleased the Goddess. Perhaps one way to deal with the apparent scandal of Lawrence's treatment of pain and discipline amongst his bodyguard in particular, is to deploy a non-psychological, instrumental approach. One such can be found in Ernst Jünger's essay *On Pain*. He points out that:

'... the estimation of pain is not the same throughout time. There are apparently attitudes that enable man to become detached from the realms of life where pain reigns as absolute master. This detachment emerges wherever man is able to treat the space through which he experiences pain, i.e. the body, as an object. Of course, this presupposes a command centre, which regards the body as a distant outpost that can be deployed and sacrificed in battle. Henceforth, all measures are designed to master pain, not to avoid it. The heroic and cultic world presents an entirely different relation to pain than does the world of sensitivity... the point is to integrate pain and organize life in such a way that one is always armed against it... The secret of modern sensitivity is that it corresponds to a world in which the body is itself the highest value.'

Whether discipline is:

'of the priestly-ascetic kind, directed toward abnegation or of the warlike-heroic kind, directed toward hardening oneself like steel. In both cases, it is a matter of maintaining complete control over life, so that at any hour of the day it can serve a higher calling.'[30]

In some respects this fits Lawrence surprisingly well: he certainly had an attitude of instrumentality to the body, and it has been sufficiently demonstrated that he did not regard the body as the highest value, and that he was willing to serve a higher calling, whether in the war, or later, in the RAF. Indeed, strangely, Lawrence combined the priestly-ascetic, and the warlike-heroic, although his modesty would have repudiated both.

Looking back to the Spartans associated with Xenophon, or forwards to the Chivalry and dedication of the Military Orders in the Middle Ages, we can see the coherence and logic of Lawrence's valuations expressed in his Gospel or the turn towards the purity of the wilderness celebrated in his 1913 article. Looking even further back in the Western Philosophical tradition, it does seem that there were antecedents in the thought and practices of the Stoics and Cynics of ancient Greece.

Endnotes

[1]   *Seven Pillars*, Ch. CIII, p. 579, Penguin Edn. In the Oxford Edition, Chapter 118, p. 677, entitled *A Birthday*.

[2]   *Seven Pillars*, Oxford Edn., p. 678.

[3]   See Ronald Storrs, *Orientations*, p. 459. Quotation from Shelley.

[4]   *Seven Pillars*, Oxford Edn., p. 681.

[5]   *Seven Pillars*, Oxford Edn., p. 682.

[6]   *Seven Pillars*, Oxford Edn., p. 683.

[7]   *Seven Pillars*, Oxford Edn., p. 679.

[8]   *Seven Pillars*, Oxford Edn., p. 684.

[9]   Compare Porphry on the life of the great Neoplatonist Plotinus [205-270 AD]. 'Plotinus, the philosopher of our times, seemed ashamed of being in the body.' See *Enneads*.Vol I, p. 3.

[10] *Seven Pillars*, Oxford Edn., pp. 684-685.

[11] 'Fasting… is not an exclusively Christian discipline; all the major religions of the world recognise its merit. Zoroaster practised fasting as did Confucius and the yogis of India. Plato, Socrates and Aristotle all fasted. Even Hippocrates.' See R. Foster, *Celebration of Discipline*, p. 62.

[12] Kierkegaard, *Papers and Journals*, p. 577.

[13] *Seven Pillars*, Oxford Edn., p. 197, and Penguin Edn., p. 199.

[14] *Seven Pillars*, Oxford Edn., p. 13, and Penguin Edn., p. 37.

[15] Gertrude Bell, *Letters*,Vol 2, p. 342. 'The edges of the desert are always stormy and difficult.'

[16] *Seven Pillars*, Oxford Edn., p. 19.

[17] *Seven Pillars*, Oxford Edn., pp. 19-20.

[18] Lowell Thomas, *With Lawrence in Arabia*, p. 305.

[19] *Seven Pillars*, Oxford Edn., p. 20.

[20] Surely he intends this the other way round?

[21] *Seven Pillars*, Oxford Edn., p. 20.

[22] Letter to Lionel Curtis, 14.v. 23. *Letters*, Brown Edn., p. 237.

[23] *Seven Pillars*, Oxford Edn., p. 21.

[24] *Seven Pillars*, Oxford Edn., p. 21.

[25] *Seven Pillars*, Oxford Edn., p. 528.

[26] *Letters*, Ed. Garnett, p. 746. To Mrs. Kennington, explaining, inter alia, the significance of the Greek inscription carved over the doorway, 'ου φροντις', from *Herodotus*,VI, p. 129. The Greek actually says, 'Not think', or 'Not worry'.

[27] *Seven Pillars*, Oxford Edn., p. 525.

[28] *Seven Pillars*, Oxford Edn., p. 525. Penguin Edn., p. 476.

[29] See *Plutarch on Sparta*, Penguin. Also Paul Cartledge, *The Spartans*.

[30] Ernst Jünger, *On Pain*, pp. 16-17.

Cynics and Stoics

CLASSICAL ROOTS OF THE GOSPELS OF BARENESS AND SIMPLICITY

⤴

I F we examine the Western Philosophical tradition, there are antecedents for the philosophy of simplicity/bareness/austerity as espoused by Lawrence, and as a feature of the culture of some of the Arabs which he 'discovered' while he lived and fought with them. It appears that amongst these antecedents, or roots, there are the intellectual resources for elaborating a philosophy in which a warrior ethos, such as Chivalry, with its emphasis on The Deed, and a certain distanciation on the world (and the flesh) like the views of the early Christian mystics, can be combined. Just such resources can be found in the writings and practices of the ancient Stoics and Cynics, so that even when the Christian faith fades, a similar comportment towards life and the world can still be maintained.

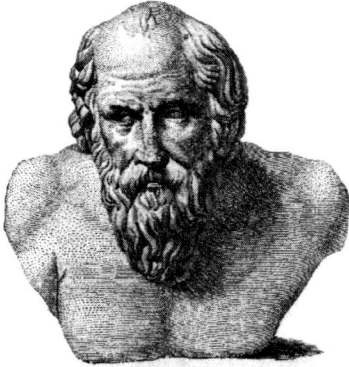

Diogenes of Sinope, c. 400-325 B.C. Seeing a mouse eating crumbs at a feast, and noticing that it was not in need of any dainties, and apparently unafraid, Diogenes was converted to a simple, austere way of life. Alexander the Great visited him, and asking if he wanted anything was told, 'Get out of my light.' Alexander said that if he had not been Alexander, he would have liked to have been Diogenes.

The Cynics

In the first place, the ancient Greek Cynics maintain a particular attitude to the body which is notably harmonious with the performative emphasis of Chivalry, and any warrior ethos. Classical Cynicism is not highly developed theoretically and, like Chivalry, and some early Christianity, is largely sustained by the Deeds of Exemplary lives and their reception, celebration, and emulation. So, while the Cynics do not offer an elaborated doctrine, their followers and proponents can be recognised by a basic orientation towards happiness and freedom, which entails a radical austerity. Cynics are led to this orientation through their acute awareness of the difference between natural and cultural values. D.R. Dudley, in his influential history of the subject, points out the sheer otherness of Cynic practice for us: 'The Cynics represented a standard with which we are unfamiliar – that of the *minimum*… In the modern world no one voluntarily lives, as did the Cynics, at subsistence level.' The comments of Emeritus Professor of Greek, I.G. Kidd, on Cynicism in the *Encylopaedia of Philosophy*, (Macmillan Publishing), brings out the same features:

'... the most characteristic feature of Cynicism was an asceticism which sought to reduce physical wants to a minimum, as in the case of animals... and to achieve spiritual independence like Gods.'

Thus Cynic practice amounted to existence as a critique of culture. They offered practical examples of autonomy of the Will which were to be very influential on the development of Stoicism – from Zeno to Epictetus, and on Christianity itself. Lawrence draws precisely on this Cynic/Stoic philosophy.

The origins of this constellation of attitudes, values, and practices go back at least as far as Socrates, particularly the Socrates represented in Xenophon rather than in Plato (although Xenophon as one of the primary sources, is pertinent too). Xenophon particularly evokes the physical courage and toughness of Socrates in battle, his self-discipline rather than his dialectical skills. As previously noted, Xenophon quotes Socrates as saying that 'many people's minds are invaded by forgetfulness, despondency, irritability and insanity because of their poor physical condition', and that 'every man ought to regard self-discipline as the foundation of moral goodness, and cultivate it in his character before anything else'.[1] The key figure after Socrates, whose thought and personality marks the Cynic tradition, is Diogenes of Sinope (c. 412/403-324/321 BC).

Diogenes approaches what he sees as the ubiquitous slavery to illusion and hypocrisy all around him by taking Nature (φύσις) as an ethical norm. By doing this he aims at a truth 'beneath' or 'beyond' the cultural values of the society in which he finds himself. This truth can be inferred by cross-cultural comparison and animal behaviour. It is worth recalling that the Greek historians, Herodotus and Thucydides, were almost contemporaries, and the kind of history they wrote took in the practices of other cultures and times, and thereby provided new and larger perspectives to their readers, effectively by writing ethnography or anthropology. Thus Herodotus records how Darius brought Greeks and Indians together to compare burial customs – to the shock and surprise of both parties. The upshot is that the confrontation between differing value systems robs both of any claim to universal validity (or tends to). Lawrence remarks on the effect of seeing through two traditions early in *Seven Pillars*.[2] It has been argued that Cynicism is, amongst other things, 'a form of voluntary cultural estrangement, in which the individual comes to see the customs and values of his society as arbitrary in nature and distains to observe them.'[3] Perhaps it can be said that Lawrence was already somewhat 'estranged' culturally before the war, partly by choice and personality, and that the experience of the war increased it.

Returning to Diogenes and the genesis of his particular philosophy, as well as its distanciation on the culture of the times, there is a legend from Theophrastus recorded by Diogenes Laertius in *Lives of Eminent Philosophers*, that Diogenes of Sinope was inspired by watching a mouse running about, '... not looking for a place to lie down in, not afraid of the dark, not seeking any of the things which are considered to be dainties'. Diogenes discovered the means of adapting himself to circumstances.[4] Perhaps this can be taken as the first episode in which reflection on animal behaviour led to inferential lessons for Cynic Philosophers; the second moment in their developing critique after, or alongside, cross-cultural comparison. According to these Cynic perspectives, the values of any society, since they are not those of Nature, are not only false, but counter-productive. Accordingly, human beings can only realise their true nature, and any possibility of happiness, by following a regime of rigorous mental and physical training (see

Introduction). The analogy with the training of athletes is taken up by both Cynics and Stoics. In other words, just as athletes pursue a path of rigorous discipline in pursuit of their goals, just so the discipline (known to the Greeks as 'Askesis' – from the Classical Greek, meaning 'training' or 'exercise', origin of asceticism, meaning self-discipline/austerity) of the philosophers not only leads to freedom, but also prepares for the possible vicissitudes of human life, e.g. shipwreck, slavery, prison, injury, and poverty. One definition of the goal was to be superior to pain and toil, and to maintain the serenity of one's ruling faculty. The practicalities of Cynic philosophy not only emerge in the stories about Diogenes, (for example about how he discarded his cup when seeing a child drink from its hands), but can also be seen in his education of the sons of Xeniades. Although he had been bought as a slave by Xeniades, he said to him, 'You must obey me, although I am a slave; for if a physician or a steersman were in slavery, he would be obeyed.'

And he was entrusted with the education of Xeniades' sons. Interestingly, he educated them in military skills as well as their other studies: 'After their other studies he taught them to ride, to shoot with the bow, to sling stones and to hurl javelins. Later, when they reached the wrestling school, he would not permit the master to give them full athletic training, but only so much as to heighten their colour and keep them in good condition. The boys used to get many passages from poets, historians, and the writings of Diogenes himself by heart; and he would practise them in every short cut to a good memory. In the house too he taught them to wait upon themselves, and to be content with plain fare and water to drink. He used to make them crop their hair close and to wear it unadorned, and to go lightly clad, barefoot, silent, and not looking about them in the streets. He would also take them hunting.'[5]

There is more than a hint of the Spartan education and its values here, and it is relevant to point out that Diogenes expressed positive views about Sparta on more than one occasion, but with a critical implication for both Sparta and the rest of Greece. For example, on being asked where in Greece he saw good men, he replied: 'Good men nowhere, but good boys at Lacedaemon.'[6]

To demonstrate that these perspectives are not just Diogenes' eccentric personality, an excerpt from the later Cynic *Epistles* strikes a similar note in a letter from Crates to The Youths (*tois veaviskos*):

> 'Accustom yourselves to wash with cold water, to eat nothing that has not been earned by toil, to wear a cloak, and to make it a habit to sleep on the ground. Then the baths will never be closed to you, the vineyards and flocks fail, the fish shops and couch shops go broke, as they will to all those who have learnt to wash with hot water, to drink wine, to eat without having toiled, to wear purple clothing, and to rest on a couch.'[7]

Besides Diogenes himself, the great prototypical Cynic, there were those who followed in the tradition he inaugurated: a genealogy of philosophers, until recently largely in the keeping of those who read Greek and Latin, which can be represented as follows:

Socrates (469-399 B.C.)   Xenophon (428-354 B.C.)
Antisthenes (445-336 B.C.)   Aristotle (384-322 B.C.)
Plato (429-347 B.C.)   Diogenes (c. 400-c. 325 B.C.)

Crates (360-280 B.C.)   Cicero (106-43 B.C.)
Zeno (335-263 B.C.)   Epictetus (A.D. 55-135)
Cleanthes (331-231 B.C.)   Dio Chrysostom (c. A.D. 45-115)
Chrysippus (c. 290-c. 207 B.C.) Lucian (A.D. 120-c. 180)
Marcus Aurelius (161-80 B.C.)

Risking an overview of Cynicism, one might say that the classical Cynic is the reverse of the devout consumer and the domesticated pleasure-seeker. The Cynic is the anti-shopper. The Cynic cannot be led by pleasure, is undomesticated, worships no household gods, and is unenslaved by the dominant cultural values. Nevertheless he or she is concerned with truth and virtue. The mobility of the Cynic follows from his or her bypassing of the domestic, and refusing the traps of comfort and pleasure, and indeed the very distinction between public and private. Hence the scandal of Diogenes originally, and later of Crates and Hypparchia. On the other hand, the Cynic is not outside the community, but disengaged/oppositional – at the edge of the group, (Hegel points out that 'Diogenes in his tub is still conditioned',[8] but in defence, one might say that he is fighting a war against that conditioning and its deleterious effects). Cynicism is the hermeneutics of austerity. The military face of this public realm austerity is to a certain extent well-reflected in Sparta; but in Sparta, of course, it was not an individual cult of freedom, but a public and coercive austerity where foreign luxuries were excluded as a matter of state policy.

Although one can plausibly see a Cynic or quasi-Cynic practice in Lawrence's austerities, it is more awkward to demonstrate a textual connection via his books. Of course there is the Stoic Epictetus who had very favourable views of the Cynic calling. Otherwise, secondary sources such as Xenophon, Marcus Aurelius, and Lucian, and even Aristophanes, are the only late demonstrable library connections. Curiously, Lawrence had a copy of Epicurus: a gift, with an introductory essay from Frederic Manning, inscribed: 'To T.E. Shaw for the purpose of comparison, from Frederic Manning. 3.iii.1930.' What the comparison was about, we can only speculate, but it is not impossible that it may have been concerned with the difference between the nuanced views on pleasure of the Epicureans, and the repudiatory Stoic/Cynic attitude. In what amounts to a savage highlighting of this difference, in his study of hedonistic ancient Athens and its appetite for food, sex, and drink, Professor James Davidson describes the reverse of the self-discipline epitomised by the ancient Cynics in his quotations from the fragments of Aristophanes' first play, *The Banqueters*. This play deals with the differing fortunes of two brothers: one of them is self-controlled (sophron), the other is 'a complete degenerate' (katapugon). The latter spends his time 'learning about drinking and singing bad songs… and feasting, and Sybaritic sumptuousness and Chian wine from Spartan cups.' Similarly, in another play, *The Acharnians*, an envoy reporting back from Persia remarks that '… the Persians consider only those who gobble up and drink the most to be men of account: his interlocutor (one Dicaeopolis) replies cuttingly, "And we (consider such prodigious consumers) cock-suckers and Katapugones."'[9]

By contrast, the comic poets quoted by Diogenes Laertius depict Zeno, the founder of Stoicism, as:

This man adopts a new philosophy.
He teaches to go hungry: yet he gets
Disciples. One sole loaf of bread his food;
His best dessert dried figs' water his drink.[10]

Lawrence's own writings only contain one reference to Zeno, in a letter to Frederic Manning dated 15 May 1930:

'*Your seeing Jahveh and the Baalim is of course what I was trying to convey. [in Seven Pillars Ch. LXIII].* *My two years taught me the* inwardness *of all Semitic history, from its beginning: and that includes Zeno and other unexpected persons.*'[11]

Lawrence's reflections on Semitic and Christian history in Ch. LXIII are in the shorter version only, and do not provide a personal philosophical practice, so much as a view of the development and differences of the three great monotheisms: as well as suggestions for his idea of *inwardness*. Indeed he labels the pages 'Another Wash', 'A new Prophet', and 'Digression'. The reason why he digresses seems to be founded in his shock at the appearance of a strange wanderer, who sits on his clothes as he bathes and remarks 'The love is from God; and of God; and towards God.' Lawrence writes that he had believed Semites unable to use love as a link between themselves and God, and that 'Christianity had seemed… the first creed to proclaim love in this upper world, from which the desert and the Semite (from Moses to Zeno) had shut it out: and Christianity was a hybrid, except in its first root not essentially Semitic.'[12] Lawrence admits that the single sentence of 'the old man of Rumm… seemed to overturn [his] theories of the Arab Nature'. But he draws no further inferences. Unfortunately the old man never talked amongst people.

The Stoics

Closer to the Cynics, and much easier to access compared to the barely social mystic who disturbed Lawrence's wash, is the Stoic Epictetus – described by some scholars as a Cynicizing Stoic because of his idealisation of the Cynic calling, and his great personal austerity. An admirer of Zeno and Socrates, Epictetus wrote that one should ask oneself what Zeno and Socrates would have done when meeting an important person. The implication being that their conduct would be a regulatory example. In matters relating to the body, Epictetus is a very strong candidate as a source for Lawrence's 'Gospel of Bareness/Simplicity'. For example:

'*In things relating to the body take just so much as bare need requires, that is to say, in things such as meat, drink, clothing, housing, and household slaves. But cut out everything that is for show and luxury.*'[13]

'*It is a mark of an ungifted man to spend a great deal of time in what concerns the body, as in much exercise, much eating, much drinking, much evacuating of the bowels, much copulating.*[14] *But these things are to be done in passing; and let your whole attention be devoted to the mind.*'[15]

In matters of personal discipline, Epictetus advised against,

'… mere display, these are the traits of a man who has *turned to externals*, and is hunting after something other, and is seeking for spectators to exclaim "What a great man!"

[author's note: there are shades here of Lawrence's self criticism in the personal chapter of *Seven Pillars*]. Epictetus remarks that Apollonius [presumably Apollonius of Tyana: see page 175 of Epictetus] was right when he used to say, 'If you have a mind to train for your own benefit, take a little cold water in your mouth when you are thirsty in hot weather, and spit it out again, and tell nobody.'[16]

Lawrence's agreement with Manning's view of *Seven Pillars* makes the latter's 1930 letter worth pausing over. After all, they admired each other's writing, and Manning's criticism in the second half of the letter seems particularly telling. After having praised the book as magnificent, in no uncertain terms, (*'your mind spent itself without stint, even prodigally, for a great occasion'*), and dwelt on the multiple difficulties of the Arab revolt, Manning remarks:

> 'You took me right back to Genesis and Job. When you describe the action of the nomad on the town-dwellers I see that Jahveh was the desert in all its naked heat moving up to consume the baalim[17] of settled communities, who had exchanged the rigorous asceticism imposed on them by the desert life, for a sensual indulgence which the previous starving had only enhanced. Job, of course, was an Arab, and his present day progeny stand in the same relation to Allah as he stood in relation to Jahveh, so passionately asserting his individuality against that engulphing one-ness. How far the "eternal illusion" as I might call it, took hold of your own mind, I can guess, and yet in all your overt acts you are only harnessing its power to serve some temporal and even momentary ends, in which you do not altogether believe, at least not with the spirit of worship which you feel towards the power it was your business to subjugate and canalize. That's the whole moral problem: one not very different in kind from that confronting Paul on his road to Damascus. As I read your book, and it is a riddle, that is the conflict which subsists at least implicitly under the material action of the book. Or is it some bent in my own mind which forces me to consider you sub specie aeternitatis?'[18]

Lawrence's reply does not meet all Manning's points here, but is fairly self-deprecatory:

> 'As for my harnessing to my go-cart the eternal force – well no: I pushed my go-cart into the eternal stream, and so it went faster than the ones that are pushed cross-stream or up-stream. I did not believe finally in the Arab movement: but thought it necessary, in its time and place. It has justified itself hugely, since the war, too. So, even to a political or statesman, the conflict is measurable and significant. I am still puzzled as to how far the individual counts: a lot, I fancy, if he pushes the right way.'[19]

Perhaps one source of Lawrence's strange powers was that, as he admits himself, he had practised for years before the war in various austerities, not least in food and sleep, and also drink and rest, so that he could pass from Intelligence work in an office in Cairo, to the desert to assess the various leaders of the Revolt with relative ease: the askesis of 'the years of control', the 'no rules about food', the 'habit of no habit' (etc.). All this is consistent with the harder-edged doctrines of Chivalry, as it is with Xenophon, Apollonius of Tyana, and most explicitly in the Cynics and Stoics. In Epictetus we find precisely the roots of Lawrence's remark about Storrs 'training like an athlete'. To one who says 'I wish to win an Olympic Victory', Epictetus advises a consideration of 'the matters which come before that and those which follow after...'

> 'You have to submit to discipline, follow a strict diet, give up sweet cakes, train under compulsion, at a fixed hour, in heat or in cold; you must not drink cold water, nor wine whenever you feel like it; you must turn

yourself over to your trainer precisely as you would to a physician. Then when the contest comes on, you have to "dig in" [wallow in dust and mud] beside your opponent, sometimes dislocate your wrist, sprain your ankle, swallow quantities of sand, take a scourging; yes, and then sometimes get beaten along with all that.'[20]

Epictetus' point is that in the same way that people do not consider properly what is entailed in becoming an athlete, similarly, to become a philosopher, people should consider their natural ability, what they can bear: the necessity of training and the sacrifices that must be made. Just as the athlete must train, so must the philosopher. Lawrence's point is that Storrs could have been even more effective had he disciplined himself similarly. That he had indeed not done so is clear from Lawrence's private correspondence with Lieutenant Colonel W.F. Stirling, and the longer remarks in the Oxford edition of *Seven Pillars*. To Stirling he wrote:

'The falseness of Storrs'… Oh yes, I saw it, but because I knew it, and he knew that I knew it, it had no share in our relations, which were between the real Storrs and the real me. Storrs could retort about the falseness of me… and there wasn't less or more in use. Each of us was a complete dramatic actor, as dressed in appropriate sentiments as clothes.'[21]

In the Oxford edition of the *Seven Pillars*, Lawrence's view of Storrs, whilst more ambivalent than in the shortened version, is also more critical, and the detail of the critique more consistent with the renunciatory Stoicism which Lawrence invariably espoused:

'The first of us was Ronald Storrs, Oriental Secretary of the Residency, the most brilliant Englishman in the Near East, and the deepest, though his eyelids were heavy with laziness, and his eyes dulled by care of self, and his mouth made unbeautiful by hampering desires. None the less Storrs sowed what we reaped, and was always the first and greatest of us. His shadow would have covered our work and British policy in the East like a cloak, had (he ?) been able to deny himself, to leave the world, and prepare his mind and body with the sternness of an athlete for a great fight.'[22]

In the shortened version, the difference is that whilst it is conceded that Storrs was *'subtly efficient, despite his diversion of energy in love of music and letters, of sculpture, painting, of whatever was beautiful in the world's fruit. None the less… [etc.]'* and *'had he been able to deny himself the world… he would have been even more effective.'* So the Oxford version is more radical, *'… to leave the world.'* It seems that Lawrence, whilst sympathetic, is critical of Storrs' 'diversion of energy'. One is reminded of Lawrence's partially concealed impatience and 'embarrassment' with Storrs when he has a 'deep discussion of Debussy' with Aziz el Masri on board the *Lama*, a converted liner at Suez. The difference between them is not only one of character, but also of philosophy. Also, Storrs was a diplomat and a particularly brilliant linguist, speaking German, French, Arabic, Italian, Greek, Latin, and Hebrew. His autobiography, *Orientations*, describes the formation of a very talented scholar of languages and a very cultivated and sybaritic personality, with none of the military virtues and austerities of Lawrence. One might interpret Lawrence's description of Storrs' face variously as hostility or merely the Military Gaze of the ancient world. Something very similar occurs in Ernst Jünger:

'In the liberal world, what one considered a "good" face was, properly speaking, the delicate face – nervous, pliant, changing, and open to the most diverse kinds of influences and impulses. By contrast, the disciplined

face is resolute; it possesses clear direction, and it is single-minded, objective and unyielding.
One immediately notices by every kind of rigorous training how the imposition of firm and impersonal rules
and regulations is reflected in the hardening of the face.'[23]

Lawrence's views on 'habits' virtually amount to a rigorous and impersonal training itself – a consistent rule. His letters show that he was persistently against them, for example, '… *habits must be nipped in their shells'* – a remark in a letter of 1917 to a friend on why he had broken the habit of not writing private letters.[24] To Garnett in 1922: '*but 'ware letter writing. It's a bad habit.'*[25] To Lady Scott in 1923: '*… two calls so close are perilously near a habit: and there are no good habits (except riding habits): deplorable.'*[26] To Lionel Curtis in 1927: '*Your life is chaos. Chaos breeds life: whereas by habit and regularity comes death, quickly.'*[27]

As previously noted, the habit he seems most to have resisted was that of eating regularly: '*I made it a rule to avoid rules in food, not to regulate my life by hours or bells, never to have fixed meals, or a fixed number of meals.'*[28]

This unusual resistance to routine dated back to at least his undergraduate days. One result must have been a degree of detachment – at least from mealtimes and timetables – from the kind of matters dubbed 'external' by the Stoics (and others) which would have resulted in an independence of mind and action, and a lack of predictability. Another result was a hard stare at the usual definition of hunger.

Endnotes

[1] Xenophon, *Conversations with Socrates,* pp. 94, 172.
[2] *Seven Pillars,* p. 30, Penguin Edn. pp. 11-12, Oxford Edn.
[3] *The Cynics,* Ed. by R. Bracht Branham and Marie-Odile Goulet-Caze, p. 122.
[4] Diogenes Laertius, *Lives of Eminent Philosopher,* Vol 2, p. 25. [VI. 23.]
[5] Diogenes Laertius, *Lives,* Vol 2, p. 33. VI. 30-31.
[6] Ibid., p. 29.
[7] Abraham J. Malherbe, *The Cynic Epistles,* p. 69.
[8] Hegel, *Phenomenology,* p. 319.
[9] James Davidson, *Courtesans and Fishcakes,* p. 173. The more literal dictionary definition is 'lewd, lustful, brutal', and the word evidently acquired a more extended sense of decadent/degenerate.
[10] Diogenes Laertius, p. 139. Zeno. VII. 27.
[11] *Letters,* Ed. Garnett, p. 693.
[12] *Seven Pillars,* Penguin Edn. pp. 364-365.
[13] Epictetus, *The Discourses,* p. 199, Ed. Chris Gill.
[14] The order of these bodily activities is also revelatory.
[15] Epictetus, p. 527, Vol 2, Loeb Edn.
[16] Epictetus, *The Discourses,* p. 175, Ed. Chris Gill.
[17] Baalim. The plural of Baal, a god of the Phoenicians. Features in the Old Testament: now signifying a false god.
[18] *Letters to T.E. Lawrence,* Ed. A.W. Lawrence, p. 135.
[19] *Letters of T.E. Lawrence,* Ed. Garnett, p. 693.
[20] Epictetus, Vol 2, p. 101, Book III. xv. 1-6, Loeb Edn.
[21] *Letters,* Edited by Malcolm Brown, p. 275.
[22] *Seven Pillars,* Oxford Edn., p. 37.
[23] Ernst Jünger, *On Pain,* p. 22.
[24] *Selected Letters,* Ed. Garnett, p. 106.
[25] Ibid., p. 156.
[26] Ibid., p. 170.
[27] *Letters,* Ed. Garnett, p. 529.
[28] *Seven Pillars,* Oxford Edn., p. 527.

CHAPTER TWELVE

Food and Drink

✧

A LTHOUGH Lawrence's most austere attitudes to food seem to have emerged during his time with the Bedouin, (e.g. '*it was thought effeminate by the Arabs to carry a provision of food for a little journey of one hundred miles…*'[1]), his restraint in this matter shows as early as his cycle rides in France in 1906. In a letter to his mother of that year from Dinard, he dwells on:

'*… the great difficulty in getting a decent drink in France: milk is not obtainable anywhere and eau de Seltz only occasionally. The result is that one gets very thirsty and the only fruits are plums and pears, their apples are uneatable: I have not had a good one yet… I ate a glorious feast of blackberries.*'

But he escaped the guide who was supposed to have accompanied him around the castle he was exploring by visiting at the dinner hour. His letters reveal that he was cycling long distances, subsisting mainly on fruit, bread, and milk – from wherever he could obtain it. The following year, while on a cycling tour to look at castles in Wales, he wrote to his mother from Caerphilly that:

'*I have come to the conclusion that two meals a day with a glass of milk at one o'clock, suit me better than three. At any rate I have always felt fresh on this trip in spite of very hard journeys, and the number of castles has not palled on me. I am fresh for any amount more, and could continue for months.*'[2]

The next year (1908), again in France to study castles for his thesis, he wrote from Cussy-Les-Forges:

'*I am riding very strongly, & feel very fit, on my diet of bread, milk & fruit (peaches [best] 3 a 1d: apricots 5 or 6 a 1d. if very special: cherries don't count). I begin on 2 pints of milk and bread & supplement with fruit to taste till evening, when more solid stuff is consumed.*'[3]

It is almost as if Lawrence is trying to reassure his mother both that he is well, and that he is not falling into gluttony:

'*… one eats a lot when riding for a week on end at my pace. My day begins early (it's fearfully hot at midday) there is usually a chateau to work at from 12.0 to 2.0 and then hotel at 7.0 or 8.0.*'

His long letter of the same year from the Hotel du Nord at Cordes in Tarn to C.F.C. Beeson (a.k.a. 'Scroggs'), full of details of places seen between Avignon and Cordes, includes the following passage which combines a characteristic mix of disgust and humour (he had already dismissed Carcassone-Toulouse as '… *a dirty industrial dung-heap of factories and plate glass*'):

> '*One's hotel dinners in Tarn (I'm degenerating into a commis-voyageur, and ça criticisera a 'plat' with the best) are weird: I don't in the least know what I ate last night: I fancy a plough-ox or two (is it a nightmare?) some potatoes were they? Stewed infant or monkey: things like paving stones but not quite so hard, haven't the faintest idea what; and to finish something indescribable, described apparently in patois as clargh-bult: they were quite possible, but anything from snail to ortolan. The bread – can you 'degust' in fancy (blessing your stars 'tis only so), leather, steeped in brine and bitter aloes, boiled till soft, with a crust like iron, and an aroma like brandy snap? Milk they say is to be imported from Europe next year: butter was brought in the year before last, and is now turned into cream cheese. I should be dead by now only for the Roquefort: 'tis as common as possible, and with enough of it anything is disguised, even the bread tastes not unlike charcoal. If you're bored or overworn, come to Tarnais hotel for a week.*'[4]

From Beyrout (Beirut) in 1909, after a month's walking in northern Palestine, Lawrence wrote a very long letter – nearly 12 pages – to his family, which again included details of his bread and fruit diet, and the social interactions which accompanied obtaining it. He describes how he left Beyrout in early July '… *and walked straight to Sidon* [approximately 30 miles], *finally arriving at Heldua* [now Khan el Khalde]' where he first tasted native bread and leben (sour milk, yoghurt). He emphasised that the diet he followed was:

> '… *only my lunacy, and the native habit: no other European would think of it: if I have slept the night in a native house then [breakfast] will be 'Haleeb' ordered overnight. The people do not usually take this, since it is fresh milk, (boiled, or heated rather, they fight shy of it cold), with quantities of sugar in it… With this will be eaten a sheet of bread no. ii. [previously described, as 'light grey… very large… circular… very thin… as ordinary brown paper, tough, and pliable, almost leathery when fresh.']. If still thirsty this is followed by prickly pears. At midday … I eat another sheet of bread… next a spring, if there is one: if not it is consumed on the march, moistened with an occasional drop of water from my water bottle.*'[5]

Lawrence goes on to detail the various fruits which could be obtained: '*Still one can get along in Palestine for fruit*' but, in essence, he is eating the food of '*the peasant class at this time of year*'. So far as drinking is concerned, '*Nobody drinks anything but water, except coffee for visitors.*' The diet that Lawrence followed on these travels almost closely resembled the ideal Cynic of Classical times – apart from their ubiquitous Lupins. Lucian remarks that the true Cynic would carry beans, barley, bread, and a book: the false one would carry mirrors, razors, dice, gold and perfume.[6] Lawrence does seem closer to the former: when he did carry gold later, it was for strategic purposes. Indeed, on his return from walking 1,100 miles through Syria and Palestine examining castles in 1909, a lecturer at Oxford who was also a family friend described Lawrence on his return as 'thinned to the bone by privation'.[7] By the time Lawrence was at Carchemish excavating a Hittite site, the references to the local food, essentially bread and leben, pass without elaboration, although during this period of the exploring, later written up as *The Wilderness of Zin*, he did produce a parody menu based on an apparent surfeit of Turkish delight:

> *Soup, Bread soup.*
> *Then, Turkish delight on toast*

Then until yesterday, Eggs
Then, sweet, Turkish delight, Dessert, Turkish delight

The most telling phrase from the same letter to his friend, E. T. Leeds, dated 24 January 1914, contains the above parody menu and the 'flesh-potter' remark below and tells us more about Lawrence's self-definition:

'… *over the consequences of much riding on camels I draw thick veils: but take it as a summing up that we are very unhappy. Woolley is the more uncomfortable, since he is a flesh-potter: I can travel on a thistle, and sleep in a cloak on the ground.'*[8]

On the way to Feisal's camp for the first time, Lawrence tastes the basic bread cooked from flour and water 'warmed' in the ashes of a brushwood fire, and clapped to shake off the dust before sharing.[9] The more sophisticated version of this bread is discovered on the way to Feisal's camp, and is described in *Seven Pillars* on the same journey, symptomatically sweetened and offered by a man in the employ of the Turks as an informant:

'*It was made of the unleavened dough cake of yesterday, crumpled while still warm between the fingers, and moistened with liquid butter… sweetened with ground sugar and scooped up to be eaten like damp sawdust in pressed pellets with the fingers.*'

Lawrence and his companions' next meal was bread and dates. Later, when travelling from Wejh to El Kurr, Lawrence describes the minimal supply of flour they carried:

'*Sherif Yusuf, now back in charge of supply, gave us each a half-bag of flour, whose forty-five pounds were reckoned a man's pinched ration for six weeks. This went slung on the riding saddle, and Nasir as well took enough on baggage camels to distribute a further fourteen pounds per man when we had marched the first fortnight out from Wejh, and had eaten enough room for it in our bags.*'

Lawrence dwells for a moment on the relative luxury of rice:

'*Nasir, a great Emir in his own place, also carried a good tent in which to receive visitors and a camel load of rice for their entertainment: but the last we ate between us, with huge comfort, for the unrelieved diet of water-bread and water, week after week, grew uninspiring. We were beginners in this style of travelling, not understanding that dry flour, as the lightest food which could be carried, was the best for a long journey. Six months later, neither Nasir nor myself wasted transport on rice-luxury.*'[10]

Lawrence's own view of the real meaning of hunger emerges clearly in Chapter 59 of the Oxford *Seven Pillars*, also entitled '*Across Sinai*' when, having arrived in Akaba (Aqaba), and not having eaten a meal for two days, the Arabs are confronted by palms heavy with dates which were yet small and green:

'*Cooking made them better in the taste but still deplorable afterwards, and we and our prisoners went about sadly, faced with the dilemma of constant hunger or of violent diurnal pains.*'

Characteristically, Lawrence turns the situation to account by using it as an opportunity to practise his own austerity, and in a sense to continue perfecting the 'spiritual equipment' referred to earlier in this text and which I take to mean 'moral' qualities like endurance, self-discipline, willpower etc.[11] Lawrence goes on to remark that:

'... it was good to be sparing, a great aid to continence, and the grosser forms of gluttony fell away from us... [Close readers may notice that the implication here is that the subtle forms of gluttony remain.] The assiduous food-habit of a lifetime had trained the English body to the pitch that it could produce a punctual nervous excitation in the upper belly a few minutes before the fixed hour of each meal: and we sometimes gave the honoured name of hunger to this sign that our gut had cubic space for more stuff. Arab hunger was not a pain but the cry of a long-empty labouring body fainting with weakness. They lived on a fraction of our bulk food, and their systems made exhaustive use of what they got. A nomad army did not dung the earth richly with by-products.'[12]

For many reasons, including the need to obtain more food, it was necessary to travel the 150 miles to Suez. In the event, this would mean a 50-hour march at walking pace to spare the camels, with only one point of water on the way:

'to excuse us cooking-halts upon the road we carried lumps of boiled camel, and some broiled dates tied up in a rag behind our saddles: also two skins (about eight gallons) of water. This for a group of eight men.'

One piece of good fortune was the accidental discovery of a field of melons near the end of the journey: '... we cracked the unripe melons and cooled our chapped lips on their pith.'[13]

Finally arriving at the Suez Canal, Lawrence found himself, essentially, obstructed by bureaucracy, and signals his impatience and frustration, having spent most of the previous four months in Arabia, and on the move:

'In the last four weeks I had ridden some fourteen hundred miles by camel, not sparing myself anything necessary to advance the war: but I was not going to spend one unnecessary night with my familiar vermin. I wanted a bath, and something cold with ice in it to drink: and to change these clothes, all sticking to my saddle sores in filthiness: and to eat something more tractable than green date and camel sinew. I got through again to the Inland Water Transport, and talked to them like Chrysostom.'[14]

Mentioning 'Chrysostom' without specifying whether he meant Saint John Chrysostom, or Dio Chrysostom, is pure Lawrence mischief. Either is plausible and leads to interesting connections. In the first place, chrysostomos is Greek for 'golden-mouthed' (i.e. very eloquent) and St. John Chrysostom [A.D. 347-407] was known for his eloquence in preaching, and his impact on the public at Antioch and Constantinople, as well as for his ascetic practices. Editions of his works are available in Greek, Latin, English, and French. Alternatively, Lawrence could have meant Dio Chrysostom, also known as Dio of Prusa [c. A.D. 40-120], a Greek orator, writer, and philosopher, who actually put on the cloak of a travelling Cynic and journeyed widely. A leading figure in the Second Sophistic, (i.e. the resurgence of Greek culture and politics under the Roman Empire, which amounted to a renaissance of Greek cultural interests), Dio Chrysostom is also a source for our knowledge of classical Stoicism and Cynicism. There is even a textual cross-link with another interest of Lawrence – Philostratus' Life of Apollonius of Tyana (Apollonius of Tyana and Chrysostom/Dio of Prusa were friends). Given that Lawrence was to dwell on the superiority of Greek literature, one might elect Dio as the intended reference if there was not the suspicion that Lawrence may have been playing on the ambiguity and fertility of evoking both figures; with their connections to the Classical and Christian past.

Lawrence's philosophy of minimalism in material things, a 'Gospel' perfectly instantiated in the diets described above, tied readily into the strategic doctrines he developed to turn the apparent weaknesses of the Bedouin into strengths. A droll feature of Lawrence's thinking about desert war was his recognition and exploitation of its resemblance to naval war:

'In character our operations… should be like naval war, in their mobility, their ubiquity, their independence of bases and lack of communication, their ignoring of ground features, of strategic areas, of fixed directions, of fixed points.'[15]

Of course, Lawrence's Classical background provided him with the perfectly apposite quote from Thucydides' *History of the Peloponnesian War*:

'He who commands the sea is at great liberty, and may take as much or as little of the war as he will… and we who commanded the desert might be equally fortunate. Camel raiding parties, self-contained like ships, might cruise without danger along the enemy's cultivation-frontier, and tap or raid into his lines where it seemed easiest or fittest or most profitable, with always a sure retreat behind them into the desert element which the Turks could not explore.'

Lawrence's personal and fortuitous advantage was that he *'had traversed most of the country many times on foot before the war, working out the movements of Saladin or Ibrahim Pasha…'* – an oblique, backwards glance to the time spent on his *Crusader Castles* thesis. In a sense, the key concept ruling these strategic desert war ideas is Mobility:

'We should use the smallest force in the quickest time, at the furthest place. If the action continued till the enemy had changed his dispositions to resist it, we would be breaking the spirit of our fundamental rule of denying him targets.'

Lawrence achieves the implementation of these goals by using,

'… the extreme frugality of the desert men, and their high efficiency when mounted on their female riding camels… We had found that on camels we were independent of supply for six weeks if each man left the sea base with a half-bag of flour, forty-five pounds in weight, slung in his riding saddle: and for shorter marches luxurious feeders might also have rice.'

A similar logic applied to water:

'… we would not want to carry more than a pint each… Some of us never drank between wells, but those were hardy men: most drank fully at each well, and carried a drink for the intermediate dry day.'

The extraordinary mobility which these minimal resources made possible are drawn out by Lawrence: *'Our six weeks' food would give us capacity for a thousand miles out and home, which would be, like the water-figure, more than ever we required.'* A year later, Lawrence was to refer back to the motto of the Akaba base – *'No Margins'*; an exact statement of the ruling idea over all material things and particularly in the conduct of desert warfare.[16] With weapons, Lawrence applied a similar line of thought: *'The equipment of the raiding parties should aim at simplicity, with nevertheless a technical superiority over the Turks in the most critical department.'*[17]

Sometimes there was respite from the monotony of bread, water, dates, and camel meat, and Lawrence describes some of the episodes when gazelle were shot and sometimes hare, jerboa, and lizards. Nevertheless they are seen as almost weakness by Lawrence: *'These indulgences amid the exertion and slow fatigue of long unbroken marches gave grateful moments to the delicate townsfolk among us.'*[18]

One of the rarest delicacies of the food Lawrence notes is the ostrich egg cooked on shredded blasting gelatine. It turns up at a time of particular difficulty. Lawrence has had to share his bread with his tired and hungry camel, they have had burning head winds, and dust blizzards, and have run out of water. Also the hot, flinty ground is laming to the delicate foot pads of camels brought up on the sandy coast or in south-central Arabia. One of their men finds two ostrich eggs, but the desert is so barren that they can only find a wisp of dry grass with which to cook them.

> '*The baggage train passed, and my eye fell on the blasting gelatine. We broached a packet, shredding it carefully into a fire beneath eggs propped on stones, till the experts pronounced the cookery complete. They eat it with a silver-hilted dagger from flint flakes which serve as platters.*'[19]

Where circumstances changed, there also the diet varied, and a sharp contrast to the foregoing austerities occurs when Lawrence is sent '… two forceful sergeant-instructors from the army school at Zeitun' to teach the Arabs how to use trench-mortars and Lewis guns. Their names are Yells and Brooke, but they get called Lewis and Stokes after the names of their respective weapons. Although they are warned that they would have to give up their British Army comforts and privileges; they would share with the Arabs an equal treatment. There were no rules, and could be no mitigations of the marching, feeding and fighting inland.[20]

In fact, Lawrence writes that '… they were fitted with clothes, and were lent two of my best camels, and stuffed their saddle bags with bully-beef.'[21] These kindly concessions to the inexperienced sergeants amount to relative luxury for Lawrence and the Arabs: '… we were comfortable with cans of hot tea, and rice and meat.'[22] It should be recorded that 'meat' here is bully beef, and Lawrence was aware of its strategic implications – at least, presumably, for Europeans: '*Our cards were speed and time, not hitting power. The invention of bully-beef had profited us more than the invention of gunpowder, but gave us strategical rather than tactical strength.*'[23] Nevertheless, Lawrence's attitude to food shows through in the small details of journeying; for example in Chapter 78 of the Oxford Edition and Chapter LXXI, page 403 of the Penguin *Seven Pillars,* where, travelling through Wadi Rum with a mixed party of Arabs, Indians, and some English Officers (Wood, Lloyd and Thorne), he ascribes the failure of the group to reach a 'stiff' pass leading on to the heights of Batra to 'laziness and a craving for comfort'. Similarly, eating rice while the English eat bully beef and biscuits, is 'feasting' and 'abundance'. He twice paints a vivid picture of the grandeur of Wadi Rum '*whose giant hill-shapes are full of design and as far above Nature as great architecture, but beautiful too, as though God had built them ready for some great pageant to which the sons of men were insufficient.*' The next day, having reached the crest, the group looks back to the:

> '… *fantastic grey domes and glowing pyramids of the mountains of Rum, prolonged today into even wider fantasies by the cloud-masses brooding over them… Very pleased, we plumped ourselves down in the first green valley over the crest.*'

They sheltered from the wind and were warmed by the faint sunshine. Lawrence has set the mood up very carefully for the bathos of his final sentence: '*Someone began to talk again about food.*'[24]

Although Lawrence and the Bedouin were perfectly aware that their mobility and power depended on the health and number of camels in their possession, they were also very clear that each of the men '*sat on two hundred pounds of potential meat. If food lacked, we halted and ate our worst camel.*'[25] Or, in some instances, this was an injured camel:

> '*The Howeitat killed them where they lay broken, stabbing a keen dagger into the throat artery near the chest, while the neck was strained tight by pulling the head round to the saddle. The wound soon made them collapse from loss of blood, they were at once cut up and shared as meat.*'[26]

But apart from the bully beef and camel meat feasts produced by accidents, Lawrence describes episodes of great privation, as in Chapter 53, where the lowness of food supply had reduced them to chewing raw parched corn. Lawrence's teeth were not up to this: '… *a trial too steep for me, and mostly I had ridden fasting.*'[27] That is, until friendly peasants provide the 'luxury' of a bag of corn – a day's bread. Where exotic foods erupted into the desert world bringing real luxury, it was usually a side-effect of blowing up trains, a situation described in Chapter 92: '*Nuri Said and the officers had artificial tastes, and rescued tinned meats and liquors from the wilder men.*' The Bedouin did not even want 'olives and other Syrian food' [page 532]. Again, as with Lawrence's 1913 College Magazine article, *The Kasr of Ibn Wardani*, and his letter to Vyvyan Richards in July 1918, there is a view, in this instance behind the phrase 'artificial tastes', about the legitimacy or value of certain tastes, even culture itself, which is almost Cynic in its purity and severity. Curiously, Said and the officers rely on the Islamic distinction between 'allowed' (*Halal*) and 'forbidden' to ensure that the luxury foods are rejected ('thrown in disgust at their heads') so that they themselves can enjoy them. On the other hand, having obtained a whole truck of tobacco destined for the Turks in the Medina garrison, Feisal, himself a smoker, sends some pack-camels loaded with cheap cigarettes to them, out of compassion.[28]

Where Lawrence meets troops who eat regularly and well, he registers amazement, as with the Egyptian Army near the railway line between Deraa and Damascus. There the expectation is that the troops will demolish large amounts of line. Then Lawrence finds out that nothing is happening because:

> '*Peake's Egyptians [were] having breakfast… like Drake's game of bowls… The Egyptian Army, proud of its regularity, indeed one of the most formally beautiful alive, fed gigantically several times a day. To the men, food was a solemn duty, enjoined, an exigency of service. No doubt it did them good, but today they vexed me. We others in these scrambling days of action ate nothing, or ate something unseen as we went, whenever the raiding halted for a moment, and gave leisure for fatigue or hunger.*'[29]

In other words, the Bedouin exemplify the Stoic views expressed by Epictetus: 'In things relating to the body take just as much as bare need requires', and 'It is the mark of an ungifted man to spend a great deal of time in what concerns the body.' Both Lawrence and Epictetus' attitude (and the Cynics for that matter), is that these bodily things should be dealt with *en passant* and are not, and should not be, ends in themselves. Militarily, Lawrence has turned the Bedouin minimalism, essentially based on poverty, to account to achieve an extraordinary strategic mobility. Philosophically and morally, Lawrence seems to turn away from the body – at least the pleasure-seeking, domesticated body, with its slavery to habits and routines, towards an existence oriented towards a personal mobility valuing mind and aesthetic experience, and duty, in time of war.

None of the foregoing strictures seem to apply to coffee and tea, although Lowell Thomas records that Lawrence did not drink these at home and was a devotee of water. Perhaps this is because coffee and tea are relatively blameless and, furthermore, much important hospitality and sociality is built round their consumption. Even so, when describing camp routine in the early days with Feisal, Lawrence makes a point of remarking that: '*Sugar for the first cup in the chill of dawn was considered fit.*'[30] That is, not taken for granted: permitted.

The only group who out-distance the Bedouin and are described by Lawrence as 'a race', not a tribe, are the Sherat: '*To look upon, they were Arab, only perhaps better made, and stronger of body.*' Their various excellencies seem to confirm Lawrence's usual opinions about the merits of the desert over the town:

> '*They were harder-living and more ascetic than any Bedouin. Often they spent years in the open without visiting a market, existing on samh* [a kind of flour, as described earlier], *and dates, and camel milk.*'

Earlier Lawrence had remarked that '*… they made it their pride to find the desert sufficient for their every need.*'[31] Characteristically, Lawrence establishes their low social standing by writing that they were '*an enigma*' and '*brave fighters*', but with no blood enemies or tribal organisation, but also that they '*… were split up all over the northern desert as helots among the Arabs. They were outcasts… Other men had hopes or illusions. The Sherat knew that nothing better than physical existence was permitted them by mankind in this world or another.*' Climbing a hill with a Sherari youth gives Lawrence enough respite to reflect that:

> '*The austerity of these great heights had shamed back the vulgar baggage of our daily cares. In the place of Consequence, it set Freedom, power to be alone, to slip the escort of our manufactured selves; a rest and complete forgetfulness of being.*'

As if to balance the ways of the desert-dwelling Sherat, within two pages Lawrence describes the character and hospitality of one Mohammed el Dheilan who is camped with Auda. Auda is in the midst of a violent money dispute with Toweiha Bedouin. Lawrence sketches Mohammed el Dheilan's merits: '*a better diplomat because less open than most Arabs… we were made very welcome by him, and given a luscious platter of rice and meat and dried tomatoes.*' However, the sting at the end of the paragraph, signals Lawrence's judgement, somehow not unconnected with the idea of freedom (from the 'manufactured self'): '*Mohammed was a villager at heart, and fed too well.*'[32]

As a counter-balance to the near cult of desert minimalism, with which Lawrence clearly had great affinity, a whole chapter of *Seven Pillars* is devoted to feasting with the Howeitat tribe, a level of hospitality, virtually unlimited, being provided in the form of twice a day feasts for an indefinite period. Lawrence describes the cooked mutton and rice, and the rituals attendant upon its consumption in great detail: enough to evoke nausea in the fastidious, or relish in the hearty:

> '*… they ladled out over the main dish all the inside and outside of the sheep, little bits of yellow intestine, the white tail cushion of fat, brown muscles and meat and skin, all swimming in the liquid butter and grease of the seething… they poured the gravy… till it was running over and a little pool congealing in the dust. That was the final touch of splendour, and the host called us to come and eat.*'[33]

It is almost as if Lawrence wants to draw the contrast between the Sherat and the Howeitat as starkly as possible. In his first person reflections a few pages later, Lawrence writes:

> *'Of course it was monotonous, but in return the crystal happiness of our hosts was a visual satisfaction, and to have shattered it a crime. Our education had been to cure us of prejudice and superstition, our culture to make us understand the simple. These people were achieving for our sake the height of nomadic ambition, a continued orgy of seethed mutton, and it was our duty to live up to it. My heaven might have been a lonely soft armchair, a book rest, and the works of poets, hand-set in Caslon, hand-printed on the best paper: but I had been for twenty-eight years well-fed, and if Arab imagination ran on food-bowls, so much the better for them. They had been provident expressly on our account.'*

In fifteen meals a week, they had eaten fifty sheep.[34]

Lawrence's private views about food pre-date his time in Arabia, and were quite firm as early as 1913 when he was digging at Carchemish. For example, in a letter to his family on 15 June he wrote,

> *'As for poor appetite, which in Arnie Father deplores, it is a thing to be above all thankful for. If it were himself who felt no desire to eat, would he not rejoice aloud. To escape the humiliation of loading in food, would bring one very near the angels. Why not let him copy that very sensible Arab habit, of putting off the chewing of bread till the moment that instinct makes it desirable. If we had no fixed meal-hours, and unprepared food, we would not fall into middle age.'*[35]

Here we have an interesting anticipation of the views expressed in *Seven Pillars* over having no rules about food, and not living by bells and timetables (and death being hastened by regularity and habit). Also, an attitude completely harmonious with the standards set by the Stoic Epictetus: the things concerning the body to be done in passing. Later, writing to his mother from Cairo in January 1917, and evidentially replying to her enquiries, he writes:

> *'I live with him [Feisal], in his tent, so our food and things (if you will continue to be keen on such rubbish!) is as good as the Hejaz can afford. Personally I am more and more convinced that it doesn't matter a straw what you eat or drink, so long as you do not do either oftener than you feel inclined.'*[36]

Consistent also with Epictetus' teaching were the views of the early Christian saint and mystic, St. Anthony of the Desert [251-356 A.D.] who, taking an even stronger line, which Lawrence may have known, would eat alone on account of a certain shame at concessions to the body:

> *'For when going to food and sleep and the other needs of the body, shame came upon him, thinking of the spirituality of the soul… He used to say that we should give all our time to the soul, rather than to the body.'*

The same biography of St. Anthony[37] then quotes from the Gospel of St. Luke, 12:29-31, the words of Jesus Christ:

> *'Be not solicitous for your life what you shall eat, nor for your body what you shall put on, [Luke 12:22]. And seek not what you may eat or what you may drink, and be not lifted up; for all these things do the nations of the world seek. But your Father knoweth that you have need of all these things. But seek ye first his kingdom, and all these things will be added to you.'*

By the time Lawrence has entered into the post-war world, his views on bodily activities in general, and food in particular, harden, and become almost doctrinaire. This is especially so after his ejection from the RAF and his entry into the Tank Corps. Lawrence was incredibly idealistic about the RAF and loathed the Army even though he stayed in it for two years. He described the army as having:

> '... a pervading animality of spirit, whose unmixed bestiality frightens me and hurts me... I react against their example into an abstention even more rigorous than of old. Everything bodily is now hateful to me (and in my case hateful is the same as impossible)... I sleep less than ever, for the quietness of night imposes thinking on me: I eat breakfast only, and refuse every possible distraction and employment and exercise.'[38, 39]

Here it is as if Lawrence is retreating within, away from the body, to a kind of inner citadel. His practice of fasting, and near fasting, seems to empower him, and it is an equation seen by the M.P. Ernest Thurtle – wherever there is a choice between comfort and freedom, comfort is always sacrificed. Of course, socially, joining in activities, including meals, would have drawn him nearer to these men whose bestiality so distressed him.

The space outside the Tank Corps at Bovington where Lawrence found some respite was, of course, his famous cottage at Clouds Hill. E.M. Forster, who was a visitor, has left an account of the place, including Lawrence's arrangements for feeding his guests. As might be expected, Lawrence compromised, not offering his selected guests the bread and cheese he would have eaten himself, nor falling into taking the 'loading in of food' too seriously:

> 'We drank water only or tea – no alcohol ever entered Clouds Hill... and we ate... out of tins. T.E. always laid in a stock of tinned dainties for his guests. There were no fixed hours for meals and no one sat down. If you felt hungry you opened a tin and drifted about with it.'

Forster also remarks that:

> 'To think of Clouds Hill as T.E.'s home is to get the wrong idea of it. It wasn't his home, it was rather his pied-à-terre, the place where his feet touched the earth for a moment, and found rest.'[40]

Lawrence confirms this in a letter to Mrs Charlotte Shaw: '*I do not wish to feel at home... Homes are ties...*'[41] In a letter to A.E. Chambers, Lawrence also emphasised the style of the place, being consistently with Forster: '*No food, except what a grocer & the camp shop & canteens provide.*'[42] As always, Lawrence is resisting the 'household gods' of domesticity: routine, comfortable 'excessive' feeding – in short, anything which would hold him down and compromise his freedom and mobility. Lawrence's detachment from food emerges in a minor reminiscence of the couple who ran the fish and chip shop at Bovington Camp. Apparently, Lawrence was fond of fish and chips, and Mrs. Knowles, the mother of Pat Knowles, his neighbour at Clouds Hill, would buy them for him. However, if Lawrence came into the shop to buy them himself, he would leave rather than queue if there was anyone else in the shop. Mrs. White told the local historian, Harry Broughton, that she solved the problem by ignoring the other customers, and instantly making up a parcel of fish and chips as if he had ordered them in advance.[43]

By the time Lawrence was out of the Army, and finally back in the RAF, he registered his happiness in a letter from Cranwell to Tank Corps friend, E. Palmer. After itemising the various duties he would be undertaking, he writes, *'Feel odd and strange: exhilarated: crazy sometimes. Is it going to meals does that?'*[44] Evidentally, proper meals had become such a rarity for Lawrence, that he ascribed his reaction to getting what he had wanted for years — entry into the RAF — to meals.

Lawrence's views on food, and the danger of over-eating, emerge even when translated into a semi-humorous key, and are addressed to a 14-year old. To S.L. Newcombe in 1934, he wrote:

'May you have a quiet Christmas with nothing abnormal to eat. Avoid gluttony, above all. Remember your figure, and the figures your parents ought to have. If you observe them over-eating, clear your throat gently to attract attention, and say "A bit high this bird?" That will put them off it. If they bring in plum puddings and things, remark in a blasé accent… the normal speech, I mean, of Eton… "Isn't it jolly, papa, to keep up these old customs? It's like Dickens, isn't it, I mean, what?" That will throw a chill over the whole meal-time — I mean orgy. You owe a duty to your family at Christmas.'[45]

Endnotes

[1] *Seven Pillars*, Oxford Edn., p. 70.
[2] *Letters*, Ed. Garnett, p. 47.
[3] Ibid., p. 53.
[4] Ibid., p. 59.
[5] *Letters*, Ed. Garnett, pp. 65-66.
[6] See *Cynics*, William Desmond, p. 79. Compare also, 'My Arabs were turning their backs on perfumes and luxuries, and looking out towards the wilderness, choosing the things in which mankind had had no share or part.' *Seven Pillars*, Oxford Edn., p. 20. Penguin Edn., p. 38.
[7] *Letters*, Malcolm Brown, p. 23.
[8] See *Cynic Epistles* quoted earlier: 'make it a habit to sleep in a cloak on the ground.'
[9] *Seven Pillars*, Oxford Edn., p. 68.
[10] Ibid., p. 242.
[11] See *Safety Last*, Col. W.F. Stirling, p. 83. 'His powers of endurance, too, were phenomenal. Few of even the most hard-bitten Arabs would ride with him from choice. He never tired. Hunger, thirst and lack of sleep appeared to have little effect on him. He had broken all the records of the dispatch riders of the Caliph Haroun al Raschid which had been sung for centuries in the tribal sagas.'
[12] *Seven Pillars*, Oxford Edn., Ch.59, p. 339. Penguin Edn., p. 323.
[13] *Seven Pillars*, Penguin Edn., p. 325.
[14] *Seven Pillars*, Oxford Edn., p. 344. Penguin Edn., p. 326.
[15] *Seven Pillars*, Oxford Edn., Ch.65, 'Irregular War', pp. 367-373.
[16] *Seven Pillars*, Oxford Edn., pp. 645-646. Penguin Edn., p. 557.
'I crossed out forage for the camels after Bair, cut down ammunition, and the petrol, and the number of cars, and everything else, to the exact point which would meet the precise operations we planned.' p. 645.
[17] *Seven Pillars*, Oxford Edn., p. 369. Penguin Edn., p. 346.
[18] *Seven Pillars*, Oxford Edn., p. 266.
[19] Ibid., Oxford Edn., p. 269.
[20] Ibid., Oxford Edn., Ch.67, p. 380.

21 i.e. canned or pickled beef; corned beef.

22 *Seven Pillars*, Oxford Edn., p. 381.

23 Ibid., p. 201.

24 *Seven Pillars*, pp. 440-441.

25 Ibid., p. 369.

26 Ibid., pp. 248-249.

27 Ibid., pp. 309-310.

28 *Seven Pillars*, Oxford Edn., Ch.92, p. 532.

29 Ibid., Ch.125, p. 723.

30 *Seven Pillars*, Oxford Edn., Ch. 21, p. 112.

31 Ibid., pp. 271 and 442-447.

32 Ibid., p. 447.

33 *Seven Pillars*, Oxford Edn., pp. 283-288.

34 Ibid., p. 291.

35 *Home Letters*, 15.6.1913. Also quoted in Wilson, *Lawrence of Arabia. The Authorised Biography*, p. 124.

36 *Letters*, Ed. Malcolm Brown, p. 103.

37 *St. Anthony of the Desert* by St. Athanasius, pp. 56, 65.

38 The idea of 'abstemption' looms in the *Seven Pillars*, but occurs as early as 1916. 'It's a bad life this, banging about strange seas with a khaki crowd very intent on banker and parades and lunch. I am a total abstainer from each, and so a snob.' *Selected Letters*, Ed. Garnett, p. 91. See also 'We abstinents… in the friendly silence of the desert.' *Seven Pillars*, p. 564, Penguin Edn.

39 *Letters*, Ed. Garnett, pp. 415- 416, [1923].

40 E.M. Forster, quoted in *Letters*, Ed. Garnett, pp. 435-6. From an article in *The Listener*, 1 September 1938.

41 *Letters*, Ed. Malcolm Brown, 1929, p. 424.

42 *Letters*, Ed. Garnett, p. 436.

43 Rodney Legg, *Lawrence of Arabia in Dorset*, p. 38.

44 *Letters*, Ed. Garnett, pp. 481-2.

45 *Letters*, Ed. Garnett, pp. 837-838.

CHAPTER THIRTEEN

Philosophy, Metaphysics and the Self

꩜

MALCOLM BROWN, the editor of a large collection of Lawrence's letters, rightly remarks that it was rare for Lawrence to deal with his beliefs. I take him to mean 'beliefs' in the philosophical sense, because the letters are replete with other kinds of belief; on food, for example, or the merits and demerits of the RAF and the Army.

One place where such philosophical beliefs emerge – views on larger questions – is in a letter to his old friend from his time at university, Vyvyan Richards, dated 26 June 1924 from Clouds Hill, and thus from his Tank Corps time and his maturity at 36:

> 'My new feeling (a dreaded conviction is looming up in the near distance) is that the basis of life, the raison d'etre of us, the springs of our actions, our ideals, ambitions, hopes, are as carnal as our lusts: & that the oppositions of mind and body, of flesh and spirit, are delusions of our timid selves.'[1]

As recorded in Chapter Four, this view has already been met in *Seven Pillars*, but only in the abbreviated version, and there under the rubric of 'self-surrender':

> 'The conception of antithetical mind and matter, which was basic to Arab self-surrender, helped me not at all… I achieved surrender (so far as I did achieve it) by the very opposite road, through my notion that mental and physical were inseparably one: that our bodies, the universe, our thoughts and tactilities were conceived in and of the molecular sludge of matter, the universal element through which form drifted as clots and patterns of varying density.'[2]

It is difficult, if not impossible, to put a date on the above passage, since the text for the *Seven Pillars* was begun (notionally) in 1919 and published in 1926. Whatever may be the case in the dating of these ideas, it is clear that Lawrence was articulating a kind of monist materialism as his metaphysical overview; perhaps in reaction against the near Platonism which seems to be the background to his thought before the war. One aspect to notice in these two quotations is not only their anti-Platonism, but also the conspicuous absence of the Soul, or any room in such thought for it. And this may signal the decline or end of his faith in the Christianity in which he had been raised, which had been such a powerful formative influence. Perhaps it is not an accident that in the paragraph following the 'molecular sludge' discussion, Lawrence remarks that, '*The practice of our revolt fortified the nihilist attitude in me.*' He ends the chapter:

'While we rode we were disembodied, unconscious of flesh or feeling: and when at an interval this excitement faded and we did see our bodies, it was with some hostility, with a contemptuous sense that they reached their highest purpose, not as vehicles of the spirit, but when, dissolved, their elements served to manure a field.'[3]

It is not immediately clear what sense Lawrence is giving the word 'nihilist'. It may be that it just signifies 'no beliefs', 'belief in nothing', rather than any larger epistemological view about knowledge as such. It is the case that the word turns up elsewhere in Lawrence's correspondence. One aspect of these views is that they do fit harmoniously with Lawrence's downgrading of the body, and it may be part of his character to feel better when engaged with a larger projected goal – such as the Arab revolt, the RAF, the conquest of the air (all quasi-Crusades) – where it is his experience that 'while we rode we were disembodied'. The danger is 'when the excitement fades.'

In February 1924, this time in a letter to Harley Granville-Barker about Granville-Barker's play, *The Secret Life*, Lawrence propounds a materialism very similar to that contained in his letter to Vyvyan Richards in June of the same year:

'Also you have missed out the animal. All your characters are intelligences… but they couldn't be as witty as all that without cracking sometimes, and letting the roar and growling of the beast be heard. Here in camp it's the lesson stamped into me with nailed feet hour after hour: that at bottom we are carnal: that our appetites and tastes and hopes and ideals are beast – qualities, coloured or shaped somewhat fancifully, but material always, things you can cut with a knife: and you have hidden that, out of shame perhaps: out of fear perhaps: or, like Shaw, in revenge.'[4]

Perhaps one of the roots for these later post-war views of Lawrence may lie in the kind of life he had chosen to lead. Earlier in his letter to Granville-Barker, Lawrence had written: 'I get up in the morning, and clean boots and make beds and carry coal and light fires, and then all day long I work till five o'clock.'[5] Ten years later, a similar practicality is announced in a letter to the poet and novelist, Cecil Day-Lewis:

'I can't feel that knowledge matters at all. There must be theories, apparently: but one can spend the few active years one has so much more enjoyably out of doors on practicalities – like my RAF boat-building. So I try not to want to think. By "recantation" I didn't mean a change of politics, but that I hoped you were getting bored with politics. The ideals of a policy are entrancing, heady things: the translating them into terms of compromise with the social structure as it has evolved is pretty second-rate work. I have never met people more honest and devoted than our politicians—but I'd rather be a dustman. A decent nihilism is what I hope for, generally. I think an established land, like ours, can do with 1% monists or nihilists. That leaves room for me. The trouble with Communism is that it accepts too much of today's furniture. I hate furniture.'[6]

Interestingly, Lawrence seems to use the phrase 'monists or nihilists' to indicate that they are the same thing: and, taking a hint from the formulation in the *Seven Pillars*, i.e., that 'the practice of our revolt fortified the Nihilist in me…' (as quoted above), he appears to be conjuring up a materialist monism with no essential freight of ideals – no more mind/body dualism. The explicit hatred of 'furniture' is more awkward to interpret. It may be related to the 'gospel of bareness in material things' as announced to Vyvyan Richards, or perhaps the bareness of Clouds Hill with its lack of a toilet and cooking facilities. 'Furniture' may also serve as a metaphor for the useless and obstructive clutter – of things or views – with which Lawrence had little sympathy, and which are obviously a feature of a civilisation based on consumption; a civilisation which was to take the very idea of 'shopping' seriously, not so long after Lawrence's death in 1935. Of course, the great theorist of 'Nihilism' in the 19th century was Nietzsche, but Lawrence makes no reference to him in this connection, and indeed Nietzsche's sense of the word ('highest values devalue themselves') is not really consonant with Lawrence's use. Provocatively, Lawrence goes on to write: *'Your inclination to re-value theme is very significant…'* Immediately after his remarks about 'furniture', this Nietzsche theme – the Revaluation of Values – is not to be found in Lawrence. Perhaps we have to be content to assign these Nietzschean themes as 'latent', or as unelected affinities between two solitary, but unlike minds.

Perhaps, to be included under Lawrence's idea of 'Nihilism', is the very absence of emphatic views, or of the kind of necessity which drove him to write the *Seven Pillars*. In a letter to F.L. Lucas in 1929, evidently in reply to the question of his writing more, Lawrence replied, *'I have nothing now to tell anyone: nothing to preach: nothing believed. Wherefore I cannot go on writing, can I?'*[7] Of course, this cannot be taken literally because he continued to conduct his life ethically and conscientiously, and with the austerity which had always been his mode of living. The sense of 'nothing believed' must surely be of no 'public' or ideological views, such as the preaching of 'Arab Freedom' which he had come to see as a lie propagated by the government. There is an even stronger statement of this position (or lack of position) in an earlier letter to Charlotte Shaw in 1926:

> *'I haven't any convictions or disbeliefs – except the one that there is no "is". You can go about the earth being interested in itself, for its own sake, because you believe in many things. Whereas I can't be interested in Durham, even, or in Boanerges, except I wish to interest another person in them.'* [Malcolm Brown points out that Lawrence had just ridden south from Edinburgh and explored Durham on the way.][8]

The phrase 'there is no "is"' takes us into much deeper water philosophically: it is almost the reverse of Being – suggesting that Lawrence did not believe in entities as such, but saw impermanence and process. Extraordinary as it may seem, it is a view which is Buddhist, and one which it is very unlikely that even Lawrence would have met at that time, and for which there is no evidence in his reading, friendships, or travels. Alternatively it could be treated as a 'throw-away' remark, or as an authentic insight which he had reached himself. There is one other place in Lawrence's writings where similar perspectives are found, and that is in his letter to Charlotte Shaw in 1927. It is a response to a pamphlet she had written about the ideas of Dr. James Porter Mills, an American author and lecturer on 'spiritual' matters and Christianity. Lawrence does not really engage with Charlotte Shaw's pamphlet, but his responses register how far he had moved away from the Christian orthodoxies of his youth, and how strikingly original his own attitude to Christianity and personal existence had become. Also, how kind Lawrence was being to a friend whose views must have seemed implausible, if not bizarre:

'I've made a beginning on your little book. A slow beginning, as throughout it will be slow progress, for my mind is inert, rather than curious or contemplative. Only abrupt contact with some flinty edge of actuality will strike a thought out of me. If I strive to dwell upon pure idea, my brain gets quickly moidered, and wanders dreamily away down the broader problems of conduct. Conduct (doing) is really so much larger a subject than existence – not larger, perhaps, in the sense of feet and inches, but – well, you can explore Arabia, whereas we speculate vainly about Mars. To do a day's work, as I do, is only possible by taking for granted that we exist, a **white lie** *[author emphasis] which discourages us being abstract-minded. Christianity has handicapped itself with a growing proportion of people since 1600 by apparently assuming (i) that we exist, (ii) that man is the centre of his universe, and (iii) that God is, more or less, analogous to man. When you say "not proven" to (i), "impossible" to (ii) and "ridiculous" to (iii), then you lose patience with a crowd which fusses over details like transubstantiation. However, your little book isn't so interested in superstructure as to neglect the foundations, so I have a better chance of liking it, than of liking S. Thomas Aquinas, who feels to me more like the founder of European dogmatic Christianity than its rather pitiful eponym.'*[9]

Given that Lawrence joined the RAF in 1922, it is possible to date his withdrawal from most of the orthodoxies of Christianity, as recorded in *The Mint*, to at least five years before the Charlotte Shaw letters. In *The Mint*, as previously remarked, Lawrence writes that the padre read a lesson from Saint Paul:

'… prating of the clash of flesh and spirit… For the rest we were just uncomprehending. Our ranks were too healthy to catch this diseased Greek antithesis of flesh and spirit. Unquestioned life is a harmony, though then not in the least Christian.'[10]

Later in *The Mint*, Lawrence writes: *'Contact with natural man leads me to deplore the vanity in which we thinking people sub-infeudate*[11] *ourselves.'* So far as orthodoxy of belief is concerned, he writes, *'Hungry time has taken from me year by year more of the Creed's clauses till now only the first four words remain. Them I say defiantly, hoping that reason may be stung into new activity when it hears there's yet some part of me which escapes its rule…'*[12]

Perhaps from this recapitulation of Lawrence's opinions well before the letters to Charlotte Shaw, his kindness and patience can be inferred, as well as his almost Buddhistic views on the nature of 'the self' – 'a white lie' – an extraordinary opinion for a man immersed in military life to hold.

With the foregoing in mind it is easier to understand the sense of Lawrence's repudiation of economics and social organisation in his letter to Ezra Pound of 1934 and, incidentally, to give the lie to those who have any belief in his interest in right wing politics.

'I don't care a hoot for economics, or our money system, or the organization of society. Such growths are like our stature; what time I have for thinking (not enough, I agree) goes, or tries to go, upon themes within my governance. A fig for financiers.'[13]

Not only does Lawrence repudiate Pound's views on the 'money system, and the organization of society', but also he gives a principled reason why he does so, and the reason is fundamentally Stoic – going back to Epictetus. To discern what is within our power and what is not: *'To make the best of what is in our power, and take the rest as it naturally happens.'*[14] In a sense Lawrence is refusing the 'political' and directing his attention to that which lies within his power or 'governance'. He goes on to write, in the same letter:

'... *some instinct tells me that the people who fuss about the money of the world are on the wrong track. Money only serves to keep us alive: and people like you and me wouldn't impair the usefulness of the world if we went down. I incline to resent our presuming to tell our physical betters what ought to be done. Disposing other people's minds is an infectious activity.'*[15]

There is a consistency of view here going back to the pages in *Seven Pillars*, Penguin Edition, page 477 on 'self-surrender', a thread that passes through the letters to Vyvyan Richards and Granville-Barber in 1924, on to *The Mint*, and then to his correspondence with Cecil Day-Lewis in 1934.

In these passages from *Seven Pillars*, *The Mint*, and the letters, two main, but related, themes can be seen. Firstly, various versions of monism/nihilism, and secondly, attempts to escape the mind/body dualism. As if these issues were not complicated enough, a close reader will notice that Lawrence moves between two main 'voices', 'I' and 'We'. Even so, we can ascribe all these views and formulations, about 'the body', 'the spirit', 'our physical betters' to Lawrence himself. In passing, perhaps it should be recalled that Lawrence is not reflecting in some serene academic situation, but against a background of basic, military training and his own asceticism.

At the same time Lawrence seemed to become more contented as time passed in the RAF.

'*I think many of us go wrong by being too exclusively cerebral. I've spent the last twelve years in the ranks of the Air Force; and nobody so in daily contact with people who work at crafts could get so heated as the N.E. [New English Weekly, a magazine] does about the regimentation of the world. My own job has been producing motor boats: and I fancy that each concrete thing I launched took away some of my bile. Whereas the uttering of a poem only increases it. Old Gandhi would prescribe for you a daily wrestle with the spinning wheel, to grow contentment. The English working men are another creation from us. Abstract ideas are another name for maggots of the brain. Heads are happy when they employ hands, not when they earn idleness for them.'*[16]

It may be that Lawrence was in flight from the kind of intellectual milieu which he had inhabited up until, roughly, the time of the post-war Paris Peace Conference. That conference had exposed, finally, the bad faith and duplicity of the geopolitics of the great powers, especially Britain and France. He had come to the conviction that, '*what [he] did in Arabia [was] morally indefensible.*' He refused pay while it lasted and decorations, and any personal profit from his part in the Arab Revolt or his war reputation.[17] These convictions had shut out the likely future employments which his reputation made possible. However, his retrenchment towards the practical was not essentially downward social mobility, despite the self-punishing tone of some of his letters, but rather a return to the practical skills he had always shown from boyhood onwards, and particularly at Carchemish. Besides, he had discovered the satisfactions of meaningful practical activities again. Even after leaving the RAF, when leisure would have attracted many, he wrote to Bruce Rogers, '*I prefer engrossment to comfort. Perhaps comfort is an acquired taste which grows with its indulgence?*'[18] The year before, in a letter to Charlotte Shaw, Lawrence had clearly signalled that his near Cynic austerity was still as lively as ever. Discussing the composer, Edward Elgar's complaints about the smallness of the financial rewards of making music, he remarks,

'... by now he should be seeing that bank-books will not interest him much longer. I feel more and more, as I grow older, the inclination to throw everything away and live on air. We all allow ourselves to need too much.'[19]

Endnotes

[1] *Letters,* Ed. Malcolm Brown, pp. 208, 269.
[2] *Seven Pillars,* Penguin Edn., p. 477.
[3] *Seven Pillars,* Penguin Edn., p. 477.
[4] *Letters,* Ed. Garnett, p. 453.
[5] Ibid., Garnett.
[6] Ibid., Garnett, p. 839.
[7] *Letters,* Ed. Malcolm Brown, p. 407.
[8] *Letters,* Ed. Malcolm Brown, p. 305.
[9] *Letters,* Ed. Malcolm Brown, p. 317-318.
[10] *The Mint,* Penguin Edn., p. 77.
[11] An odd use of the word. Chambers' definition 'the putting of an estate in fee: the granting of tithes to layman.' Yet the sense is of 'subdivide' or 'analyse'.
[12] *The Mint,* p. 171.
[13] *Letters,* Ed. Malcolm Brown, p. 506.
[14] Epictetus, *The Discourses,* p. 6.
[15] *Letters,* Ed. Malcolm Brown, p. 507.
[16] *Letters,* Ed. Malcolm Brown, p. 507.
[17] Ibid., Malcolm Brown, p. 343.
[18] Ibid., Malcolm Brown, p. 536.
[19] Ibid., Malcolm Brown, p. 475.

CHAPTER FOURTEEN

The Military Philosophers

ᢙᢥᢗ

L AWRENCE devotes the brief Chapter 35 of the Oxford text of the *Seven Pillars* to his reflections on Strategy and Tactics. With very little change, the same material can be found in the shortened Penguin edition in Chapter XXXIII, page 193. Perhaps significantly, Lawrence endured about ten days of illness at Abu Markha in April 1917 during which he lay in his tent and reflected upon the strategy and tactics of the Arab Revolt: '*I began at last to think continuously of the Arab Revolt, as an accustomed thing to rest upon against the pain.*' Hitherto, the priority had been:

'*… a crying need for action, and we had just done what seemed to instinct best, without probing into the why, or formulating what we really wanted at the end of all. Instinct so abused, without its basis of past knowledge and reflection, had grown merely feminine, and was now destroying my confidence: so I snatched the opportunity of this forced idleness to look for the equation between my book-reading and my movements.*'

Carl von Clausewitz, 1780-1831. According to Clausewitz, in war, 'One might say that the physical seems little more than the wooden hilt, while the moral factors are the precious metal, the real weapon, the finely-honed blade.'

Lawrence writes that, unfortunately, he is as much in command as he pleases, but is untrained. On the other hand he is 'tolerably read' in military theory. Strikingly, he admits that his interest had been '… *abstract, concerned with the philosophy and theory of warfare, especially from its metaphysical side.*'[1] What this means is not immediately clear, but perhaps indicates an interest in the broader, governing ideas behind strategic thinking, and the relation of military thought to other areas of human activity.

The major thinkers that Lawrence studied form a somewhat different list compared to those mentioned in answer to his biographers' questions (for example, Liddell Hart had asked two questions: 1. *When did you begin to read books on the theory of war as distinct from history? 2. What books did you begin with?*) In answer to Robert Graves and Liddell Hart, he had listed Creasey, Henderson, Mahan, Napier, Coxe, Procopius (for Belisaurus), and Demetrius Poliorcetes.

In the Oxford Edition of *Seven Pillars*, he writes,

> '… *my Oxford curiosity* [had] *taken me past Napoleon to Clausewitz and his school, to Caemmerer and Moltke,* [von der] *Goltz and the recent Frenchmen.*[2] *They had seemed partial books, and after looking at Jomini and Willisen, I had found broader principles in Saxe and Guibert and the eighteenth century. However, Clausewitz was intellectually so much the master of them all, and his book so logical and fascinating that unconsciously I had accepted his finality until a comparison of Kuhne and Foch had disgusted me with soldiers, made me weary of their officious glory, critical of all their light.*'

In the Oxford edition, the first list of military thinkers, in Chapter 19, which is entitled 'Yenbo', (page 103), is slightly different to the shortened text in the Penguin *Seven Pillars*:

> '… *of course I had read the usual books, too many books, Clausewitz and Jomini, Mahan and Foch, and had played with Napoleon's Campaigns, worked on Hannibal's tactics, and followed the wars of Belisarius, like any other man at Oxford: but I had never thought myself into the mind of a real commander compelled to fight a campaign of his own.*'[3]

However, by the time of the second enumeration of military writers in the chapter on Strategy and Tactics (Ch. 35), the Oxford edition is the same as the shortened *Seven Pillars*. One striking feature of these lists of military thinkers is their historical range: back as far as Belisaurus (AD. 505-565) and Hannibal (274-183 BC.), and forward to Mahan (1840-1914) and Foch (1851-1929). This range and the theoretical depth provided by Carl von Clausewitz, the great 'Philosopher of War', as the military historian Walter Goerlitz has described him, make it difficult to believe Lawrence's claim never to have thought himself into the mind of a real commander. After all, we have his own word, on his thirtieth birthday, that, '*as little as four years ago I had meant to be a general, and knighted, when I was thirty.*'[4] Furthermore, it is clear from the seven explicit references to Clausewitz in the *Seven Pillars* that Lawrence had studied him very thoroughly – even to the extent of making semi-jokes, quoting Clausewitz whilst under fire:

> '… *I retorted with a word from Clausewitz, about a rearguard effecting its purpose by being more than by doing: but he was past laughter, and perhaps with justice, for the little flinty bank behind which we sheltered was crackling with fire.*'[5]

That Lawrence was fluent in at least parts of this literature is demonstrated by the darker mood in the account of the battle at Tafileh (Chapters 94-95). There he is concerned to offer a parody, not only of battle maxims, but also of the standard conventions which governed reports of battles.

Lawrence's own views on war itself, scattered through his letters, are neither bellicose nor pacifist: he seems to have accepted it as a permanent feature of human existence. In a late letter to Cecil Day-Lewis in 1934, he remarks that:

'As a historian by training I shouldn't like to think that accidental participation in this *one war of the infinite series past and to come* had put it bigly in the foreground of any but its victims.'[6]

Without further comment, evidently Lawrence accepts that the war in which he participated was just one of an infinite series. Perhaps this throws some light on his aside to Robert Graves about the 83-year old Thomas Hardy in a letter of 1923. Having stated all kinds of admiring things about Hardy, Lawrence writes:

'... *and yet he entertains so many illusions, and hopes for the world, things which I, in my disillusioned middle age* [Lawrence was 35], *feel to be illusory. They used to call this man a pessimist. While really he is full of fancy expectations.*'[7]

It may be, of course, that this evaluation of Hardy was an expression of Lawrence's 'Nihilism'.

Much earlier, in a letter of 1915 to his mentor, D.G. Hogarth, a Fellow of Magdalen College, a scholar of considerable talents, an archaeologist, and Chief of the influential Arab Bureau, Lawrence had again accepted the fact of 'the next war' without comment. Here it is merely a part of his geopolitical analysis written from Cairo, in which he is dwelling, among other matters, on the strategic importance of Alexandretta to Britain and its allies: 'If Russia has Alexandretta it's all up with us in the Near East. And in any case *in the next war* the French will probably be under Russia's finger in Syria.'[8]

On the other hand, in his 1929 letter to the M.P. Ernest Thurtle, Lawrence enlarges upon the (alleged) causes of wars, and their 'madness':

'*It is the peace-army & navy & air force which is the concern of Parliament. War is a madness, for which no legislation will suffice. If you damage the efficiency of war, by act of Parliament, then when the madness comes Parliament will first of all repeal its damaging acts. Wars, in England, well up from below: from the ignorant: till they carry away the (reluctant) Cabinet.*'[9]

So far as Clausewitz's *On War* is concerned, Lawrence owned the first full English translation, by Colonel J.J. Graham, in a new and revised edition published by Kegan Paul in 1911. This edition includes an Introduction written in 1908 by Colonel F.N. Maude of the British Army (see Appendix 2). This revised version was based on the first English version which had been brought out in London in 1873. Clausewitz's original text '*Vom Kriege*' dated back to 1832 (Dummlers Verlag, Berlin). It is worth noting how recently available in English this classic text had been to Lawrence: it had only been translated into English when he was 23. This demonstrates how up to the minute Lawrence was in this respect, and how he was ahead of the scholarship which has subsequently been undertaken on Clausewitz. Whilst later scholars have pointed out that deficiencies in the Graham translation derive mostly from corruptions of the third German edition which he used, nevertheless the Graham translation has certain advantages: 1) The introduction by F.N. Maude which includes a discussion of Moltke;

2) The useful index; 3) Graham's closer adherence to the German sentence structure, and, in places, the powerful language of the original; 4) The appendix, '*Instructions for the [Hohenzollern] Crown Prince.*'

Some scholars have argued that Colonel Maude's introduction may have influenced the way the book was read and understood. He not only divided it into three volumes, but added footnotes and a discussion of Moltke's influence. Maude was also overtly hostile to Germany, beginning his piece:

'*The Germans interpret their new national colours – black, red and white – by the saying, "Durch Nacht und Blut zur licht," ("Through night and blood to light"), and no work yet written conveys to the thinker a clearer conception of all that the red streak in their flag stands for than this deep and philosophical analysis of "War" by Clausewitz.*'[10]

Maude also goes on to write that:

'*What Darwin accomplished for Biology, generally Clausewitz did for the Life History of Nations nearly half a century before him, for both have proved the existence of the same law in each case, viz., "The survival of the fittest" – the "fittest" as Huxley long since pointed out, not being necessarily synonymous with the ethically "best".*'

Whether this Social-Darwinist perspective is a valid reading of Clausewitz is arguable, but it is the case that where Clausewitz discusses the importance of, for example, Boldness in Chapter 6, he eulogises it, writing that:

'*Boldness governed by superior intellect is the mark of the hero. This kind of boldness does not consist in defying the natural order of things and in crudely offending the laws of probability; it is rather a matter of energetically supporting that higher form of analysis by which genius arrives at a decision: rapid, only partly conscious weighing of the possibilities. Boldness can lend wings to intellect and insight...*'

'*Today practically no means other than war will educate a people in this spirit of boldness; and it has to be a war waged under daring leadership. Nothing else will counteract the softness and the desire for ease which debase the people in times of growing prosperity and increasing trade. A people and nation can hope for a strong position in the world only if national character and familiarity with war fortify each other by continual interaction.*'[11]

A conviction is being expressed here that could have been voiced by Agesilaus in ancient Sparta.

Lawrence was aware of the debilitating effects of town life on some of the Arabs he met and describes, with approval, the measures taken to overcome them in the case of Sherif Hussein's sons. Whilst not exactly warfare, the methods whereby Sherif Hussein 'counteracted the softness and desire for ease' which he detected in his sons, clearly drew Lawrence's approval and were a kind of preliminary training or hardening for war. Originally the sons had been made to live in Constantinople, where they had acquired an education as good as the city could provide:

'*Then they came back to the Hejaz, young Levantine effendis, in European clothes, with Turkish manners. The father at once changed them into Arab dress and, to rub up their Arabic, gave them Meccan companions and sent them out into the wilds in command of small bodies of Ageyl Camel Corps, to patrol the pilgrim roads against robbers. The young men thought it might be an amusing trip, but were rather dashed when their father forbade them special food, bedding, and soft-padded saddles. He would not let them back to Mecca even for the feast, but kept them out for months in all seasons guarding the roads day and night, learning to handle all manner of men, and their methods of riding and fighting. Soon they hardened, and became self-reliant and self-content.'*[12]

Lawrence's assessment of Feisal's troops in 1916, echoes this language:

'They were a tough-looking crowd, dark-coloured, some negroid in face. Their physical condition was very good. They were thin, but exquisitely made, moving about with a free activity which was altogether delightful to watch. It did not seem possible that men could be hardier or harder. They could ride immense distances day after day, run through sand and over rocks barefoot in the heat for hour after hour without pain, and climb their hills like goats… they shot well and carefully but were limited to short ranges, since they had no measure of length, to help them, with the sighting… My conclusions were that the value of the tribesmen was defensive only, and their real element guerrilla warfare.'[13]

Lawrence, with his knowledge of history and reading of the great military strategists, culminating in Clausewitz, was aware of the irony of the situation:

'The Hejaz war meanwhile would be one of dervishes against regular troops, and for the first time the British had found themselves on the side of the dervishes, with their textbooks applying only by contrary. It was the fight of a rocky, mountainous, barren country (reinforced by a wild horde of mountaineers) against an enemy so enriched in equipment by the Germans as almost to have lost virtue for rough-and-tumble war.'[14]

Lawrence's assessments of the condition and morale of Feisal's troops were not only generated by his explicit military/political duty, the results of which can be seen in '*Secret Dispatches From Arabia*'. There, in the 27 Articles first published in the *Arab Bulletin* in August 1917, the strengths and weaknesses of the Bedouin are clearly laid out. In addition, it is almost as if Lawrence has a 'military gaze' which can see the tactical and strategic possibilities of men and situations, and which can see also the presence or absence of what Nietzsche called the Military Virtues. For example, in the passage quoted above, Lawrence writes of the 'virtue for rough-and-tumble war', the virtue here being an echo of Machiavelli's 'Virtu' as well as the Nietzschean Virtue. On the one hand, Lawrence's judgement of the Bedouin is that '… *they are splendid scouts, their mobility gives you the advantage that will win this local war… and the gazelle-hunters, who form a proportion of the better men, are great shots at visible targets.*' On the other hand, '*they cannot sit still without slacking.*' And yet, on a very Clausewitzian note, he turns all this to account around the importance of 'initiative', a favourite concept and value of military thinkers: '*The more unorthodox and Arab your proceedings, the more likely you are to have the Turks cold, for they lack initiative, and expect you to. Don't play for safety.*'[15] In short, this is the spirit of 'boldness' lauded by Clausewitz. Even so, within the same Articles, we have, '*Do not let them ask you for things, since their greed will then make them look upon you only as a cow to milk.*' Two years later, describing the 'preaching' of the Revolt by Feisal and himself, evoking the new Nationalism amongst the tribes:

'He… conjured up for them the trammeled enemy on the eternal defensive, whose best end was to have done no more than necessary. While we abstinents swam calmly and coolly in the friendly silence of the desert, till pleased to come ashore.'[16]

The 'greed' has apparently vanished. Here, we see a clear instance of Lawrence either selecting or projecting a private value which happened to be deeply harmonious with the poverty and austerity of some of the Bedouin, and at the same time signalling that the strategies applicable to naval war could be applied to the desert.

The discussion of Moltke in the introduction to Clausewitz written by Colonel Maude in 1908 would have had a particular contemporary relevance. *Graf* Helmuth von Moltke (1800-1891) had been the victor in wars against Denmark, Austria and France, and was both a noted military theorist and an organiser of the Prussian and Imperial German Army. His claim to be a disciple of Clausewitz encouraged the reputation of the latter.

Whilst Lawrence praises Clausewitz in the *Seven Pillars*, his later opinions seem increasingly critical. For example, he wrote to Liddell Hart that his book *The Ghost of Napoleon* which called Clausewitz 'The Mahdi of Mass' – really an indefensible judgement – was a '… *very good little book: modest, witty, and convincing.*'[17] It may be that by the time he was corresponding with Liddell Hart, his own recollection of Clausewitz was becoming foggy; after all he had first read *On War* in 1906-7.[18] Clausewitz had advanced arguments and views which Lawrence himself had either replicated or could be presumed to share. For example, on the importance of 'Moral Factors', Lawrence had said that in view of the material weaknesses of the Arabs, the 'Moral' weapon could not be allowed to rust. Clausewitz devotes a brief, but telling, chapter to Moral Factors, '… the moral elements are among the most important in war. They constitute the spirit that permeates war as a whole, and at an early stage they establish a close affinity with the will that moves and leads the whole mass of force, practically merging with it, since the will is itself a moral quantity.'[19] Furthermore, '… most of the matters dealt with in this book are composed in equal parts of physical and of moral causes and effects. One might say that the physical seems little more than the wooden hilt, while the moral factors are the precious metal, the real weapon, the finely honed blade.'

Perhaps even closer to Lawrence are Clausewitz's scattered observations on willpower. In a letter to the Crown Prince of Prussia, the future Frederick William IV, Clausewitz wrote, '*only the will, which governs strong natures like an absolute ruler, can prevent unusual gifts and abilities from being lost among the multitude of daily phenomena, like a single ray of light losing itself in immeasurable space.*' Neither the study of history, nor that of any other discipline, possessed meaning unless the student was determined to perfect himself.[20] Willpower comes into play in connection with Clausewitz's well-known examination of the importance of 'friction' in war. By 'friction' Clausewitz means the countless 'minor incidents' that 'distinguish real war from war on paper', and which make 'Action in war like movement in a resistant element':

> '*Iron will power can overcome this friction; it pulverizes every obstacle, but of course it wears down the machine as well… The proud spirit's firm will dominates the art of war as an obelisk dominates the town square on which all roads converge.*'[21]

Along with the Military Virtues themselves, other affinities between Clausewitz and Lawrence can be seen in the former's discussion of exertion and suffering. Here, Vyvyan Richards almost echoes the words of Clausewitz 'hardening for a great endeavour'. Having singled out 'danger, physical exertion, intelligence, and friction' as the elements that form 'the atmosphere of war' and which add up to 'friction', Clausewitz designates 'combat experience' as the only lubricant that will reduce the 'abrasion'. Nevertheless, 'Habit hardens the body for great exertions, strengthens the heart in great peril, and fortifies judgement against first impressions. Habit breeds that priceless quality, calm…'[22]

Again:

'War is the realm of physical exertion and suffering. These will destroy us unless we can make ourselves indifferent to them, and for this, birth or training must provide us with a certain strength of body and soul. If we do possess those qualities, then even if we have nothing but common sense to guide them we shall be well equipped for war: it is exactly these qualities that primitive and semi-civilised people usually possess.'[23]

Where Clausewitz discusses 'Genius' in Book One, Chapter III of his book under the title '*The Genius for War*', he surveys '… *all those gifts of mind and temperament that in combination bear on military activity.*'[24] He argues that although the warrior spirit is far more common in any primitive, warlike race than among civilised people, the truly great commander – the military genius – does not appear before a high level of civilisation has been reached, '*as the Romans and the French have shown us.*' We know from recent scholarship that Clausewitz had been sufficiently impressed by Fichte's study of Machiavelli to write to him about it, and Machiavelli had written at length on Livy in his *Discourses*. Of course, Clausewitz's military career had been dominated by the impact of the French armies under Napoleon. Thus, along with courage, determination, rapid and accurate decision-making, strength of will, energy, and the longing for honour and renown, the '*vital contribution of intelligence is clear throughout*', though '*war may appear to be uncomplicated, it cannot be waged with distinction except by men of outstanding intellect*' capable of '*outstanding effort, the kind that gives men a distinguished name.*'[25]

Clausewitz's own character can be inferred from the kind of judgements he made of personalities in the elite circles of Prussian society, as well as his diagnoses of the ills of that society which the wars with the French had exposed. His view of Louis Ferdinand, the talented nephew of Frederick the Great, is particularly telling, given that since his appointment as adjutant to Prince August, he had ample opportunity to observe such personalities in Berlin. There is a resemblance between the psychological and political acuity of both Lawrence and Clausewitz's judgements. Of Louis Ferdinand, Clausewitz wrote:

'He was the Prussian Alcibiades. A somewhat disorderly way of life had prevented him from maturing fully. As though he were the first-born son of Mars, he possessed huge gifts of courage, daring, determination; but like the head of an old family, who, proud of his wealth, neglects other matters, he too had not done enough to educate and develop his mind seriously… He continued his gay life, made heavy debts, wasted his energies on nothing but pleasure, did not always keep the best company; nevertheless he never succumbed to these forces, but kept his head above water, and in spirit remained in nobler regions.'[26]

Other aspects of Clausewitz's personality emerge where his intense identification with the future of Germany in general, and the status of Prussia in particular, are concerned. Connected to this one could say that – with the powerful British Empire in the background – Lawrence identified himself with the Arabs during the war, but with the RAF afterwards: the British Empire then being still unchallenged. When Clausewitz surveyed the condition of Germany after defeat at the hands of Napoleon, he remarked that:

> 'The poverty of the German spirit… [and] the feebleness of character and principle emerging everywhere is enough to make one weep… That the attitudes of our people are not marked by greater nobility is not the fault of nature, but of men. Had those who led the nation shown themselves to be better men, then the nation would have been animated by a different spirit… With whips I would stir the lazy animal and teach it to burst the chains with which out of cowardice and fear it permitted itself to be bound.'[27]

Despite the apparent belligerence which Clausewitz expressed at the time of Prussia's defeat, his remarks demonstrate his dislike of routine 'square-bashing' – an attitude which almost echoes that of Lawrence in *The Mint*:

> 'An object of real sadness to me is the petty drill-spirit that now engulfs us… it is a real misfortune that the Landwehr is being repaid for its goodwill with this torture, which destroys its spirit and involves so much that is personally disagreeable.'[28]

Where Lawrence may have learned from Clausewitz strategically, or at least been inspired to develop his own doctrines for the unique conditions he faced in the desert, the chapter in *On War* devoted to 'The People In Arms', unsurprisingly, provides the richest materials. In that chapter Clausewitz argues that where

> '… a whole nation renders armed resistance, the question then is no longer "of what value is this to the people?", but "what is its potential value, what are the conditions it requires, and how is it to be utilized?" By its very nature, such scattered resistance will not lend itself to major actions, closely compressed in time and space. Its effect is like that of the process of evaporation: it depends on how much surface is exposed. The greater the surface and the area of contact between it and the enemy forces, the thinner the latter have to be spread, the greater the effect of a general uprising.'[29]

Whether Lawrence recalled this from his study of Clausewitz, or worked it out for himself, it is evident that he realised how to apply it to the Arab cause:

> 'In the Arab case the algebraic factor (= known variables, fixed conditions) would first take practical account of the area we wished to deliver… perhaps one hundred and forty thousand square miles. And how would the Turks defend all that?… no doubt by a trench across the bottom, if we came like an army with banners. But suppose we were (as we might be) an influence, an idea, a thing intangible, invulnerable, without front or back, drifting about like a gas? Armies were like plants, immobile as whole, firm-rooted, nourished through long stems to the head. We might be a vapour, blowing where we listed. Our kingdoms lay in each man's mind, and as we wanted nothing material to live on, so we might offer nothing material to the killing.'[30]

Clausewitz's line of argument is very similar to Lawrence's here:

> 'A general uprising, as we see it, should be nebulous and elusive; its resistance should never materialize as a concrete body, otherwise the enemy can direct sufficient force at its core, crush it and take many prisoners… On the other hand, there must be some concentration at certain points: the fog must thicken and form a dark and menacing cloud out of which a bolt of lightning may strike at any time.'[31]

In passing, the injustice of Liddell Hart's description of Clausewitz as 'The Mahdi of Mass,' can be seen: it is quite clear that Clausewitz explicitly repudiates 'mass' in general/popular uprisings. Another advantage that Lawrence's knowledge of Clausewitz may have given him is the conceptual clarity which marks the text of *On War*. It should be recalled that Clausewitz was writing at a time of great intellectual ferment in Germany. At the Berlin Institute for the Study of Military Affairs, founded in 1802, where Clausewitz, along with other ambitious young officers, pursued a course of studies including logic, geography, military history, mathematics, defence and attack of fortified places, he would have met Johann Gottfried Kiesewetter, an influential populariser of Kantian philosophy, and have been influenced by him. Whilst no evidence can be adduced that Clausewitz had actually read Kant, the fact is that their lives overlapped – Clausewitz 1780-1831, and Kant 1724-1804. Along with Kiesewetter, the influence of the Enlightenment and of German Idealism permeated the intellectual atmosphere of the time. Besides, Kant, Herder, Fichte and Schiller (frequently mentioned in Clausewitz's letters) were also contemporaries. This background, along with his immersion in the wars against Napoleon and the French Revolutionary armies, and his intense preoccupation with the foreign policy of Prussia, in parallel with the obstructed attempts to reform the military institutions, produced a unique mind. Clausewitz was able to theorise war as a combination of violence, chance, genius, and politics. It appears that he could use 'Absolute War' as a Kantian Regulatory Idea, but maintain contact with military experience via his deep study of military history (and his own experience in the army from the age of twelve). As Peter Paret remarks in his study of Clausewitz, '… his historical writings contain theoretical discussions, and his essays and chapters on theory are filled with historical material.'[32]

Lawrence would have necessarily read Clausewitz as an historian himself; by training he was an archaeologist/historian. His brother, A.W. Lawrence, remarks on him being '… mentally at home in biblical Palestine, in Medieval France and Ancient Egypt and Mesopotamia.'[33] One might add ancient Greece and Byzantine civilisation as well – in any case, from the Hittites (Carchemish) onwards, Lawrence knew these cultures, all of which were marked by that ubiquitous institution – war. Clausewitz's appeal to someone with Lawrence's background must have been immense because Clausewitz's project was not to produce rules or maxims for fighting wars, but to produce a greater understanding, a deeper theoretical penetration into war as such, and to test this understanding against the 'bottled experience' of history.

The other great philosopher of German Idealism, exerting a considerable influence on European culture, and a contemporary of Clausewitz, was Georg Wilhelm Friedrich Hegel (1770-1831). There have been some attempts to argue for a connection between Hegel's dialectic, and the dialectical nature of some of Clausewitz's thought – between history, theory, and experience. However, the tenor of Clausewitz, and his declared positions on philosophy, make this implausible. For example, in 1808 he wrote:

> '*Contempt and derision are merited by presumptuous philosophy, which seeks to raise us high above the activities of the day, so that we can escape their pressures and cease all inner resistance to them… Generations do not exist in order to observe the world; by constantly striving for rational goals they are the world… The times belong to you; what they will become, they will become through you!*'[34]

Clausewitz was too close to the realities of war as an experience through which he lived and also because of his study of military history, and too close to the politics of his time, to go very far into the abstractions of speculative Reason. On the other hand, his analytical and critical drives, coupled with the dialectical movement of thought between the concept and social reality, almost conjure up the presence of the great Idealist philosophers of his times. In a sense Clausewitz was far closer to Lawrence's early Chivalrous cult of the Deed than to the metaphysicians. It may well be that the nearest point of contact for Lawrence with the great metaphysicians of modern European philosophy was precisely Clausewitz's *On War*. Clausewitz – the greatest military intellectual the West has produced – was also not only a product of the culture that produced Kant, Hegel, and Goethe, but he was also in contact with the Classical tradition via its military history. His reading of Machiavelli, for example, saturated in references to Livy, along with Xenophon, Frontinus, Plutarch, Polybius, Tacitus and Vegetius, would have (re)connected Clausewitz with the Classical world. Lawrence, in a sense, came from this Classical world via his own education from childhood onwards. It is, therefore, almost with a sense of shock, that one comes across any reference to The Absolute or The Ideal – language from the German Idealist tradition – in Lawrence's writings. There seem to be only two occasions where this is so. Firstly, in a letter to Edward Garnett in 1922 about the writing of the *Seven Pillars*:

'... there's no absolute in the imaginative world, and so journeymen like myself are confused and miserable in it.'[35]

Secondly, in a letter to Eric Kennington in 1934, toward the end of his time in the RAF, and somewhat depressive in tone:

'I do not care for relatives, for matching myself against my kind. There is an ideal standard somewhere and only that matters: and I cannot find it. Hence this aimlessness.'[36]

Of course, it could be argued that Lawrence deploys 'absolute' and 'ideal' because they indicate his meaning, and are innocent of any philosophical baggage. On the other hand, it is the case that the study of Clausewitz entails contact with the world of 18th and 19th century philosophy since his thought developed in that culture and uses some of its conceptual resources. Perhaps it is symptomatic of a greater awareness of this philosophical background that Jean Beraud Villars – the French biographer of Lawrence – entitled his book *Le Colonel Lawrence ou la Recherche de l'Absolu* (published in English in 1959 as *T.E. Lawrence or The Search for the Absolute*).[37]

Another voice from outside the Anglophone world who also sheds light on Lawrence, particularly on the problematic area between asceticism and masochism, is the Argentian, Victoria Ocampo. She remarks that Lawrence was one of those, '... to rediscover the efficacy of the ascetic life outside the religious rules which exact its observance... (yet) condemned to die, like Christopher Columbus, without knowing on what continent they are stranded.' Also, Ocampo remarks that '... sadism, masochism, neuroses, suppressed desires, complexes, all those things which psychoanalysis invents in order to debunk the scruples and ardent aspirations of mankind and their rebirth in secular disguises, are not sufficient to explain them.'[38] What exactly this 'efficacy' is or was, is not entirely clear. Perhaps, before we have explored it for ourselves, we may ascribe some of Lawrence's energy and 'genius' to it.

Endnotes

1   *Seven Pillars,* Oxford Edn., p. 191. Penguin Edn., p. 193.

2   Lawrence had the 1911 translation of Clausewitz by Col.J.J. Graham in his library at Clouds Hill.

3   *Seven Pillars,* Oxford Edn., p. 103, Ch. 19.

4   *Seven Pillars,* Oxford Edn., p. 678.

5   Ibid., p. 542.

6   *Selected Letters*, Ed. Garnett, p. 360. Italics added.

7   Quoted in Wilson, p. 722.

8   *Selected Letters,* Ed. Garnett, p. 86. Italics added.

9   Ibid., p. 304.

10 *Clausewitz, On War,* Pelican Classics. Edited by Anatol Rapoport, p. 83.

11 *Clausewitz, On War.* Edited and translated by Michael Howard and Peter Paret, pp. 225–226, Everyman Edition. Emphases added.

12 *Seven Pillars,* Oxford Edn., p. 84. Once again, the constellation of features which harks back to the Classical Cynics: but here is a precursor to military skills.

13 *Seven Pillars,* Oxford Edn., pp. 88, 89.

14 Ibid., p. 91.

15 *Twenty-Seven Articles,* Quoted *in Secret Despatches,* pp. 157, 158, 159.

16 *Seven Pillars,* Penguin Edn., p. 564, Ch. XCIX. Oxford Edn., p. 656. Italics added.

17 *TE's notes on The Ghost of Napoleon.* Quoted in the Journal of the T.E. Lawrence Society, Vol X, No.2, Spring 2001.

18 Journal. Ibid., p. 69.

19 Clausewitz, *On War,* pp. 216-217, Everyman Edition. Edited and translated by Michael Howard and Peter Paret, 1976.

20 Clausewitz letter to the Crown Prince, 1812. Quoted in *Clausewitz and the State,* Peter Paret, 1976.

21 Clausewitz, *On War,* p. 138.

22 *On War,* p. 141.

23 Ibid., p. 116-117.

24 Ibid., p. 115.

25 Clausewitz, *On War,* pp. 128-129.

26 Clausewitz, *Nachrichten,* pp. 437–440. Quoted *in Clausewitz and the State,* Peter Paret, p. 108.

27 Clausewitz letter to Marie v. Bruhl, 1807. Quoted in Paret, p. 129.

28 Clausewitz letter to Gneisenau, 1815. Quoted in Paret, p. 251.

29 Clausewitz, *On War,* p. 579, Ch. 26.

30 *Seven Pillars,* Oxford Edn., pp. 195-196, Ch. 35, *Strategy and Tactics.*

31 Clausewitz, *On War,* p. 581.

32 *Clausewitz and the State,* Peter Paret, p. 328.

33 *T.E. Lawrence by His Friends,* p. 591.

34 Clausewitz, *Politische Schriften und Briefe,* pp. 65–66. Quoted in Paret, p. 151.

35 *Selected Letters of T.E. Lawrence,* Garnett, p. 147.

36 *Letters of T.E. Lawrence,* Garnett, p. 814.

37 *T.E. Lawrence or The Search for The Absolute,* Jean Beraud Villars. Trans. Peter Dawnay, 1959.

38 Victoria Ocampo, *338171 T.E. [Lawrence of Arabia],* pp. 87-88.

CHAPTER FIFTEEN

Sex and Pain

ᴄⱴᴐ

SOONER or later, the examination of our heroes' or heroines' lives reveals that they too are flawed, they too struggle with 'the world, the flesh, and the devil', and that they too are more or less marked by that struggle. So it is also with Lawrence. My contention is that the dark side of Lawrence's personality does not vitiate his extraordinary achievements, or the interesting complexity of his mind and the originality and rarity of his philosophy of life. Even so, the emergence of the knowledge of his masochism is impossible to contemplate without sadness; and perhaps not without almost a suspicion that the beatings he organised for himself were an attempt – perhaps partially successful – to destroy his own legendary reputation for posterity.

The two main public sources for the arrangements Lawrence made to encounter more pain are *The Secret Lives of Lawrence of Arabia* by Phillip Knight and Colin Simpson, and *A Prince of Our Disorder* by John E. Mack. *The Secret Lives* is partly based on a typescript written by John Bruce, a Scotsman, who had joined the Tank Corps around the time that Lawrence joined in 1923. John E. Mack offers additional evidence of the involvement of another service companion in the beatings, and to 'material left at Clouds Hill by Lawrence himself' (diary notes).[1] With this 'material', the story darkens further, as Mack notes how '... Lawrence wrote to various institutions and individuals, including a riding and hunting establishment, a swimming instructor, physiotherapists, a diet expert, and a "remedial gymnasium" specialising in Swedish massage and "medical electricity".'[2] The arrangements Lawrence made seem to be almost a parody of his skills in organising, or manipulating men to do his will. Lawrence represents himself as a delinquent called 'Ted' who has stolen money from an 'uncle' or 'old man' who was threatening to reveal Lawrence's illegitimacy to the world unless he returned the money or submitted to severe floggings. Lawrence chose tough, but relatively simple, service colleagues to administer these punishments – naïve enough, but trustworthy enough. Reading about these punitive arrangements, one has the feeling of intrusion upon a private disorder bordering on the tragic, despite its grotesque elements. The attempt to understand this downward spiral into humiliation and pain is not necessarily linked to Lawrence's philosophy of life, but may be connected to his attitude to the body, along with other determinants, other causes more deeply rooted in his past. It seems, at most, to be the crossing of a line between austerity and masochism: the spilling over of a minimalist discipline into perversity, the collapse of a rare freedom into a circle of punishment, strange satisfaction, and atonement. To step back from the bizarre details and make some sense of it, to come to some rational understanding of the motives and causality which drove it is, perhaps, the most difficult challenge for anyone engaged by the life and mind of this extraordinary person.

Two markers, at least, are relatively easy to establish. One is the complicated relationship with his mother; the other is the self-aware record Lawrence has left us in his letters and in the *Seven Pillars*. Mack argues that Lawrence's 'psychological vulnerabilities may be traced in large part' to his relationship with his mother.[3] Evidently a very strong personality, the struggle Lawrence had to distance from her may be inferred from his letter to Charlotte Shaw in 1927:

> 'Mother is rather wonderful: but very exciting… I have a terror of her knowing anything about my feelings, or convictions, or way of life. If she knew they would be damaged, violated, no longer mine. You see, she would not hesitate to understand them: and I do not understand them, and do not want to… She has given me a terror of families and inquisitions. And you'll understand that she is my mother and an extraordinary person. Knowledge of her will prevent my ever making any woman a mother, and the cause of children.'[4]

It is also clear from another letter to Charlotte, later in the same year, that relations between mother and son were fraught enough for Lawrence to use the language of warfare to describe them:

> 'No trust ever existed between my mother and myself. Each of us jealously guarded his or her own individuality, whenever we came together. I always felt that she was laying siege to me, and would conquer, if I left a chink unguarded.'[5]

No accident, of course, that Lawrence, who had studied castles so intensely, should use the language of siege warfare, or the image of 'the citadel' in the Deraa episode.

Mack relates in *Prince of our Disorder* the account he had received from Lawrence's brother Arnold of the discipline administered by their mother when they were children. According to Arnold, their mother went in for 'severe whippings on the buttocks', never having to administer them to Bob, once to Frank and frequently to T.E. Arnold was convinced that they were given for the purpose of breaking T.E.'s will. Mack also remarks that apparently Sarah Lawrence never lost her faith in such punishments, saying in later years that the reason Lord Astor's horses never won was because he wouldn't whip them.[6] Without falling into the glibbery of our psychological contemporary culture, it seems plausible to see in these early experiences marked by pain, the struggle for autonomy, and the theme of the triumph of the personal Will; certain themes which seem to be a partly hidden counterpoint to Lawrence's undoubted achievements. The beating also seems to be the prototype for the kind of encounter which Lawrence organised to take place in an exclusively male setting in the last decade or so of his life.

The 'bridge', so to speak, which seems to have sexualised the beatings, was the notorious Deraa episode, recounted in the *Seven Pillars*, and remarked upon in the letters. Much ink has been spent on questioning the veracity of Lawrence's account: but if, as a hermeneutic principle, it is assumed that he is telling the truth, then more sense and meaning can be found in his post-war behaviour, than is the case if it is assumed that he is either lying or fantasising.

In the Oxford edition of the *Seven Pillars*, the Deraa episode is recounted in Chapter
87, sardonically subtitled 'Being Taught'. (Chapter 80, page 450 in the Penguin edition,
there is additionally labelled 'A Turkish Conscript', 'Recruit's Training', 'Further Lessons',
'Passing Out', 'Life Again', 'Hiding a Secret'.) Both editions describe the brutal thrashing
and rape, the near out-of-the-body experience:

> '*I had strung myself to learn all pain until I died, and no longer an actor but a spectator, cared not how
> much my body jerked and squealed in its sufferings. Yet I knew or imagined what passed about me.*'

Next Lawrence describes how he was kicked with a nailed boot by the corporal:

> '*I remembered smiling idly at him, for a delicious warmth, probably sexual, was swelling through me: and
> then he flung up his arm and hacked with the full length of his whip into my groin.*'[7]

In the two editions, the ending of the chapter is very different. In the Penguin edition:
'... *how in Deraa that night the citadel of my integrity had been irrevocably lost*' (page 456).
In the Oxford edition, a far more revelatory ending, and perhaps an anticipation of the
disorder of the last years:

> '*I was feeling very ill, as though some part of me had gone dead that night in Deraa, leaving me maimed,
> imperfect, only half myself. It could not have been the defilement, for no one ever held the body in less honour
> than I did myself: probably it had been the breaking of the spirit by that frenzied nerve-shattering pain
> which had degraded me to beast-level when it made me grovel to it; and which had journeyed with me
> ever since, a fascination and terror and morbid desire, lascivious and vicious perhaps, but like the striving
> of a moth towards its flame.*'[8] [November 1917]

It seems that here we have the turning point which, together with Lawrence's
knowledge of the duplicity of the Sykes-Picot Agreement, marks the difference between
the early Lawrence, and the disillusioned figure of later years. The worn and traumatised
figure hovering on the point of entry into the RAF, as depicted in the first pages of
The Mint. It may be that Lawrence's self-hatred, fed by both his disgust with his own
role in the Arab rebellion – and the attendant public adulation – together with the
traumatic discovery of the 'morbid desire', set him up, so to speak, for the beating disorder
of his last years. It would be very easy, here, to speak of the Return of the Repressed, for
one who had not only fled from contact, but who also had attitudes to the body which
are strange to modern narcissism, and seem to belong to another time: the monasteries
of the Middle Ages. There are indeed times when Lawrence seems to be the reincarnation
of a Monk or a Crusader. His attitude to his own body usually seems to have been
severely instrumental, e.g., in *The Mint*:

> '*Till this year my insignificant body has met life's demands. If it fails me now I shall break it; but I hope
> it may scrape through.*'[9]

And:

> '*I hate cozening my body, even by order.*'[10]

More savagely still:

> '*Airmen are so healthy and free of the joints, that they exult to fling their meat about. Activity does not
> remind them, yet, how man hangs in his body, crucified.*'[11]

Here, in this strange image, Lawrence registers a view of the body very far from the quasi-medical hedonism of modernity: instead he evokes a kind of internalisation of crucifixion – the self-hanging crucified in permanent pain within the body. Even so, Lawrence's friends noticed that his health and equanimity returned during his RAF years; and we can also notice that the decompression he achieved at times of stress was the rapture of speed on one of the largest and fastest motorcycles of the times. In *The Mint*, Lawrence announced his fondness for speed:

'The extravagance in which my surplus emotion expressed itself lay on the road. So long as roads were tarred blue and straight; not hedged; and empty and dry, so long I was rich.'[12]

Readers may notice that this pleasure and release is full of risk and danger, and involves no bodily contact. A similar mood occurs in the prose poem called '*Confession of Faith*' found at Clouds Hill after Lawrence's death. Essentially about the conquest of the air, it contains the telling lines, '*In speed we hurl ourselves beyond the body. Our bodies cannot scale the heavens except in a fume of petrol.*'[13]

In the *Seven Pillars*, these themes of the body, pain, risk and punishment, are lit up in a more elaborate prose against the horizon of warfare in the desert. Famously, or notoriously, depending upon one's perspective, Lawrence offered a near-apologia for such homosexuality as there was amongst the tribes:

'The public women of the rare settlements we entered in our months of wandering would have been nothing to our numbers, even had their raddled meat been palatable to a man of healthy parts. In horror of such sordid commerce our youths began indifferently to slake one and other's needs in their own clean bodies – a cold convenience that by comparison seemed sexless and even pure. Later, some began to justify this sterile process, and swore that friends quivering together in the yielding sand, with intimate hot limbs in supreme embrace, found there hidden in the darkness a sensual coefficient of the mental passion which was welding our souls and spirits in one flaming effort.'[14]

Next, to end the paragraph, there is a transition to a darker note, evoking something more punitive. A modulation from the previous sentence, from '*some began…*' to '*Some few…*', unlike Lawrence's more usual practice of drifting between 'I' and 'we':

'Some few, thirsting to punish the appetites they could not wholly prevent, took a savage pride in degrading the body, and offered themselves fiercely in any habit which promised physical pain or filth.'[15]

While Lawrence seems the least likely candidate for 'filth' of any kind, the question which floats behind these sentences, is not only 'how did he know these things?', but also whether, given his extraordinary austerity and toughness, he also was one of those who 'offered themselves fiercely in any habit which promised physical pain'? Undecidable as this may be, the several passages in the *Seven Pillars* dealing with pain and punishment have a particular searing quality – part of which may be attributable to the wrought-up tone of the writing:

'The sorrow of living was so great that the sorrow of punishment had to be pitiless. We lived for the day, and died for it also. When we needed to punish we wrote our lesson with gun or whip immediately in the sullen flesh of the sufferer, and the case was beyond appeal. The desert did not afford the refined slow penalties of courts and gaols.'[16]

Again, where Lawrence discusses monotheism in general, and the particular forms it took in the desert tribes, his analysis moves from the ineffable, and large abstract negations, to abnegation, renunciation, self-restraint and, finally, cruelty:

'This creed of the desert seemed inexpressible in words and indeed in thought… The desert dweller could not take virtue for his belief… His sterile experience robbed him of compassion and perverted his human kindness to the image of the waste in which he hid. Accordingly he hurt himself, not merely to be free, but to please himself. There followed a delight in pain, a cruelty which to him was more than goods. The desert Arab found no joy like the joy of voluntarily holding back. He found luxury in abnegation, renunciation, self-restraint. He made nakedness of the mind as sensuous as nakedness of the body. He saved his own soul, perhaps, and without danger, but in a hard selfishness.'[17]

Lawrence argues that 'the ground belief' of all the Semitic creeds was waiting in the desert, ('… the emptiness of the world and the fullness of God'), but that it had to be 'diluted' to be made comprehensible in towns and villages: like the scream of a bat 'too shrill for many ears' escaping 'through our coarser texture'.[18]

Lawrence's own pains – for example his description of a scorpion sting – are revelatory of his own attitude to the body and its sufferings, and give some substance to Ernst Jünger's remarks on the subject:

'Whenever one approaches the points where man proves himself to be equal or superior to pain, one gains access to the sources of his power and the secret hidden behind his dominion. Tell me your relation to pain, and I will tell you who you are!'[19]

Lawrence's observations on the effects of pain on himself, emerge in his reflections on a scorpion sting:

'We waited that day, and all night. At sunset a scorpion scuttled out of my saddlebags under the bush by which I had lain down to make note of the day's weariness, and stung me – it seems repeatedly. The pain was very great, and my arm swelled up, and kept me uneasily awake until the second dawn. It checked thought, and so was a not unwelcome relief to my overburdened mind, for seldom was the body claimant enough to interrupt my self-questioning, and then only by the help of some such surface injury sweeping all the sluggish nerves like fire. Nor did pain of this quality ever endure long enough really to be a cure. On this occasion, after distracting me for the night, it gave way to that unattractive and not honourable internal ache which, after a little, in itself provoked thought, and left me yet weaker to endure it unharmed.'[20]

One feature of this episode is Lawrence's clarity in seeing that, even against the background of sleeplessness, the pain disrupts thought in an exchange which is 'not unwelcome'. Another is the description of this pain as 'unattractive and not honourable', which subtly evokes the idea that there might be pains which are 'attractive and honourable'. And the latter, along with its aura of masochism, also suggests the honourable pains of Chivalry registered in *Lancelot of the Lake* and the *Song of Roland*. Should this seem fanciful, it can be demonstrated that even in *The Mint* Lawrence refers back to Chivalrous texts; for example where discussing the serving of food, and his practice of serving himself short (more Christian self-abnegation), he writes: *'No virtue there. Like the Lady of Shalot, I prefer my world backwards in the mirror.'*[21] Similarly, Lawrence also refers to William Morris's *Siguard,* thereby demonstrating that these texts remained in his mind, early and late.[22]

Where Lawrence comes to discuss his bodyguard in the *Seven Pillars*, he again strikes the same unsettling note first heard in the pages on monotheism. In the first place, Lawrence describes how 'all applicants for my service' were examined and proved by Abdullah and 'the Zaagi' (the commander of Lawrence's bodyguard), thanks to whom '… *a wonderful gang of experts grew about me… The British at Akaba called them cut-throats, but they cut throats only to my order.*' The austerities which the bodyguard had to embrace in daily life and warfare seem largely to have been generated by Lawrence's own activities: '… *my rides were customarily very long and hard and sudden.*' Consequently the bodyguard were 'picked riders', paid and mounted on the fastest and strongest camels, however hard and exhausting they might be to ride.[23] However, in matters of discipline, their regime appears harsh to the point of sadism, and the rationale for it odd:

'*Abdulla and the Zaagi ruled them, by my authority, with an unalloyed savagery which could only be excused by the power of each man to quit the service if he wished. [As mentioned in Chapter 10.] Yet we had only one resignation. The others, though adolescents full of carnal passion, tempted by their irregular life, well-fed, exercised, rich, seemed to sanctify their fear, to be fascinated by their physical suffering. Servitude in the East was based, like other conduct, on their obsession with the antithesis between body and spirit,[24] and these took pleasure in subordination, in the utter degrading of the body, to throw more into relief the freedom and equality of mind: almost they preferred servitude, as richer in experience than authority. So the relation of master and man in Arabia was at once more free and more subject than elsewhere. Servants were afraid of the sword of justice, and of the whip, not because the one might put an arbitrary term to their existence, and the other print red rivers of pain about their sides, but because these were the symbols and the means to which their obedience was vowed. They had a gladness of abasement, a freedom of consent to yield to their masters the last service and degree of their flesh and blood, because their spirits were equal, and the contract voluntary… Pain was to them a solvent, a cathartic, almost a decoration to be fairly worn, so long as they survived it.*'[25]

One of the few moderns to address the evaluation of pain outside the problematic of psychology, is Ernst Jünger, the conservative critic of bourgeois German culture, and the Weimar Republic in particular. An ex-stormtrooper, Jünger, in an almost Schopenhauerian language, argues for the idea that pain is ubiquitous:

'*No claim, however, is more certain than the one pain has on life. Where people are spared pain, social stability is produced according to the laws of a very specific economy… one can speak of a "cunning of pain" that never fails to reach its aim… Boredom is nothing other than the dissolution of pain in time.*'[26] [Author note: one can note, in passing, Jünger's echo of Hegel's 'cunning of Reason'.]

Jünger takes the view that there has been a growth in sensitivity in the last 150 years and that the secret of this modern sensitivity is that 'it corresponds to a world in which the body is itself the highest value.'[27] It is very evident that Lawrence shares some of Jünger's views: he certainly did not regard the body as the 'highest value'. By paying attention to a writer and thinker like Jünger – one who had earned the right to speak on questions of pain from his own wounds suffered on the Western Front – we can perhaps begin to distinguish what, in Lawrence, is a disorder we are forced to call masochistic, there being no other word for the sexualisation of pain, from a near-warrior ethos of material minimalism; to use a modern phrase, a militant refusal of 'the comfort zone'. Jünger argues that: 'The heroic and cultic world presents an entirely different relation to pain than does the world of sensitivity.'[28] The detachment from the realms of life where pain is absolute master is only possible where the body is treated as a distant 'outpost' that can be deployed and sacrificed in battle. Lawrence appears to have shared the view of the body as expressed by Jünger, but without the cultural baggage of continental Reactionary Modernism. To be sure, Lawrence eulogises the way of life of the engineers and servicemen amongst whom he spent his later years, but the tone in which he does so merely overlaps with the Nietzschean worker of Jünger's writings. In his 1922 essay, *Battle as Inner Experience*, Jünger develops his idea that 'courage is the only virtue of man', a view Lawrence might have entertained:

> '*Courage is the effort of one's own person to the last consequence, the jump start of an idea against matter, without care for what comes of it. Courage means to let oneself be nailed to the cross for one's cause. Courage means, in the last moment of life, to still show allegiance to the thought for which one stood and fell.*'[29]

Where Lawrence reflects on these things, he registers doubts, reservations, and complications, in some of his most impacted and awkward prose:

> '*To suffer in simplicity for another gave a sense of greatness, of super-humanity. There was no such loftiness as a Cross from which to contemplate the world. The pride and exhilaration of it were beyond conceit. Yet each one occupied, robbed the late-comers of all but the poor part of copying, and the meanest of things were those done by example. The virtue of sacrifice lay within the victim's soul. Honest redemption must have been free and child-minded. When the expiator was conscious of the under-motives and the after-glory of his act, both were wasted on him.*'[30]

Impossible that Jünger, fighting battles as a stormtrooper on the Western Front, would have had time or resources or motives for such considerations, even if both he and Lawrence would have taken the Choice of Achilles – the short, heroic life full of deeds and glory, rather than the dull, long haul. The crowning irony, of course, was Jünger's extended life and his death at 102.

Where Lawrence does speak explicitly of women and sex in the *Seven Pillars*, he is dismissive, having become 'full of vexation' with various organisational frustrations:

> '*I… burst into Auda's tent. He was sitting on its sand floor feeding on boiled bread with his latest wife, a jolly, good-humoured girl… I laid aside my purpose in order to gain ground with Auda, and began to jeer at the old man, provokingly, for being so old and yet so foolish, like the rest of his race, who regarded our comic reproductive processes not as merely an unhygienic pleasure, but as a main business of life. He retorted with his desire for children, and I asked him if he had found life good enough to thank his parents for bringing him into it or wantonly to confer the doubtful gift upon an unborn spirit?*'[31]

Turning to the letters, we find a similar, if moderated tone from 1929:

> '*Women? I like some women. I don't like their sex: any more than I like the monstrous regiment of men. Some men. There is no difference that I can feel between a woman and a man. They look different, granted: but if you work with them there doesn't seem any difference at all. I can't understand all the fuss about sex. It's as obvious as red hair: and as little fundamental, I fancy.*'[32]

In the same year Lawrence writes, briefly, to Edward Marsh in reply to the latter's remarks about Lady Chatterley. Obviously impressed, Lawrence comments apologetically, that his is the 25th letter of the night, but that:

'Yours wasn't a letter but something very magnificent: Lady Chatterley. *I'm re-reading it with a slow deliberate carelessness: going to fancy that I've never read a D.H.L. before, and that it's up to me to appraise this new man and manner. D.H.L. has always been so rich and ripe a writer to me, before, that I'm deeply puzzled and hurt by this* Lady Chatterley *of his. Surely the sex business isn't worth all this damned fuss? I've met only a handful of people who really cared a biscuit for it.'*[33]

Lawrence had finished *The Mint* by 1928 and in it he strikes a similar note about sex, but with a grain more humour. In the chapter entitled 'The Four Senses' (curiously he omits 'taste'), he admits that, of his senses, he fears and shuns touch most. And yet his account of the 'select preacher' at Oxford, speaking of venery, is not without its droll note:

'And let me implore you, my young friends, not to imperil your immortal souls upon a pleasure which, so I am credibly informed, lasts less than one and three-quarter minutes.'

However, Lawrence admits that:

'Of direct experience I cannot speak, never having been tempted so to peril my mortal soul: and six out of ten enlisted fellows share my ignorance despite their flaming talk.'[34]

Lawrence follows this by going deeper into the possibilities of an experience he never had:

'But if the perfect partnership, indulgence with a living body, is as brief as the solitary act, then the climax is indeed no more than a convulsion, a razor-edge of time, which palls so on return that the temptation flickers out into the indifference of tired disgust once a blue moon, when nature compels it.'[35]

Whatever else one may make of this, the intransigent distance from the hysterically sexualised culture of our own times is as evident as the reasoned nausea with which Lawrence defends his own asceticism. Similarly with homosexuality; but here the refusal is more grounded in experience:

'Report accuses us of sodomy, too: and anyone listening into a hut of airmen would think it a den of infamy. Yet we are too intimate, and too bodily soiled, to attract one another. In camps all things, even if not public, are publicly known: and in the four large camps of my sojourning there have been five fellows actively beastly. Doubtless their natures tempted others: but they fight its expression as the normal airman fights his desire for women, out of care for physical fitness.'[36]

The reasons Lawrence has lined up for his own, and his fellow airmen's chastity, are simply 'shyness', 'the wish to be clean', and 'care for physical fitness'. Perhaps we have here the voice of another more sexually naïve time; a culture perhaps less enthralled by the dominant myth of romantic sexual coupledom (or, one might say, a culture less preoccupied with sex and gender than ours). In any case it is evident from the foregoing that Lawrence was well defended against it; not only by upbringing and lack of opportunity, but also by predilection and personal philosophy; in a sense walled-off from any possibility of hetero- or homosexual encounter.

Continuing with the principle that Lawrence was, indeed, telling the truth about the beating and rape by Turks at Deraa, much light can now be shed on the changes seen in his character and aspirations, particularly after the war, if the effects now known as Rape Trauma Syndrome are taken into account. For the purposes of clarity, it seems best to separate Lawrence's masochism from the after-effects of the rape. Also, with the tragic knowledge of the 20th century's wars behind us, and the horrors which have occurred subsequently, we know that irrespective of the sexual orientation of its perpetrators, rape was, and is, a policy for degrading and wrecking the personality and morale of its victims. Therefore the sexual orientation of the Bey, over which there has been some speculation and argument, can be put on one side.

Dr. Andrew Norman, in his book on Lawrence, quotes from Richie J. McMullen's study of male rape, to useful effect, listing some of the effects of that traumatic experience.[37] These effects line up strikingly with many of the aspects of Lawrence's post-war problems. McMullen lists guilt, unworthiness, fear, bewilderment, self-blame, depression: 'Being a victim of rape means being powerless. It means not being able to control or direct one's body, life, or circumstances. It means lacking autonomy and the freedom to self-govern or self-regulate. It also means not having the power to self-determination.' Norman draws the almost inevitable conclusion, 'And so we see Lawrence content to live thereafter in relative obscurity in the lower ranks of the armed services; where others would provide his meals, make decisions for him, and in short, absolve him from having to take responsibility for his own life.'[38] In the light of these considerations, we can begin to see how extraordinary Lawrence's subsequent achievements were. The war which had killed two of his brothers had indeed damaged him too, but in more complex and hidden ways.

From all this, perhaps some of the tangled motives that led to the beating disorder can be inferred. McMullen remarks that '… for some male victims, rape might constitute their first ever sexual experience.'[39] Together with the savage beating, and Lawrence's reaction to it – a reaction perhaps pre-formed by his childhood beatings, and entrenched by his own austerities – the stage is set for an indissoluble link between pain and arousal. Lawrence's first sexual experience was to be the last which involved direct human contact, but not the last as such. Norman suggests that the subsequent beatings occurred on or around the anniversary of the Deraa episode.[40] Whether this is so or not, the pattern in which Lawrence had become trapped is evident: the repetition of the preamble to his first sexual experience. Of course, the problem with the explanation of the beatings as 'the search for mastery by repetition', is that whilst it has a certain psychological plausibility, not all of Lawrence's arrangements fit the pattern of beating. That is, not only the enquiries about riding schools, medical electricity and gymnasia, but also the swimming in the North Sea in February followed by more horse riding, and other austerities. One can note that medieval monks had indeed punished their bodies by singing hymns whilst freezing in the same waters; and that flogging and scourging as punishments were practices of the Military Orders in the Middle Ages – and Lawrence would have known this.[41] Indeed, his brother, Arnold, attests that 'his subjection of the body was achieved by methods advocated by the saints whose lives he had read.'[42] The question inescapably arises: is this really 'subjection'? Or can we say that, in the light of Lawrence's extraordinary achievements, and undoubted austerity, there was a partial subjection? Subjection 'to the extent that…' After all, the disciplines of the saints and their followers were not at all restricted to beatings. Traditionally, in the Christian Church there was also Fasting, Prayer, Meditation, Study, Solitude, Simplicity, Poverty, Submission, and Confession.[43] In fact, the Evangelical Movement, as represented by the person of Canon

Alfred Christopher, a strong influence on Lawrence's childhood, had a version of this tradition which listed 'the five Rs of the Evangelical Society: Ruin, Redemption, Regeneration, Righteousness and Responsibility.'[44] Perhaps Lawrence's struggles after the war, and his entry into the RAF, can be understood as attempts at Redemption, if not Righteousness, after the morally compromising experience of fomenting Revolt whilst knowing about the Sykes-Picot Agreement. The view of the Argentine biographer, Victoria Ocampo, is that 'Lawrence was voluntarily hiding anonymously in a barracks because that was his hair shirt' – his expiation for being a 'false counsellor'.[45] Thereby he breaks a Chivalry precept.

Perhaps we can also take all the foregoing culture of Christian austerity as the deeply formative atmosphere of Lawrence's youth. And this highly braced mentality, having been forced to make the brutal discovery of the eros of pain in Deraa, was also struggling with the guilt of having used the Bedouin – some of whom were close friends – for the purposes of the British war effort. We can recall Lawrence's awareness of the Sykes-Picot deal, and his sense of being a 'standing court-martial' on himself. If we add the possibility that these war experiences made Lawrence leave his asexual self, then the only direction of displacement, given his formation, was towards homosexuality. Perhaps then, the beatings were a kind of compromise between 'simple' masochism and homosexuality; a kind of agonised nearness without physical contact. The sign of 'classical' masochism, as Deleuze points out, is its Contractual nature.[46] The masochist is ultimately in control, whatever his sufferings. On the other hand the masochist scene usually involves the beating woman, and this is very much not Venus in Furs, but Jock in Uniform. The complex arrangements, involving the imaginary 'Old Man' and the unreal transgression certainly are 'contractual', and even involve payment, but the men who enter the contract are under the impression that they are helping Lawrence evade worse things – public exposure of his illegitimacy and extreme embarrassment for his family. The sign that these ceremonies are more than masochism are there in the small details. For example, after an initial beating, Bruce reports that, 'The Old Man said it was not good enough and it was to be done with trousers down… After I had given him the twelve he [Lawrence] said "Give me another one for luck".'[47] This was as if Lawrence was reaching out across the distance between them, but still avoiding actual bodily contact. The other marker of the disavowed eros present in these encounters was that they were to be administered until there was a seminal emission.[48] Even so, Bruce states that Lawrence seemed to get no pleasure from the beatings and that he was not 'homosexual'.[49] Lawrence seems to have organised a ritual which not only had its roots in the medieval past, but was also the perfect compromise between homosexuality and masochism, providing punishment for various real and imagined sins: the betrayal of the Arabs (and possibly Dahoum); complicity with the Sykes-Picot deal; confirming his badly-damaged self-perception after the Deraa episode; repeating the 'glow' of perverse satisfaction which he had inadvertently discovered there; and at the same time involving a kind of closeness to those administering it – without contact. Consistent with this area between homosexuality and masochism is Lawrence's idealisation of certain strong and authoritative military figures, such as Allenby and Trenchard. Edward Garnett's letter to Lawrence about his lunch with Trenchard, curiously droll and insightful by turns, throws light on these issues from a sympathetic and knowledgeable angle:

'I liked him [Trenchard] on the whole, but I should not care to be under him. He might sit for a picture of Mars. But then your feminine side has a passion for being under these heavy military men. Trenchard is one of the innumerable types of fighting men who are glorified by your clean young privates.' [50]

Garnett was a very experienced editor at the Jonathan Cape publishing house, who must have known Lawrence at least since 1922 when the latter sent him one of the first three copies of the *Seven Pillars*. It is plausible that he knew Lawrence quite well.

Lastly, given that Lawrence held the body in very low esteem, one way to understand the masochistic rites of his later years is to see them as a strategy. A strategy in which the ultimate object was, by violence, to restore some balance between the pain and sense of pollution he must have felt within – especially after the debacle of the Paris Conference and Feisal's subsequent ejection from Damascus by the French – and the outer world where he was feted as a hero, particularly in the wake of Lowell Thomas's famous illustrated show, 'With Lawrence in Arabia', which was partly the source of Lawrence's early celebrity. For someone with Lawrence's highly braced sense of ethics, the cumulative effects of the war, and the disjunction between his inner world and the outer myth, must have been almost unbearable.

Endnotes

[1] John E. Mack, *Prince of our Disorder*, p. 433.
[2] Mack, p. 437.
[3] Mack, p. 33.
[4] *Letters*, Ed. Malcolm Brown, p. 325.
[5] *Letters*, Ed. Malcolm Brown, p. 344.
[6] John. E. Mack, *Prince of our Disorder*, p. 33.
[7] *Seven Pillars*, Oxford Edn., pp. 498- 499. Penguin Edn., pp. 454-455.
[8] *Seven Pillars*, Oxford Edn., pp. 501-502.
[9] *The Mint*, p. 65.
[10] *The Mint*, p. 160.
[11] *The Mint*, p. 218.
[12] *The Mint*, p. 225.
[13] Published in Garnett Edn., *Selected Letters*, p. 301.
[14] *Seven Pillars*, Oxford Edn., p. 10.
[15] Ibid., p. 10.
[16] Ibid., p. 11.
[17] *Seven Pillars*, Oxford Edn., p. 21.
[18] Ibid., p. 22.
[19] Ernst Jünger, *On Pain*, p. 1.
[20] *Seven Pillars*, Oxford Edn., p. 420.
[21] *The Mint*, p. 157.
[22] *The Mint*, p. 169.
[23] *Seven Pillars*, Oxford Edn., p. 524.
[24] In *The Mint* this is described as '... this diseased Greek antithesis', p. 77.
[25] *Seven Pillars*, Oxford Edn., pp. 524-526.
[26] Ernst Jünger, *On Pain*, p. 13.
[27] Ibid., p. 17.

28 Ibid., p. 16.
29 Quoted in '*On Pain*', p. xxxvi.
30 *Seven Pillars*, Oxford Edn., p. 661.
31 *Seven Pillars*, Oxford Edn., p. 385.
32 *Letters,* Ed. Garnett, p. 305.
33 Ibid., *Letters,* Garnett, p. 652.
34 *The Mint,* p. 129.
35 *The Mint,* p. 130.
36 Ibid., p. 130.
37 Andrew Norman, *T.E. Lawrence: The Enigma Explained,* Ch. 22.
38 Ibid., pp. 78–80.
39 Quoted in Norman, p. 78.
40 Ibid., p. 88.
41 Desmond Seward, *The Monks Of War: The Military Religious Orders*, p. 237.
42 *Friends,* p. 592.
43 Richard Foster, *Celebration Of Discipline.*
44 *The Secret Lives of Lawrence of Arabia*, p. 23.
45 Victoria Ocampo, *338171 T.E.*, p. 87.
46 Gilles Deleuze, *Sacher-Masoch: an Interpretation.*
47 *Secret Lives,* p. 223.
48 *Prince of Our Disorder,* p. 433.
49 Ibid., p. 433.
50 *Letters to T.E. Lawrence,* Ed. A.W. Lawrence.

CHAPTER SIXTEEN

Speed and Politics

⚭

I F Lawrence had one addiction that stayed with him during his early life and in his later life, none of those things covered by the previous chapters compared with his love of speed. Certainly he was a devotee of books and music, but his love of speed stayed with him and, if anything, it grew. Beginning with racing bicycles, and then moving on to Triumph motorcycles, this passion included the speedboats which he helped develop for the RAF, and reached its apotheosis with a series of seven Brough motorcycles. It should be said that although he had his share of crashes, the accident that killed him did not occur at speed but was, characteristically, a function of the technical limitations of the machine (weak brakes), and a concern for the boy cyclists concealed by a dip in the road. There has been some speculation and rumour about Lawrence's final crash and his death. The basic facts are that on the morning of 13 May 1935 he rode to the post office at Wool in order to post a parcel of books to a friend, and to send a telegram to Henry Williamson, author of *Tarka the Otter*, a book Lawrence admired. The return to his cottage at Clouds Hill near Bovington, involved riding a narrow, steep-sided, country road with three dips in it. The latter dips are deep enough to conceal a vehicle briefly. The consensus of informed opinion is that although Lawrence was a very experienced rider who knew the road well, he did not see the two boy cyclists concealed in one of the dips, who were riding side-by-side, until the last few seconds. Lawrence was travelling at about 28 mph, and must have swerved and braked hard to avoid hitting the cyclists. He hit the back wheel of one of the cycles, lost control of his motorcycle, and was thrown over the handlebars. Lawrence was not wearing a helmet, landed on his head, and ended up against a tree trunk. It is worth recording that the motorcycle was still in second gear after the crash. Anyone who has seen the large, powerful motorcycle will probably have noticed the weak braking capacity. In sum, Lawrence was not speeding, and was apparently trying to save the lives of the cyclists.

There is a rapture of speed, and Lawrence is good at describing it. He even had a quasi-theory of its appeal:

> '*Speed is the second oldest craving in our nature. Every natural man cultivates the speed that appeals to him. I have a motor-bike income.*' [Lawrence doesn't bother to say what the first craving is, or was being dismissive, but it was probably sex of whatever orientation – author][1]

To Robert Graves he wrote:

'When I open out a little more, as for instance across Salisbury Plain at 80 or so, I feel the earth moulding herself under me. It is me piling up this hill, hollowing this valley, stretching out this level place. Almost the earth comes alive, heaving and tossing on each side like the sea. That is a thing the slow coach will never feel. It is the reward of speed. I could write you pages on the lustfulness of moving swiftly.'[2]

Lawrence explores this vein for about five pages in *The Mint*, including a race with a Bristol fighter, one of the best evocations of the feeling of flashing across the English countryside in the Thirties before rules and density of traffic made it impossible to say, '*I slowed to 90: signaled with my hand for him to overtake.*'[3] We may feel some incredulity at this race with a Bristol fighter, but Lawrence records it clearly, adding that '... *the pilot pointed down the road toward Lincoln*', presumably inviting a race (*The Mint*, Penguin Edition, page 226). He also adds the plausible detail of the rude gesture of the aeroplane's passenger as he passed him: '*Over he rattled. His passenger, a helmeted and goggled grin, hung out of the cock-pit to pass me the "Up Yer" Raf* (sic. – RAF) *randy greeting.*' Considering that the race probably took place in the mid-1920s, around 1925-26, the rudimentary level of aircraft can be taken into consideration when assessing this story.

On a somewhat darker note, Lawrence is quite clear about the risks he took during the difficult times he spent in the Tank Corps, when riding at high speeds was obviously a relief:

'When my mood gets too hot and I find myself wandering beyond control, I pull out my motor-bike and hurl it top speed through these unfit roads for hour after hour. My nerves are jaded and gone near dead, so that nothing less than hours of voluntary danger will prick them into life.'[4] (*Letters*, page 416.)

All this is consistent with Lawrence's downgrading of the body, '... *no one ever held the body in less honour than I did myself.*'[5] The joy of speed for Lawrence is partly summed up in his phrase contained in verse he wrote to Lord Carlow, '*In speed we hurl ourselves beyond the body*'. The full verse is:

In speed we hurl ourselves beyond the body.
Our bodies cannot scale the heavens except in a fume of petrol.
Bones. Blood. Flesh. All pressed inward together.[6]

Here he speaks of flight – in what must be one of the earliest expressions of the experience of G forces – but characteristically (because although Lawrence always toughened himself, he invariably denigrates the body and praises the mind) as a projection beyond the body. Anyone who has driven fast will know the exhilaration he evokes; and the sense of being beyond one's mundane earthbound self.

This curious combination of machine-based transcendence has led at least one writer to suggest that Lawrence was in some way connected to the phenomenon of Reactionary Modernism: an ideological comportment to modernity with right wing political implications.

Professor Azar Gatt, in his magisterial *History of Military Thought*, notes that the 'active public enthusiasm for the air in inter-war Britain was disproportionately associated with the radical right.' And Lawrence was indeed very enthusiastic about 'the conquest of the air.'[7] Reactionary Modernism, a term coined by the writer Jeffery Herf in 1984 in his book of that title, sums up this feature of right wing thought in the mid-twentieth century, as characterised by 'an enthusiasm for technology coupled with a rejection of the Enlightenment and the values and institutions of liberal democracy.' Gatt lines Lawrence up with other devotees of flight and air power, like H.G. Wells, Gabriele d'Annunzio, Filippo Tommaso Marinetti, and J.F.C. Fuller. The only figure he cites who is outside this right wing company is Antoine de Saint-Exupéry, and even he 'has been charged with being susceptible to the ideal of 'Airman-as-Fascist' with his 'code of hardship, duty, discipline, and sacrifice.'[8]

It is clear that several issues are tangled up in this assessment of Lawrence: and perhaps the most immediate, for liberals, is the guilt by association with some right wing figures. Firstly, it is a fact that Lawrence was enthusiastic for certain technologies: bicycle gears as boy and, later, motorcycles, speedboats and aircraft. Whether Lawrence '… rejected the Enlightenment and the values and institutions of liberal democracy' is doubtful and more awkward to establish. And, although some have seen him as an agent of British Imperialism (his effigy was burnt by the League of Socialists), his political beliefs are not immediately evident. Also, his view of the world was not a consistent philosophical position: hence he could try to defend the 'native things' both in Arabia and India, resist the introduction of anything 'Franji'[European] into Arabia, and yet enjoy motorcycles, Rolls Royces, and flight. Even in 1927, he was sensitive to the signs of Western industry in India. To Miss Fareedah El Akle, he expressed his dislike of India,

'… also it is squalid, with much of the dirty industrialization of Europe, with all its native things decaying, or being forcibly adjusted to Western conditions.'[9]

Orwell has argued that Lawrence was perhaps 'the last right wing intellectual', going on to write that, '… since about 1930 everyone describable as an 'intellectual' has lived in a state of chronic discontent with the existing order. Necessarily so, because society as it was constituted, had no room for him.'[10] But this is to pigeonhole Lawrence in a curiously unconvincing manner – almost a form of conceptual anachronism, since Lawrence did not and would not fit into the Left/Right political schema. And this was because he was either orientating his life and decisions by his sense of what was ethically right (consider his anguish about the Sykes/Picot duplicity), or whatever geopolitical or military matters were under consideration at any given point in time and reflected, for example, in his strategies for trying to oust the French from Syria, or in the logic of developing Britain's airports between the wars.

If I am right about Lawrence's formation by Classical culture and Chivalry, then he was outside the conceptual space of conventional politics, and he reached back to values which did not map onto the orthodox axis of Liberal/Conservative, or Left/Right. Furthermore, as Harold Orlans has pointed out:

'It is hazardous to judge anyone's political outlook from their wartime activity. In World War One, men of all political viewpoints served in the military and thereby served the Empire. What else could they do? The only alternatives were flight, prison, or conscientious objection.'[11]

In short, now that the hegemony of Marxism has waned, the possibility of posing the question, 'What is wrong with defending one's country?' can again be posed. Nationalism with (almost) a good conscience is again possible as it was for the millions of men '… on the political left or right or with no political interest at all, (who) enlisted and fought.'[12] Such political views as Lawrence had are rather to be found on the level of the great Politics of The Round Table – the ideas acquired from Hogarth of the Empire as a 'commonwealth of free peoples'. To be sure, the old Left would argue that Lawrence 'objectively' served Imperialism – and perhaps he did. However, reading his letters at the time of the deaths of his brothers early in the [First World] war, it is impossible to evade the directness and sincerity of his wish to serve in the struggle against the Axis powers. If even St. Exupéry is tarred with the innuendo of Fascism because of his code of 'hardship, duty, discipline, sacrifice', (and what is wrong with these things?), then it seems that the characterisation of Lawrence as left or right wing is implausible, if not impossible. Indeed, it is as difficult to see what is wrong with Exupéry's code as it is to see what is wrong with Lawrence's – which led him to such efforts in pursuit not only of Arab freedom from the Turks, but his own country's success in the First World War.

As a student of Clausewitz, Lawrence was obviously aware of his famous dictum that 'War is a continuation of Politics by other means.' In other words, politics and war form a continuum; there is no war outside a political context. But knowing this, and subscribing to a party political ideology are two different things, and Lawrence's own views on politics at the local level were particularly cutting. Ralph Isham, who was an American serving in the British Army as a Lieutenant-Colonel in 1918, relates how, in 1920, Winston Churchill asked him to 'prevail' on Lawrence to help him sort out the Middle East, where things were not going well. Apparently Lawrence's reply to Churchill had been 'flippant'. Isham and Lawrence met and Isham explained that Churchill was ready to make Lawrence Governor-General, possibly of Arabia (Mesopotamia) because Isham reports '… *things were not going very well in the Middle East*' and '… *Mr Churchill said he meant to put the matter, in so far as he could, in Lawrence's hands; that he would make him Governor-General, and would back him to the utmost*' (*Friends*, page 301). Lawrence's reply was that he liked Winston…

'… *he writes well. But he's a politician. I'd rather be a chimney sweep than a politician. Their job makes them second-rate. Too much necessity for compromise. All ours that I know, are honest and devoted, but they have an eye on the weather and they reek of red herrings.*'[13]

Isham adds that Lawrence '… was like Kipling in the intensity of his patriotism, but disliked the jingo tenor of Kipling's writings.' Lawrence and Kipling had, in fact, met and spent the day together, and talked mainly about engines, getting on very well.

The Labour M.P. Ernest Thurtle relates how he sounded Lawrence out about the possibility of him being 'beguiled into the necessary political activity', and discovered that he was 'definitely not interested'. Thurtle reflects that those who aspire to leadership have to come into contact with 'the sordid, the petty and the mean'. Strikingly, Thurtle is convinced that '… T.E. would have had the contempt of Coriolanus for these things. He would have scorned to achieve power at the price of his own self-respect, and so democratic leadership would never have been his.'[14] Thurtle also notices the pessimism in Lawrence's more general views. Here, Lawrence would have agreed about the 'discontent of intellectuals'. He was convinced, on the one hand, that the people were contented enough to refuse revolution, but added:

'Don't fly off with the idea that I laud this contentment: I think the planet is in a damnable condition, which no change of party, or social reform, will do more than palliate insignificantly. What is wanted is a new master species – birth control for us, to end the human race in fifty years – and then a clear field for some cleaner mammal. I suppose it must be a mammal.'[15]

It is difficult to estimate how seriously Lawrence meant this, but his opinions about the near impossibility of social reform or change were firm, despite his keen sympathy for the underdog – something noticed by Alec Dixon who reports Lawrence as saying:

'... that the charabanc was a heaven-sent gift to the poorer folk of England since it gave them an opportunity to see something of their country. He seldom discussed social problems, and when he did it was with detachment, for he seemed to be strongly opposed to any kind of organized social reform. But for the under-dog, as an individual, he had the keenest sympathy, which he frequently displayed in queer, angry little comments as we passed through a village or the dismal slums of some coast town.'[16]

In a letter to Charlotte Shaw he wrote:

'It is not possible to change the organic structure of society: or at least it would be easier to reform the single man of his kidneys, leg, or hair.'[17]

In passing, the Nietzschean flavour of 'new master species' can be noted, along with the old Lawrence valuation of 'clean', 'cleaner'. There is indeed almost an echo here of the anti-animal rhetoric of the *Seven Pillars*. And yet the Thurtle letter was written in 1929, and the Charlotte Shaw letter in 1926. Lawrence's low estimate of politics – at least at the party level, is again registered in a letter of 1934 to Captain Lloyd-James, a supporter of Oswald Mosley, in which Lawrence declines an invitation to dinner with various Fascists. Half-seriously, Lawrence writes,

'I want your movement to hurry up and put an end to the license of the daily Press. It will be glorious to dance on the combined cess-pit that holds the dead Daily Express, Daily Chronicle and Daily Herald. My dictatorship programme would also uproot all telegraph poles and bury the wires, assume ownership of all sea-beaches – and scrag the police. Yours not very seriously. T.E. Shaw.'[18]

A week later, evidently following another letter from the Fascists, Lawrence wrote less frivolously:

'Politics in England mean either violent change (I care not enough for anything to lead me into that) or wasting twenty years of one's time and all one's strength on pandering to the House of Commons.[19]

'The meanest Government servant has more power than unofficial M.P. (i.e. a Member of Parliament not holding Ministerial office). So I can't afford politics, either. I'm sorry you think the youth now growing up lacking in character and guts. I have served for twelve and a half years in the R.A.F. and nearly lost what withered heart I possess, (at forty-five), to my fellows, here. They are so definite and happy, I think. They seem to get much more out of life than my contemporaries did, twenty-five years ago. I should have called them a cleaner and better generation. I don't see how anybody in daily touch with working fellows could have dismal thoughts of England… No, please don't make me any part of your Club, I'm prepared only to serve… and I'm very tired: even of serving.'

Similarly, in a letter to Cecil Day-Lewis, also written in 1934, Lawrence's view, as noted in Chapter 13, was:

'The ideals of a policy are entrancing, heady things: the translating them into items of compromise with the social structure as it has evolved is pretty second-rate work. I have never met people more honest and devoted than our politicians – but I'd rather be a dustman. A decent nihilism is what I hope for, generally. I think an established land, like ours, can do with 1% monists or nihilists. That leaves room for me. The trouble with Communism is that it accepts too much of today's furniture. I hate furniture.'[20]

One other telling perspective on politicians as individuals emerges from his remarks to his close friend, Eric Kennington:

'He fed me with jokes and recounted, in great detail, the story of his visit to the House of Commons to beard the Socialists. It is well known, but I have only heard the finale, from his lips. "Well, goodnight gentlemen. I hope you all lose your seats at the next Election." "What should we do then?" said one simpleton. "Join the R.A.F. — but no. They would not take you. There's not a fit man in the room." [Giggle, giggle, giggle.] It was told to amuse me, and it did. But it bored him utterly.'[21]

Strikingly, over a period of 14 years, from 1920 to 1934, Lawrence not only uses jobs usually accorded very low social esteem – such as chimney sweep and dustman – to express his opinion of politics, but he also reiterates the connection between compromise and being 'second-rate', however honest and devoted the individual politician may be. Furthermore, engaging in politics would waste years of his time and strength. He is not a Reactionary Modernist in the German or Italian mode – rejecting democracy and its associated institutions, dwelling on the importance of 'blood and soil' or the *Geist* of the nation and its folk traditions. None of these things are part of his mental furniture, or part of the culture he emerged from. Instead he rejects politics in his own terms, and not without a hint of elitist distain. They are not what he wants to give his time and energy to. He aligns himself explicitly with 'the 1% monists or nihilists', i.e. a minority of *non-believers*. He will not subscribe to political orthodoxy, but his practice is to identify with the R.A.F. as a project worth his efforts. So he is not a 'nihilist' in the sense of having no allegiances at all. Even as he considers Communism (in answer to Day-Lewis), he puts his finger on its great weakness, in his eyes: *'It accepts too much of today's furniture. I hate furniture.'* By 'furniture' we may take Lawrence to mean the clutter and 'household gods' which clog up most ordinary lives. As mentioned previously, the stuff and things which we are led to believe are necessary, and which he was concerned to avoid, such as in his criteria of selection for things at Clouds Hill (and the things he would *not* have – 'No kitchen, no food, no cooking equipment, no bed, no drains, no sanitation' [etc.]).[22] Here we have a late echo of the Gospel of Simplicity in material things, and the exchange of comfort for freedom which Lawrence always preached. Curiously, a similar philosophy of life was expressed by Marguerite Yourcenar in an interview in 1968: 'If a young man or woman hopes to succeed according to the technocrats' formulas – automobiles – television – washing machine – then they will be trapped like slaves.'[23] It may be that Yourcenar's long immersion in the Latin and Greek literature of antiquity – which prepared her for *Memoirs of Hadrian* – also gave her a similar distanciation on contemporary culture as that which Lawrence possessed. One thing is clear: they were both formed by a long education in the Classics.

If Lawrence's references to 'nihilism' and 'monism' are to be taken seriously – especially the former – then the resonances of the words in the mid-1930s should be noted. In general, 'nihilism' argues that Life has no intrinsic purpose, meaning, or value. Philosophically, it has been defined as an extreme form of Scepticism. Lawrence may have got his sense of the word from Turgenev's novel of 1862, *Fathers and Sons*, where a character remarks, '*A nihilist is a man who does not bow to any authorities, who does not take any principle on trust, no matter with what respect that principle is surrounded.*' Once again, the Lawrence use of the word seems to point to *unbeliever*. Thus, the positive sense of nihilist here would be 'one who is free of beliefs,' and therefore not trapped in certain orthodoxies and routine practices. One may reasonably question whether Lawrence had always had such views, or had gradually arrived at them. Perhaps one can say that he had always had a cult of self-hardening and freedom – freedom in the sense of 'freedom from' certain reliances and orthodox habits. And this theme so to speak, was always there; but the years, and experience, added clarity and cut away unnecessary accretions. As he wrote in *The Mint*:

> '*Hungry time has taken from me year by year more of the Creed's clauses till now only the first four words remain. Them I say defiantly, hoping that reason may be stung into new activity when it hears there's a part of me which escapes its rule.*'[24]

These words thus mark the last stand of the Christianity in which he had been raised, but not the end of his sense of the Ethical. For the record, in our uneducated times, by the Creed, Lawrence must have meant the 4th century declaration of Christian Faith, the Nicene Creed, which begins '*We believe in one God*'. The fact that this is five words does not vitiate the point that Lawrence is making; the end of his faith in the elaborated doctrine of his youth. In a sense, Lawrence's new faith was the simple touchstone invented by Major General Sir Hugh Trenchard by which all activities were tried: '*Will this, or will it not, promote the conquest of the air?*'[25] In its service he deployed all the powers that his self-hardening, self-discipline, and austerity, had perfected.

Endnotes

[1]   *Lawrence to his Biographer Liddell Hart,* Quoted in John E. Mack, p. 450.
[2]   John. E. Mack, p. 450.
[3]   *The Mint*, p. 227.
[4]   *Letters,* Ed. Garnett, pp. 414–415. To Lionel Curtis 1923.
[5]   Quoted from *The Seven Pillars* in *The Secret Lives of Lawrence of Arabia*, p. 245.
[6]   Quoted in *Secret Lives*, p. 307.
[7]   Azar Gatt, *History of Military Thought*, p. 594.
[8]   Gatt, p. 596.
[9]   *Letters*, Ed. Malcolm Brown, p. 316.
[10] George Orwell, *England Your England*, N.Y. Harcourt Brace Jovanovich, 1953, p. 274. Quoted in *Lawrence Journal*, Vol VIII, No.1.
[11] Harold Orlans. Lawrence's Political Outlook. *Lawrence Journal*. Vol VIII, No.1, p. 28.
[12] Ibid.
[13] *Friends*, pp. 301-302.
[14] *Friends*, p. 355.
[15] *Selected Letters*, Ed. Garnett, pp. 316-317.
[16] *Friends*, p. 371.
[17] Quoted In *Journal of the T.E. Lawrence Society*, Vol VIII, No.1, p. 31.

[18] Wilson, *Authorised Biography,* p. 917, and *Journal* Vol VIII, p. 32.

[19] Harold Orlans in *The Journal* substitutes 'pandering' for 'parading'. Cf. Wilson, p. 917.

[20] *Letters,* Ed. Garnett, p. 839.

[21] *Friends,* p. 280.

[22] Letter to Frederic Manning, in *Letters.* Ed. Brown, p. 499 [1934].

[23] Marguerite Yourcenar: *Inventing a Life,* Josyane Savigneau, p. 301.

[24] *The Mint,* p. 171.

[25] *The Mint,* p. 118.

Envoi
OR
A LETTER TO LAWRENCE

ᴄᐯᴐ

19th May 1935 [Date of Lawrence's death]

*Quite a long time you've been gone from this world. How much has changed in 75 years.
The dirty modernity you saw beginning in India — well, its time has truly come. So first the
bad news. The silliest (celebrity), dirtiest (plutonium), Civilisation there has ever been: how many
have there been? Five, ten, twenty? This one lurches towards the abyss, babbling to itself about
shopping (shopping!), celebrity things, and sex and drugs. On its knees before the electronic
golden calf, and believing itself to be unique and free.*

*The very idea of 'the trivial' has vanished. Our leaders fly to their endless meetings, and smile.
Or stand briefly beneath foreign suns — where you sweated and struggled —their ties briefly
removed, and in their leaderly poses. Hands on hips, and a concerned frown focused on an empty
middle distance. Surrounding them, the patient troops. Like the patient English at home.
Politely enduring the failing charade of our institutions and the impertinence of some of our latest
guests. And in the deepest English countryside, still the old taciturn dream of the old England.
It has never spoken, and never will, although some composers have caught its fleeting mood.
You understood this in Elgar. It's also there in Butterworth, and Vaughan Williams, and best
not articulated in these giggly times.*

*And the positive? A greater mobility, a growing restlessness amongst the best of the young — still
young enough to feel injustice and bad ethics. And as the growing ecological problems start to bite,
and the paper boat of our unearnt prosperity grows soggy, the face of the next future can be
discerned, despite our flights and disavowals, and stoned laughter. And its first name is Austerity.
True austerity. The great lessness. The simplicity in material things which you noticed so early.
And it will be so hard for most of us. In fact impossible, if it were not inevitable. And this is the
crowning irony. The only answer to our slavery to things, and our confusion of happiness with
pleasure, will be the compulsory austerity of the future. Amidst all your struggles and affectations,
your greatest lesson. How to prepare mind and body, like an athlete, for the fight.
How to be free. Askesis.*

Appendix 1

TWENTY-SEVEN ARTICLES

[ARAB BULLETIN, 20 AUGUST 1917]

THE following notes have been expressed in commandment form for greater clarity and to save words. They are, however, only my personal conclusions, arrived at gradually while I worked in the Hejaz and now put on paper as stalking horses for beginners in the Arab armies. They are meant to apply only to Bedu; townspeople or Syrians require totally different treatment. They are of course not suitable to any other person's need, or applicable unchanged in any particular situation. Handling Hejaz Arabs is an art, not a science, with exceptions and no obvious rules. At the same time we have a great chance there; the Sherif trusts us, and has given us the position (towards his Government) which the Germans wanted to win in Turkey. If we are tactful, we can at once retain his goodwill and carry out our job, but to succeed we have got to put into it all the interest and skill we possess.

1. Go easy just for the first few weeks. A bad start is difficult to atone for, and the Arabs form their judgments on externals that we ignore. When you have reached the inner circle in a tribe, you can do as you please with yourself and them.

2. Learn all you can about your Ashraf and Bedu. Get to know their families, clans and tribes, friends and enemies, wells, hills and roads. Do all this by listening and by indirect inquiry. Do not ask questions. Get to speak their dialect of Arabic, not yours. Until you can understand their allusions, avoid getting deep into conversation, or you will drop bricks. Be a little stiff at first.

3. In matters of business deal only with the commander of the army, column, or party in which you serve. Never give orders to anyone at all, and reserve your directions or advice for the C.O., however great the temptation (for efficiency's sake) of dealing direct with his underlings. Your place is advisory, and your advice is due to the commander alone. Let him see that this is your conception of your duty, and that his is to be the sole executive of your joint plans.

4. Win and keep the confidence of your leader. Strengthen his prestige at your expense before others when you can. Never refuse or quash schemes he may put forward; but ensure that they are put forward in the first instance privately to you. Always approve them, and after praise modify them insensibly, causing the suggestions to come from him, until they are in accord with your own opinion. When you attain this point, hold him to it, keep a tight grip of his ideas, and push him forward as firmly as possibly, but secretly, so that no one but himself (and he not too clearly) is aware of your pressure.

5. Remain in touch with your leader as constantly and unobtrusively as you can. Live with him, that at meal times and at audiences you may be naturally with him in his tent. Formal visits to give advice are not so good as the constant dropping of ideas in casual talk. When stranger sheikhs come in for the first time to swear allegiance and offer service, clear out of the tent. If their first impression is of foreigners in the confidence of the Sherif, it will do the Arab cause much harm.

6. Be shy of too close relations with the subordinates of the expedition. Continual intercourse with them will make it impossible for you to avoid going behind or beyond the instructions that the Arab C.O. has given them on your advice, and in so disclosing the weakness of his position you altogether destroy your own.

7. Treat the sub-chiefs of your force quite easily and lightly. In this way you hold yourself above their level. Treat the leader, if a Sherif, with respect. He will return your manner and you and he will then be alike, and above the rest. Precedence is a serious matter among the Arabs, and you must attain it.

8.   Your ideal position is when you are present and not noticed. Do not be too intimate, too prominent, or too earnest. Avoid being identified too long or too often with any tribal sheikh, even if C.O. of the expedition. To do your work you must be above jealousies, and you lose prestige if you are associated with a tribe or clan, and its inevitable feuds. Sherifs are above all blood-feuds and local rivalries, and form the only principle of unity among the Arabs. Let your name therefore be coupled always with a Sherif's, and share his attitude towards the tribes. When the moment comes for action put yourself publicly under his orders. The Bedu will then follow suit.

9.   Magnify and develop the growing conception of the Sherifs as the natural aristocracy of the Arabs. Intertribal jealousies make it impossible for any sheikh to attain a commanding position, and the only hope of union in nomad Arabia is that the Ashraf be universally acknowledged as the ruling class. Sherifs are half-townsmen, half-nomad, in manner and life, and have the instinct of command. Mere merit and money would be insufficient to obtain such recognition; but the Arab reverence for pedigree and the Prophet gives hope for the ultimate success of the Ashraf.

10.   Call your Sherif 'Sidi' in public and in private. Call other people by their ordinary names, without title. In intimate conversation call a Sheikh 'Abu Annad', 'Akhu Alia' or some similar by-name.

11.   The foreigner and Christian is not a popular person in Arabia. However friendly and informal the treatment of yourself may be, remember always that your foundations are very sandy ones. Wave a Sherif in front of you like a banner and hide your own mind and person. If you succeed, you will have hundreds of miles of country and thousands of men under your orders, and for this it is worth bartering the outward show.

12.   Cling tight to your sense of humour. You will need it every day. A dry irony is the most useful type, and repartee of a personal and not too broad character will double your influence with the chiefs. Reproof, if wrapped up in some smiling form, will carry further and last longer than the most violent speech. The power of mimicry or parody is valuable, but use it sparingly, for wit is more dignified than humour. Do not cause a laugh at a Sherif except among Sherifs.

13.   Never lay hands on an Arab; you degrade yourself. You may think the resultant obvious increase of outward respect a gain to you; but what you have really done is to build a wall between you and their inner selves. It is difficult to keep quiet when everything is being done wrong, but the less you lose your temper the greater your advantage. Also then you will not go mad yourself.

14.   While very difficult to drive, the Bedu are easy to lead, if you have the patience to bear with them. The less apparent your interferences the more your influence. They are willing to follow your advice and do what you wish, but they do not mean you or anyone else to be aware of that. It is only after the end of all annoyances that you find at bottom their real fund of goodwill.

15.   Do not try to do too much with your own hands. Better the Arabs do it tolerably than that you do it perfectly. It is their war, and you are to help them, not to win it for them. Actually, also, under the very odd conditions of Arabia, your practical work will not be as good as,   . perhaps, you think it is.

16.   If you can, without being too lavish, forestall presents to yourself. A well-placed gift is often more effective in winning over a suspicious sheikh. Never receive a present without giving a liberal return, but you may delay this return (while letting its ultimate certainty be known) if you require a particular service from the giver. Do not let them ask you for things, since their greed will then make them look upon you only as a cow to milk.

17. Wear an Arab headcloth when with a tribe. Bedu have a malignant prejudice against the hat, and believe that our persistence in wearing it (due probably to British obstinacy of dictation) is founded on some immoral or irreligious principle. A thick headcloth forms a good protection against the sun, and if you wear a hat your best Arab friends will be ashamed of you in public.

18. Disguise is not advisable. Except in special areas, let it be clearly known that you are a British officer and a Christian. At the same time, if you can wear Arab kit when with the tribes, you will acquire their trust and intimacy to a degree impossible in uniform. It is, however, dangerous and difficult. They make no special allowances for you when you dress like them. Breaches of etiquette not charged against a foreigner are not condoned to you in Arab clothes. You will be like an actor in a foreign theatre, playing a part day and night for months, without rest, and for an anxious stake. Complete success, which is when the Arabs forget your strangeness and speak naturally before you, counting you as one of themselves, is perhaps only attainable in character: while half-success (all that most of us will strive for; the other costs too much) is easier to win in British things, and you yourself will last longer, physically and mentally, in the comfort that they mean. Also then the Turks will not hang you, when you are caught.

19. If you wear Arab things, wear the best. Clothes are significant among the tribes, and you must wear the appropriate, and appear at ease in them. Dress like a Sherif, if they agree to it.

20. If you wear Arab things at all, go the whole way. Leave your English friends and customs on the coast, and fall back on Arab habits entirely. It is possible, starting thus level with them, for the European to beat the Arabs at their own game, for we have stronger motives for our action, and put more heart into it than they. If you can surpass them, you have taken an immense stride toward complete success, but the strain of living and thinking in a foreign and half-understood language, the savage food, strange clothes, and stranger ways, with the complete loss of privacy and quiet, and the impossibility of ever relaxing your watchful imitation of the others for months on end, provide such an added stress to the ordinary difficulties of dealing with the Bedu, the climate, and the Turks, that this road should not be chosen without serious thought.

21. Religious discussions will be frequent. Say what you like about your own side, and avoid criticism of theirs, unless you know that the point is external, when you may score heavily by proving it so. With the Bedu, Islam is so all-pervading an element that there is little religiosity, little fervour, and no regard for externals. Do not think from their conduct that they are careless. Their conviction of the truth of their faith, and its share in every act and thought and principle of their daily life is so intimate and intense as to be unconscious, unless roused by opposition. Their religion is as much a part of nature to them as is sleep or food.

22. Do not try to trade on what you know of fighting. The Hejaz confounds ordinary tactics. Learn the Bedu principles of war as thoroughly and as quickly as you can, for till you know them your advice will be no good to the Sherif. Unnumbered generations of tribal raids have taught them more about some parts of the business than we will ever know. In familiar conditions they fight well, but strange events cause panic. Keep your unit small. Their raiding parties are usually from one hundred to two hundred men, and if you take a crowd they only get confused. Also their sheikhs, while admirable company commanders, are too 'set' to learn to handle the equivalents of battalions or regiments. Don't attempt unusual things, unless they appeal to the sporting instinct Bedu have so strongly, or unless success is obvious. If the objective is a good one (booty) they will attack like fiends, they are splendid scouts, their mobility gives you the advantage that will win this local war, they make proper use of their knowledge of the country (don't take tribesmen to places they do not know), and the gazelle-hunters, who form a proportion of the better men, are great shots at visible targets. A sheikh from one tribe cannot give orders to men from another; a Sherif is necessary to command a mixed tribal force. If there is plunder in prospect, and the odds are at all equal, you will win.

Do not waste Bedu attacking trenches (they will not stand casualties) or in trying to defend a position, for they cannot sit still without slacking. The more unorthodox and Arab your proceedings, the more likely you are to have the Turks cold, for they lack initiative and expect you to. Don't play for safety.

23. The open reason that Bedu give you for action or inaction may be true, but always there will be better reasons left for you to divine. You must find these inner reasons (they will be denied, but are none the less in operation) before shaping your arguments for one course or other. Allusion is more effective than logical exposition: they dislike concise expression. Their minds work just as ours do, but on different premises. There is nothing unreasonable, incomprehensible, or inscrutable in the Arab. Experience of them, and knowledge of their prejudices will enable you to foresee their attitude and possible course of action in nearly every case.

24. Do not mix Bedu and Syrians, or trained men and tribesmen. You will get work out of neither, for they hate each other. I have never seen a successful combined operation, but many failures. In particular, ex-officers of the Turkish army, however Arab in feelings and blood and language, are hopeless with Bedu. They are narrow-minded in tactics, unable to adjust themselves to irregular warfare, clumsy in Arab etiquette, swollen-headed to the extent of being incapable of politeness to a tribesman for more than a few minutes, impatient, and, usually, helpless without their troops on the road and in action. Your orders (if you were unwise enough to give any) would be more readily obeyed by Beduins than those of any Mohammedan Syrian officer. Arab townsmen and Arab tribesmen regard each other mutually as poor relations, and poor relations are much more objectionable than poor strangers.

25. In spite of ordinary Arab example, avoid too free talk about women. It is as difficult a subject as religion, and their standards are so unlike our own that a remark, harmless in English, may appear as unrestrained to them, as some of their statements would look to us, if translated literally.

26. Be as careful of your servants as of yourself. If you want a sophisticated one you will probably have to take an Egyptian, or a Sudani, and unless you are very lucky he will undo on trek much of the good you so laboriously effect. Arabs will cook rice and make coffee for you, and leave you if required to do unmanly work like cleaning boots or washing. They are only really possible if you are in Arab kit. A slave brought up in the Hejaz is the best servant, but there are rules against British subjects owning them, so they have to be lent to you. In any case, take with you an Ageyli or two when you go up country. They are the most efficient couriers in Arabia, and understand camels.

27. The beginning and ending of the secret of handling Arabs is unremitting study of them. Keep always on your guard; never say an unnecessary thing: watch yourself and your companions all the time: hear all that passes, search out what is going on beneath the surface, read their characters, discover their tastes and their weaknesses, and keep everything you find out to yourself. Bury yourself in Arab circles, have no interests and no ideas except the work in hand, so that your brain is saturated with one thing only, and you realize your part deeply enough to avoid the little slips that would counteract the painful work of weeks. Your success will be proportioned to the amount of mental effort you devote to it.

Appendix 2

BOOKS AT CLOUDS HILL

A list of the books T.E.Lawrence had in his cottage at the time of his death on 13th May 1935. First published in *T.E.Lawrence by His Friends*, edited by A.W. Lawrence, Jonathan Cape, London, 1937.

BOOKS AT CLOUDS HILL

THE following is probably a complete list of the books, other than his own writings, in the possession of T. E. Lawrence at the close of his life; it includes a few volumes returned after his death by borrowers, but excludes any which he had left elsewhere with the apparent intention of never reclaiming them. Matter which appears in the printed list within quotation marks consists solely of inscriptions written at the beginning of certain volumes. *N.pl.* means 'No place'.

ADAMS, H. The Degradation of the Democratic Dogma, intro. by B. Adams. *New York, Macmillan Co.*, 1919, 8 *in.* Review of this book from 'Statesman', March 13, 1920, pinned to fly-leaf

—— The Education of Henry Adams: an autobiography [pop. ed]. *London, Constable*, 1928, 7½ *in.*

AESCHYLUS. Tragoediae, ed. Lewis Campbell [Parnassus lib.]. *London, Macmillan*, 1898, 7 *in.* Vellum. 'T. E. L.'

—— Oresteia Text, ed. by R. Proctor [type prepared from Alcala fount [lim. ed.]. *London, Chiswick Press.* 1904, 10½ *in.* 2 *copies* 'T. E. L.'

AESOP. Aesop's Fables. Samuel Croxall's translation with a bibliographical note by Victor Scholderer and numerous facsimiles of Florentine woodcuts [lim. ed. arranged by B. Rogers. No. 1363, signed Bruce Rogers]. *N. pl., Limited Editions Club*, 1933, 10½ *in.* 'To T. E. Shaw with best wishes from W. Merler, Jan. 1934'

AGAR, W. AND OTHERS. One hundred and one ballades, contributed by W. Agar, etc., with illustrations by John Nash [1st ed.]. *London, Cobden-Sanderson*, 1931, 8½ *in.*

AIKEN, C. The Jig of Forslin. *London, Secker*, 1921, 7½ *in.*

AKHMATOVA, A. Forty-seven love poems, trans. from the Russian by Natalie Duddington [lim. ed. Presentation copy]. *London, Jonathan Cape*, 1927, 8 *in.*

ALDINGTON, R. Death of a Hero: a novel. *New York, Covici, Friede*, 1929, 8 *in.*

ALLINGHAM, W. Sixteen poems, by William Allingham: selected by William Butler Yeats. *Dundrum, Dun Emer Press*, 1905, 8½ *in.* Uncut

ANACREON. The Odes with the fragments of Sappho and Alcaeus, trans. T. Orger. *London, R. Hunter*, 1825, 7 *in.* [Inside front cover: Bookplate of John Morgan. Flyleaf: Bookplate of Maurice Baring. 'Maurice Baring: 1914'. 'T. Shaw from Maurice Baring, 1929']

ANDERSON, S. Horses and Men: tales from our American life. *New York, Huebsch*, 1923, 7½ *in.*

ANTHOLOGIA. Ανθολογια διαφορων επιγραμματων . . . Florilegium diversorum epigrammatum in septem libros distinctum. *Venetiis, apud Aldifilios*, 1550, 6 *in.* Leather. 'T. E. L. Aleppo 1912'

ANTHOLOGY. I vol. 10 *in.* [Selections from vols. I and II of Firmin-Didot, with Latin translation, Anthologia Platina]. 'Arab Bureau Cairo' in rubber stamp. 'T. E. L. 1914'

ANTIOCH. La Conquête de Jérusalem: faisant suite à la chanson d'Antioche composée par le pèlerin Richard et ren. par Graindor de Douai au XIIIe siècle pub. par C. Hippeau [Coll. des poètes fr. du moyen age]. *Paris, A. Aubry*, 1868, 8 *in.* Half calf. 'T. E. L.'

—— La chanson d'Antioche, composée au commencement du XIIe siècle par le pèlerin Richard. publiée pour la première fois par P. Paris, 2 vols. [Romans des

ANTIOCH (*continued*) douze pairs de France, Nos. XI and XII]. *Paris, J. Techener*, 1848, 8½ *in.* Both vols. uncut. 'T. E. L.'

APULEIUS. The Golden Asse of Apuleius, done into English by William Adlington, with an introduction by Thomas Seccombe [lim. ed.]. *London, Grant Richards*, 1913, 9 *in.* 'T. E. L.'

—— The Golden Ass, trans. out of Latin by William Adlington, anno 1566, intro. by Charles Whibley [Tudor Translations IV]. *London, D. Nutt*, 1893, 8½ *in.*

ARISTOPHANES. Comoediae accedunt perditarum fabularum fragmenta ex rec. G. Dindorfii, vol. I. *Oxonii, Typ. Academ*, 1835, 8½ *in.* MS. list of contents on flyleaf. 'T. E. L. Oxford 1914. This copy went with me through the Arab war. T. E. L.'

—— Comedies, a new and literal translation by William James Hickie, vol. I [Bohn's Classical Library]. *London, G. Bell*, 1905, 7 *in.*

ARRAS, J. D'. Melusine, Nouvelle ed. rev. par M. Ch. Bonnet. *Paris, P. Jannet*, 1854, 6½ *in.* Red leather. 'T. E. L. Paris, 1919'

ARRIAN. History of the expedition of Alexander the Great, and conquest of Persia, trans. by Mr. Rooke, corrected and enlarged. *London, J. Davis*, 1812, 9½ *in.*

ASQUITH, M. Margot Asquith, an autobiography. 4 vols. *New York, G. H. Doran*, 1920-22, 9 *in.*

AUCASSIN ET NICOLETE. Aucassin et Nicolete. Edited and revised by F. W. Bourdillon. Frontispiece by L. Pissarro. [Last book printed in Vale type by E. and L. Pissarro at the Eragny Press, lim. ed.] *Hammersmith, Eragny Press*, 1903, 8½ *in.* 'T. E. L.'

AUDEN, W. H. The Dance of Death. *London, Faber*, 1933, 8 *in.*

—— The Orators: an English study. *London, Faber*, 1932, 8½ *in.*

—— Poems. *London, Faber*, 1930, 8 *in.* 2 copies

AUGUSTINE, ST. (Bishop of Hippo). The Confessions of S. Augustine. Illustrations designed by Paul Woodroffe and engraved upon wood by Clemence Housman, by whom the title-page has also been engraved from the design of Laurence Housman [lim. ed., no. 80]. *London, Kegan Paul*, 1900, 9 *in.* Limp white vellum. 'T. E. L.'

BACHARACH, A. L. The Musical Companion, ed. by A. L. Bacharach. *London, Gollancz*, 1934, 7½ *in.*

BACON, F. Philosophical Works edited by John M. Robertson. *London, Routledge*, 1905, 9 *in.* 'T. E. L.'

BAERLEIN, H. On the Forgotten Road: a chronicle of the crusade of children, 1212. *London, J. Murray*, 1909, 7½ *in.*

BAKER, SIR H. Cecil Rhodes, by his architect. *London, Oxford University Press*, 1934, 8½ *in.* [Slip 'With the author's compliments']

BALDWIN, S. On England, and other addresses. *London, Philip Allan*, 1926, 9 *in.*

BALZAC, H. DE. The Wild Ass's Skin. [Everyman's Library]. *London, J. M. Dent & Co.*, 1906, 7 *in.*

BANDELLO. Certain tragical discourses of Bandello, trans. by Geffraie Fenton, 1567, introduction by Robert Langton Douglas, 2 vols. [Tudor Trans.] *London, D. Nutt*, 1898, 8 *in.* [Pages mostly uncut. Slip 'With Prof. R. L. Douglas' compliments']. 'T. E. L.'

BARBELLION, W. N. P. The Journal of a Disappointed Man. Introduction by H. G. Wells [2nd imp.]. *London, Chatto & Windus*, 1919, 7½ *in.* 'T. E. L.'

—— A Last Diary. Preface by A. J. Cummings. *London, Chatto & Windus*, 1920, 7½ *in.*

BARBUSSE, H. Le Feu. *Paris, Flammarion*, 1917, 7½ *in.*

—— Under fire: the story of a squad. Trans. by Fitzwater Wray [reprint]. *London, Dent*, 1917, 7½ *in.*

BARING, M. Das retrospective Gepäck [an anthology made by M. Baring of English, Latin, French, Spanish, Italian, Russian and Greek verse, mainly from pages of the Oxford Books of Verse. 'T. E. Shaw from Maurice Baring, April 9th, 1929']

—— Algae: An anthology of phrases. *London, Heinemann*, 1928, 7½ *in.* 2 copies. ['By order of Major Baring' on jacket of one. The other inscribed on flyleaf 'T. S. from M. B. 1929']

—— Collected poems. *London, Heinemann*, 1925, 8 *in.*

—— Flying Corps Headquarters 1914-1918. *London, Heinemann*, 1930, 8 *in.* 'T. Shaw from Maurice Baring, 1931'

—— Friday's Business. *London, Heinemann*, 1932, 7 *in.* 'T. S. from M. B. 1932'

—— Lost Lectures, or the fruits of experience. *London, P. Davies*, 1932, 8 *in.* 'T. S. from M. B. 1932'

—— Per ardua MCMXIV - MCMXVIII [lim. ed.]. *Long Crendon, Seven Acres Press*, 1929, 10 *in.* 'T. S. from M. B. 1929'

—— Poems: 1914-1919. *London, Secker*, 1920, 9 *in.*

——The Puppet Show of Memory [new imp.]. *London, Heinemann*, 1922, 9 *in.* 'From Major Baring'

LITERATURE

BARING, M. Poems 1892-1929 [lim. ed.]. *London, privately printed at Fanfare Press,* 1929, 10 *in.*

—— R. F. C., H. Q., 1914-1918. *London, G. Bell,* 1920, 7 *in.* 'T. E. L.'

—— Tinker's Leave. *New York, Doubleday, Doran,* 1928, 7½ *in.* 'T. E. Shaw from Maurice Baring 1928'

—— When They Love. *New York, Doubleday, Doran,* 1928, 7½ *in.* ['T. E. S.' on fly-leaf. 'T. S. from M. B. 1928' on half-title. On title-page, title is crossed out, and above it written 'Comfortless memory'. English title: 'Title changed because American publishers would not have it' in M. Baring's hand]

—— Unreliable History. *London, Heinemann,* 1934, 8 *in.* 'from Maurice Baring'

BARKER, H. GRANVILLE. The Secret Life: a play in three acts [1st ed.]. *Boston, Little, Brown,* 1923, 7½ *in.* 'For T. E. Shaw from Harley Granville-Barker—Nov. 1923. You might hand it on to Lawrence sometime'

—— Waste: a tragedy, in four acts. *London, Sedgwick & Jackson,* 1927, 7 *in.* 'T. E. S.-L. from H. G.-B. 2.6.27. T. H.'s birthday: they being here and to dispatch this to you'

BARRIE, SIR J. M. Margaret Ogilvy, by her son, J. M. Barrie [2nd ed.] *London, Hodder & Stoughton,* 1897, 7½ *in.*

BASHKIRTSEFF, M. The journal of Marie Bashkirtseff. Trans. with an introduction by Mathilde Blind. *London, Cassell,* 1891, 8 *in.*

BATES, H. E. The Black Boxer: tales. [Pharos ed.]. *London, Cape,* 1932, 7½ *in.*

—— Charlotte's Row [1st ed.]. *London, Cape,* 1931, 7½ *in.*

BAUDELAIRE, C. Les fleurs du mal. [Oeuvres complètes]. *Paris, A. Lemerre,* n.d., 6½ *in.* Half calf

BAX, C. Twenty Chinese poems paraphrased by Clifford Bax [Orpheus Series, no. 3]. *London, Orpheus Press,* 1910, 8½ *in.*

BAYARD. The Right Joyous & Pleasant History of the Chevalier Bayard, by the Loyal Servant. Trans. S. Coleridge [Newnes' Pocket Classics]. *London, George Newnes Ltd.,* 7 *in.* 'T. E. L. Beyrout, 1911'

BEACHCROFT, T. O. A Young Man in a Hurry: and other stories [1st. ed.]. *London, Boriswood,* 1934, 7½ *in.*

BEATON, G. Doctor Partridge's Almanack for 1935. *London, Chatto & Windus,* 1934, 9 *in.* ['Gerald Brennan' written below author's name on title-page]

—— Jack Robinson: a picaresque novel. *London, Chatto & Windus,* 1933, 7½ *in.*

BEAUMONT and FLETCHER, J. Beaumont and Fletcher, 2nd ed. by J. St. Loe Strachey [Mermaid Series]. *London, Fisher Unwin,* n.d., 7 *in.* 'T. E. L.'

BEDDOES, T. L. The Complete Works of Thomas Lovell Beddoes. Edited with a memoir by Sir Edmund Gosse and decorated by the Dance of Death of Hans Holbein [lim. ed., no. 5]. *London, Fanfrolico Press,* 1928, 10 *in.* Brown leather. Uncut

BEERBOHM, M. The Works of Max Beerbohm. With a bibliography by J. Lane [3rd ed.]. *London, Lane,* 1921, 7½ *in.* 'T. E. L.'

—— Works [signed and lim. ed., no. 761]. *London, Heinemann,* 1922, 8 *in.*

—— And Even Now. *London, Heinemann,* 1920, 8 *in.* 'T. E. L.'

—— A Christmas Garland [reprint]. *London, Heinemann,* 1918, 7½ *in.* 'T. E. L.'

—— More [3rd ed.]. *London, Lane,* 1921. 7 *in.* 'T. E. L.'

—— More [lim. ed.]. *London, Heinemann,* 1922, 8 *in.*

—— Seven Men [lim. ed. of works, vol. 7]. *London, Heinemann,* 1922, 8 *in.*

—— Zuleika Dobson: or an Oxford love story [new imp.]. *London, Heinemann,* 1922, 7½ *in.*

BEETHOVEN, L. VAN. Symphonie IX [Philharmonic Scores]. *Wien, Philharmonischer Verb.,* n.d., 7½ *in.* [Note enclosed 'Best wishes H. A. Ford, F/Sergt. 19.5.28']

BELLOC, H. The Cruise of the 'Nona'. *London, Constable,* 1925, 9 *in.*

—— The Eye-witness. *London, E. Nash,* 1908, 7½ *in.*

—— The Old Road, illus. by William Hyde. *London, A. Constable,* 1904, 11 *in.*

—— The Path to Rome [4th ed.]. *London, Allen & Unwin,* 1916, 7½ *in.* 'T. E. L.'

—— Short talks with the dead and others. *New York, Harper,* 1926, 9 *in.*

—— Verses [new ed.]. *London, Duckworth,* 1911, 8½ *in.* 'T. E. S.'

—— The Benefits Moral and Secular of Assassination [Leviatian Fry Series]. *London, C. Lahr,* 1932, 8 *in.* 2 copies: 1 lim. ed.

BENET, S. V. John Brown's Body. *New York, Doubleday, Doran,* 1929, 8 *in.*

BENNETT, A. 'The Clayhanger Family.' I Clayhanger; II Hilda Lessways; III Those Twain. *London, Methuen,* 1925, 7½ *in.* ['V. W. R. from E. S. and E. A. B. 18.xi.27.']

BENSON, S. Good-bye, Stranger. *London, Macmillan,* 1926, 7½ *in.*

—— Hope against Hope and other stories. *London, Macmillan,* 1931, 10½ *in.*

—— Pipers and a Dancer. *New York, Macmillan Co.,* 1924, 7½ *in.*

BEOWULF. The Tale of Beowulf. *Hammersmith, Kelmscott Press,* 1895, 11½ *in.* Bound in white parchment. Bookplate of Emery Walker inside cover. ['To T. E. Shaw from

478

BOOKS AT CLOUDS HILL

BEOWULF (*continued*)
Emery Walker November 3rd, 1932' on 4th flyleaf]

BERKELEY, G. A New Theory of Vision and other select philosophic writings [Everyman's Library]. *London, J. M. Dent,* 1919, 7 *in.*

BETJEMAN, J. Ghastly Good Taste [1st ed.]. *London, Chapman and Hall,* 1933, 7½ *in.* 'T. E. S. from J. E. 10.8.33'

BIBLE. The Holy Bible newly trans. out of the original tongues and with the former trans. diligently compared and revised by His Majesties command. *London, Charles Bill,* 1702, 5 *in.* Red tooled leather

—— The English Bible. Containing the old testament and the new translated out of the original tongues by special command of His Majesty King James I and now reprinted with the text revised by a collation of its early and other principal editions and edited by the late Rev. F. H. Scrivener, M.A., LL.D., for the Syndics of the University Press, Cambridge. 5 vols. *London, Doves Press,* 1903, 13 *in.* 'T. E. L.'

—— The Holy Bible. *London, British and Foreign Bible Society,* 1921, 5½ *in.*

BICKLEY, F. True Dialogues of the Dead, compiled by Francis Bickley [lim. ed.]. *London, G. Chapman,* 1925, 7½ *in.*

BINYON, L. The Secret: sixty poems. *London, Elkin Mathews,* 1920, 7½ *in.* 'T. E. L.'

BLACK, G. A Beggar and other fantasies [lim. ed. no. 159]. *Holmwood, Surrey, E. Garnett,* 1889, 7½ *in.* 'Nov. 11. T. E. Shaw from Edward Garnett. This little book was published by me in 1889! The frontispiece is my book plate done for me by Ford Madox Brown'

BLACKWOOD, A. The Centaur. *London, Macmillan,* 1911, 8 *in.*

—— Dudley and Gilderoy: a nonsense [1st ed.]. *London, Benn,* 1929, 8½ *in.* 'T. E. S.'

—— Dudley and Gilderoy: a nonsense [1st ed.]. *London, Benn,* 1929, 8½ *in.* 'T. E. S.': on half-title 'The secret of a successful elevated life . . . is to remain inconspicuous while yet obtaining one's objective', p.68

BLAKE, W. The Drawings and Engravings of William Blake by Laurence Binyon. *London, Studio,* 1922, 11½ *in.*

—— Poetry and Prose, ed. by Geoffrey Keynes [Century ed.]. *Bloomsbury, Nonesuch Press,* 1927, 7½ *in.*
'T. E. S. August, 1927.
He who bends to himself a joy
Does the winged life destroy;
But he who kisses the joy as it flies
Lives in eternity's sunrise'

—— The Book of Thel. Songs of Innocence and Songs of Experience, illus. by Charles Ricketts [lim. ed.] *N. pl., Ballantyne Press,* 1897, 8 *in.* 'T. E. L.'

BLAKE, W. Illustrations of the Book of Job intro. by Laurence Binyon and Geoffrey Keynes *New York, Pierpont Morgan Library,* 1935, 15 *in.* 'T. E. Shaw from Geoffrey Keynes.' [Only the text: no facsimiles]

—— Jerusalem. Ed. by E. R. D. Maclagan and A. G. B. Russell [The Prophetic Books of William Blake]. *London, A. H. Bullen,* 1904, 10½ *in.* 'T. E. L.'

—— The Marriage of Heaven and Hell and a Song of Liberty. Intro. by Francis Griffin Stokes. *London, Florence Press,* 1911, 7½ *in.* 'T. E. L.'

—— The Marriage of Heaven and Hell. [Facsimile edition. Also contains facsimile of his Index to Songs of Innocence and of Experience. Copy no. 45, signed Wm. Muir.] *N. pl., W. Muir,* 1885, 11½ *in.*

—— Milton. Ed. by E. R. D. Maclagan and A. G. B. Rusell. [The Prophetic Books of William Blake.] *London, A. H. Bullen,* 1907, 10½ *in.* 'T. E. L.'

—— Poetical sketches illus. by Charles Ricketts. *N. pl., Ballantyne Press,* 1899, 8 *in.* 'T. E. L.'

BLUNDEN, E. The Harbingers: poems by E. C. Blunden, *privately printed* 1916, 5½ *in.* Original paper covers. 'T. E. Lawrence from Robert Graves 1920'

—— The Shepherd and other poems of peace and war. *Thavies Inn, Cobden-Sanderson,* 1922, 9 *in.* 'T. E. L.'

—— Undertones of War [rev. ed.]. *London, Cobden-Sanderson,* 1930, 9 *in.* 'Edmund Blunden, Jan. 31, 1934'

—— The Waggoner and other poems. *London, Sidgwick & Jackson,* 1920, 7½ *in.*

BLUNT, LADY A. The celebrated romance of The Stealing of the Mare, trans. from the original Arabic by Lady Anne Blunt and done into verse by Wilfrid Scawen Blunt. Decorations designed and engraved by R. A. Maynard [lim. ed., no. 49]. *Newton, Montgomeryshire, Gregynog Press,* 1930, 12½ *in.* ['Nov. 1930. T. E. Shaw from Edward Garnett']

BLUNT, W. S. The Poetical works of Wilfrid Scawen Blunt. A complete edition. 2 vols. *London, Macmillan,* 1914, 8 *in.* ['T. E. L.' in vol. I. 'to T. E. Lawrence in admiration of his courage and honesty in public life and much else, from Wilfrid Scawen Blunt, New-buildings, July 28th, 1922' in vol. 2]

—— In Vinculis. *London, Kegan Paul,* 1889, 6½ *in.* 'T. E. L.'

—— The Love-lyrics and Songs of Proteus, with the love-sonnets of Proteus, now

479

BLUNT, W. S. (*continued*) reprinted in their full text with many sonnets omitted from the earlier editions. *London Kelmscott Press*, 1892, 8 *in.* Vellum. 'T. E. L.'

—— My diaries: being a personal narrative of events 1888-1914. 2 vols. [lim. ed. no. U] [Borzoi books]. *New York, Knopf*, 1921, 9 *in.* 'Thomas Edward Lawrence from Wilfrid Scawen Blunt. New-buildings, January 13th, 1922'

—— A New Pilgrimage, and other poems. *London, Kegan Paul*, 1889, 6½ *in.* 'T. E. L.'

BOCCACCIO, G. Il libro di messer Giovanni Boccaccio cittadino Fiorentino chiamato il Decameron cognominato Prencipe Galeotto nel quale si contengono cento novelle in diece di dette da sette donne e da tre giovani uomini. *Chelsea, Ashendene Press*, 1920, 16½ *in.* 'T. E. L.'

BORROW, G. Lavengro [new ed.]. *London, Murray*, 1900, 8 *in.*

—— The Zincali: an account of the Gypsies of Spain [Everyman's Library]. *London, Dent*, n.d., 7 *in.* ['V. W. R.']

BOSWELL, J. The Life of Samuel Johnson. Intro. by Herbert Askwith [Modern Library of World's best books]. *London, Lane*, n.d., 8 *in.*

BOURGOGNE, A. J. B. F. Memoirs of Sergeant Bourgogne, 1812-1813, trans., ed. by Paul Coffin and Maurice Hénault. *London, Heinemann*, 1899, 8½ *in.*

BRAITHWAIT, R. Barnabae itinerarium: Barnabees Journall to which is added the Song of Bessie Bell, by Richard Braithwait [lim. ed., no. 12]. *London, Penguin Press*, 1932, 9 in. Vellum. 'T. E. S.'

BRERETON, C. Mystica et lyrica. *London, Elkin Mathews*, 1919, 7½ *in.* 'T. E. S.' ['To Alex: Devine a XXth century Knight-errant. C. B.']

BRIDGES, R. Poems written in the year MCMXIII, by Robert Bridges, poet laureate [lim. ed.]. *London, Ashendene Press*, 1914, 9 *in.* 'T. E. L.'

—— The Testament of Beauty: a poem in four books. *Oxford, Clarendon Press*, 1930, 9 *in.*

BRIEUX. Three plays by Brieux, with a preface by Bernard Shaw. The English versions by Messrs. Bernard Shaw, St. John Hankin and John Pollock [4th ed.]. *London, Fifield*, 1917, 7½ *in.* [Half-title 'T. E. Lawrence from C. F. S. January, 1924']

BRITISH POWER BOAT CO. [1 vol. of photographs showing developments and construction of Power Boats]. 10½ *in.*

BROOKE, C. F. TUCKER. The Shakespeare apocrypha, being a collection of fourteen plays which have been ascribed to Shakespeare, edited by C. F. Tucker Brooke. *Oxford, Clarendon Press*, 1908, 7½ *in.* ['V. W. R.']

BROWN, ALEC. Cranes at sunrise: poems [1st ed.]. *London, Boriswood*, 1934, 7½ *in.*

BROWNE, B. The devil and X.Y.Z. *London, Gollancz*, 1931, 7½ *in.*

BROWNE, SIR T. Religio medici, Urn Burial, Christian morals and other essays [Ballantyne Press]. *London, Hacon & Ricketts*, 1902, 11½ *in.* 'T. E. L.'

BROWNING, R. The poetical works of Robert Browning, vol. I. *London, Smith Elder*, 1906, 7½ *in.* 'T. E. L.'

—— Dramatis personae [Text from 1st ed., 1864, lim. ed.]. *Hammersmith, Doves Press*, 1910, 9½ *in.* Vellum. 'T. E. L.'

—— Men and Women. 2 vols. [Text from 1st ed., 1855, lim. ed.]. *Hammersmith, Doves Press*, 1908, 9½ *in.* 'T. E. L.'

BUCHAN, J. Montrose. *London, T. Nelson*, 1928, 9 *in.* 'T. E. S.'

—— A Prince of the Captivity [1st ed.]. *London, Hodder & Stoughton*, 1933, 7½ *in.*

BUCK, P. S. The Good Earth [11th ed.]. *London, Methuen*, 1934, 7½ *in.*

BULLEN, A. H. Lyrics from the dramatists of the Elizabethan age: edited by A. H. Bullen [lim. ed., no. 201]. *London, Nimmo*, 1889, 8½ *in.* Quarter-calf. 'T. E. L.'

BUNIN, I. A. The Gentleman from San Francisco, and other stories, trans. by S. S. Koteliansky and Leonard Woolf [corrig. slip: 'The first story is trans. by D. H. Lawrence and S. S. Koteliansky]. *Richmond, L. & V. Woolf*, 1922, 7 *in.* 'T. E. L.'

BUNYAN, J. The Pilgrim's Progress. Pt. I. collated by Janet E. Ashbee [lim. ed., no. 407]. *Bow, Essex House Press*, 1899, 6 *in.* Vellum

—— The Pilgrim's Progress. 2vols. Engraving by Blair Hughes-Stanton and Gertrude Hermes [lim. ed., no. 13]. *London, Cresset Press*, 1928, 14 *in.*

BURMAN, B. L. Then there's Cripple Creek. *London, Thornton Butterworth*, 1930, 7½ *in.*

BURNS, R. The Complete Works of Robert Burns, containing his poems, songs and correspondence, with a new life of the poet, and notices, critical and biographical, by Allan Cunningham, illustrated. *Boston, Phillips, Sampson*, 1854, 9½ *in.* Brown leather

BURTON, SIR R. F. The Kasîdah of Hâjî Abdû el Yezdi: a lay of the higher law. *London, Hutchinson*, 1914, 7 *in.* 'T. E. L.'

BURY, G. W. Arabia Infelix, or the Turks in Yamen. *London, Macmillan*, 1915, 8½ *in.*

BUTLER, S. Alps and Sanctuaries of Piedmont and the Canton Ticino. [Op. 6.] New and

BUTLER, S. (*continued*) enlarged ed. with author's revisions and index, and an intro. by R. A. Streatfield, illus. *London, Fifield*, 1913, 8 *in.*

—— Erewhon, wood engravings by Blair Hughes-Stanton [lim. ed., no. 70]. *Newtown, Montgomeryshire, Gregynog Press*, 1932, 9 *in.* Leather

—— Erewhon Revisited twenty years later [3rd imp.]. *London, Fifield*, 1903, 7½ *in.*

—— A First Year in Canterbury Settlement, with other early essays, ed. by R. A. Streatfield. *London, Fifield*, 1914, 7½ *in.*

—— Further extracts from the note-book of Samuel Butler, chosen and edited by A. T. Bartholomew [1st ed.]. *London, Cape*, 1934, 7½ *in.*

—— The Way of All Flesh [2nd. ed., 11th imp.]. *London, Fifield*, 1919, 7½ *in.* 'T. E. L.'

BYRON, G. G., LORD. Don Juan. *London, Sisley*, n.d., 7 *in.*

CAESAR. Commentarii cum supplementis Auli Hirtii et aliorum [Oxford Pocket Classics]. *Oxonii, J. Parker*, 1880, 5 *in.* 'T. E. S.'

—— Gai Iuli Caesaris commentarii rerum in Gallia gestarum VII accedit Auli Hirti commentarius ex rec. T. Rice Holmes [Scrip. class. bibliotheca Riccardiana v.] [lim. ed. no. 86]. *London, Medici Soc.*, 1914, 9½ *in.* Limp vellum. 'T. E. L. 1919'

CALDERON, G. Tahiti, by Tihoti [G. Calderon]. *London, Grant Richards*, 1921, 8½ *in.* 'T. E. L.'

CAMPBELL, J. Earth of Cualaun with 21 designs by the author [lim. ed., no. 193]. *Dublin, Maunsel*, 1917, 9 *in.*

CAMPBELL, R. Adamastor: poems. *London, Faber*, 1930, 7½ *in.*

—— Broken Record: reminiscences. *London, Boriswood*, 1934, 7½ *in.*

—— Broken Record. Reminiscences by Roy Campbell. *London, Boriswood*, 1934, 7½ *in.* Proof

—— The Flaming Terrapin [1st ed.]. *London, Cape*, 1924, 7½ *in.* 'T. E. S.'

—— Flowering Reeds: poems [1st ed.]. *London, Boriswood*, 1933, 7½ *in.*

—— The Georgiad: a satirical fantasy in verse [special signed ed.]. *London, Boriswood*, 1931, 9 in.

—— The Wayzgoose: a South African satire [1st ed.]. *London, Cape*, 1928, 8 *in.*

CAMPION, T. Fifty Songs. Decorated by C. Ricketts. *London, Hacon & Ricketts*, 1906, 9 *in.* 'T. E. L.'

CAPAJON. Fifty-four Short Stories — 1921-1932. Selected with an introduction by Edward Garnett. *London, Cape*, 1933, 7½ *in.*

CARLYLE, T. Sartor Resartus [Temple Classics]. *London, Dent*, n.d., 6 *in.*

CASALE PILGRIM. The Casale pilgrim: a sixteenth-century illustrated guide to the holy places reproduced in facsimile notes by Cecil Roth. *London, Soncino Press*, 1929, 10 *in.* MS. note on half-title:

'We climbed the steep ascent to heaven
Through trouble, toil and pain
Oh Lord! To us may strength be given
To scramble back again'

CASTIGLIONE, B. The Courtyer of Count Baldessar Castilio very necessary and profitable for younge gentilmen done into Englyshe by Thomas Hoby, ed. by J. E. Ashbee: Essex House Press [lim. ed., no. 65]. *London, E. Arnold*, 1900, 9 *in.* Vellum. 'T. E. L., Pole Hill, Chingford, E.4'

CATULLUS. Catulli, Tibulli, Properti carmina quae extant onmia, cura Robinson Ellis, Joannis P. Postgate, Joannis S. Phillimore [Scrip. Class. bibl. Riccardiana] [lim. ed., no. 240]. *London, Medici Soc.*, 1911, 9½ *in.* Vellum. 'T. E. L.' 2nd flyleaf ['H. R. Walker, Greek Iambic Prize, Eton, 1912']

CAVENDISH, G. The Life of Thomas Wolsey, Cardinal Archbishop of York, written by George Cavendish. *Hammersmith, Kelmscott Press*, 8½ *in.* Bound limp vellum. 'T. E. L.'

CELLINI, B. The Life of Benvenuto Cellini, trans. by John Addington Symonds. 2 vols. [Ballantyne Press.] *London, Hacon & Ricketts*, 1900, 11½ *in.* Morocco, Mcleish. 2 vols. bound together. 'T. E. L.'

CERVANTES. El Ingenioso hidalgo Don Quijote de la Mancha. *Paris, Garnier Hermanos*, 1886, 7 *in.*

CHAUCER, G. The Works of Geoffrey Chaucer, edited by F. S. Ellis, ornamented with pictures designed by Sir Edward Burne-Jones, and engraved on wood by W. H. Hooper. Printed by William Morris at the *Kelmscott Press*, 1896, 17½ *in.* 'T. E. L.'

—— Canterbury Tales, ed. A. W. Pollard. *London, Kegan Paul, Trench & Co.*, 1887, 6½ *in.* 'T. E. L.'

CHESTERTON, G. K. Collected Poems [signed lim. ed., no. 236]. *London, C. Palmer*, 1927, 9½ *in.* 'T. E. S.'

—— The Ballad of the White Horse [7th ed.]. *London, Methuen*, 1925, 6½ *in.*

CHILDERS, E. The Riddle of the Sands. *London, Smith Elder*, 1903, 7½ *in.* 'T. E. L.' ['W. H. Myers']

CHURCHILL, W. S. Marlborough, His life and times. 2 vols. *London, Harrap*, 1933-34, 9½ *in.* [Vol. I, on half-title 'Lurens from W., Oct. 1933'; Vol. II, on 2nd flyleaf 'To Lurens from Winston, Oct. 21, 1934']

—— My Early Life; a roving commission.

CHURCHILL, W. S. *(continued)*
London, Thornton Butterworth, 1930, 9 *in.* 'To Lurens from Winston S. Churchill, Oct. 14, 1930'
—— The World Crisis – 1911-1914. *London, Thornton Butterworth*, 1923, 9 *in.* 'Inscribed by Winston S. Churchill for Lurens to replace stolen property, February, 1934'
—— The World Crisis – 1915. *London, Thornton Butterworth*, 1923, 9 *in.* [On 2nd flyleaf 'Inscribed by Winston S. Churchill for Lurens to replace stolen property, February, 1934']
—— The World Crisis – 1916-1918. 2 vols. *London, Thornton Butterworth*, 1927, 9 *in.* 'Lurens from W. S. C. 1. 3. 27'
—— The World Crisis: the aftermath. *London, Thornton Butterworth*, 1929, 9 *in.* [On 2nd flyleaf 'To Colonel Lawrence, from his friend Winston S. Churchill, 1 Mar. 1929]

CLAUSEWITZ, C. VON. On War, trans. by Col. J. J. Graham. New and rev. ed. with intro. by F. N. Maude. 3 vols. *London, Kegan Paul*, 1911, 8½ *in.* 'T. E. L.'

CLIFTON, V. The Book of Talbot. *London, Faber*, 1933, 9 *in.*

COLBOURNE, N. Economic Nationalism [2nd ed.]. *London, Figurehead*, 1934, 7½ *in.*

COLDICOTT, R. London Men in Palestine and how they marched to Jerusalem. *London, E. Arnold*, 1919, 9 *in.*

COLERIDGE, S. T. Poems chosen out of the works of Samuel Taylor Coleridge [ed. by F. S. Ellis]. *Hammersmith, Kelmscott Press*, 1896, 8½ *in.* Limp vellum. 'T. E. L.'
—— The Rime of the Ancient Mariner [lim. ed. Designed by Bruce Rogers]. *Oxford, Oxford University Press*, 1930, 9 *in.*

COLLIER, J. Tom's a-cold: a tale [1st ed.]. *London, Macmillan*, 1933, 7½ *in.*

COLUM, P. The Children of Odin, illus. *New York, Macmillan*, 1920, 7½ *in.*
—— Dramatic Legends and other poems [1st ed.]. *London, Macmillan*, 1922, 8½ *in.*
—— Mogu the Wanderer, or the Desert. *Boston, Little, Brown*, 1917, 7½ *in.*
—— Wild Earth and other poems [reprint]. *New York, Macmillan*, 1922, 7½ *in.*
—— Wild Earth: a book of verse. *Dublin, Maunsel*, 1907, 7 *in.*

COMINES, P. DE. The History of Comines, Englished by T. Danett; intro. by C. Whibley. 2 vols. [Tudor Translations, ed. by W. E. Henley, vols. 17 and 18]. *London, D. Nutt*, 1897, 8½ *in.* 'T. E. L.'

CONGREVE, W. Works, ed. by F. W. Bateson. *London, P. Davies*, 1930, 7½ *in.*

CONRAD, J. Almayer's Folly [8th ed.]. *London, T. Fisher Unwin*, 1920, 7½ *in.* 'T. E. L.'

CONRAD, J. The Arrow of Gold [1st ed.]. *London, T. Fisher Unwin*, 1919, 8 *in.*
—— The Arrow of Gold: a story between two notes. *New York, Doubleday Page*, 1919, 7½ *in.* 'T. E. L.'
—— Chance [13th ed.]. *London, Methuen*, 1919, 7 *in.* 'T. E. L.'
—— Letters from Conrad, 1895 to 1924. Ed. with introduction and notes by E. Garnett. *London, Nonesuch Press*, 1927, 9 *in.* 'T. E. L. from E. G. Oct. 1929'
—— Lord Jim [reprint] *London, Dent*, 1917, 7½ *in.* 'T. E. L., Paris, 1919'
—— The Mirror of the Sea [3rd ed.]. *London, Methuen*, 1913, 7 *in.* 'T. E. L. Signed for T. E. Lawrence with the greatest regard by Joseph Conrad 1922'
—— The Nigger of the 'Narcissus' [new imp.]. *London, Heinemann*, 1898, 7½ *in.*
—— Notes on life and letters [uniform ed.]. *London, Dent*, 1924, 8½ *in.* 'T. E. S. from E. G.'
—— The Shadow-line [reprint]. *London, Dent*, 1919, 7½ *in.*
—— Typhoon [reprint] [Heinemann's 2*s.* net novels]. *London, Heinemann*, 1919, 7 *in.* 'T. E. L.'
—— Victory: an island tale [1st ed.]. *London, Methuen*, 1915, 7½ *in.*
—— Within the Tides [Wayfarer's Library]. *London, Dent*, n.d., 7 *in.* 'T. E. L.'
—— Youth: a narrative; and two other stories [popular ed.]. *Edinburgh, W. Blackwood*, 1919, 7 *in.* 'T. E. L.'

COON, C. S. The Riffian. *London, Cape*, 1934, 7½ *in.*

COPPARD, A. E. Adam and Eve and Pinch me: tales [lim. ed.]. *Waltham St. Lawrence, Golden Cockerel Press*, 1921, 7½ *in.*
—— Clorinda walks in Heaven: tales. *Waltham St. Lawrence, Golden Cockerel Press*, 1922, 7½ *in.* 'T. E. L.'
—— Hips and Haws: poems [lim. ed. no. 69]. *Waltham St. Lawrence, Golden Cockerel Press*, 1922, 7½ *in.*

CORNISH, G. W. Beneath the Surface and other stories. *London, Grant Richards*, 1917, 7½ *in.* Pages uncut

COUCH, A. QUILLER. The Oxford Book of English verse, 1250-1900; ed. by Arthur Quiller-Couch. *Oxford, Clarendon Press*, 1915, 6½ *in.* [Vellum. 'Bought in Cairo 1916. Carried through Hejaz and Syria 1917-1918. T. E. Lawrence, Damascus, 1. 10' on 2nd flyleaf]
—— The Oxford Book of Ballads; chosen and edited by Arthur Quiller-Couch. *Oxford, Clarendon Press*, 1910, 7½ *in.*
—— The Oxford Book of Victorian Verse; chosen by Arthur Quiller-Couch. *Oxford, Clarendon Press*, 1913, 6½ *in.* 'T. E. L.'

COUNTRYMAN. The Countryman, Jan.-Feb.-March, 1930. No. 4, Vol. III. *Idbury, Kingham, Oxford, J. W. Robertson Scott*, 7½ *in.*
—— The Countryman, April-May-June, 1930. No. 1. Vol. IV. *Idbury, Kingham, Oxford, J. W. Robertson Scott*

COWARD, N. Post-mortem: a play in eight scenes [1st ed.]. *London, Heinemann*, 1931, 7½ *in.*

CRANE, S. Collected poems, ed. by Wilson Follett. *New York, Knopf*, 1930, 7½ *in.*
—— Bowery Tales [Heinemann's Colonial Library of Popular Fiction]. *London, W. Heinemann*, 1901, 7½ *in.*
—— George's Mother. *London, E. Arnold*, 1896, 7 *in.* ['T. E. L. from E. G.']
—— The Little Regiment [Pioneer Series]. *London, Heinemann*, 1897, 7½ *in.*
—— Maggie. *London, Heinemann*, 1896, 6½ *in.* '18.9.33. T. E. Shaw from Edward Garnett'
—— Maggie. *London, Heinemann*, 1918, 7 *in.* 'T. E. Lawrence from Edward Garnett'
—— The Open Boat and other stories. *London, Heinemann*, 1918, 7½ *in.*
—— The Red Badge of Courage. Preface by J. Conrad [reprinted]. *London, W. Heinemann*, 1925, 7½ *in.*
—— The Third Violet. *London, Heinemann*, 1897, 7½ *in.*
—— Wounds in the Rain: a collection of stories relating to the Spanish-American War of 1898. *London, Methuen*, 1900, 7½ *in.*

CRANE, W. An artist's reminiscences, with illustrations by the author, and others from photographs. *London, Methuen*, 1907, 9 *in.*

CRESSWELL, W. D'A. Poems 1921-1927 [1st ed.]. *London, Wells Gardner*, 1928, 7 *in.* ['W. D'A. Cresswell' on flyleaf. Sonnet 'The Bay of Biscay, written by author in pencil on flyleaf at end of book. Two letters from Cresswell in book, loose]
—— Time Lags Abed [priv. signed ed., no. 10]. *n. pl. privately printed*, 1930, 7½ *in.* [Back of title-page 'For T. E. Shaw']

CRIPPEN, L. Olympus and Fuji Yama; a study in transcendental history. *London, E. Green*, 1910, 10 *in.* 'T. E. L.'

CROSBY, C. Poems for Harry Crossby by C. C. *Paris, Black Sun Press*, 1931, 9½ *in.*

CUMMINGS, E. E. Eimi [2nd print]. *New York, Covici, Friede*, 1933, 8½ *in.* Review slip in front

CURTIS, L. Civitas Dei [1st ed.]. *London, Macmillan*, 1934, 8½ *in.* [Contains author's complimentary slip]

DAHLBERG, E. Bottom Dogs, with an intro. by D. H. Lawrence [lim. ed., no. 296]. *London, Putnam's*, 1929, 7½ *in.*

DANE, C. Broome Stages [new imp.]. *London, Heinemann*, 1931, 8½ *in.* 'Dear Mr. Shaw. Effendi told me you liked this in its rough state — and that so cheered me, (for it was only half done at the time) that I can't deny myself the pleasure of sending you a completed copy. Yours very sincerely Clemence Dane. Monday 2nd'

DANTE. The Vita Nuova and Canzoniere [Temple Classics]. *London, Dent*, 1924, 6 *in* Leather

DAVID, ST. The Life of Saint David [lim. ed., no. 172]. *Newtown, Montgomeryshire, Gregynog Press*, 1927, 10 *in.* Vellum

DAVIDSON, J. Ballads and Songs. *London, Lane*, 1894, 7 *in.*
—— The Last Ballad and other poems. *London, Lane*, 1899, 7 *in.*
—— A Rosary. *London, Grant Richards*, 1903, 7½ *in.*
—— The Pilgrimage of Strongsoul and other stories. *London, Ward & Downey*, 1896, 8 *in.*
—— A Second series of Fleet Street eclogues. *London, Lane*, 1896, 7 *in.*
—— The Testament of John Davidson. *London, Grant Richards*, 1908, 7½ *in.* 'T. E. L.'

DAVIES, R. Rings on her Fingers [Collectors ed., no. 172]. *London, Harold Shaylor*, 1930, 9 *in.*

DAVIES, W. H. Collected Poems. Portrait by Will Rothenstein [2nd imp.]. *London, Fifield*, n.d. 7½ *in.* 'T. E. L. 1919'
—— Farewell to Poesy and other pieces [1st ed.]. *London, Fifield*, 1901, 7 *in.*
—— Jewels of Song: an anthology of short poems. Compiled by W. H. Davies. *London, Cape*, 1930, 8 *in.* [On half-title 'T. E. S. from C. F. S. Oct. 1930 p. 38' (on p. 38: 'Dominus illuminatio mea' by R. D. Blackmore). Note from C. F. S. loose in book. 'Think you may like to know what interested me in this, though you did not ask. Books of another class will go in a day or two. I read Rose Macaulay's new one yesterday']
—— A Poet's Pilgrimage. *London, A. Melrose*, 1918, 7½ *in.*
—— Selected Poems, arranged by Edward Garnett, foreword by the author [lim. ed., no. 51]. *Newtown, Montgomeryshire, Gregynog Press*, 1928, 9 *in.* 'T. E. L. from E. G.' [Pages uncut]

DEATH IN THE AIR. The war diary and photographs of a flying corps pilot. *London, Heinemann*, 1933, 9 *in.*

DEFOE, D. A Journal of the Plague Year. [Everyman's Library]. *London, Dent*, n.d., 7 *in.* 'T. E. L.'

DE LA BÈRE, R. A History of the Royal Air Force College, Cranwell. *Aldershot, Gale & Polden*, 1934, 7½ *in.*

DE LA MARE, W. The Listeners and other poems [4th imp.]. *London, Constable*, 1918, 6½ *in.* 'T. E. L. 1919'

—— Motley and other poems [2nd im.]. *London, Constable*, 1918, 7½ *in.* 'T. E. L.'

—— Peacock Pie: a book of rhymes [5th imp.]. *London, Constable*, 1919, 9 *in.* 'T. E. L. 1919'

—— The Fleeting and other poems [lim. and signed ed., no. 53]. *London, Constable*, 1933, 9 *in.*

—— The Veil and other poems [signed lim. ed., no 78]. *London, Constable*, 1921, 9 *in.* 'T. E. L.'

DENNIS, G. Bloody Mary's. *London, Heinemann*, 1934, 7½ *in.*

—— Declaration of Love. *London, Heinemann*, 1927, 7½ *in.*

—— The End of the World. *London, Eyre & Spottiswoode*, 1930, 9 *in.*

—— Harvest in Poland. *London, Heinemann*, 7 *in.* No title page

—— Mary Lee. *London, Heinemann*, 1922, 7 *in.*

DE QUINCEY, T. Confessions of an English Opium-eater, together with their sequels, The English mail-coach and Suspiria de profundis, with an introductory essay by G. Saintsbury. *London, Constable*, 1927, 9 *in.*

—— Confessions of an English Opium-eater [World's Classics]. *London, Oxford University Press*, 1910, 6 *in.*

DICKINSON, E. The Poems of Emily Dickinson. Ed. by M. D. Bianchi and A. L. Hampson [definitive complete ed.]. *London, Secker*, 1933, 8½ *in.*

DIEHL, E. Anthologia lyrica Graeca, ed. Ernestus Diehl [vols. 1-20 suppl.] [Bibl. Teubner]. *Lipsiae, B. B. Teubner*, 1925, 6½ *in.*

DIGBY, K. H. The Broadstone of Honour, or the true sense and practice of chivalry. Godefridus. *London, E. Lumley*, 1844, 7½ *in.* [Bookplate of William Hopetown, Earl of Northesk, inside front cover. On flyleaf 'T. E. S.']

DIXELIUS, H. The Minister's Daughter, trans. by A. C. Sethergren, with a foreword by E. Garnett. *New York, E. P. Dutton*, 1926, 7½ *in.*

DONNE, J. X sermons preached by that late learned and rev. divine John Donne, Doctor in Divinity, once Dean of the Cathedral Church of St. Paul's. Chosen from the whole body of Donne's sermons by Geoffrey Keynes [lim. ed., no. 181]. *London, Nonesuch Press*, 1923, 12 *in.*

DORGELÈS, R. Wooden Crosses. *London, Heinemann*, 1920, 7½ *in.*

DOSTOÏEFFSKY, F. The Brothers Karamazov, trans. by Constance Garnett [new imp.] [Novels, I]. *London, Heinemann*, 1920, 7½ *in.*

—— Crime and Punishment. [Everyman's Library]. *London, Dent*, 1915, 7 *in.* ['V. W. Richards from H. L. S. Savory, Xmas 1917. I think you will find this a most interesting and clever if rather lurid picture of life']

—— Crime and Punishment: a Russian realistic novel [2nd ed.] [Vizetelly's one-volume novels]. *London, Vizetelly*, 1886, 7½ *in.*

—— Letters from the Underworld, trans. by C. J. Hogarth. [Everyman's Library no. 654]. *London, Dent*, 1919, 7 *in.*

—— The Possessed: a novel in three parts; trans. by Constance Garnett [new imp.] [Novels]. *London, Heinemann*, 1916, 7½ *in.* 'T. E. L.'

—— A Raw Youth: a novel in three parts; trans. by Constance Garnett [Novels]. *London, Heinemann*, 1916, 7½ *in.* 'T. E. L.'

DOUBLEDAY, F. N. He's Done it Again: more indiscreet recollections privately printed. [Edition limited to 99 copies.] *N. pl., n. pub.* 1933, 7½ *in.* [Slip 'With the compliments of Mr. F. N. Doubleday']

DOUGHTY, C. M. Adam Cast Forth. *London, Duckworth*, 1908, 7½ *in.* [Title-page stamped 'Presentation Copy.' Flyleaf 'V. W. R.' stamped 'Bancroft's School Upper Library.' 'Presented by Mr. Richards']

—— Adam Cast Forth. *London, Duckworth*, 1908, 7½ *in.*

—— The Clouds. *London, Duckworth*, 1912, 8½ *in.* 'T. E. L., Beyrout, 1912'

—— The Dawn in Britain [6 vols.]. *London, Duckworth*, 1906. 'T. E. L. 13.11.20 *ex libris* [illegible].'

—— Mansoul, or the Riddle of the World. *London, Selwyn & Blount*, 1920, 7 *in.* 'T. E. Lawrence with C. M. Doughty's kind regards'

—— Mansoul or the Riddle of the World [2nd and rev. ed. Lim. ed., presentation copy]. *London, Cape* and *the Medici Society*, 1923, 8 *in.* [On half-title 'Colonel T. E. Lawrence with Charles M. Doughty's kind regards']

—— Travels in Arabia Deserta [2 vols.]. *Cambridge, Cambridge University Press*, 1888, 9 *in.* [On half-title 'T. E. Lawrence with Charles M. Doughty's very kind regards. Feb. 1921']

—— Travels in Arabia Deserta [vol. I]. *Cambridge, Cambridge University Press*,

DOUGHTY, C. M. (*continued*)
1888, 9 *in.* [Photo of Doughty, signed underneath, on flyleaf.] 'T. E. L.'

—— Travels in Arabia Deserta, with a new preface by the author, introduction by T. E. Lawrence [2 vols. thick paper]. *London, Lee Warner* and *Jonathan Cape*, 1921, 10 *in.* [Vol. I 'Charles M. Doughty, T. E. Lawrence.' Vol. 2 'T. E. L.']

—— Travels in Arabia Deserta, intro. by T. E. Lawrence [2 vols.]. *London, Lee Warner* and *Cape*, 1921, 9 *in.* 'T. E. L.'

—— Travels in Arabia Deserta. With a new preface by the author [Vol. II]. *London, Cape* and *The Medici Society*, 1923, 9 *in.*

—— Under Arms. *Westminster, A. Constable*, 1900, 8½ *in.* ['T. E. Lawrence with Ch. M. Doughty's kind regards. 2 Feb. '21.' Pasted in, a cutting from *Morning Post* Jan. 14, 1896, 'This letter I wrote from Italy, Jan. 1896, to the *Morning Post.*' The German emperor's aims]

DOUGLAS, LORD A. The City of the Soul [2nd ed.]. *London, Grant Richards*, 1899, 7 *in.* 'T.E.L.'

DOUGLAS, G. The House with the Green Shutters; illus. *London, Collins*, n.d., 7½ *in.* Pages nearly all uncut

DOUGLAS, N. Alone. *London, Chapman & Hall*, 1921, 8½ *in.* 'T. E. L.'

—— Experiments. *London, Chapman & Hall*, 1925, 9 *in.* 'T. E. S.'

—— Fountains in the Sand: rambles among the oases of Tunisia. *London, Secker*, 1912, 8½ *in.* 'T. E. L.'

—— In the Beginning. *New York, J. Day*, 1928. 7½ *in.*

—— In the Beginning. *London, Chatto & Windus*, 1928, 7½ *in.* 'T. E. S.'

—— Looking Back: an autobiographical excursion [2nd print]. *New York, Harcourt Brace*, 1933, 8½ *in.* 'T. E. S.'

—— Old Calabria. *London, Secker*, 1915, 9 *in.* 'T. E. L.'

—— South Wind [4th imp.]. *London, Secker*, 1918, 7½ *in.* 'T. E. L.'

—— South Wind [signed lim. ed., no. 149]. *London, Secker*, 1922, 8½ *in.* 'T. E. L.'

—— Summer Islands, Ischia and Ponza. *London, D. Harmsworth*, 1931, 7½ *in.*

—— They Went [cheap ed.]. *London, Chapman & Hall*, 1930, 7½ *in.*

—— They Went. *London, Chapman & Hall*, 1920, 7½ *in.* 'T. E. L.'

—— Together. *New York, R. M. McBride*, 1923, 9 *in.* 'T. E. S.'

DOWSON, E. The poems of Ernest Dowson, with a memoir by Arthur Symons, four illustrations by Aubrey Beardsley and a portrait by William Rothenstein. *London, Lane*, 1913, 7½ *in.* 'T. E. L.'

DOYLE, J. The Marmosites' miscellany. *London, Hogarth Press*, 1925, 9 *in.* [By Robert Graves]. 'T. E. S. from R. G.'

DREISER, T. A History of myself: Dawn. *London, Constable*, 1931, 8 *in.*

DRINKWATER, J. Persephone [lim. ed., designed by Bruce Rogers]. *New York, W. E. Rudge*, 1926, 10½ *in.*

DUNCAN, ISADORA. My life [reprint]. *London, Gollancz*, 1932, 7½ *in.*

DUNN, G. W. M. Poems – Group One. *London, Cape*, 1934, 7½ *in.* 2 copies

—— [Manuscript book of poems. Blue morocco. 'For T. E. Shaw from G. W. M. Dunn. 3.4.33']

—— Poems – Group one [1st ed.]. *London, Cape*, 1934, 7½ *in.* 'For T. E. Shaw from G. W. M. Dunn. For the only encouragement I ever received'

DUNSANY, LORD. The Book of Wonder, a chronicle of little adventures at the edge of the world. Illustrations by S. H. Sime [2nd ed.]. *London, Elkin Mathews*, 1919, 8 *in.* 'T. E. L.'

—— The Gods of Pegana. Illus. by S. H. Sime [3rd ed.]. *London, Elkins Mathews*, 1919, 8 *in.*

—— Tales of War. *Dublin, Talbot Press*, 1918, 7½ *in.*

—— Tales of Wonder [2nd ed.]. *London, Elkin Mathews*, 1917, 7½ *in.*

—— Time and the Gods, with 10 full-page illustrations by S. H. Sime. *London, Heinemann*, 1906, 8½ *in.*

—— The Travel Tales of Mr. Joseph Jorkens. *London, Putnam's*, 1931, 7½ *in.* 'T. E. S.'

—— Unhappy Far-off Things. *London, Elkin Mathews*, 1919, 7½ *in.*

ECCLESIASTICUS. The Wisdom of Jesus, the son of Sirach commonly called Ecclesiasticus. *Chelsea, Ashendene Press*, 1932, 11½ *in.* [Red leather: W. H. Smith]

EDE, H. S. A Life of Gaudier-Brzeska [lim. ed., no. 77]. *London, Heinemann*, 1930, 13½ *in.*

—— Henri Gaudier-Brzeska, to 'T. E. S.' [MSS. of book publ. by Heinemann, 1930: with presentation letter]

EDWARD THE CONFESSOR. La Estoire de Seint Aedward le rei. Reproduced in facsimile from the unique MS. Intro. by M. R. James [Roxburghe Club]. *Oxford, Oxford University Press*, 1920, 12 *in.*

ELIOT, T. S. Poems 1909-1925 [4th imp.]. *London, Faber*, 1930, 7½ *in.*

ELMER, R. P. and **SMART, C. A.** The Book of the Longbow, ed. by Robert P. Elmer and Charles Allen Smart, with illus. by Will Crawford [lim. ed., no. 135]. *New York, Doubleday Doran*, 1929, 9½ *in.* Pages uncut

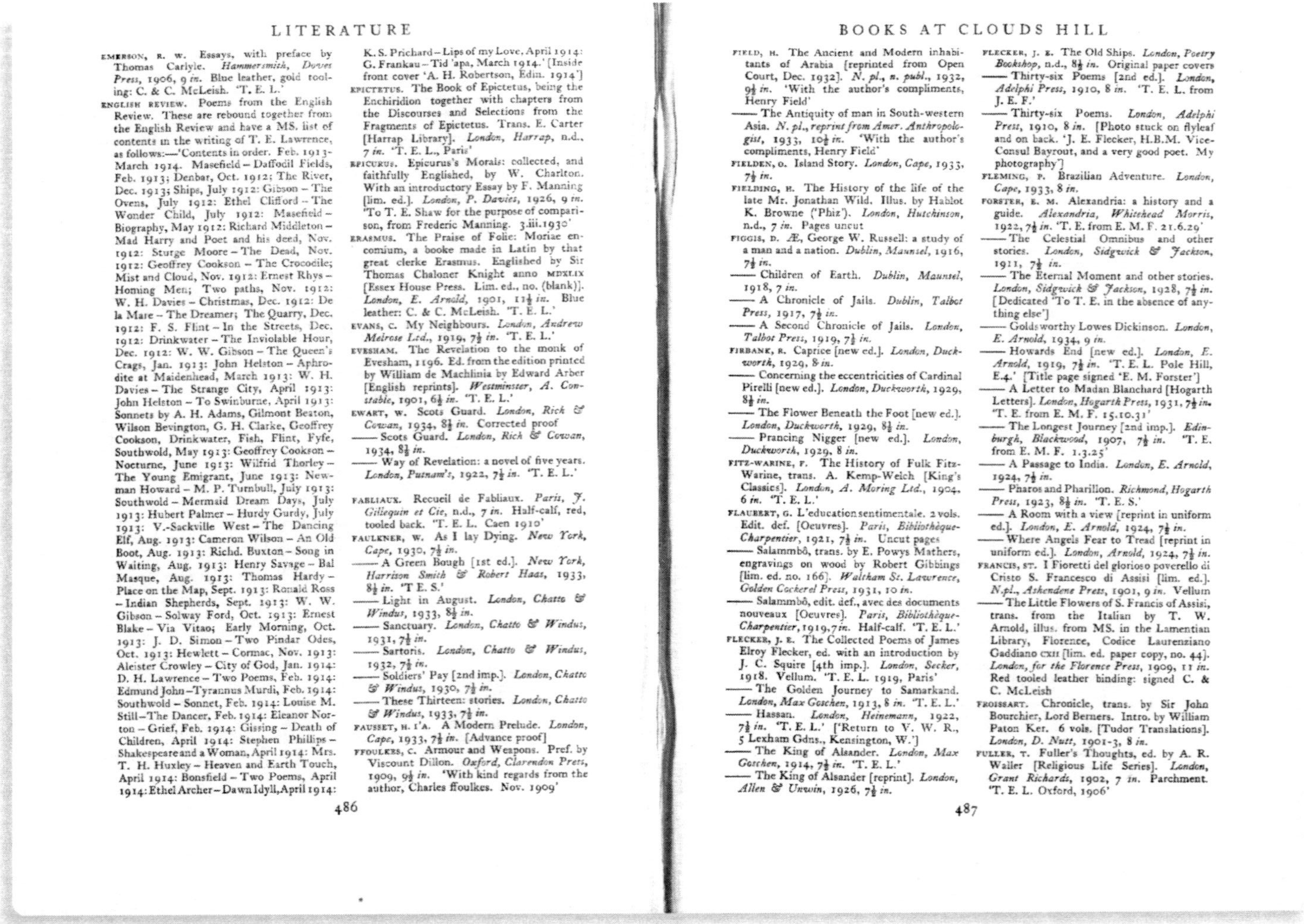

LITERATURE

EMERSON, R. W. Essays, with preface by Thomas Carlyle. *Hammersmith, Doves Press*, 1906, 9 *in.* Blue leather, gold tooling: C. & C. McLeish. 'T. E. L.'

ENGLISH REVIEW. Poems from the English Review. These are rebound together from the English Review and have a MS. list of contents in the writing of T. E. Lawrence, as follows:—'Contents in order. Feb. 1913–March 1914. Masefield – Daffodil Fields, Feb. 1913; Denbar, Oct. 1912; The River, Dec. 1913; Ships, July 1912: Gibson – The Ovens, July 1912: Ethel Clifford – The Wonder Child, July 1912: Masefield – Biography, May 1912: Richard Middleton – Mad Harry and Poet and his deed, Nov. 1912: Sturge Moore – The Dead, Nov. 1912: Geoffrey Cookson – The Crocodile; Mist and Cloud, Nov. 1912: Ernest Rhys – Homing Men; Two paths, Nov. 1912: W. H. Davies – Christmas, Dec. 1912: De la Mare – The Dreamer; The Quarry, Dec. 1912: F. S. Flint – In the Streets, Dec. 1912: Drinkwater – The Inviolable Hour, Dec. 1912: W. W. Gibson – The Queen's Crags, Jan. 1913: John Helston – Aphrodite at Maidenhead, March 1913: W. H. Davies – The Strange City, April 1913: John Helston – To Swinburne, April 1913: Sonnets by A. H. Adams, Gilmont Beaton, Wilson Bevington, G. H. Clarke, Geoffrey Cookson, Drinkwater, Fish, Flint, Fyfe, Southwold, May 1913: Geoffrey Cookson – Nocturne, June 1913: Wilfrid Thorley – The Young Emigrant, June 1913: Newman Howard – M. P. Turnbull, July 1913: Southwold – Mermaid Dream Days, July 1913: Hubert Palmer – Hurdy Gurdy, July 1913: V.-Sackville West – The Dancing Elf, Aug. 1913: Cameron Wilson – An Old Boot, Aug. 1913: Richd. Buxton – Song in Waiting, Aug. 1913: Henry Savage – Bal Masque, Aug. 1913: Thomas Hardy – Place on the Map, Sept. 1913: Ronald Ross – Indian Shepherds, Sept. 1913: W. W. Gibson – Solway Ford, Oct. 1913: Ernest Blake – Via Vitao; Early Morning, Oct. 1913: J. D. Simon – Two Pindar Odes, Oct. 1913: Hewlett – Cormac, Nov. 1913: Aleister Crowley – City of God, Jan. 1914: D. H. Lawrence – Two Poems, Feb. 1914: Edmund John – Tyrannus Murdi, Feb. 1914: Southwold – Sonnet, Feb. 1914: Louise M. Still – The Dancer, Feb. 1914: Eleanor Norton – Grief, Feb. 1914: Gissing – Death of Children, April 1914: Stephen Phillips – Shakespeare and a Woman, April 1914: Mrs. T. H. Huxley – Heaven and Earth Touch, April 1914: Bonsfield – Two Poems, April 1914: Ethel Archer – Dawn Idyll, April 1914: K. S. Prichard – Lips of my Love, April 1914: G. Frankau – Tid 'apa, March 1914.' [Inside front cover 'A. H. Robertson, Edin. 1914']

EPICTETUS. The Book of Epictetus, being the Enchiridion together with chapters from the Discourses and Selections from the Fragments of Epictetus. Trans. E. Carter [Harrap Library]. *London, Harrap*, n.d., 7 *in.* 'T. E. L., Paris'

EPICURUS. Epicurus's Morals: collected, and faithfully Englished, by W. Charlton. With an introductory Essay by F. Manning [lim. ed.]. *London, P. Davies*, 1926, 9 *in.* 'To T. E. Shaw for the purpose of comparison, from Frederic Manning. 3.iii.1930'

ERASMUS. The Praise of Folie: Moriae encomium, a booke made in Latin by that great clerke Erasmus. Englished by Sir Thomas Chaloner Knight anno MDXLIX [Essex House Press. Lim. ed., no. (blank)]. *London, E. Arnold*, 1901, 11½ *in.* Blue leather: C. & C. McLeish. 'T. E. L.'

EVANS, C. My Neighbours. *London, Andrew Melrose Ltd.*, 1919, 7½ *in.* 'T. E. L.'

EVESHAM. The Revelation to the monk of Evesham, 1196. Ed. from the edition printed by William de Machlinia by Edward Arber [English reprints]. *Westminster, A. Constable*, 1901, 6½ *in.* 'T. E. L.'

EWART, W. Scots Guard. *London, Rich & Cowan*, 1934, 8½ *in.* Corrected proof

—— Scots Guard. *London, Rich & Cowan*, 1934, 8½ *in.*

—— Way of Revelation: a novel of five years. *London, Putnam's*, 1922, 7½ *in.* 'T. E. L.'

FABLIAUX. Recueil de Fabliaux. *Paris, J. Gillequin et Cie*, n.d., 7 *in.* Half-calf, red, tooled back. 'T. E. L. Caen 1910'

FAULKNER, W. As I lay Dying. *New York, Cape*, 1930, 7½ *in.*

—— A Green Bough [1st ed.]. *New York, Harrison Smith & Robert Haas*, 1933, 8½ *in.* 'T E. S.'

—— Light in August. *London, Chatto & Windus*, 1933, 8½ *in.*

—— Sanctuary. *London, Chatto & Windus*, 1931, 7½ *in.*

—— Sartoris. *London, Chatto & Windus*, 1932, 7½ *in.*

—— Soldiers' Pay [2nd imp.]. *London, Chatto & Windus*, 1930, 7½ *in.*

—— These Thirteen: stories. *London, Chatto & Windus*, 1933, 7½ *in.*

FAUSSET, H. I'A. A Modern Prelude. *London, Cape*, 1933, 7½ *in.* [Advance proof]

FFOULKES, C. Armour and Weapons. Pref. by Viscount Dillon. *Oxford, Clarendon Press*, 1909, 9½ *in.* 'With kind regards from the author, Charles ffoulkes. Nov. 1909'

486

BOOKS AT CLOUDS HILL

FIELD, H. The Ancient and Modern inhabitants of Arabia [reprinted from Open Court, Dec. 1932]. *N. pl., n. publ.*, 1932, 9½ *in.* 'With the author's compliments, Henry Field'

—— The Antiquity of man in South-western Asia. *N. pl., reprint from Amer. Anthropologist*, 1933, 10½ *in.* 'With the author's compliments, Henry Field'

FIELDEN, O. Island Story. *London, Cape*, 1933, 7½ *in.*

FIELDING, H. The History of the life of the late Mr. Jonathan Wild. Illus. by Hablot K. Browne ('Phiz'). *London, Hutchinson*, n.d., 7 *in.* Pages uncut

FIGGIS, D. Æ, George W. Russell: a study of a man and a nation. *Dublin, Maunsel*, 1916, 7½ *in.*

—— Children of Earth. *Dublin, Maunsel*, 1918, 7 *in.*

—— A Chronicle of Jails. *Dublin, Talbot Press*, 1917, 7½ *in.*

—— A Second Chronicle of Jails. *London, Talbot Press*, 1919, 7½ *in.*

FIRBANK, R. Caprice [new ed.]. *London, Duckworth*, 1929, 8 *in.*

—— Concerning the eccentricities of Cardinal Pirelli [new ed.]. *London, Duckworth*, 1929, 8½ *in.*

—— The Flower Beneath the Foot [new ed.]. *London, Duckworth*, 1929, 8½ *in.*

—— Prancing Nigger [new ed.]. *London, Duckworth*, 1929, 8 *in.*

FITZ-WARINE, F. The History of Fulk Fitz-Warine, trans. A. Kemp-Welch [King's Classics]. *London, A. Moring Ltd.*, 1904, 6 *in.* 'T. E. L.'

FLAUBERT, G. L'education sentimentale. 2 vols. Edit. def. [Oeuvres]. *Paris, Bibliothèque-Charpentier*, 1921, 7½ *in.* Uncut pages

—— Salammbô, trans. by E. Powys Mathers, engravings on wood by Robert Gibbings [lim. ed. no. 166]. *Waltham St. Lawrence, Golden Cockerel Press*, 1931, 10 *in.*

—— Salammbô, edit. def., avec des documents nouveaux [Oeuvres]. *Paris, Bibliothèque-Charpentier*, 1919, 7 *in.* Half-calf. 'T. E. L.'

FLECKER, J. E. The Collected Poems of James Elroy Flecker, ed. with an introduction by J. C. Squire [4th imp.]. *London, Secker*, 1918. Vellum. 'T. E. L. 1919, Paris'

—— The Golden Journey to Samarkand. *London, Max Goschen*, 1913, 8 *in.* 'T. E. L.'

—— Hassan. *London, Heinemann*, 1922, 7½ *in.* 'T. E. L.' ['Return to V. W. R., 5 Lexham Gdns., Kensington, W.']

—— The King of Alsander. *London, Max Goschen*, 1914, 7½ *in.* 'T. E. L.'

—— The King of Alsander [reprint]. *London, Allen & Unwin*, 1926, 7½ *in.*

FLECKER, J. E. The Old Ships. *London, Poetry Bookshop*, n.d., 8½ *in.* Original paper covers

—— Thirty-six Poems [2nd ed.]. *London, Adelphi Press*, 1910, 8 *in.* 'T. E. L. from J. E. F.'

—— Thirty-six Poems. *London, Adelphi Press*, 1910, 8 *in.* [Photo stuck on flyleaf and on back. 'J. E. Flecker, H.B.M. Vice-Consul Bayrout, and a very good poet. My photography']

FLEMING, P. Brazilian Adventure. *London, Cape*, 1933, 8 *in.*

FORSTER, E. M. Alexandria: a history and a guide. *Alexandria, Whitehead Morris*, 1922, 7½ *in.* 'T. E. from E. M. F. 21.6.29'

—— The Celestial Omnibus and other stories. *London, Sidgwick & Jackson*, 1911, 7½ *in.*

—— The Eternal Moment and other stories. *London, Sidgwick & Jackson*, 1928, 7½ *in.* [Dedicated 'To T. E. in the absence of anything else']

—— Goldsworthy Lowes Dickinson. *London, E. Arnold*, 1934, 9 *in.*

—— Howards End [new ed.]. *London, E. Arnold*, 1919, 7½ *in.* 'T. E. L. Pole Hill, E.4.' [Title page signed 'E. M. Forster']

—— A Letter to Madan Blanchard [Hogarth Letters]. *London, Hogarth Press*, 1931, 7½ *in.* 'T. E. from E. M. F. 15.10.31'

—— The Longest Journey [2nd imp.]. *Edinburgh, Blackwood*, 1907, 7½ *in.* 'T. E. from E. M. F. 1.3.25'

—— A Passage to India. *London, E. Arnold*, 1924, 7½ *in.*

—— Pharos and Pharillon. *Richmond, Hogarth Press*, 1923, 8½ *in.* 'T. E. S.'

—— A Room with a view [reprint in uniform ed.]. *London, E. Arnold*, 1924, 7½ *in.*

—— Where Angels Fear to Tread [reprint in uniform ed.]. *London, Arnold*, 1924, 7½ *in.*

FRANCIS, ST. I Fioretti del glorioso poverello di Cristo S. Francesco di Assisi [lim. ed.]. *N.pl., Ashendene Press*, 1901, 9 *in.* Vellum

—— The Little Flowers of S. Francis of Assisi, trans. from the Italian by T. W. Arnold, illus. from MS. in the Lamentian Library, Florence, Codice Laurenziano Gaddiano CXII [lim. ed. paper copy, no. 44]. *London, for the Florence Press*, 1909, 11 *in.* Red tooled leather binding: signed C. & C. McLeish

FROISSART. Chronicle, trans. by Sir John Bourchier, Lord Berners. Intro. by William Paton Ker. 6 vols. [Tudor Translations]. *London, D. Nutt*, 1901–3, 8 *in.*

FULLER, T. Fuller's Thoughts, ed. by A. R. Waller [Religious Life Series]. *London, Grant Richards*, 1902, 7 *in.* Parchment. 'T. E. L. Oxford, 1906'

487

GALSWORTHY, J. Five Tales. *London, Heinemann*, 1918, 7½ *in.*

—— The Island Pharisees [Heinemann's 1s. net Novels]. *London, W. Heinemann*, 1915, 7 *in.* 'T. E. L.'

—— Letters from John Galsworthy 1900–1932. Edited and with introduction Edward Garnett [lim. ed., presentation copy]. *London, Cape*, 1934, 8 *in.* 'Nov. '34. T. E. Shaw from Edward Garnett'

—— A Modern Comedy [signed lim. ed., no. 1018]. *London, Heinemann*, 1929, 8½ *in.* Vellum. [After author's signature 'Of the English: "Wonderful the way the English keep their humour" ']

—— Moods, Songs and Doggerels [2nd ed.]. *London, Heinemann*, 1913, 9 *in.* 'T. E. L. Paris 1919'

—— Saint's Progress. *London, Heinemann*, 1919, 7½ *in.* 'T. E. L.'

GARNETT, D. The Grasshoppers Come, wood-engravings by R. A. Garnett. *London, Chatto & Windus*, 1931, 7½ *in.* 'T. E. Shaw from David Garnett'

—— Lady into Fox, illus. by R. A. Garnett. *London, Chatto & Windus*, 1922, 7½ *in.*

—— Pocahontas or the Nonpareil of Virginia. *London, Chatto & Windus*, 1933, 8 *in.* 'T. E. Shaw from David Garnett. Jan 6, 1933'

—— A Rabbit in the Air: notes from a diary kept while learning to handle an aeroplane. *London, Chatto & Windus*, 1932, 7½ *in.* 'T. E. Shaw from David Garnett, April 7, 1932'

—— The Sailor's Return, with a frontispiece by Ray Garnett. *London, Chatto & Windus*, 1925, 7½ *in.*

GARNETT, E. The Breaking Point, with preface and a letter to the Censor. *London, Duckworth*, 1907, 7½ *in.* 'E. L. from E. G. Dec. 1922'

—— The Feud: a play in three acts. *London, A. H. Bullen*, 1909, 7½ *in.* 'T. E. Lawrence from E. G.'

—— Friday Nights. Literary criticisms and appreciations [first series]. *London, Cape*, 1922, 7½ *in.* 'June, 1922. T. E. Lawrence from Edward Garnett'

—— An Imaged World: poems in prose, with five drawings by William Hyde. *London, Dent*, 1894, 7½ *in.* 'Oct. 1933. T. E. Shaw from E. G.'

—— Papa's War, and other satires. *London, Allen & Unwin*, 1918, 8½ *in.* 'T. E. Lawrence from E. G.'

—— The Trial of Jeanne d'Arc: an historical play in five acts. *London, Sidgwick & Jackson*, 1912, 7½ *in.* 'T. E. Shaw from E. G. Jan. 1930'

GARNETT, E. The Trial of Jeanne d'Arc and other plays. *London, Cape*, 1931, 7½ *in.* 'Oct. 1931. T. E. Shaw from E. G.'

—— Turgenev: a study, with a foreword by Joseph Conrad. *London, Collins*, 1917, 7½ *in.* 2 copies. ['T. E. Shaw from E. G. Jan. 1931' on flyleaf of one. 'T. E. L.' on flyleaf of other, which has a half-title 'T. E. Lawrence from E. G.']

GARNETT, R. The Twilight of the Gods, and other tales. *London, Fisher Unwin*, 1888, 7½ *in.*

—— The Twilight of the Gods, and other tales. *London, Lane*, 1911, 7½ *in.* 'T. E. L.'

GARRARD, A. CHERRY. The Worst Journey in the World. Antarctic 1910-1913, with panoramas, maps and illustrations by the late Dr. E. A. Wilson and other members of the expedition. 2 vols. *London, Constable*, 1922, 9 *in.*

GARROD, H. W. The Oxford Book of Latin Verse. *Oxford, Clarendon Press*, 1912, 7 *in.* 'T. E. L.'

GAUTIER, T. Oeuvres. Poésies 3. Émaux et Camées, Théatre en vers. *Paris, A. Lemère*, n.d., 6½ *in.* Half-calf

—— Un Trio de romans: Les Roués innocents. Militona. Jean et Jeannette [Oeuvres]. *Paris, Charpentier*, 1914, 7½ *in.*

—— Voyage en Espagne [nouvelle éd.] [Oeuvres]. *Paris, Charpentier*, 1922, 7½ *in.* Pages uncut

GAWSWORTH, J. Poems 1930-1932. End papers designed by Frederick Carter [1st ed.]. *London, Rich & Cowan*, 1933, 7½ *in.*

GAYA, L. DE. Gaya's Traité des Armes, 1678, ed. by C. ffoulkes [Tudor and Stuart Library]. *Oxford, Clarendon Press*, 1911, 7½ *in.*

GEOGRAPHICAL JOURNAL. Geographical Journal, vol. XLIV, no. 6. Dec. 1914 [contains The Baghdad Railway, by Capt. S. F. Newcombe]. *London, Royal Geographical Society*, 1914, 9½ *in.*

GEORGIAN POETRY. Georgian poetry 1911-1912 [10th thousand]. *London, Poetry Bookshop*, 1917, 7½ *in.*

GERHARDI, W. Futility. A novel on Russian themes. Preface by Edith Wharton. *New York, Duffield & Co.*, 1922, 7½ *in.* 'T. E. S.'

GIBBON, E. The History of the Decline and Fall of the Roman Empire, ed. by J. B. Bury, 7 vols. [6th ed.]. *London, Methuen*, 1912, 7½ *in.* All vols. uncut. 'T. E. L.'

GIBBON, M. The Seals [1st ed.]. *London, Cape*, 1935, 8 *in.*

GILLIGAN, E. One Lives to tell the Tale [1st ed.]. *London, Cape*, 1931, 8½ *in.* 'T. E. L.'

GISSING, G. The Private Papers of Henry Ryecroft [3rd imp.]. *Westminster, A. Constable*, 7½ *in.*

GISSING, G. The Private Papers of Henry Ryecroft [reprint]. *London, Constable*, 1915, 8 *in.*

GODEFREY OF BOLOYNE. The History of Godefrey of Boloyne and of the conquest of Jherusalem [from Caxton's ed.]. *Hammersmith, Kelmscott Press*, 1893, 11½ *in.* 'T. E. L.'

GOETHE, J. W. VON. Faust: eine Tragödie. *München, Bremer Press*, 1925, 9 *in.* Red leather. 1929 on back

—— Faust, 2 vols. *Hammersmith, Doves Press*, 1906-10, 9½ *in.* Vol. 1, 'J. H. R.' Vol. 2, 'T. E. S.' sic.

GOGARTY, O. Wild Apples, preface by William Butler Yeats [lim. ed.]. *Dublin, Cuala Press*, 1930, 8½ *in.*

GOLDEN LEGEND. The Golden Legend, 3 vols. [ed. by F. S. Ellis from Caxton's edition]. *Hammersmith, Kelmscott Press*, 1892, 11½ *in.* Vols. 2 and 3 uncut. 'T. E. L.'

GORKY, M. Reminiscences of Leo Nicolayevitch Tolstoi, trans. S. S. Koteliansky and L. Woolf [2nd ed.]. *Richmond, L. & V. Woolf at the Hogarth Press*, 1920, 7½ *in.* 'T. E. L.'

GOSSE, E. Father and Son: a study of two temperaments [Windmill Library]. *London, Heinemann*, 1933, 6½ *in.*

GRAHAM, R. B. CUNNINGHAME. Brought Forward. *London, Duckworth*, 1916, 7½ *in.* 'T. E. L.'

—— Cartagena and the Banks of the Sinu. *London, Heinemann*, 1920, 10 *in.* 'From R. B. Cunninghame Graham with kind regards and best wishes, Dec. 15, 1920'

—— Faith [reprint]. *London, Duckworth*, 1913, 7½ *in.* 'T. E. L.'

——A Hatchment [Reader's Library]. *London, Duckworth*, 1920, 7½ *in.*

—— Mogreb - el - Acksa. A Journey in Morocco. *London, Heinemann*, 1898, 9 *in.* 'T. E. L.'

—— Notes on the district of Menteith for tourists and others [reprint]. *London, A. & C. Black*, 1895, 7 *in.*

—— Progress and other sketches [Reader's Library]. *London, Duckworth*, 1911, 7½ *in.*

—— Scottish stories [New Reader's Library]. *London, Duckworth*, 1929, 7 *in.*

—— Thirteen Stories [2nd imp.]. *London, Heinemann*, 1901, 7½ *in.* 'T. E. L.'

—— Writ in Sand. *London, Heinemann*, 1932, 7½ *in.*

GRAHAM, S. A Private in the Guards. *London, Macmillan*, 1919, 8½ *in.* 'T. E. L.'

GRAHAME, K. The Golden Age [Nelson's Library of General Literature]. *London, Nelson*, n.d., 7½ *in.* 'T. E. L.'

GRAVES, P. P. The Pursuit [Hauran, Autumn 1918]. *London, Faber*, 1930, 8 *in.* 2 copies. [One inscribed 'To T. E. Shaw with best wishes from Philip Graves']

GRAVES, R. Claudius the God, and his wife Messalina. *London, A. Barker*, 1934, 8½ *in.*

—— I, Claudius. *London, A. Barker*, 1934, 8½ *in.*

—— Country Sentiment [1st ed.]. *London Secker*, 1920, 7½ *in.* 'T. E. L.' ['Robert Graves 1920']

—— The Feather Bed, with a cover design by William Nicholson [lim. ed.]. *Richmond, Hogarth Press*, 1923, 9 *in.* [On back of flyleaf is stuck a slip with the words printed 'This edition of The Feather Bed is limited to 250 signed copies of which this is number' followed by, in MS. 'less, a bibliographic rarity: from Robert Graves to T. E. Lawrence']

—— Fairies and Fusiliers [2nd imp.]. *London, Heinemann*, 1919, 7 *in.* 'T. E. L.' ['Robert Graves 1920']

—— Good-bye to all that: an autobiography [1st ed.]. *London, Cape*, 1929, 8 *in.*

—— On English Poetry [1st ed.]. *New York, Knopf*, 1922, 8 *in.* Dedicated to T. E. Lawrence and W. H. R. Rivers. 'T. E. L.' on top of flyleaf, 'R. G.' at bottom

—— The Pier-glass. *London, Secker*, 1921, 7½ *in.* 'T. E. L. from Robert Graves 1921'

—— Poems 1914-27 [lim. ed., no. 35, signed by author]. *London, Heinemann*, 1927, 9 *in.*

—— Poems 1926-1930. *London, Heinemann*, 1931, 8 *in.*

—— Poems 1929 [Seizin 3, lim. ed., no. 83]. *London, Seizin Press*, 1929, 8 *in.*

—— Poems 1930-1933. *London, A. Barker*, 1933, 8½ *in.* 'T. E. S.'

—— Ten Poems More [lim. ed., signed by author but copy not numbered. Covers by Len Lye]. *Paris, Hours Press*, 1930, 11½ *in.*

—— To Whom Else? [lim. ed., signed: out of series: cover by Len Lye]. *Deyá, Majorca, Seizin Press*, 1931, 11 *in.*

—— Treasure Box. *N. pl., no publ.*, n.d. 'Colonel Lawrence from Robert Graves in admiration. Dingle Cottage, Boars Hill'

—— Whipperginny [1st ed.]. *London, Heinemann*, 1923, 7½ *in.* [Author's name on title page crossed out and 'Robert Graves' in autograph beneath. On flyleaf:

'Lawrence, of virtuous mother virtuous son,
Now that the fields are dark and ways are mire,
Where shall we sometimes meet . . .etc . . .?'
John Milton, Islip, March 17th, 1923]

—— and RIDING, L. No Decency Left, by Barbara Rich. *London, Cape*, 1932, 7½ *in.*

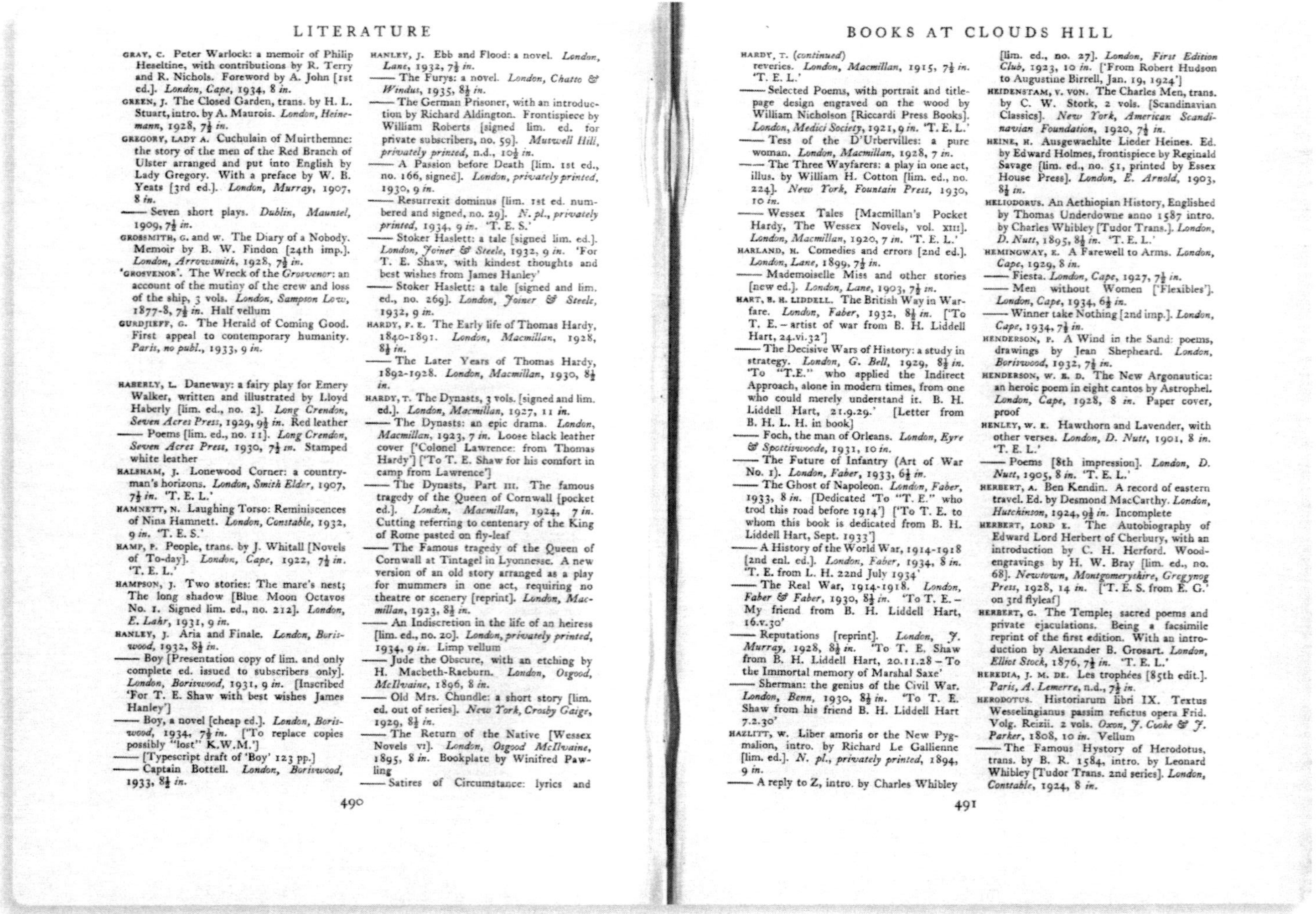

LITERATURE

GRAY, C. Peter Warlock: a memoir of Philip Heseltine, with contributions by R. Terry and R. Nichols. Foreword by A. John [1st ed.]. *London, Cape,* 1934, 8 *in.*

GREEN, J. The Closed Garden, trans. by H. L. Stuart, intro. by A. Maurois. *London, Heinemann,* 1928, 7½ *in.*

GREGORY, LADY A. Cuchulain of Muirthemne: the story of the men of the Red Branch of Ulster arranged and put into English by Lady Gregory. With a preface by W. B. Yeats [3rd ed.]. *London, Murray,* 1907, 8 *in.*

—— Seven short plays. *Dublin, Maunsel,* 1909, 7½ *in.*

GROSSMITH, G. and W. The Diary of a Nobody. Memoir by B. W. Findon [24th imp.]. *London, Arrowsmith,* 1928, 7½ *in.*

'GROSVENOR'. The Wreck of the *Grosvenor*: an account of the mutiny of the crew and loss of the ship, 3 vols. *London, Sampson Low,* 1877-8, 7½ *in.* Half vellum

GURDJIEFF, G. The Herald of Coming Good. First appeal to contemporary humanity. *Paris, no publ.,* 1933, 9 *in.*

HABERLY, L. Daneway: a fairy play for Emery Walker, written and illustrated by Lloyd Haberly [lim. ed., no. 2]. *Long Crendon, Seven Acres Press,* 1929, 9½ *in.* Red leather

—— Poems [lim. ed., no. 11]. *Long Crendon, Seven Acres Press,* 1930, 7½ *in.* Stamped white leather

HALSHAM, J. Lonewood Corner: a countryman's horizons. *London, Smith Elder,* 1907, 7½ *in.* 'T. E. L.'

HAMNETT, N. Laughing Torso: Reminiscences of Nina Hamnett. *London, Constable,* 1932, 9 *in.* 'T. E. S.'

HAMP, P. People, trans. by J. Whitall [Novels of To-day]. *London, Cape,* 1922, 7½ *in.* 'T. E. L.'

HAMPSON, J. Two stories: The mare's nest; The long shadow [Blue Moon Octavos No. 1. Signed lim. ed., no. 212]. *London, E. Lahr,* 1931, 9 *in.*

HANLEY, J. Aria and Finale. *London, Boriswood,* 1932, 8½ *in.*

—— Boy [Presentation copy of lim. and only complete ed. issued to subscribers only]. *London, Boriswood,* 1931, 9 *in.* [Inscribed 'For T. E. Shaw with best wishes James Hanley']

—— Boy, a novel [cheap ed.]. *London, Boriswood,* 1934, 7½ *in.* ['To replace copies possibly "lost" K.W.M.']

—— [Typescript draft of 'Boy' 123 pp.]

—— Captain Bottell. *London, Boriswood,* 1933, 8½ *in.*

HANLEY, J. Ebb and Flood: a novel. *London, Lane,* 1932, 7½ *in.*

—— The Furys: a novel. *London, Chatto & Windus,* 1935, 8½ *in.*

—— The German Prisoner, with an introduction by Richard Aldington. Frontispiece by William Roberts [signed lim. ed. for private subscribers, no. 59]. *Mutwell Hill, privately printed,* n.d., 10½ *in.*

—— A Passion before Death [lim. 1st ed., no. 166, signed]. *London, privately printed,* 1930, 9 *in.*

—— Resurrexit dominus [lim. 1st ed. numbered and signed, no. 29]. *N. pl., privately printed,* 1934, 9 *in.* 'T. E. S.'

—— Stoker Haslett: a tale [signed lim. ed.]. *London, Joiner & Steele,* 1932, 9 *in.* 'For T. E. Shaw, with kindest thoughts and best wishes from James Hanley'

—— Stoker Haslett: a tale [signed and lim. ed., no. 269]. *London, Joiner & Steele,* 1932, 9 *in.*

HARDY, F. E. The Early life of Thomas Hardy, 1840-1891. *London, Macmillan,* 1928, 8½ *in.*

—— The Later Years of Thomas Hardy, 1892-1928. *London, Macmillan,* 1930, 8½ *in.*

HARDY, T. The Dynasts, 3 vols. [signed and lim. ed.]. *London, Macmillan,* 1927, 11 *in.*

—— The Dynasts: an epic drama. *London, Macmillan,* 1923, 7 *in.* Loose black leather cover ['Colonel Lawrence: from Thomas Hardy'] ['To T. E. Shaw for his comfort in camp from Lawrence']

—— The Dynasts, Part III. The famous tragedy of the Queen of Cornwall [pocket ed.]. *London, Macmillan,* 1924, 7 *in.* Cutting referring to centenary of the King of Rome pasted on fly-leaf

—— The Famous tragedy of the Queen of Cornwall at Tintagel in Lyonnesse. A new version of an old story arranged as a play for mummers in one act, requiring no theatre or scenery [reprint]. *London, Macmillan,* 1923, 8½ *in.*

—— An Indiscretion in the life of an heiress [lim. ed., no. 20]. *London, privately printed,* 1934, 9 *in.* Limp vellum

—— Jude the Obscure, with an etching by H. Macbeth-Raeburn. *London, Osgood, McIlvaine,* 1896, 8 *in.*

—— Old Mrs. Chundle: a short story [lim. ed. out of series]. *New York, Crosby Gaige,* 1929, 8½ *in.*

—— The Return of the Native [Wessex Novels VI]. *London, Osgood McIlvaine,* 1895, 8 *in.* Bookplate by Winifred Pawling

—— Satires of Circumstance: lyrics and

490

BOOKS AT CLOUDS HILL

HARDY, T. (*continued*)
reveries. *London, Macmillan,* 1915, 7½ *in.* 'T. E. L.'

—— Selected Poems, with portrait and title-page design engraved on the wood by William Nicholson [Riccardi Press Books]. *London, Medici Society,* 1921, 9 *in.* 'T. E. L.'

—— Tess of the D'Urbervilles: a pure woman. *London, Macmillan,* 1928, 7 *in.*

—— The Three Wayfarers: a play in one act, illus. by William H. Cotton [lim. ed., no. 224]. *New York, Fountain Press,* 1930, 10 *in.*

—— Wessex Tales [Macmillan's Pocket Hardy, The Wessex Novels, vol. XIII]. *London, Macmillan,* 1920, 7 *in.* 'T. E. L.'

HARLAND, H. Comedies and errors [2nd ed.]. *London, Lane,* 1899, 7½ *in.*

—— Mademoiselle Miss and other stories [new ed.]. *London, Lane,* 1903, 7½ *in.*

HART, B. H. LIDDELL. The British Way in Warfare. *London, Faber,* 1932, 8½ *in.* ['To T. E. – artist of war from B. H. Liddell Hart, 24.vi.32']

—— The Decisive Wars of History: a study in strategy. *London, G. Bell,* 1929, 8½ *in.* 'To "T.E." who applied the Indirect Approach, alone in modern times, from one who could merely understand it. B. H. Liddell Hart, 21.9.29.' [Letter from B. H. L. H. in book]

—— Foch, the man of Orleans. *London, Eyre & Spottiswoode,* 1931, 10 *in.*

—— The Future of Infantry (Art of War No. 1). *London, Faber,* 1933, 6½ *in.*

—— The Ghost of Napoleon. *London, Faber,* 1933, 8 *in.* [Dedicated 'To "T. E." who trod this road before 1914'] ['To T. E. to whom this book is dedicated from B. H. Liddell Hart, Sept. 1933']

—— A History of the World War, 1914-1918 [2nd enl. ed.]. *London, Faber,* 1934, 8 *in.* 'T. E. from L. H. 22nd July 1934'

—— The Real War, 1914-1918. *London, Faber & Faber,* 1930, 8½ *in.* 'To T. E. – My friend from B. H. Liddell Hart, 16.v.30'

—— Reputations [reprint]. *London, J. Murray,* 1928, 8½ *in.* 'To T. E. Shaw from B. H. Liddell Hart, 20.11.28 – To the Immortal memory of Marshal Saxe'

—— Sherman: the genius of the Civil War. *London, Benn,* 1930, 8½ *in.* 'To T. E. Shaw from his friend B. H. Liddell Hart 7.2.30'

HAZLITT, W. Liber amoris or the New Pygmalion, intro. by Richard Le Gallienne [lim. ed.]. *N. pl., privately printed,* 1894, 9 *in.*

—— A reply to Z, intro. by Charles Whibley [lim. ed., no. 27]. *London, First Edition Club,* 1923, 10 *in.* ['From Robert Hudson to Augustine Birrell, Jan. 19, 1924']

HEIDENSTAM, V. VON. The Charles Men, trans. by C. W. Stork, 2 vols. [Scandinavian Classics]. *New York, American Scandinavian Foundation,* 1920, 7½ *in.*

HEINE, H. Ausgewaehlte Lieder Heines. Ed. by Edward Holmes, frontispiece by Reginald Savage [lim. ed., no. 51, printed by Essex House Press]. *London, E. Arnold,* 1903, 8½ *in.*

HELIODORUS. An Aethiopian History, Englished by Thomas Underdowne anno 1587 intro. by Charles Whibley [Tudor Trans.]. *London, D. Nutt,* 1895, 8½ *in.* 'T. E. L.'

HEMINGWAY, E. A Farewell to Arms. *London, Cape,* 1929, 8 *in.*

—— Fiesta. *London, Cape,* 1927, 7½ *in.*

—— Men without Women ['Flexibles']. *London, Cape,* 1934, 6½ *in.*

—— Winner take Nothing [2nd imp.]. *London, Cape,* 1934, 7½ *in.*

HENDERSON, P. A Wind in the Sand: poems, drawings by Jean Shepheard. *London, Boriswood,* 1932, 7½ *in.*

HENDERSON, W. B. D. The New Argonautica: an heroic poem in eight cantos by Astrophel. *London, Cape,* 1928, 8 *in.* Paper cover, proof

HENLEY, W. E. Hawthorn and Lavender, with other verses. *London, D. Nutt,* 1901, 8 *in.* 'T. E. L.'

—— Poems [8th impression]. *London, D. Nutt,* 1905, 8 *in.* 'T. E. L.'

HERBERT, A. Ben Kendin. A record of eastern travel. Ed. by Desmond MacCarthy. *London, Hutchinson,* 1924, 9½ *in.* Incomplete

HERBERT, LORD E. The Autobiography of Edward Lord Herbert of Cherbury, with an introduction by C. H. Herford. Wood-engravings by H. W. Bray [lim. ed., no. 68]. *Newtown, Montgomeryshire, Gregynog Press,* 1928, 14 *in.* ['T. E. S. from E. G.' on 3rd flyleaf]

HERBERT, G. The Temple; sacred poems and private ejaculations. Being a facsimile reprint of the first edition. With an introduction by Alexander B. Grosart. *London, Elliot Stock,* 1876, 7½ *in.* 'T. E. L.'

HEREDIA, J. M. DE. Les trophées [85th edit.]. *Paris, A. Lemerre,* n.d., 7½ *in.*

HERODOTUS. Historiarum libri IX. Textus Wesselingianus passim refictus opera Frid. Volg. Reizii. 2 vols. *Oxon, J. Cooke & J. Parker,* 1808, 10 *in.* Vellum

—— The Famous Hystory of Herodotus, trans. by B. R. 1584, intro. by Leonard Whibley [Tudor Trans. 2nd series]. *London, Constable,* 1924, 8 *in.*

491

LITERATURE

HERRICK, R. Poems chosen out of the works of Robert Herrick. Ed. by F. S. Ellis from the text of the edition put forth by the author in 1648. *Hammersmith, Kelmscott Press*, 1895, 8 *in.* Limp vellum. 'T. E. L.'

HEWLETT, M. The Agonists: a trilogy of God and man. *London, Macmillan*, 1911, 7½ *in.* 'T. E. L.'

—— Fond Adventures [Macmillan's Colonial Library]. *London, Macmillan*, 1905, 7½ *in.*

—— The Forest Lovers: a romance [reprint]. *London, Macmillan*, 1899, 7½ *in.*

—— In a Green Shade: a country commentary *London, Bell*, 1920, 7½ *in.*

—— The Life and Death of Richard Yea-and-Nay. *London, Macmillan*, 1900, 7½ *in.*

—— New Canterbury Tales [copyright ed.]. *Leipzig, Tauchnitz*, 1901, 6½ *in.* Half vellum. 'T. E. L. Rouen 1910'

—— The Queen's Quair; or, the six years' tragedy [reprint]. *London, Macmillan*, 1912, 7½ *in.*

—— The Song of the Plow [1st ed.]. *London, Heinemann*, 1916, 8½ *in.*

HEYWARD, DU B. Porgy, decorated by Theodore Nadejen. *N. pl., Grosset & Dunlap*, 1925. 'T. E. S.'

HILTON, J. Lost horizon. *London, Macmillan*, 1933, 7½ *in.* 'T. E. S.'

HODGSON, R. Poems. 2 copies. *London, Macmillan*, 1917, 7 *in.* 'T. E. L. Cairo 1917'

HOGARTH, D. G. Accidents of an Antiquary's Life. *London, Macmillan*, 1910, 9 *in.*

—— Hittite Seals, with particular reference to the Ashmolean collection. *Oxford, Clarendon Press*, 1920, 12½ *in.*

—— A Wandering Scholar in the Levant. *London, J. Murray*, 1896, 7½ *in.*

HOMER. Ilias, ed. W. Leaf [Parnassus Library of Greek and Latin Texts]. *London, Macmillan*, 1895, 7 *in.*

—— Ilias, ed. by Walter Leaf [Parnassus Library]. *London, Macmillan*, 1895, 7 *in.* Suède

—— Ilias, the first twelve staves, trans. by Maurice Hewlett. *London, Cresset Press*, 1928, 11 *in.* Pages uncut

—— 'Ομηρου Οδυσσεια, intro. by James M. Paton, 2 vols. [Chiswick ed.] [lim. ed., no. 11]. *London, Pickering & Chatto*, n.d., 6½ *in.* Vellum. 'T. E. L. Oxford 1911'

—— The Odyssey of Homer, done into English verse by W. Morris. *London, Longmans, Green*, 1897, 8 *in.*

—— Odyssey, trans. by T. E. Lawrence [lim. ed.]. *London, Emery Walker*, 1932, 11½ *in.* Black calf

—— The Odyssey of Homer, newly trans. into English prose by T. E. Lawrence [lim. ed. copy extra seriem]. *New York, Oxford University Press*, 1932, 10 *in.* 'T. E. S.'

HOMER. Ομηρου Οδυσσεια, text of 1896 ed. by D. B. Monro: type designed by R. Proctor [lim. ed.]. *Oxford, University Press*, 1909, 11½ *in.* Pages uncut. 'To T. E. Lawrence from Sydney C. Cockerell Mar. 27, 1922'

HOPKINS, G. M. Poems, ed. by R. Bridges, with an appendix of additional poems and a critical introduction by C. Williams [2nd ed. lim. ed., no. 86]. *Oxford, Oxford University Press*, 1930, 8½ *in.*

HORACE. Horati carminum libri IV [lim. ed.]. *Londini. Peter Davies*, 1926, 9 in. Pages uncut

—— Quintus Horatius Flaccus. *Londini, G. Pickering*, 1824, 3½ *in.* Leather ['T. E. L. Shaw from Ronald Storrs']

—— Opera, ed. F. W. Cornish. *London, Kegan Paul, Trench et Soc.* 1888, 6½ *in.* 'T. E. L.'

—— Quinti Horati Flacci carmina Sapphica. Chelsea, in aed. St. J. Hornby, *Ashendene Press*, 1903, 7 *in.*, on Japanese vellum

—— Carminum librum quintum a R. Kipling et C. Graves Anglice redditum ed. A. D. Godley. *Oxonii, B. Blackwell*, 1920, 7½ *in.*

HOUGHTON, C. A Hair Divides. *London, Thornton Butterworth*, 1930, 7 *in.*

—— The Riddle of Helena [new ed.]. *London, Collins*, 1934, 7½ *in.* [Note on wrapper 'Please disregard this quite unsuitable dust wrapper. B. R.']

HOUSMAN, A. E. A Shropshire Lad [lim. ed., no. 36] [Riccardi Press Booklets]. *London, for the Medici Society*, 1914, 9 *in.* [Green tooled leather, binding signed 'C. & C. McLeish'. 'T. E. L. from C. F. B. 1914']

—— A Shropshire Lad [lim. ed., no. 396 [Riccardi Press Booklets]. *London, Medici Society*, 1914, 9 *in.* 'T. E. L.'

—— Last Poems. *London, Grant Richards*, 1922, 7½ *in.*

—— A Shropshire Lad [reprint]. *London, Richards Press*, 1930, 7½ *in.* Uncut

HOUSMAN, L. All Fellows: seven legends of lower redemption. *London, Kegan Paul*, 1896, 7½ *in.*

—— Bethlehem, a nativity play: The pageant of our Lady and other poems. *London, Macmillan*, 1902, 8 *in.* 'T. E. L.'

—— Gods and their Makers [1st ed.]. *London, Lane*, 1897, 8 in.

—— Green Arras. *London, Lane*, 1896, 7½ *in.* 'T. E. L. 1919'

—— The Heart of Peace and other poems. *London, Heinemann*, 1918, 7½ *in.* 'T. E. L.'

—— The Little Land, with songs from its four rivers. *London, Grant Richards*, 1899, 8 *in.* 'T. E. L.'

492

BOOKS AT CLOUDS HILL

HOUSMAN, L. Rue. *London, Unicorn*, 1899, 7½ *in.* Bookplate O. Brett. 'T. E. L.'

HOW, B. Into the Wilderness. *London, Houghton Publishing Co.*, 1931, 7½ *in.*

HOWARD, HENRY, EARL OF SURREY. The original poems of Henry Howard, Earl of Surrey [lim. ed., no. 137]. *London, Aquila Press*, 1929, 9 *in.* Brown leather ['M. to L. 25.12.29.'] 'T. E. S.'

HUBER, C. Journal d'un voyage en Arabie, 1883-1884. *Paris, Impr. Nationale*, 1891, 11 *in.*

HUDSON, W. H. Adventures among Birds [Collected works in 24 vols. lim. ed.]. *London, Dent*, 1923, 8½ *in.* 'T. E. S.'

—— El Ombu [Greenback Library]. *London, Duckworth*, 1902, 7 *in.* Red leather: C. & C. McLeish. ['T. E. L.' 'W. H. Hudson']

—— El Ombu [Greenback Library, no. 2]. *London, Duckworth*, 1902, 7½ *in.* Bookplate of Edward Garnett. ['T. E. L.' from E. G. 1919' on page before title-page. 'David Garnett' in pencil on flyleaf]

—— British Birds [Collected Works in 24 vols. lim. ed.]. *London, Dent*, 1923, 8½ *in.* 'T. E. S.'

—— Far Away and Long Ago: a history of my early life. *London, Dent*, 1918, 8½ *in.* 'T. E. L.'

—— Far Away and Long Ago: a history of my early life [Complete works in 24 vols. lim. ed.]. *London, Dent*, 1923, 8½ *in.* 'T. E. S.'

—— Green Mansions [New Reader's Library]. *London, Duckworth*, 1930, 7 *in.*

—— Green Mansions: a romance of the tropical forest. *London, Duckworth*, 1904, 7½ *in.* 'T. E. L.'

—— Green Mansions: a romance of the tropical forest [Reader's Library]. *London, Duckworth*, 1919, 7½ *in.*

—— A Hind in Richmond Park. *London, Dent*, 1922, 8½ *in.* 'T. E. L.'

—— Idle days in Patagonia, illustrated. *London, Chapman & Hall*, 1893, 9 *in.* 'T. E. L.'

—— Idle days in Patagonia [Coll. Works in 24 vols. lim. ed.]. *London, Dent*, 1933, 8½ *in.* 'T. E. S.'

—— Men, Books and Birds, Notes by Morley Roberts. *London, Eveleigh Nash*, 1925, 8½ *in.*

—— Nature in Downland, with a note by Edward Garnett [Collected works in 24 vols. lim. ed.]. *London, Dent*, 1923, 8½ *in.* 'T. E. L. c/o V. W. Richards, Pole Hill, Chingford, E.4'

—— The Naturalist in La Plata [Collected works in 24 vols. lim. ed.]. *London, Dent*, 1923, 8½ *in.* 'T. E. S.'

—— The Purple Land that England Lost. 2 vols. *London, Sampson, Low*, 1885, 7½ *in.*

HUDSON, W. H. A Shepherd's Life: impressions of the south Wiltshire downs [Collected works in 24 vols. lim. ed.]. *London, Dent*, 1923, 8½ *in.* 'T. E. S.'

HUEFFER, F. M. (F. M. FORD). It was the Nightingale [1st ed.]. *London, Heinemann*, 1934, 9 *in.*

—— Last Post [1st ed.]. *London, Duckworth*, 1928, 7½ *in.*

—— A Man could Stand Up: a novel. *London, Duckworth*, 1926, 7½ *in.*

—— No More Parades: a novel. *London, Duckworth*, 1925, 7½ *in.*

—— Some Do Not: a novel [4th impression]. *London, Duckworth*, 1929, 7½ *in.*

—— Thus to Revisit: some reminiscences. *London, Chapman & Hall*, 1921, 8½ *in.*

HUGHES, R. Gypsy-night, and other poems [8th book from Golden Cockerel Press. lim. ed.]. *Waltham St. Lawrence, Golden Cockerel Press*, 1922, 7 *in.* 'T. E. L.'

—— A High Wind in Jamaica [6th impression]. *London, Chatto & Windus*, 1931, 7½ *in.*

HUGO, V. Les Misérables, illus. par Brion. *Paris, Hekel & Lacroix*, 1869, 11½ *in.*

HUTCHINSON, LUCY. Memoirs of the Life of Colonel Hutchinson, by his widow, revised by C. H. Firth [new ed.]. [London Library] *London, Routledge*, 1906, 7½ *in.*

HUXLEY, A. Leda. *London, Chatto & Windus*, 1920, 8½ *in.* 'T. E. L.'

—— Little Mexican, and other stories. *London, Chatto & Windus*, 1924, 7½ *in.*

HUYSMANS, J.-K. Là-Bas. *Paris, Plon-Nourrit*, n.d., 7½ *in.* 'T. E. L.'

—— La Cathédrale. *Paris, Plon-Nourrit*, n.d., 7½ *in.* 'T. E. S.'

HYDE, D. The Love Songs of Connacht, being the fourth chapter of the songs of Connacht, col. and trans. by Douglas Hyde. *Dundrum, Dun Emer Press*, 1904, 8½ *in.*

IBSEN, H. The Pillars of Society, and other plays. Ed. with an introduction, by Havelock Ellis [Scott Library]. *London, Walter Scott Publishing Co.*, n.d., 7 *in.* 'T. E. L.'

IONICA. Ionica. *London, G. Allen*, 1891, 6½ *in.*

IRVING, W. Voyages and Discoveries of the companions of Columbus, with an introduction by the author, a foreword by Van Wyck Brooks and a decoration by Edward A. Wilson [Savoy Editions, issue no. 4, lim. ed., no. 77]. *New York, Rimington & Hooper*, 1929, 9½ *in.*

ISHAM, J. C. Winds and Tides. *New York, G. P. Putnam's Sons*, 1925, 8½ *in.* ['T. E. Shaw—from Ralph Isham—It's been hell—but worth it']

493

JACCACI, A. F. On the Trail of Don Quixote: rambles in La Mancha. *London, Lawrence & Bullen*, 1897, 8½ *in.*

JACOBSEN, J. P. Niels Lyhne, trans. by H. A. Larsen [2nd printing] [Scandinavian Classics, vol. 13]. *New York, American-Scandinavian Foundation*, 1930, 7½ *in.*

—— Marie Grubbe, a lady of the seventeenth century, trans. H. A. Larsen [Scandinavian Classics, vol. 7]. *New York, American-Scandinavian Foundation*, 1917, 7½ *in.* ['Edward Garnett']

JAMES, H. A Little tour in France, illus. by Joseph Pennell. *London, Heinemann*, 1900, 8 *in.* Bookplate of Richard Oliver

JEAN LE HOUX. The Vaux-de-Vire of Maître Jean le Houx, ed. and trans. by James Patrick Muirhead. *London, Murray*, 1875, 9 *in.* [Letter from J. P. Muirhead to H. Hamersley stuck in front]

JEFFERS, R. Cawdor [Hogarth living poets, 12]. *London, Hogarth Press*, 1929, 8 *in.*

—— Give your Heart to the Hawks, and other poems [2nd pr.]. *New York, Random House*, 1933, 8 *in.*

JEFFERIES, R. After London, or Wild England [pop. ed.]. *London, Duckworth*, 1908, 8 *in.*

—— Amaryllis at the fair: a novel. *London, Sampson Low*, 1887, 7½ *in.*

—— Bevis, the story of a boy [Reader's Library]. *London, Duckworth*, 1910, 7½ *in.*

—— Field and Hedgerow: last essays. *London, Longmans*, 1889, 7½ *in.*

—— The Life of the Fields. *London, Chatto & Windus*, 1884, 7½ *in.*

—— Nature near London. *London, Chatto & Windus*, 1893, 7½ *in.*

—— The Open Air. *London, Chatto & Windus*, 1885, 7½ *in.*

—— The Story of my Heart: my autobiography [7th imp.]. *London, Longmans, Green*, 1901, 7½ *in.*

JERUSALEM. Photographs of Jerusalem by J. Benor-Katter

—— 1920-1922. Being the records of the Pro-Jerusalem Society during the first two years of the civil adminstration. Ed. by C. R. Ashbee with a preface by Sir Ronald Storrs. *London, for Council of the Pro-Jerusalem Society*, 1924, 11½ *in.* 'T. E. L. from R. S. 7.11.24'

JOBSON, R. The golden trade, or, A discovery of the river Gambia and the golden trade of the Aethiopians. Set down as they were collected in travelling part of the years 1620 and 1621 [lim. ed., no. 39]. *London, Penguin Press*, 1932, 9 *in.* Vellum. 'T. E. S.'

JOCELIN OF BRAKELOND. The Chronicle of Jocelin of Brakelond, monk of St. Edmundsbury, trans. ed. L. C. Jane [King's Classics]. *Chatto & Windus*, 1907, 6 *in.* [Covered parchment paper: L. C. Jane '"He who strives to please all men, deserves to please none". Jocelin de Brakelond, p. 65. L. Cecil Jane']. 'T. E. L.'

JOHN, R. The Seventh Child: a retrospect [1st ed.]. *London, Heinemann*, 1932, 7½ *in.*

JOHNSON, L. Poetical works of Lionel Johnson [reprint]. *London, Elkin Mathews*, 1917, 7½ *in.*

—— Twenty-one poems written by Lionel Johnson: selected by William Butler Yeats. *Dundrum, Dun Emer*, 1904, 8½ *in.*

JONES, E. H. and HILL, C. W. The Road to En-dor: being an account of how two prisoners of war at Yozgad in Turkey won their way to freedom. *London, Lane*, 1920, 7½ *in.*

JONES, I. King of Air Fighters: biography of Major 'Mick' Mannock, V.C., D.S.O., M.C. [1st ed.]. *London, Ivor Nicholson & Watson*, 1934, 8½ *in.* ['With the compliments and very best wishes of the author. The story of one *Great* man to be read by another, please! Ira Jones. April 18th, 1935 (author's 39th birthday')]

JONSON, B. Masques and Entertainments, ed. by H. Morley [Carisbrooke Library, IX]. *London, Routledge*, 1890, 8 *in.*

JOYCE, J. Anna Livia Plurabelle, with a preface by Padraic Colum [lim. ed. signed by author, no. 652]. *New York, Crosby Gaige*, 1928, 7 *in.*

—— Dubliners [2nd print]. *New York, Huebsch*, 1917, 7½ *in.* 'T. E. L.'

—— Haveth Childers Everywhere [Criterion miscellany no. 26]. *London, Faber & Faber*, 1931, 8 *in.*

—— Pomes Penyeach. *Paris, Shakespeare*, 1927, 4½ *in.*

—— A Portrait of the Artist as a Young Man [2nd ed.]. *London, Egoist*, 1917, 7½ *in.*

—— Tales told of Shem and Shaun: three fragments from work in progress [lim. ed., no. 123]. *Paris, Black Sun Press*, 1929, 8½ *in.*

—— Ulysses [signed lim. ed., no. 36]. *Paris, Shakespeare*, 1922, 9½ *in.* MS. notes in text, by W. M. M. Hurley. Red leather, gold tooled, signed C. & C. McLeish. 'T. E. L.'

KEATS, J. Poems, ed. F. S. Ellis. *Hammersmith, Kelmscott Press*, 1894, 8 *in.* Vellum. 'T. E. L.'

KEMPIS, T. A. The Imitation of Christ. *Edinburgh, T & A. Constable*, n.d., 6½ *in.* Doves Bindery: gold tooled vellum. 'T. E. L. 1919'

KENNARD, C. Suhail. *London, Richards Press*, 1927, 8 *in.*

KER, W. P. Essays on Medieval Literature. *London, Macmillan*, 1905, 8 *in.* ['A. C. Harradine 19']

KEYNES, J. M. The Economic Consequences of Mr. Churchill. *London, Hogarth Press*, 1925, 8½ *in.*

KIERNAN, R. H. Captain Albert Ball: a historical record. *London, J. Hamilton Ltd.*, 1933, 8½ *in.*

—— The First War in the Air, with a preface by Air-Marshal Sir R. Brooke-Popham [1st ed.]. *London, Davies*, 1934, 8 *in.*

—— Little Brother goes Soldiering, intro. by Stephen Gwynn. *London, Constable*, 1930, 7½ *in.*

KINGLAKE, A. W. Eothen, or traces of travel brought home from the east [2nd ed.]. *London, J. Ollivier*, 1845, 9 *in.*

KIPLING, R. Works. 12 volumes in one. *New York, W. J. Black*, n.d., 7½ *in.*

—— Verse, inclusive edition, 1885-1918. *New York, Doubleday, Page*, 1919, 8½ *in.* Blue morocco French Binders: New York. 'T. E. L.'

—— The Gods of the Copybook Headings; The Scholars. Two pamphlets bound together. *New York, Doubleday, Page*, 1919, 8 *in.* Blue morocco: French Binders: Garden City, New York

—— Just So Stories for little Children, illus. by the author. *London, Macmillan*, 1902, 9 *in.*

—— Kim [reprint]. *London, Macmillan*, 1902, 8 *in.* Bookplate of Elizabeth Frances Fortescue

KLITGAARD, K. The Holy Land and Egypt, with a reproduction in colours of a map painted by Kaj Klitgaard. *New York, W. E. Rudge, for their friends*, 1927, 11 *in.*

KROG, H. Three plays; Happily Ever After?; Triad; The Copy; trans. by Roy Campbell. *London, Boriswood*, 1934, 7½ *in.*

LA FONTAINE. Forty-two Fables of La Fontaine, trans. by Edward Marsh. *London, Heinemann*, 1924, 8 *in.* ['T. E. Lawrence from Edward Marsh Nov. 19, 1924']

LAFORGUE, J. Oeuvres complètes. Moralités Légendaires. Les Deux Pigeons [11th edit.]. *Paris, Mercure de France*, 1921, 7½ *in.*

—— Moralités Légendaires. 2 vols., illus. by L. Pissaro [lim. ed.]. *London, Hacon & Ricketts*, 1907-8, 8½ *in.*

LAGERLÖF, S. Gösta Berling's Saga, trans. from the Swedish by L. Tudeer. 2 vols. [Scandinavian Classics]. *New York, American-Scandinavian Foundation*, 1918, 7½ *in.* 'T. E. L. from Edward Garnett, 1929'

LAMB, C. Essays of Elia. Last essays of Elia. 2 vols. [Library of English prose 1 & 2.] *Edinburgh, Foulis*, 1904-5, 8 *in.*

LA MOTTE, E. N. The Backwash of War: the human wreckage of the battlefield as witnessed by an American hospital nurse [4th impression]. *New York, Putnam*, 1916, 7 *in.* 'T. E. L.'

LANDOR, W. S. The Shorter Works of Walter Savage Landor. *London, George Newnes, Ltd.*, n.d., 7 *in.* Leather. 'T. E. L.'

—— Epicurus Leontion and Ternissa, decor. by C. Ricketts: Ballantyne Press [lim. ed.]. *London, Hacon & Ricketts*, n.d., 7½ *in.* Bookplate: H. G. & M. C. Bell. 'T. E. L. 1919'

LA SALE, A. DE. Le petit Jehan de Saintré. *Paris, J. Gillequin et Cie*, n.d., 7 *in.* 'T. E. L. Beauvais 1910'

LAWRENCE, D. H. Aaron's Rod [2nd print]. *New York, T. Seltzer*, 1922, 7½ *in.*

—— Amores: poems. *London, Duckworth*, n.d., 7½ *in.*

—— Bay: a book of poems, cover and decorations by Anne Estelle Rice [lim. ed., no. 125]. *Westminster, Beaumont Press*, 1919, 7½ *in.* 'T. E. L.'

—— Birds, Beasts & Flowers: poems with wood engravings by Blair Hughes-Stanton. *London, Cresset Press*, 1930, 13½ *in.*

—— England, My England. *London, Secker*, 1924, 7½ *in.* 'T. E. S.'

—— Kangaroo. *London, Secker*, 1923, 7½ *in.* 'T. E. S.'

—— Lady Chatterley's Lover [signed lim. ed., no. 824]. *N. pl., privately printed*, 1928, 9 *in.* Bound morocco. 'T. E. S.'

—— The Ladybird; The Fox; The Captain's Doll. *London, Secker*, 1923, 7½ *in.* 'T. E. S.'

—— Last Poems, ed. by Richard Aldington and Giuseppe Orioli [lim. ed., no. 429]. *Florence, G. Orioli*, 1932, 9½ *in.* 'T. E. S.'

—— Look! We have come Through! *New York, Huebsch*, 1919, 8½ *in.* 'T. E. L.'

—— The Lost Girl [reprint]. *London, Secker*, 1930, 7 *in.* 'T. E. S.'

—— Love among the Haystacks: and other pieces. With a reminiscence by David Garnett. *London, Nonesuch Press*, 1930, 9½ *in.*

—— Love Poems, and others. *London, Duckworth*, 1913, 8½ *in.* 'T. E. L.'

—— The Lovely Lady. *London, Secker*, 1932, 7½ *in.* 'T. E. S.'

—— The Man Who Died [lim. ed.]. *London, Secker*, 1931, 10 *in.* 'T. E. S.'

—— New Poems. *London, Secker*, 1918, 7½ *in.* 'T. E. L. Paris 1919'

—— Pansies and Poems. *London, Secker*, 1929, 9 *in.* 'T. E S.'

—— The Plumed Serpent. *London, Secker*, 1926, 7½ *in.*

—— The Prussian Officer, and other stories. *London, Duckworth*, 1914, 7½ *in.* 'Nov. 31. T. E. Shaw from Edward Garnett'

LAWRENCE, D. H. Sea and Sardinia, with eight pictures in colour by Jan Juta. *New York, Seltzer*, 1921, 9½ *in*. Picture from jacket stuck inside back cover. 'T. E. L.'

—— Sons and Lovers. *London, Duckworth*, 1913, 7½ *in*. 'T. E. L.'

—— Twilight in Italy [1st ed.]. *London, Duckworth*, 1916, 7½ *in*. 'T. E. L.'

—— The White Peacock. *London, Heinemann*, 1911, 7½ *in*. 'T. E. L.'

—— The Woman Who Rode Away, and other stories. *London, Secker*, 1928, 7½ *in*. 'T. E. S.'

—— Women In Love [signed ed., no. 6]. *New York, privately printed*, 1920, 9 *in*. 'T. E. L.'

—— and SKINNER, M. L. The Boy in the Bush [1st ed.]. *New York, Seltzer*, 1924, 7½ *in*. 'T. E. S.'

LECONTE DE LISLE. Oeuvres, 3 vols. Poèmes barbares. Poèmes tragiques. Rev. edit. Derniers poèmes. *Paris, A. Lemerre*, n.d., 6½ *in*. Pages uncut. 'T. E. Cairo, 1915'

—— Oeuvres, Poèmes Antiques. *Paris, A. Lemerre*, n.d., 6½ *in*. 233-317 uncut

LE CORBEAU, A. The Forest Giant, trans. from the French by J. H. Ross [1st ed.]. *London, Cape*, 1924, 7½ *in*. 'J. H. Ross' was a name assumed by T. E. Lawrence

LEDWIDGE, F. Last Songs. *London, Jenkins*, 1918, 7½ *in*. 'T. E. L.'

—— Songs of Peace, with an introduction by Lord Dunsany. *London, Jenkins*, 1917, 8 *in*. 'T. E. L.'

LEE, V. Hortus Vitae and Essays on the gardening of life. *London, Lane*, 1904, 7½ *in*.

LETHABY, W. R. Philip Webb and his work. *London, Oxford University Press*, 1935, 7½ *in*. 'T. E. Shaw from Sydney Cockerell, 4 March 1935'

LEWIS, C. DAY. Collected Poems 1919-1933. Transitional Poem: From Feathers to Iron: The Magnetic Mountain. *London, Hogarth Press*, 1935, 8½ *in*.

—— Beechen Vigil, and other poems. *London, Fortune Press*, 1925, 9 *in*. 'T. E. S.'

—— Country Comets. *London, Martin Hopkinson*, 1928, 7½ *in*.

—— Dick Willoughby. Tales of Action No. 11. *Oxford, Blackwell*, n.d., 8 *in*.

—— From Feathers to Iron [Hogarth Living Poets 22]. *London, Hogarth*, 1921, 7½ *in*.

—— From Feathers to Iron [2nd impression], Hogarth Living Poets no. 22]. *London, Hogarth Press*, 1932, 7½ *in*.

—— A Hope for Poetry. *Oxford, Blackwell*, 1934, 9 *in*.

—— A Time to Dance, and other poems [1st ed.]. *London, Hogarth Press*, 1935, 8½ *in*. ['T. E. Shaw from C. Day Lewis, March 1935']

LEWIS, C. DAY. Transitional Poem [Hogarth Living Poets, no. 9]. *London, Hogarth Press*, 1929, 7½ *in*. 2 copies. 'T. E. S.'

LEWIS, P. WYNDHAM. The Art of Being Ruled. *London, Chatto & Windus*, 1926, 9 *in*. 'To Col. Lawrence (of *Arabia*) from Wyndham Lewis'

—— Snooty Baronet. *London, Cassell*, 1932, 7½ *in*.

—— Tarr. *London, The Egoist Ltd.*, 1918, 7 *in*. 2 copies. On flyleaf of one 'T. E. L.'

—— The Wild Body. *London, Chatto & Windus*, 1927, 7½ *in*. 2 copies. 'T. E. S.'

LIDDELL, H. G. and SCOTT, R. A Greek-English Lexicon [5th ed. rev.]. *Oxford, Clarendon Press*, 1864, 10 *in*.

LLOYD, LORD. Egypt Since Cromer. 2 vols. *London, Macmillan*, 1933, 9 *in*. Presentation slip enclosed

LOCKHART, R. H. B. Memoirs of a British Agent [reprint]. *London, Putnam*, 1932, 8½ *in*.

LOEB CLASSICAL LIBRARY. Achilles Tatius; Aeschines; Appian: Roman history 1-4; Apuleius; Boethius; Caesar: Civil war; Cicero: Letters to Atticus 1 and 3; De Finibus; Clement of Alexandria; Daphnis and Chloe; Dio Roman history 1-6; Fronto; Galen: On the natural faculties; Greek anthology, 2, 3, 5; Greek Bucolic poets; Hesiod, Homeric hymns; Homer: Odyssey; St. John Damascene; Julian 1; Ovid: Metamorphoses 1; Heroides and Amores; Pausanias 1; Philostratus 1-2; Pindar; Procopius 1-3; Quintus Smyrnaeus; Strabo: Geography 1; Tacitus: Dialogus, Agricola, Germania; Theophrastus 1-2; Thucydides 1 [This set, complete at the time, was presented by Lord Riddell]

LONGUS. Daphnis and Chloe: a most sweet and pleasant pastoral romance for young ladies, done into English by Geo. Thorley, gent, illus. by C. Shanna and C. Ricketts [lim. ed.]. *London, Elkin Mathews* and *John Lane*, 1893, 11½ *in*. 'T. E. L.'

LOWELL, J. R. My Study Windows, intro. by Richard Garnett [Scott Library]. *London, W. Scott*, n.d., 6½ *in*.

LOWRY, M. Ultramarine, a novel [1st ed.]. *London, Cape*, 1933, 7½ *in*.

LUCAS, F. L. Ariadne. *Cambridge, Cambridge University Press*, 1932, 8 *in*.

—— Marionettes. *Cambridge, Cambridge University Press*, 1930, 7½ *in*.

—— Time and Memory [Hogarth Living Poets]. *London, Hogarth Press*, 1929, 7½ *in*.

LUCIAN. Lucian's True History, trans. by F. Hickes, illus. by W. Strang, J. B. Clark and

LUCIAN (*continued*)
A Beardsley [lim. ed.]. *London, A. H. Bullen*, 1902, 9 *in*. Suède

LUCRETIUS. T. Lucreti Cari de rerum natura libri sex. *Chelsea, in aed. St. J. Hornby*, 1913, 11 *in*. 'T. E. L.'

—— De rerum natura libri sex recogn. C. Bailey. ed. altera [Scrip. class. bibl. Oxon]. *Oxonii, Typ. Clarend.*, 1921, 7 *in*.

LUTHER, M. The Book of Vagabonds and Beggars, with a vocabulary of their language, first trans. by J. C. Hotten and now ed. anew by D. B. Thomas [lim. ed., no. 39]. *London, Penguin Press*, 1932, 9 *in*. Vellum. 'T. E. S.'

LYE, L. No Trouble [lim. ed., copy not numbered but inscribed 'T. E. S.' 'Len Lye' on page after title page]. *Deyá, Majorca, Seizin Press*, 1930, 11½ *in*.

MACAULAY, R. Told by an Idiot [4th print.]. *New York, Boni & Liveright*, 1924, 7½ *in*.

MCFEE, W. Command [signed and lim. ed., no. 324]. *New York, Doubleday, Page*, 1922, 8½ *in*.

—— The Harbourmaster. *New York, Doubleday, Doran*, 1932, 8 *in*.

MACHEN, A. Far Off Things [lim. ed., no. 34, signed]. *London, Secker*, 1922, 8½ *in*. 'T. E. L.'

—— The Great God Pan, and The Inmost Light [2nd ed.]. *London, Lane*, 1895, 7½ *in*.

—— The Hill of Dreams. *London, Grant Richards*, 1907, 7½ *in*. 'T. E. L.'

—— The London Adventure or the Art of Wandering. *London, Secker*, 1924, 8½ *in*. 'T. E. S.'

—— The Secret Glory. *London, Secker*, n.d., 7½ *in*. 'T. E. L.'

MACHIAVELLI, N. Machiavelli: vol. I. The Art of War, trans. by P. Whitehorne, 1560; The Prince, trans. by E. Dacres, 1640. Vol II. The Florentine History, trans. by T. Bedingfeld, 1595 [Tudor translations, ed. by W. E. Henley, vol. v 39 and 40]. *London, D. Nutt*, 1905, 8½ *in*.

MACKENZIE, C. The Darkening Green [1st ed.]. *London, Cassell*, 1934, 7½ *in*.

—— First Athenian Memories [War Memories, vol 2]. *London, Cassell*, 1931, 7½ *in*.

—— Gallipoli Memories [War Memories, vol 1]. *London, Cassell*, 1929, 7½ *in*.

—— Greek Memories [1st ed.]. *London, Cassell*, 1932, 7½ *in*.

—— Guy and Pauline [1st ed.]. *London, Secker*, 1915, 7½ *in*. Bookplate of Capt. Mansfield Smith-Cumming. ['For C., Compton Mackenzie, August 12. 20']

MACKENZIE, C. Sinister Street, 2 vols. [vol. I 9th imp.]. *London, Secker*, 1914-16, 7½ *in*. Vol. I black cloth; vol. II red cloth

—— Vestal Fire [1st ed.]. *London, Cassell*, 1927, 7½ *in*.

—— Water on the Brain [1st ed.]. *London, Cassell*, 1933, 7½ *in*.

MACLEISH, A. Conquistador [1st ed. lim.]. *London, Gollancz*, 1933, 9 *in*.

MACLEOD, D. Memoirs of the Life and Gallant Exploits of the old Highlander Serjeant Donald Macleod (1688-1791). Reprinted from the original edition of 1791 with intro. and notes by J. G. Fyfe. *London, Blackie*, 1933, 9 *in*.

MACLEOD, J. G. The Ecliptic. *London, Faber & Faber*, 1930, 8½ *in*. Mostly uncut pages

MACMICHAEL, H. A. A history of the Arabs in the Sudan and some account of the people who preceded them and of the tribes inhabiting Dárfur. 2 vols. *Cambridge University Press*, 1922, 9½ *in*. Containing author's complimentary slip. Not cut

MACNAMARA, F. Marionettes. *London, Elkin Mathews*, 1909, 7½ *in*. 'T. E. L.'

MCPHEE, F. Apocalypse of Love. *London, Boriswood*, 1933, 8½ *in*.

MACPHERSON, IAN. Land of Our Fathers. *London, Cape*, 1933, 7½ *in*.

MAGNUS, M. Memoirs of the Foreign Legion, by M. M., intro. by D. H. Lawrence. *London, Secker*, 1924, 7½ *in*. 'T. E. S.'

MALORY, SIR T. Le Morte d'Arthur, 2 vols. [Everyman's Library]. *London, Dent*, 1908, 7 *in*.

MANDEVILLE, SIR J. Travels. Version of the Cotton MS. in modern spelling [Library of English Classics]. *London, Macmillan*, 1900, 9 *in*. 'T. E. L.'

MANN, T. The Magic Mountain, trans. by H. T. Lowe-Porter [reprint]. *London, Secker*, 1932, 7½ *in*.

—— Der Tod in Venedig. *Berlin, S. Fischer*, 1913, 7½ *in*. 'T. E. L. 1913'

MANNING, F. Eidola. *London, J. Murray*, 1917, 7 *in*.

—— The Life of Sir William White. *London, J. Murray*, 1923, 9 *in*. 'T. E. Shaw from Frederick Manning, 20.11.1932'

—— The Middle Parts of Fortune: Somme and Ancre, 1916, 2 vols. [lim. ed., no 86: ordinary ed. issued as 'Her Privates We']. *London, Piazza Press*, 1929, 7½ *in*.

—— Poems. *London, Murray*, 1910, 7 *in*.

—— Scenes and Portraits. *London, Murray*, 1909, 7½ *in*.

—— Scenes and Portraits [new rev. ed., of which 250 copies signed by author, no. 101]. *London, P. Davies*, 1930, 8½ *in*. Uncut

MANNING, F. The Vigil of Brunhild: a narrative poem. *London, Murray*, 1907, $7\frac{1}{2}$ *in.*

MANSFIELD, K. Bliss, and Other Stories. *London, Constable*, 1920, 7 *in.*

MARCH, W. Company K. *London, Gollancz*, 1933, $7\frac{1}{2}$ *in.*

MARCHESINUS J. Mamotrectus. Venice, F. de Hailbrun and N. de Frankfordia, 1476, $8\frac{1}{2}$ in. [Last 3 pp. missing]

MARIE DE FRANCE. Poésies, publiées par B. de Roquefort, 2 vols. *Paris, Chasserian*, 1820, $8\frac{1}{2}$ *in.* Half calf

MARLOWE, C. Christopher Marlowe, ed. by Havelock Ellis, intro. by J. A. Symonds [Mermaid Series]. *London, T. Fisher Unwin*, n.d., $9\frac{1}{2}$ *in.*

—— Plays and Poems. *London, Simpkin Marshall*, n.d., $6\frac{1}{2}$ *in.*

MARSON, T. B. 'Twixt Grass and Plough. *London, Pitman*, 1934, $8\frac{1}{2}$ *in.*

MARVELL, A. Miscellaneous Poems [lim. ed., no. 327]. *London, Nonesuch Press*, 1923, $10\frac{1}{2}$ *in.* 'T. E. S.'

MASEFIELD, J. Ballads and Poems [tenth thousand]. *London, Elkin Mathews*, 1918, $7\frac{1}{2}$ *in.* 'T. E. L. Paris 1919'

—— Captain Margaret. [Travellers' Library]. *London, Cape*, 1927, 7 *in.*

—— Enslaved and other Poems. *London, Heinemann*, 1920, $7\frac{1}{2}$ *in.* 'T. E. L.'

—— Salt-water Ballads [6th ed.]. *London, Elkin Mathews*, 1918, $7\frac{1}{2}$ *in.* 'T. E. L. Paris 1919'

MATTHEWS, K. Greek Salad: an autobiography of Greek travel. *London, P. Davies*, 1935, 8 *in.*

MAUGHAM, W. S. Ah King [lim. ed., no. 148 signed]. *London, Heinemann*, 1933, $8\frac{1}{2}$ *in.* Pages uncut

—— Cakes and Ale, or the Skeleton in the cupboard [new imp.]. *London, Heinemann*, 1930, $7\frac{1}{2}$ *in.*

—— Six Stories written in the first person singular. *London, Heinemann*, 1931, $7\frac{1}{2}$ *in.*

MAUPASSANT, G. DE. Boule de Suif et Le Vengeur, illus. by F. Money. [Conteurs et Poètes]. *Paris, Ferroud*, 1919, 7 *in.* Half-calf

—— Stories from de Maupassant, trans. by E. M., pref. by Ford M. Hueffer [re-issue]. *London, Duckworth*, 1910, 7 *in.* 'T. E. L.'

MELVILLE, H. The Works of Herman Melville, Standard edition, vols. 1-12, 16. Vol. I, Typee [lim. ed., no. 51]19 22; vol. II, Omoo, 1922; III and IV, Mardi and a Voyage Thither, 1922; V, Redburn, 1922; VI, White Jacket, 1922; VII and VIII, Moby Dick, 1922; IX, Pierre, 1923; X, The Piazza Tales, 1923; XI, Israel Potter, 1923; XII, The Confidence Man, 1923; XVI, Poems, containing Battle pieces, John Marr and other sailors, Timolea, and miscellaneous poems, 1924. *London, Constable*, 1923-24, 9 *in.*

MELVILLE, H. Israel Potter: his fifty years of exile. *Lndon, Jarrolds*, 1925, 8 *in.*

—— Moby Dick or the whale, illus. by Rockwell Kent. *London, Cassell*, 1930, 7 *in.*

MEREDITH, G. The Ordeal of Richard Feverel. *London, Constable*, 1919, $6\frac{1}{2}$ *in.* 'T. E. L.'

—— Selected Poems. *Westminster, Archibald Constable*, 1897, 8 *in.* 'T. E. L.'

MEREJKOWSKI, D. The Death of the Gods, trans. by Herbert Trench [3rd ed.]. *London, Constable*, 1904, 7 *in.* 'T. E. L.'

MÉRIMÉE, P. Carmen, etc. [62nd ed.] [Oeuvres compl.]. *Paris, Callmann-Lévy*, n.d., $7\frac{1}{2}$ *in.*

—— Colomba: La Vénus d'Ille: Les Ames du purgatoire [Oeuvres compl.]. *Paris, Calmann-Lévy*, 1920, $7\frac{1}{2}$ *in.* Pages uncut

MEW, C. The Rambling Sailor [1st ed.]. *London, Poetry Bookshop*, 1929, 8 *in.*

MEYER, K. Selections from Ancient Irish Poetry, trans. by Kuno Meyer [2nd ed.]. *London, Constable*, 1913, $7\frac{1}{2}$ in.

MEYNELL, A. Last Poems. *London, Burns Oates*, 1923, $7\frac{1}{2}$ *in.* [Pages uncut]

MEYNELL, E. The Life of Francis Thompson. *London, Burns Oates*, 1918, 8 *in.*

MICHAEL ANGELO BUONARROTI. The Sonnets of Michael Angelo Buonarroti, trans. into English by John Addington Symonds [3rd ed.]. *London, Smith Elder*, 1912, 7 *in.*

MILTON, J. Areopagitica: a speech of Mr. John Milton for the liberty of unlicensed printing, to the parliament of England [lim. ed., 2nd issue]. *London, Eragny Press*, 1904, 11 *in.*

—— Paradise Lost [Harrap Library]. *London, Harrap*, 1909, 7 *in.*

—— Paradise Lost: a poem in XII books. *Hammersmith, Doves Press*, 1902, $9\frac{1}{2}$ *in.* Vellum

—— Paradise Regain'd: a poem in IV books to which are added Samson Agonistes and Poems both English and Latin compos'd on several occasions. *Hammersmith, Doves Press*, 1905, $9\frac{1}{2}$ *in.* Vellum. 'T. E. L.'

MOALLAKA. The Seven Poems, suspended in the temple at Mecca, trans. from the Arabic by F. E. Johnson. *Bombay, Education Society*, 1893, $8\frac{1}{2}$ *in.* 'T. E. L.'

—— The Seven Golden Odes of Pagan Arabia, known also as the Moallakat, trans. by Lady Anne Blunt: done into English verse by Wilfrid Scawen Blunt. *London, Chiswick Press*, 1903, $9\frac{1}{2}$ *in.* Half-title cut. Blue calf: C. & C. McLeish. 'T. E. L.' 4th flyleaf 'T. E. Lawrence'

—— The Poem of Amriolkais: one of the

MOALLAKA (*continued*)
seven Arabian poems or Moallaka which were suspended on the temple at Mecca, rendered into English by Sir William Jones. Reprint. Wood-engravings by Eileen Mayo [lim. ed., 134]. *Shaftesbury, High House Press*, 1930, 9 *in.* 'T. E. S.'

MONARDES, N. Joyfull newes out of the new founde worlde. Englished by J. Frampton, intro. by S. Gaselee. 2 vols. [lim. ed.]. *London, Constable*, 1925, $8\frac{1}{2}$ *in.*

MONTAGUE, C. E. Dramatic Values. *London, Methuen*, 1911, 7 *in.* ['Edward Garnett, Feb. 1911.'] Review copy

—— A Hind let Loose [4th ed.]. *London, Methuen*, 1923, $7\frac{1}{2}$ *in.*

MONTAIGNE. The Essays of Montaigne done into English by J. Florio anno 1603, with an intro. by Saintsbury. 3 vols. [Tudor translations, ed. by W. E. Henley, vols. 1-3]. *London, D. Nutt*, 1892-3, $8\frac{1}{2}$ *in.* 'T. E. L.'

MONTESQUIEU. Oeuvres, 2 vols. *Paris, Jean Gilleguin*, n.d., 7 *in.* 'Carentan, -.8.10' on 3rd flyleaf. 'T. E. L.'

MOORE, G. Aphrodite in Aulis [new and rev. ed.]. *London, Heinemann*, 1931, 9 *in.*

—— Avowals. *London, Heinemann*, 1924, $8\frac{1}{2}$ *in.*

—— The Brook Kerith: a Syrian story, with twelve engravings by Stephen Gooden [lim. ed., no 344. Signed George Moore, Stephen Gooden]. *London, Heinemann*, 1929, $10\frac{1}{2}$ *in.* Vellum

—— Esther Waters: a novel [1st ed.]. *London, W. Scott*, 1894, $7\frac{1}{2}$ *in.* 'T. E. L.'

—— Evelyn Innes [1st ed.]. *London, Fither Unwin*, 1898, 8 *in.* 'T. E. L.'

—— Hail and Farewell. 3 vols. [var. ed.]. *London, Heinemann*, 1912-19, $7\frac{1}{2}$ *in.*

—— The Lake. *London, Heinemann*, 1905, $7\frac{1}{2}$ *in*

—— The Untilled Field [1st ed.]. *London, Fisher Unwin*, 1903, $7\frac{1}{2}$ *in.* 'T. E. L.'

—— Vain Fortune, with eleven illustrations by Maurice Greiffenhagen [1st ed.]. *London, Henry*, n.d., 8 *in.*

MOORE, T. Lalla Rookh, an oriental romance, illustrated with engravings [20th ed.]. *London, Longmans*, 1842, 9 *in.* Gold tooled leather: A. R. K.

MORE, SIR T. Utopia [trans. by Ralph Robinson 1551: reprinted lim. ed. on vellum]. *Chelsea, Ashendene Press*, 1906, 11 *in.* Green morocco: W. H. S. 'T. E. L.'

MORGAN, C. Portrait in a Mirror. *London, Macmillan*, 1929, $7\frac{1}{2}$ *in.* ['T. E. L. from E. G.']

MORIER, J. The Adventures of Hajji Baba of Ispahan. 2 vols. [English Classics]. *London, Methuen*, 1895, $7\frac{1}{2}$ *in.* 'T. E. L. Oxford, 1909'

MORLEY, C. 'Effendi', Frank Nelson Doubleday, 1862-1934. *N. pl., privately printed*, 1934, 8 *in.*

MORLEY, F. and F. V. Inversive Geometry. *London, Bell*, 1933, $8\frac{1}{2}$ *in.* 'For T. E. S. F. V. M.'

MORRIS, W. Art and its Producers, and The Arts and Crafts of to-day: two addresses delivered before the National Association for the Advancement of Art. *London, Longmans*, 1901, $8\frac{1}{2}$ *in.*

—— The Earthly Paradise. *London, Longmans, Green & Co.*, 1910, $8\frac{1}{2}$ *in.* ['H. B.']

—— The Earthly Paradise, 8 vols. *Hammersmith, Kelmscott Press*, 1896-7, $9\frac{1}{2}$ *in.* Limp vellum. 'T. E. L.'

—— The Hollow Land, and other contributions to the Oxford and Cambridge Magazine [reproduced at Chiswick Press with the Golden type designed by W. Morris for Kelmscott Press]. *London, Longmans*, 1903, $8\frac{1}{2}$ *in.* Vellum. 'T. E. L. Finals 1910'

—— The Life and Death of Jason: a poem. [9th ed.]. *London, Longmans*, 1897, $7\frac{1}{2}$ *in.* Brown suède. 'T. E. L.'

—— Love is Enough, or the Freeing of Pharamond: a morality. *Hammersmith, Kelmscott Press*, 1897, $11\frac{1}{2}$ *in.* Vellum. Book plate 'Ex libris: T. J. Cobden-Sanderson.' 'T. E. L.'

—— News from Nowhere. *Hammersmith, Kelmscott Press*, 1892, 8 *in.* Vellum limp. 'T. E. L.'

—— Poems by the Way. *Hammersmith, Kelmscott Press*, 1891, 8 *in.* Vellum. 'T. E. L.'

—— The Roots of the Mountains, wherein is told somewhat of the lives of the men of Burgdale [reproduced at Chiswick Press with Golden type designed by W. Morris]. *London, Longmans*, 1901, $11\frac{1}{2}$ *in.*

—— The Story of Sigurd the Volsung and the Fall of the Niblungs, with two pictures designed by E. Burne-Jones and engraved by W. H. Hooper. *Hammersmith, Kelmscott Press*, 1898, 13 *in.* Limp vellum. 'T. E. L.'

—— The Story of the glittering plain which has also been called the land of living men or the acre of the undying [reprinted]. *London, Longmans, Green & Co.*, 1904, $7\frac{1}{2}$ *in.* ['T. E. L.' 'V. W. R.']

—— A Tale of the House of the Wolfings and all the kindreds of the Mark, written in prose and in verse by William Morris. [Printed at the Chiswick Press with the Golden type designed by Morris for the Kelmscott Press.] *London, Longmans, Green & Co.*, 1901, $11\frac{1}{2}$ *in.* 'T. E. L.'

LITERATURE

MORRIS, W. The Sundering Flood. *Hammersmith, Kelmscott Press*, 1897, 8½ *in.* 'T. E. L.'

—— The Water of the Wondrous Isles. *Hammersmith, Kelmscott Press*, 1897, 11½ *in.* Vellum. 'T. E. L.'

—— The Well at the World's End. *Hammersmith, Kelmscott Press*, 1896, 11 *in.* Vellum: gold stamped crest stuck inside back cover. 'T. E. L. 1911, Carchemish'

—— The Wood Beyond the World. *London, Longmans*, 1904, 7½ *in.* 'T. E. L. Salisbury, 1910'

MOTTRAM, R. H. The Spanish Farm Trilogy 1914-1918 [reprint]. *London, Chatto & Windus*, 1927, 7½ *in.*

MÜCKE, H. VON. The 'Ayesha', a great adventure. The escape of the landing squad of the *Emden*. Ed. by J. G. Lockhart [2nd ed., Nautilus Library]. *London, P. Allan*, 1933, 7 *in.*

MUNRO, H. H. Reginald, by Saki [4th ed.]. *London, Methuen*, 1915, 6½ *in.* 'T. E. L.'

—— Short Stories of Saki, complete with an intro. by Christopher Morley [reprint]. *London, Lane*, 1932, 7½ *in.*

MYERS, E. Gathered Poems. *London, Macmillan*, 1904, 7½ *in.* 'T. E. L.'

MYERS, L. H. The Orissers [signed lim. ed., no. 198]. *London, Putnam's*, 1922, 10 *in.*

NAMIER, L. B. England in the Age of the American Revolution. *London, Macmillan*, 1930, 9 *in.* Contains author's complimentary slip

—— Skyscrapers and other essays. *London, Macmillan*, 1931, 8 *in.*

NAPIER, M. Songs of the Dead, with an intro. by Edward Garnett. *London, Lane*, 1920, 9 *in.* 'T. E. L.'

NASH, T. The Unfortunate Traveller, ed. by P. Henderson, illus. by H. Mackey. Hand-coloured illustrations and decorations [lim. ed., no. 62]. *London, Verona Society*, 1930, 9 *in.*

NEW TESTAMENT. Η Καινη Διαθηκη juxta exemplar millianum. *Oxonii, Typ. Clarend.*, 1825, 7 *in.*

—— Η Καινη Διαθηκη . . . acc. Canones Eusebii. *Oxonii, Typ. Clarend.*, 1863, 6½ *in.*

NICHOLS, R. Aurelia and other poems. *London, Chatto & Windus*, 1920, 7½ *in.* 'T. E. L.'

NICOLSON, H. Some People. *London, Constable*, 1927, 7½ *in.* ['Dear T. E. S., I've been sitting here with Mr. Wilson talking about you far off in Karachi, with all the Sind Desert stretching out behind you. I may be out again next year. Best of luck to you as always. Kermit Roosevelt. See p. 219 J. G. W.'] [Ref. to T. E. L. on p. 219]

NIETZSCHE, F. The Joyful Wisdom, trans. by Thomas Common [2nd ed., no. 346] [Complete Works, vol. 10]. *Edinburgh, T. N. Foulis*, 1910, 8 *in.* 'T. E. L.'

—— Thus Spake Zarathustra: a book for all and none, trans. by A. Tille [2nd imp. of this translation]. *London, T. Fisher Unwin*, 1908, 9½ *in.* ['Leonard Williams']

—— The Twilight of the Idols, The Antichrist. Notes to Zarathustra, and Eternal Recurrence, trans. by A. M. Ludovici. [2nd ed., no. 662] [Complete Works, vol. 16]. *Edinburgh, T. N. Foulis*, 1915, 8 *in.* 'T. E. L.'

O'CASEY, S. The Silver Tassie: a tragi-comedy. *London, Macmillan*, 1928, 7½ *in.*

—— Two Plays. Juno and the Paycock; The Shadow of a Gunman. *London, Macmillan*, 1925, 7½ *in.*

—— Within the Gates: a play of four scenes in a London Park. *London, Macmillan*, 1933, 7½ *in.*

O'FAOLÁIN, S. A Nest of Simple Folk. *London, Cape*, 1933, 7½ *in.*

O'FLAHERTY, L. The Fairy Goose and two other stories [lim. ed. signed by author, no. 524]. *New York, Crosby Gaige*, 1927, 6½ *in.*

O'GRADY, S. The Bog of Stars, and other stories and sketches of Elizabethan Ireland. *London, Fisher Unwin*, 1893, 6½ *in.*

OMAR KHAYYÁM. Rubaiyat of Omar Khayyám the astronomer-poet of Persia rendered into English verse by Edward Fitzgerald [lim. ed., no. 47]. *London, for the Medici Society*, 1913, 9½ *in.* 'T. E. L.'

O'SULLIVAN, M. Twenty Years a-growing, rendered from the original Irish by Moya Llewelyn Davies and George Thomson. Intro. note by E. M. Forster. *London, Chatto & Windus*, 1933, 8½ *in.*

OWEN, W. Poems. Intro. by Siegfried Sassoon. *London, Chatto & Windus*, 1920, 8½ *in.* 'T. E. L.'

—— The Poems of Wilfred Owen. A new edition including many pieces now first published, and notices of his life and work by Edmund Blunden [special ed., no. 7]. *London, Chatto & Windus*, 1931, 9 *in.*

OXFORD DICTIONARY. The Shorter Oxford English Dictionary, revised edition by C. T. Onions, 2 vols. *Oxford, Clarendon Press*, 1933, 11 *in.*

PAGET, J. The New 'Examiner', with a critical intro. by Winston S. Churchill [signed lim. ed., no. 4]. *N. pl., Haworth Press*, 1934, 10 *in.* Red leather: Sangorski & Sutcliffe. 'To Lurens from Winston, Chartwell, February 1934'

500

BOOKS AT CLOUDS HILL

PAINE, H. S. 'Miss Britain III': Album of photos, presented by H. S. Paine

PALGRAVE, W. G. Narrative of a year's journey through Central and Eastern Arabia, 1862-63. 2 vols. *London, Macmillan*, 1865, 8½ *in.*

PALMER, H. In Autumn [lim. ed., no 55]. *London, privately printed*, 1931, 9½ *in.*

PALMER, H. E. Summit and Chasm: a book of poems and rimes. *London, Dent*, 1934, 7 *in.*

PATER, W. Imaginary Portraits [reprint]. *London, Macmillan*, 1907, 8 *in.* ['V. W. R.] MS. notes? on front cover

—— Marius the Epicurean, 2 vols. [Riccardi Press Books, lim. ed., no. 328]

PATMORE, C. The Angel in the House, 2 vols. *London, Macmillan*, 1863, 6½ *in.*

PEACOCK, T. L. Gryll Grange, intro. by George Saintsbury. *London, Macmillan*, 1896, 7½ *in.* Pages uncut

—— The Misfortunes of Elphin [lim. ed., no. 83]. *Newtown, Montgomeryshire, Gregynog Press*, 1928, 9½ *in.*

—— Songs from the novels of Thomas Love Peacock [York Library, lim. ed., no. 8]. *London, R. Brimley Johnson*, n.d., 5½ *in.* 'T. E. L.'

PEPYS, S. Diary, ed. by Lord Braybrooke. *London, Simpkin Marshall*, n.d., 6½ *in.* 'T. E. L.'

—— The Diary of Samuel Pepys, ed. with additions by H. B. Wheatley. 3 vols. *London, Bell*, 1928, 7½ *in.*

PETRIE, SIR W. M. F. Tanis: pt. 1, 1883-4. 2nd memoir of the Egypt Exploration Fund. *London, Trübner*, 1885, 12½ *in.*

PICKTHALL, M. Oriental encounters, Palestine and Syria, 1894-1896. *New York, Knopf*, 1927, 8 *in.*

—— Said the Fisherman [Blue Jade Library]. *New York, Knopf*, 1925, 8 *in.*

PILCHER, VELONA. The Searcher: a war play. Reading version with 9 wood engravings by Blair Hughes-Stanton [lim. 1st ed.]. *London, Heinemann*, 1929, 10 *in.*

'PINCHBECK LYRE'. Poems by Pinchbeck Lyre. *London, Duckworth*, 1931, 7½ *in.*

PINDAR. Carmina cum deperditorum fragmentis selectis iterum rec. W. Christ. *Lipsiae, B. G. Teubner*, 1896, 7 *in.* 'T. E. L.'

—— The Extant Odes, trans. by E. Myers. *London, Macmillan*, 1908. 7½ *in.* 'T. E. L.'

PIRANDELLO, L. Three plays: Six characters; Henry IV; Right you are [4th print]. *London, Dent*, 1925, 7½ *in.* ['C. Stirling, F. O.']

PLOMER, W. The Case is Altered [1st ed.]. *London, Hogarth Press*, 1932, 7½ *in.*

PLOMER, W. The Fivefold Screen [signed lim. ed., no. 8]. *London, Hogarth Press*, 1932, 10½ *in.*

PLUTARCH. Plutarch's lives of the noble Grecians and Romans, Englished by Sir Thomas North anno 1579, with an introduction by George Wyndham, 6 vols. [Tudor Translations, ed. by W. E. Henley, nos. 7-12]. *London, D. Nutt*, 1895-6, 8½ *in.* 'T. E. L.'

POCOCK, G. N. Modern prose, chosen by Guy N. Pocock [King's Treasuries of Literature]. *London, Dent*, 1925, 6 *in.*

POLO, M. The Travels of Marco Polo, trans. by A. Ricci, with an intro. and index by E. Denison Ross [Broadway Travellers]. *London, Routledge*, 1931, 9 *in.*

PORPHYRY. On the cave of the nymphs in the thirteenth book of the Odyssey, trans. by T. Taylor. *London, J. M. Watkins*, 1917, 7 *in.* MS. annotations

PORTER, A. The Signature of Pain, and other poems. *London, Cobden-Sanderson*, 1930, 9 *in.*

POUND, E. Selected Poems, ed. by T. S. Eliot [lim. ed., no. 5, signed]. *London, Faber & Gwyer*, 1928, 7½ *in.*

—— Canzoni. *London, Elkin Mathews*, 1911, 6½ *in.*

—— A Draft of XXX Cantos [lim. ed., no. 38). *Paris, Hours Press*, 1930, 8 *in.*

—— Exultations. *London, Elkin Mathews*, 1909, 6½ *in.* 'T. E. L.'

—— Personae of Ezra Pound [1st ed.]. *London, Elkin Mathews*, 1909, 7 *in.* 'T. E. L.'

POWYS, L. Damnable Opinions [1st ed.]. *London, Watts*, 1935, 7½ *in.*

—— Damnable Opinions [1st ed.]. *London, Watts*, 1935, 7½ *in.* [Card 'With the compliments of Mr. Llewelyn Powys, Chydyck, Chaldon Herring, Feb. 1935']

—— Skin for Skin [lim. ed., no. 657]. *London, Cape*, 1926, 9 *in.*

POWYS, T. F. Black Bryony: with five woodcuts by R. A. Garnett. *London, Chatto & Windus*, 1923, 7½ *in.* Some pages uncut

—— Fables, with four drawings by Gilbert Spencer. *London, Chatto & Windus*, 1929, 9 *in.*

—— Mark Only. *London, Chatto & Windus*, 1924, 7½ *in.*

—— Mockery Gap. *London, Chatto & Windus*, 1925, 7½ *in.*

—— Mr. Tasker's Gods. *London, Chatto & Windus*, 1925, 7½ *in.* 'T. E. S.'

—— The Two Thieves: In Good Earth; God; The Two Thieves. *London, Chatto & Windus*, 1932, 7½ *in.*

PREWETT, F. Poems. *Richmond, Hogarth Press for the author*, n.d., 9 *in.*

501

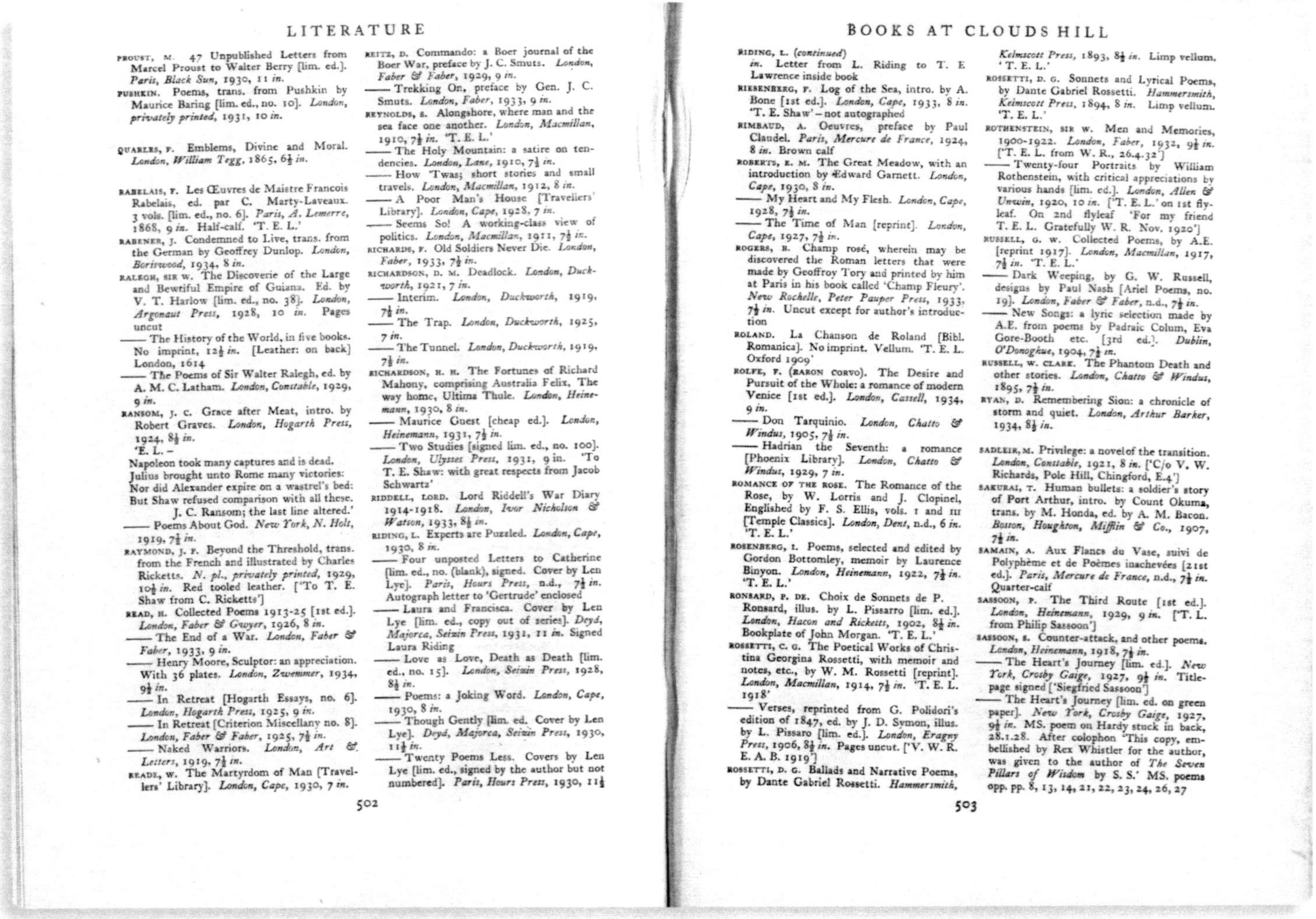

LITERATURE

PROUST, M. 47 Unpublished Letters from Marcel Proust to Walter Berry [lim. ed.]. *Paris, Black Sun*, 1930, 11 *in.*

PUSHKIN. Poems, trans. from Pushkin by Maurice Baring [lim. ed., no. 10]. *London, privately printed*, 1931, 10 *in.*

QUARLES, F. Emblems, Divine and Moral. *London, William Tegg*, 1865, 6½ *in.*

RABELAIS, F. Les Œuvres de Maistre Francois Rabelais, ed. par C. Marty-Laveaux. 3 vols. [lim. ed., no. 6]. *Paris, A. Lemerre*, 1868, 9 *in.* Half-calf. 'T. E. L.'

RABENER, J. Condemned to Live, trans. from the German by Geoffrey Dunlop. *London, Boriswood*, 1934, 8 *in.*

RALEGH, SIR W. The Discoverie of the Large and Bewtiful Empire of Guiana. Ed. by V. T. Harlow [lim. ed., no. 38]. *London, Argonaut Press*, 1928, 10 *in.* Pages uncut

—— The History of the World, in five books. No imprint, 12½ *in.* [Leather: on back] London, 1614

—— The Poems of Sir Walter Ralegh, ed. by A. M. C. Latham. *London, Constable*, 1929, 9 *in.*

RANSOM, J. C. Grace after Meat, intro. by Robert Graves. *London, Hogarth Press*, 1924, 8½ *in.*
'E. L. –
Napoleon took many captures and is dead.
Julius brought unto Rome many victories:
Nor did Alexander expire on a wastrel's bed:
But Shaw refused comparison with all these.
J. C. Ransom; the last line altered.'

—— Poems About God. *New York, N. Holt*, 1919, 7½ *in.*

RAYMOND, J. F. Beyond the Threshold, trans. from the French and illustrated by Charles Ricketts. *N. pl., privately printed*, 1929, 10½ *in.* Red tooled leather. ['To T. E. Shaw from C. Ricketts']

READ, H. Collected Poems 1913-25 [1st ed.]. *London, Faber & Gwyer*, 1926, 8 *in.*

—— The End of a War. *London, Faber & Faber*, 1933, 9 *in.*

—— Henry Moore, Sculptor: an appreciation. With 36 plates. *London, Zwemmer*, 1934, 9½ *in.*

—— In Retreat [Hogarth Essays, no. 6]. *London, Hogarth Press*, 1925, 9 *in.*

—— In Retreat [Criterion Miscellany no. 8]. *London, Faber & Faber*, 1925, 7½ *in.*

—— Naked Warriors. *London, Art & Letters*, 1919, 7½ *in.*

READE, W. The Martyrdom of Man [Travellers' Library]. *London, Cape*, 1930, 7 *in.*

REITZ, D. Commando: a Boer journal of the Boer War, preface by J. C. Smuts. *London, Faber & Faber*, 1929, 9 *in.*

—— Trekking On, preface by Gen. J. C. Smuts. *London, Faber*, 1933, 9 *in.*

REYNOLDS, S. Alongshore, where man and the sea face one another. *London, Macmillan*, 1910, 7½ *in.* 'T. E. L.'

—— The Holy Mountain: a satire on tendencies. *London, Lane*, 1910, 7½ *in.*

—— How 'Twas; short stories and small travels. *London, Macmillan*, 1912, 8 *in.*

—— A Poor Man's House [Travellers' Library]. *London, Cape*, 1928, 7 *in.*

—— Seems So! A working-class view of politics. *London, Macmillan*, 1911, 7½ *in.*

RICHARDS, F. Old Soldiers Never Die. *London, Faber*, 1933, 7½ *in.*

RICHARDSON, D. M. Deadlock. *London, Duckworth*, 1921, 7 *in.*

—— Interim. *London, Duckworth*, 1919, 7½ *in.*

—— The Trap. *London, Duckworth*, 1925, 7 *in.*

—— The Tunnel. *London, Duckworth*, 1919, 7½ *in.*

RICHARDSON, H. H. The Fortunes of Richard Mahony, comprising Australia Felix, The way home, Ultima Thule. *London, Heinemann*, 1930, 8 *in.*

—— Maurice Guest [cheap ed.]. *London, Heinemann*, 1931, 7½ *in.*

—— Two Studies [signed lim. ed., no. 100]. *London, Ulysses Press*, 1931, 9 in. 'To T. E. Shaw: with great respects from Jacob Schwartz'

RIDDELL, LORD. Lord Riddell's War Diary 1914-1918. *London, Ivor Nicholson & Watson*, 1933, 8½ *in.*

RIDING, L. Experts are Puzzled. *London, Cape*, 1930, 8 *in.*

—— Four unposted Letters to Catherine [lim. ed., no. (blank), signed. Cover by Len Lye]. *Paris, Hours Press*, n.d., 7½ *in.* Autograph letter to 'Gertrude' enclosed

—— Laura and Francisca. Cover by Len Lye [lim. ed., copy out of series]. *Deyá, Majorca, Seizin Press*, 1931, 11 *in.* Signed Laura Riding

—— Love as Love, Death as Death [lim. ed., no. 15]. *London, Seizin Press*, 1928, 8½ *in.*

—— Poems: a Joking Word. *London, Cape*, 1930, 8 *in.*

—— Though Gently [lim. ed. Cover by Len Lye]. *Deyá, Majorca, Seizin Press*, 1930, 11½ *in.*

—— Twenty Poems Less. Covers by Len Lye [lim. ed., signed by the author but not numbered]. *Paris, Hours Press*, 1930, 11½

502

BOOKS AT CLOUDS HILL

RIDING, L. (*continued*) *in.* Letter from L. Riding to T. E. Lawrence inside book

RIESENBERG, F. Log of the Sea, intro. by A. Bone [1st ed.]. *London, Cape*, 1933, 8 *in.* 'T. E. Shaw' – not autographed

RIMBAUD, A. Oeuvres, preface by Paul Claudel. *Paris, Mercure de France*, 1924, 8 *in.* Brown calf

ROBERTS, E. M. The Great Meadow, with an introduction by Edward Garnett. *London, Cape*, 1930, 8 *in.*

—— My Heart and My Flesh. *London, Cape*, 1928, 7½ *in.*

—— The Time of Man [reprint]. *London, Cape*, 1927, 7½ *in.*

ROGERS, B. Champ rosé, wherein may be discovered the Roman letters that were made by Geoffroy Tory and printed by him at Paris in his book called 'Champ Fleury'. *New Rochelle, Peter Pauper Press*, 1933, 7½ *in.* Uncut except for author's introduction

ROLAND. La Chanson de Roland [Bibl. Romanica]. No imprint. Vellum. 'T. E. L. Oxford 1909'

ROLFE, F. (BARON CORVO). The Desire and Pursuit of the Whole: a romance of modern Venice [1st ed.]. *London, Cassell*, 1934, 9 *in.*

—— Don Tarquinio. *London, Chatto & Windus*, 1905, 7½ *in.*

—— Hadrian the Seventh: a romance [Phoenix Library]. *London, Chatto & Windus*, 1929, 7 *in.*

ROMANCE OF THE ROSE. The Romance of the Rose, by W. Lorris and J. Clopinel, Englished by F. S. Ellis, vols. I and III [Temple Classics]. *London, Dent*, n.d., 6 *in.* 'T. E. L.'

ROSENBERG, I. Poems, selected and edited by Gordon Bottomley, memoir by Laurence Binyon. *London, Heinemann*, 1922, 7½ *in.* 'T. E. L.'

RONSARD, P. DE. Choix de Sonnets de P. Ronsard, illus. by L. Pissarro [lim. ed.]. *London, Hacon and Ricketts*, 1902, 8½ *in.* Bookplate of John Morgan. 'T. E. L.'

ROSSETTI, C. G. The Poetical Works of Christina Georgina Rossetti, with memoir and notes, etc., by W. M. Rossetti [reprint]. *London, Macmillan*, 1914, 7½ *in.* 'T. E. L. 1918'

—— Verses, reprinted from G. Polidori's edition of 1847, ed. by J. D. Symon, illus. by L. Pissaro [lim. ed.]. *London, Eragny Press*, 1906, 8½ *in.* Pages uncut. ['V. W. R. E. A. B. 1919']

ROSSETTI, D. G. Ballads and Narrative Poems, by Dante Gabriel Rossetti. *Hammersmith, Kelmscott Press*, 1893, 8½ *in.* Limp vellum. 'T. E. L.'

ROSSETTI, D. G. Sonnets and Lyrical Poems, by Dante Gabriel Rossetti. *Hammersmith, Kelmscott Press*, 1894, 8 *in.* Limp vellum. 'T. E. L.'

ROTHENSTEIN, SIR W. Men and Memories, 1900-1922. *London, Faber*, 1932, 9½ *in.* ['T. E. L. from W. R., 26.4.32']

—— Twenty-four Portraits by William Rothenstein, with critical appreciations by various hands [lim. ed.]. *London, Allen & Unwin*, 1920, 10 *in.* ['T. E. L.' on 1st flyleaf. On 2nd flyleaf 'For my friend T. E. L. Gratefully W. R. Nov. 1920']

RUSSELL, G. W. Collected Poems, by A.E. [reprint 1917]. *London, Macmillan*, 1917, 7½ *in.* 'T. E. L.'

—— Dark Weeping, by G. W. Russell, designs by Paul Nash [Ariel Poems, no. 19]. *London, Faber & Faber*, n.d., 7½ *in.*

—— New Songs: a lyric selection made by A.E. from poems by Padraic Colum, Eva Gore-Booth etc. [3rd ed.]. *Dublin, O'Donoghue*, 1904, 7½ *in.*

RUSSELL, W. CLARK. The Phantom Death and other stories. *London, Chatto & Windus*, 1895, 7½ *in.*

RYAN, D. Remembering Sion: a chronicle of storm and quiet. *London, Arthur Barker*, 1934, 8½ *in.*

SADLEIR, M. Privilege: a novel of the transition. *London, Constable*, 1921, 8 *in.* ['C/o V. W. Richards, Pole Hill, Chingford, E.4']

SAKURAI, T. Human bullets: a soldier's story of Port Arthur, intro. by Count Okuma, trans. by M. Honda, ed. by A. M. Bacon. *Boston, Houghton, Mifflin & Co.*, 1907, 7½ *in.*

SAMAIN, A. Aux Flancs du Vase, suivi de Polyphème et de Poèmes inachevées [21st ed.]. *Paris, Mercure de France*, n.d., 7½ *in.* Quarter-calf

SASSOON, P. The Third Route [1st ed.]. *London, Heinemann*, 1929, 9 *in.* ['T. L. from Philip Sassoon']

SASSOON, S. Counter-attack, and other poems. *London, Heinemann*, 1918, 7½ *in.*

—— The Heart's Journey [lim. ed.]. *New York, Crosby Gaige*, 1927, 9½ *in.* Title-page signed ['Siegfried Sassoon']

—— The Heart's Journey [lim. ed. on green paper]. *New York, Crosby Gaige*, 1927, 9½ *in.* MS. poem on Hardy stuck in back, 28.1.28. After colophon 'This copy, embellished by Rex Whistler for the author, was given to the author of *The Seven Pillars of Wisdom* by S. S.' MS. poems opp. pp. 8, 13, 14, 21, 22, 23, 24, 26, 27

503

SASSOON, S. Lingual exercises for advanced vocabularians, by Siegfried Sassoon [lim. ed.]. *Cambridge, privately printed at University Press*, 1925, 8½ *in.* On back of title-page ['T. E. L., S. S.']

—— Memoirs of a Fox-hunting Man. *London, Faber*, 1928, 7½ *in.*

—— Memoirs of an Infantry Officer [1st ed.]. *London, Faber & Faber*, 1930, 7½ *in.*

—— The Old Huntsman, and other poems. *London, Heinemann*, 1917, 8½ *in.* 'T. E. L.'

—— Picture Show [lim. ed.]. *Cambridge, privately printed at University Press*, 1919, 9½ *in.* Colophon signed by author. On front flyleaf 'T. E. L.' 'Some extra things written in for me by S.S. in December 1919. T. E. L.' These are: Limitations (opposite p. 10); Early Chronology (opposite p. 16); Phantom (opposite p. 23)

—— Recreations, by Siegfried Sassoon [lim. ed.]. *N.pl., privately printed*, 1923, 7½ *in.* On back of title-page ['T. E. L., S. S., 2.8.1923']

—— The Road to Ruin. *London, Faber*, 1933, 9 *in.*

—— Satirical Poems [new ed.]. *London, Heinemann*, 1933, 7½ *in.* [Slip pasted over imprint. Half-title 'T. E. S. from S. S.']

—— Vigils, by S. S. [lim. ed. engraved on copper, no. 255 signed]. *N. pl., privately printed*, 1934, 9 *in.*, 2nd flyleaf ['T. E. salutamus, S. S.']

—— War Poems. *London, Heinemann*, 1919, 6½ *in.* 2 copies

SCHILLER, F. C. S. Humanism: philosophical essays. *London, Macmillan*, 1903, 9 *in.* ['V. W. R.']

SCOTT, G. Poems. *London, Oxford University Press*, 1931, 8 *in.*

SCOTT, M. Tom Cringle's Log. *London, Macmillan*, 1895, 7½ *in.*

SAVOY. The Savoy, nos. 1 and 2, Jan. and April 1896. *London, L. Smithers*, 1896, 10 *in.* MS. remarks, undecipherable on fly-leaves

SHAKESPEARE, W. The Works of Shakespeare. The text of the First Folio with Quarto variants and a selection of modern readings: edited by Herbert Farjeon, 7 vols. [lim. ed., copy out of series]. *New York, Nonesuch Press*, 1929-33, 9½ *in.* Bound red leather. 'T. E. Shaw from D. Garnett'

—— Comedies, histories, and tragedies, faithfully reproduced in facsimile from the edition of 1623. *London, Methuen*, 1910, 14½ *in.* Suède

—— Venus and Adonis [lim. ed., no. 239]. *Stratford-on-Avon, Shakespeare Head Press*, 1905, 7½ *in.*

SHANKS, E. The Queen of China, and other poems. *London, Secker*, 1919, 7½ *in.* 'T. E. L.'

SHARP, W. The Dominion of Dreams. Under the Dark Star. By 'Fiona Macleod' [The Works of 'Fiona Macleod', uniform ed., vol. III]. *London, Heinemann*, 1910, 7½ *in.* Vellum. Crest of Jesus College, Oxford, stuck inside front cover. 'T. E. L. Finals 1910'

—— The Sin-eater; the Washer of the Ford, and other legendary moralities, by 'Fiona Macleod'. *London, Heinemann*, 1910, 7½ *in.* Vellum. Jesus crest stuck in front cover

SHAW, C. F. MS. notebook of quotations. Brown tooled leather. ['T. E. S. C. F. S. 1927']

SHAW, G. B. The Complete Plays of Bernard Shaw. *London, Constable*, 1931, 10 *in.*

—— Selected passages from the Works of Bernard Shaw, chosen by Charlotte F. Shaw. *London, Cape*, 1921, 7 *in.*

—— The Adventures of the Black Girl in her search for God [1st ed.]. *London, Constable*, 1932, 8½ *in.* [On half-title 'T. E. S. from C. F. S. . . . But who may abide the day of His coming: and who shall stand when He appeareth. For He is like a refiner's fire . . . Christmas and New Year 1932-3']

—— The Adventures of the Black Girl in her search for God [advance copy]. *London, Constable*, 1932, 8½ *in.* [On half-title: 'T. E. S. from C. F. S.' On paper enclosed 'This is the first copy! It won't be published until Dec. 5th. So keep it secret till then. C. F. S.' Below this note is written in pencil 'Identical with published first edition, except that a new stereo was made for the cut on p. 58, 1932. T. E. S.']

—— The Apple Cart: a political extravaganza [1st ed.]. *London, Constable*, 1930, 7 *in.*

—— Back to Methuselah: a metabiological pentateuch. *London, Constable*, 1922, 7 *in.* [On half-title: 'To T. E. Lawrence from G. Bernard Shaw 15.1.24']

—— Candida: a mystery. *London, Constable*, 1908, 7 *in.* ['V. W. R.']

—— Heartbreak House; Great Catherine, and Playlets of the War [3rd imp.]. *London, Constable*, 1921, 7 *in.* 'T. E. L.'

—— Imprisonment. *New York, Brentano's*, 1925, 7½ *in.* On title-page ['T. E. L. from C. F. S.']

—— The intelligent woman's guide to socialism and capitalism. The foundation of the seven pillars, being the word of a western prophet to the deliverer of Damascus; Shaw born Shaw to Shaw that took that name upon him. *Privately printed for the author*, 1928. *Printed in Great Britain by R. & R. Clark, Ltd., Edinburgh*, 9½ *in.* Type-

SHAW, G. B. (*continued*)
written letter from G. B. to T. E. stuck in end

—— John Bull's Other Island and Major Barbara: also How he lied to her husband [7th imp.]. *London, Constable*, 1921, 7 *in.*

—— Music in London 1890-94: criticisms contributed week by week to the *World*, 3 vols. [Works, vols. 26-8, lim. ed.] *London, Constable*, 1931, 9 *in.*

—— Saint Joan. *London, Constable*, 1924, 7 *in.* ['To Shaw from Shaw to replace many stolen copies until this, too, is stolen. 7th Feb. 1934'] 'G.B.S. gave me first a copy of the acting version of S. Joan. It was borrowed from me by an R.T.C. reader, who lent it to another, and he to a third. So it disappeared. Then G.B.S. sent me another Joan, like this, inscribed 'To Pte. Shaw from Public Shaw'. This was one of my chief joys at Clouds Hill: but in 1932 it also vanished. Hence this third copy, with its pessimistic inscription. 2.34. T. E. S.'

—— Three Plays for Puritans [10th imp.]. *London, Constable*, 1920, 7 *in.*

—— Too True To Be Good: a collection of stage sermons by a Fellow of the Royal Society of Literature. Rough proof, unpublished. *N. pl., privately printed*, 1931, 8 *in.*

—— Too True To Be Good; Village Wooing; and On the Rocks: three plays [1st ed.]. *London, Constable*, 1934, 8 *in.* On half-title ['T. E. S. from C. F. S. Feb. 19']

—— [Proof of 'Immaturity' stitched up in trial binding by Cockerel for the collected ed. Loose sheets of 2nd proof of the Preface]

SHELLEY, P. B. The Poetical Works of Percy Bysshe Shelley. 3 vols. *Hammersmith, Kelmscott Press*, 1895, 8½ *in.* Limp white vellum. 2 copies of vol. 3. ['To H. M. Ellis from his loving father, Sept. 15, 1897. Aetat, suae. 33.' 'T. E. L.']

—— Prometheus Unbound: a lyrical drama in four acts [lim. ed.]. *N. pl., De Zilverdistel*, 1917, 9½ *in.* Vellum

SHIEL, M. P. Cold Steel. *London, Grant Richards*, 1899, 7½ *in.* Book plate of Harry Rendall

—— Dr. Krasinski's Secret. *New York, Vanguard Press*, 1929, 7½ *in.*

—— How the Old Woman got Home. *London, Richards Press*, 1927, 7½ *in.*

—— The Isle of Lies. London, *Werner Laurie*, n.d., 7½ *in.* 2 copies

—— The Last Miracle. *London, Werner Laurie*, 1906, 7½ *in.*

—— The Lord of the Sea. *London, Grant Richards*, 1901, 7½ *in.* Book plate: J. R. Miles

SHIEL, M. P. The Purple Cloud [reprint]. *London, Gollancz*, 1929, 7½ *in.* 'T. E. S.'

—— The Purple Cloud. *London, Chatto & Windus*, 1901, 7½ *in.* 'T. E. S.'

—— Shapes in the Fire. *London, Lane*, 1896, 7 *in.* 'T. E. L.'

—— The Yellow Peril [reprint. First published in 1913 under the title 'The Dragon']. *London, Gollancz*, 1929, 7½ *in.*

SHORTHOUSE, J. H. John Inglesant, 2 vols. [new ed.]. *London, Macmillan*, 1881, 7½ *in.*

SIDGWICK, A. H. Jones's Wedding, and other poems. *London, Arnold*, 1918, 8 *in.* 'T. E. L. 1919'

SIDNEY, SIR P. Miscellaneous Works, with a life, by William Grey. *Oxford, D. A. Talboys*, 1829, 7½ *in.* Red leather. 'T. E. L.'

—— The Sonnets of Sir Philip Sidney, ed. by John Gray; ornaments designed and cut on the wood by Charles S. Ricketts [lim. ed.]. *London, Ballantyne Press*, 1898, 9 *in.* Red tooled leather binding signed H.R. 'T. E. L.'

SIENKIEWICZ, H. In Vain, trans. by Jeremiah Curtin. *London, Dent*, 1899, 7½ *in.*

SITWELL, O. Before the Bombardment [1st ed.]. *London, Duckworth*, 1926, 7½ *in.*

SITWELL, S. Southern Baroque Art: a study of painting, architecture and music in Italy and Spain of the 17th and 18th centuries. *London, Grant Richards*, 1924, 8½ *in.*

SMITH, A. W. A Captain Departed [1st ed.]. *London, Peter Davies*, 1934, 7½ *in.*

SMITH, L. PEARSALL. The Youth of Parnassus, and other stories. *London, Macmillan*, 1895, 8 *in.*

—— Trivia. *London, Constable*, 1918, 5½ *in.* 'T.E.L.'

SNAITH, J. C. William Jordan junior. *London, Constable*, 1907, 7½ *in.* 'T. E. L.'

SOMERVILE, W. The Chace: a poem by William Somervile, Esq., an introduction by A. Henry Higginson, engravings by Thomas Bewick [lim. ed., no. 203]. *New York, Doubleday, Doran*, 1929, 12 *in.* Uncut

SOPHOCLES. Tragoediae, ed. by R. Y. Tyrrell [Parnassus Library of Greek and Latin Texts]. *London, Macmillan*, 1897, 7 *in.* 'T. E. L.'

SORLEY, C. H. Marlborough and other poems [4th ed.]. *Cambridge, Cambridge University Press*, 1919, 7 *in.* 'T. E. L.'

SPENDER, S. Poems. *London, Faber*, 1933, 8½ *in.* Proof?

—— Poems [2nd ed.]. *London, Faber*, 1934, 8½ *in.*

SPENSER, EDMUND. The Faerie Queene. *London, printed by H. L. for Mathew*

SPENSER, EDMUND (*continued*) *Lownes*, 1609, 9½ *in.* Leather. Book plate of Calwich Library inside front cover. On flyleaf 'T. E. R.'

—— The Faerie Queene, 2 vols. *Cambridge, Cambridge University Press*, 1909. 12¾ *in.* 'T. E. L.'

—— Minor poems [lim. ed.]. *Chelsea, Ashendene Press*, 1925, 17 *in.* Vellum, calf back

—— The Shepheardes Calender: containing twelve aeglogues, proportionable to the twelve monethes. Illus. *Hammersmith, Kelmscott Press*, 1896, 9½ *in.* 'T. E. L.'

SPINOZA. Spinoza's Ethics and 'De Intellectus Emendatione' [Everyman's Library]. *London, Dent*, 1916, 7 *in.*

SPRINGS, E. War Birds: diary of an unknown aviator, illus. by Clayton Knight. *London, J. Hamilton*, n.d., 9 *in.*

SQUIRE, J. C. Poems [1st series]. *London, Secker*, 1918, 9 *in.* 'T. E. L. 1918'

STANTON, W. The Journal of William Stanton, pilot, of Deal, intro. by A. H. Long. *Portsmouth, W. H. Barrell*, 1929, 8½ *in.*

STEEVENS, G. W. Monologues of the Dead. *London, Methuen*, 1896, 7½ *in.*

STEIN, G. The Autobiography of Alice B. Toklas, illus. *London, Lane*, 1933, 9 *in.*

—— Three lives. *London, J. Rodker*, 1927, 8½ *in.* Pages uncut

STEPHENS, J. Collected Poems. *London, Macmillan*, 1926, 7½ *in.* Uncut

—— The Charwoman's Daughter. *London, Macmillan*, 1912, 7½ *in.* 2 copies

—— The Crock of Gold [reprint]. *London, Macmillan*, 1913, 7½ *in.*

—— The Demi-gods. *London, Macmillan*, 1914, 7 *in.* 'T. E. S.'

—— Etched in Moonlight. *London, Macmillan*, 1928, 7½ *in.* 'T. E. S.'

—— Here Are Ladies. *London, Macmillan*, 1913, 7½ *in.*

—— The Hill of Vision. *Dublin, Maunsel*, 1912, 7½ *in.* ['P. de S. from M. P-F.']

—— A Poetry Recital. *London, Macmillan*, 1925, 7½ *in.*

—— In the Land of Youth. *London, Macmillan*, 1924, 7½ *in.*

STEVENSON, R. L. The Master of Ballantrae. *London, Cassell*, 1889, 7½ *in.*

—— St. Ives. *London, Heinemann*, 1898, 7½*in.*

—— Treasure Island, illus. ed. [29th thous.]. *London, Cassell*, 1889, 7½ *in.*

—— Virginibus Puerisque and other papers [Cameo edition]. *New York, C. Scribner's Sons*, 1896, 6½ *in.*

STOKOE, F. W. Tollkopf on Dreams, and other poems. *Cambridge, Heffer*, 1922, 7½ *in.* 'T. E. Shaw from F. W. Stokoe'

STRACHEY, J. Cheerful Weather for the Wedding. *London, Hogarth Press*, 1932, 7½ *in.*

STRACHEY, L. Queen Victoria [4th imp.]. *London, Chatto & Windus*, 1921, 8½ *in.*

STRIBLING, T. S. The Store [1st ed.]. *New York, Doubleday, Doran*, 1932, 8 *in.*

STUART, F. The Coloured Dome. *London, Gollancz*, 1932, 7½ *in.*

STURLASON, S. Heimskringla: the Olaf Sagas, trans. S. Laing [Everyman's Library]. *London, J. M. Dent*, n.d., 7 *in.*

SUCKLING, SIR J. Poems, ed. by John Gray, decor. by Charles Ricketts: Ballantyne Press. *London, Hacon & Ricketts*, 1906, 9½ *in.* 'T. E. L.'

SWEDENBORG, E. Heaven and its Wonders, and Hell: [Everyman's Library]. *London, Dent*, n.d., 7 *in.* 'T. E. L.'

SWIFT, J. The Works of Jonathan Swift containing interesting and valuable papers not hitherto published. In two volumes. With memoir of the author by Thomas Roscoe. *London, H. G. Bohn*, 1856, 9½ *in.* Brown calf

—— Selected essays, engravings on wood by John Farleigh: ed. by R. Ellis Roberts vol. 1 [lim. ed., no. 362]. *Waltham St. Lawrence, Golden Cockerel Press*, 1925, 10 *in.*

—— Travels into several remote nations of the world by Lemuel Gulliver, 2 vols. *London, Benj. Motte*, 1726, 7½ *in.* Calf, gold-tooled. 'T. E. L.'

—— Travels into several remote nations of the world by Lemuel Gulliver, 2 vols. bound as 1 [lim. ed., no. 56]. *Waltham St. Lawrence, Golden Cockerel Press*, 1925, 10 *in.*

SWINBURNE, A. C. Selections from A. C. Swinburne, ed. by E. Gosse and Thomas James Wise [lim. ed., no. 172]. *London, Heinemann*, 1919, 9 *in.* 'T. E. L.'

—— Atalanta in Calydon: a tragedy [new ed.]. *London, Chatto & Windus*, 1894, 7½ *in.* 'T. E. L. 1920'

—— A Century of Roundels [2nd ed.]. *London, Chatto & Windus*, 1883, 8 *in.* Half-parchment. 'Ex libris W. G. L.'

—— Poems and Ballads [2nd series]. *London, Chatto & Windus*, 1878, 7½ *in.*

—— Poems and Ballads [3rd series, 7th ed.]. *London, Chatto & Windus*, 1902, 7½ *in.*

—— Songs before Sunrise, by Algernon Charles Swinburne [lim. ed., paper copy, no. 39]. *London, for Florence Press*, 1909, 10 *in.* 'T. E. L. 1919'

SYKES, SIR P. A History of Exploration from the earliest times to the present day. *London, Routledge*, 1934, 10 *in.* 'To Col. T. E. Lawrence with much regard from Sir Percy Sykes'

SYKES, SIR P. Persia. *Oxford, Clarendon Press*, 1922, 7½ *in.*

SYNGE, J. M. The Aran Islands [reprint]. *Dublin, Maunsel*, 1920, 7½ *in.* 'T. E .L.'

—— Plays. *Dublin, Maunsel*, 1919, 7½ *in.* 'T. E. L.'

TENNYSON, A. In Memoriam [lim. ed., no. (blank)]. *London, Nonesuch Press*, 1933, 11 *in.* 'T. E. S. from D. G.'

—— In Memoriam [Golden Treasury series]. *London, Macmillan*, 1904, 6 *in.* Morocco

—— Poems. *London, E. Moxon*, 1857, 8½ *in.* Red leather: Nutt, Cambridge

—— Poems [Ballantyne Press]. *London, Hacon & Ricketts*, 1900, 9½ *in.* 'T. E. L. 1918'

TERRY, E. and SHAW, G. B. Ellen Terry and Bernard Shaw: a correspondence, ed. by Christopher St. John [2nd ed.]. *London, Constable*, 1931, 9 *in.*

THOMAS, B. Arabia Felix: across the empty quarter of Arabia with a foreword by T. E. Lawrence (T. E. S.) and appendix by Sir Arthur Keith [1st ed.]. *London, Cape*, 1932, 9½ *in.*

THOMAS, E. Selected Poems of Edward Thomas with an introduction by Edward Garnett [lim. ed., no. 40]. *Newtown, Montgomeryshire, Gregynog Press*, 1927, 9½ *in.* 'T. E. L. from E. G.'

—— Collected Poems with a foreword by Walter de la Mare. *London, Selwyn & Blount*, 1920, 8 *in.* 'T. E. L.'

—— The Icknield Way, illus. [Constable's Miscellany]. *London, Constable*, 1929, 7 *in.*

—— Rest and Unrest. *London, Duckworth*, 1910, 6½ *in.*

THOMAS, H. As It Was, by H. T. [new imp.]. *London, Heinemann*, 1926, 7½ *in.*

—— World Without End. *London, Heinemann*, 1931, 7½ *in.*

THOMPSON, F. The Collected Poetry of Francis Thompson [ed. de luxe]. *London, Hodder & Stoughton*, 1913, 9½ *in.* 'T. E. L. 1919'

THOMSON, J. The City of Dreadful Night, and other poems. *London, Reeves & Turner*, 1880, 7 *in.*

—— The City of Dreadful Night, and other poems, being a selection from the poetical works of James Thomson ['B.V.']. *London, Dobell*, 1910, 6½ *in.*

THUCYDIDES. Eight bookes of the Peloponnesian warre written by Thucydides the sonne of Olorus. Interpreted with faith and diligence immediately out of the Greeke by Thomas Hobbes, the author of the book De Cive, Secretary to the late Earle of Devonshire. *London, Charles Harper*, 1676, 12½ *in.* Leather. Rebacked

TOLLER, E. The Swallow-book, English version by Ashley Dukes. *Oxford, Oxford University Press*, 1924, 7½ *in.* [On title-page 'T. E. S. from F. S.']

TOLSTOI, L. N. Anna Karenina, vol. 2 [Everyman's Library]. *London, Dent*, 1914, 7 *in.*

—— The Death of Ivan Ilyitch, and other stories, trans. by Constance Garnett [pop. ed.]. *London, Heinemann*, 1915, 7 *in.*

—— A Landed Proprietor; the Cossacks; Sevastopol, ed. and trans. by Leo Wiener, illus. [lim. ed., no. 32]. *London, G. S. Howell*, 1905, 9 *in.* 'T. E. L.'

—— Ressurrection: a novel, trans. by Louise Maude. *London, Oxford University Press*, 1931, 7½ *in.*

—— War and Peace, trans. by N. H. Dole, illus. by E. H. Garrett. Four volumes in two [World's Great Novels]. *London, Walter Scott Publishing Co.*, n.d., 8 *in.* 'T. E. L.'

TOMLINSON, H. M. All our Yesterdays [signed lim. ed., no. 1019]. *London, Heinemann*, 1930, 9½ *in.*

—— All our Yesterdays. *London, Heinemann*, 1930, 8 *in.* 'To T. E. Shaw. H. M. Tomlinson 10. 1. 30.'

—— Côte d'or [Criterion miscellany no. 2]. *London, Faber*, 1929, 7½ *in.*

—— Gallions Reach: a romance [new ed.]. *London, Heinemann*, 1931, 7 *in.*

—— The Sea and the Jungle, with woodcuts by Clare Leighton [signed lim. ed., no. 474]. *London, Duckworth*, 1930, 9 *in.*

—— The Snows of Helicon [signed lim. ed. no. 172]. *London, Heinemann*, 1933, 9 *in.*

—— Tidemarks: some records of a journey to the beaches of the Moluccas and the forest of Malaya, in 1923 [3rd imp.]. *London, Cassell*, 1932, 7 *in.*

TOURNEUR, C. The Works of Cyril Tourneur, ed. by Allardyce Nicoll, with decorations by Frederick Carter [lim. ed., copy not numbered]. *London, Fanfrolico Press*, 1929, 10 *in.*

TRAHERNE, T. Centuries of Meditations, ed. by Bertram Dobell [reprint]. *London, Dobell*, 1927, 7½ *in.*

TRELAWNY, E. J. Adventures of a Younger Son, intro. by E. Garnett [popular ed.]. *London, T. Fisher Unwin*, 1897, 8 *in.*

TRENCH, H. Selected Poems. *London, Cape*, 1924, 7½ *in.*

TRISTAN. Le Roman de Tristan et Iseut, ed. J. Bedier [lim. ed., no. 280]. *Paris, H. Piazza*, 1918, 7½ *in.* 'T. E. L.'

—— The Romance of Tristan and Iseult, re-told by J. Bédier, trans. by H. Belloc. *London, G. Allen*, 1913, 7½ *in.*

TROY. The recuyell of the historyes of Troye. 2 vols. *Hammersmith, Kelmscott Press*, 1892.

TROY (*continued*)
11½ *in.* Limp vellum. Both vols. uncut. 'T. E. L.'

TWAIN, M. The Adventures of Huckleberry Finn. *London, Harrap*, 1924, 7½ *in.*

—— The Adventures of Tom Sawyer [a new ed.]. *London, Chatto & Windus*, 1900, 7½ *in.*

UNDERHILL, E. Immanence: a book of verses [reprint]. *London, Dent*, 1920, 7½ *in.*

UNRUH, F. VON. Verdun (Opfergang) trad. de Benoist-Méchin [Coll. de la Revue Européenne 5]. *Paris, S. Kra*, 1924, 7 *in.* ['T. E. S. from E. G. June, 25']

USĀMAH. An Arab-Syrian gentleman and warrior in the period of the crusades: memoirs of Usāmah Ibn-Munqidh, trans. by Philip K. Hitti [Records of Civilisation]. *New York, Columbia University Press*, 1929, 9 *in.*

VANSITTART, R. Foolery: a comedy in verse. *London, A. L. Humphreys*, 1912, 6½ *in.* 'T. E. L.'

—— The Singing Caravan: a Sufi tale, decorations and frontispiece by William MacCance [lim. ed., no. 142]. *Newtown, Montgomeryshire, Gregynog Press*, 1923, 11 *in.* Bound in leather, Gregynog Press Bindery

—— The Singing Caravan: a Sufi tale. *London Heinemann*, 1919, 8 *in.* ['T. E. L.' 2nd flyleaf 'Carried with me on Handley-Pages from Paris to Egypt in 1919. Between Paris and Marseilles the Chapter II of my *Seven Pillars of Wisdom* (Chap. I in the subscribers' edition of 1926) was written on a back cover of this book, now torn out. Its rhythm was derived from the beat of the R. R. Eagle VIII engines of our machine. Other notes from the Seven Pillars (then complete in 1st draft) are on the back flyleaf of this copy. Cranwell, 1926. T. E. S.' 4th flyleaf 'To T. E. L. from R. V. Paris 1919']

VAUGHAN, H. Vaughan's sacred poems being a selection, illus. by C. Ricketts [lim. ed.]. *N. pl., Ballantyne Press*, 1897, 8 *in.* ['W. A. to S. A.']

VERGA, G. Maestro-Don Gesualdo, trans. by D. H. Lawrence. *London, Cape*, 1925, 7½ *in.* 'T. E. S.'

VIRGIL. Publii Vergilii Maronis opera: Bucolica, Georgica, Aeneis. *London, Ashendene Press*, 1910, 10 *in.* Red stamped leather: W. H. S. 'T. E. L. 1919'

VERHAEREN, E. Oeuvres. *Paris, Mercure de France*, 1912, 8 *in.* Blue leather. 'T. E. S.'

VERINO, U. Vita di Santa Chiara vergine composta per Ugolino Verino cittadino Fiorentino: reprinted from the original MS. by Walter W. Seton [lim. ed.]. *Chelsea, Ashendene Press*, 1921, 8 *in.* Vellum. 'T. E. L.'

VIGFUSSEN, G., and POWELL, F. YORK. Corpus Poeticum Boreale. The poetry of the old northern tongue, ed. and trans. by G. Vigfussen and F. Y. Powell. 2 vols. *Oxford, Clarendon Press*, 1883, 9 *in.*

VILLIERS DE L'ISLE-ADAM, J. M. M. P. A. Axel, trans. into English by H. P. R. Finberg with a preface by W. B. Yeats, illus. by T. Sturge Moore [lim. ed., no. 62, signed H. P. R. Finberg]. *London, Jarrolds*, 1925, 9 *in.*

VILLON, F. Autres poesies de maistre François Villon et de son école, illus. by L. Pissarro [lim. ed.]. *London, Hacon & Ricketts*, 1901, 7½ *in.* 'T. E. L.'

—— Les Ballades, illus. L. Pissaro [lim. ed.]. *London, Hacon & Ricketts*, 1900, 8 *in.* 'T. E. L.'

—— Oeuvres avec préf. par Paul Lacroix. *Paris, Flammarion*, n.d., 7 *in.* 'T. E. L.'

VOLTAIRE. Voltaire's letter written from the Château de Ferney, February 11, 1765, to James Boswell [facsimile]. *N. pl., W. E. Rudge*, 1927, 11½ *in.*

WADDELL, H. Peter Abelard: a novel. *London, Constable*, 1933, 8 *in.*

WALEY, A. One hundred and seventy Chinese poems, trans. by Arthur Waley [Constable's Miscellany]. *London, Constable*, 1928, 7 *in.*

WALLER, E. Poems, ed. by G. Thorn Drury. *London, Lawrence & Bullen*, 1893, 6½ *in.* 'T. E. S.'

WALMSLEY, L. Foreigners [1st ed.]. *London, Cape*, 1935, 8 *in.*

—— Three Fevers [reprint]. *London, Cape*, 1933, 7½ *in.*

WALPOLE, H. The Apple Trees: four reminiscences, with wood-engravings by Lynton Lamb [lim. ed., no. 76]. *Waltham St. Lawrence, Golden Cockerel Press*, 1932, 9½ *in.* [Signed 'Hugh Walpole' after dedication]

WARDE, F. Bruce Rogers, designer of books. *Cambridge (Mass.), Harvard University Press*, 1925, 9 *in.*

WASSERMANN, J. The Triumph of Youth, trans. by O P. Schinnerer. [and printing]. *New York, Boni & Liberight*, 1927, 7½ *in.* ['G. R. Ashlin.'] ['H. B. Pegler']

WATSON, W. New Poems [2nd ed.]. *London, Lane*, 1909, 7½ *in.*

WAVELL, A. P. The Palestine Campaigns [Campaigns and Their Lessons, ed. by Sir C. Caldwell]. *London, Constable*, n.d., 9 *in.*

WEBSTER, J. Complete Works, ed. by F. L. Lucas. 4 vols. *London, Chatto & Windus*, 1927, 9 *in.*

WELLS, H. G. The Island of Dr. Moreau [Essex ed. Collected Works, vol. XIV]. *London, Benn*, 1927, 7 *in.*

—— The Outline of History: being a plain history of life and mankind with maps and plans by J. F. Horrabin [5th revision]. *London, Cassell*, 1930, 8½ *in.*

—— The Shape of Things to Come; the ultimate revolution. *London, Hutchinson*, 1933, 8½ *in.* [On title-page 'To Lawrence (and now you know) H. G.']

—— The Short stories of H. G. Wells [2nd impression]. *London, Benn*, 1927, 7½ *in.*

—— The Scientific Romances of H. G. Wells. *London, Gollancz*, 1933, 7 *in.*

WHEEN, A. W. Two Masters [Criterion Miscellany 1]. *London, Faber*, 1929, 7½ *in.*

WHITMAN, W. Complete Prose Works. *New York, Appleton*, 1908, 7½ *in.* Book plate: E. A. Carter. 'T. E. S.'

—— Leaves of Grass. *New York, no publisher*, 1867, 7½ *in.* Half leather

WHITTAKER, J. I, James Whittaker. *London, Rich & Cowan*, 1934, 7½ *in.* 'For T. E. L. "I. J." 19. 2. 35'

WILDE, O. The Happy Prince, and other tales, illus. by Walter Crane and Jacomb Hood [5th imp.]. *London, D. Nutt*, 1907, 9 *in.*

—— Poems, with the Ballad of Reading Gaol [13th ed.]. *London, Methuen*, 1916, 7 *in.*

—— The Soul of Man. *London, A. L. Humphreys*, 1907, 6½ *in.* 'T. E. L.'

WILLIAMS' CALENDAR. Williams' Calendar or the Utica Almanack for the year of our Lord 1829 astronomical calculations by Edwin E. Prentiss containing, besides the astronomical calculations, a great variety of woeful and entertaining pieces. *Auburn, U. F. Doubleday*, 1829, 6 *in.* Rebound green tooled leather: Hardy, Miller & Pilon

WILLIAMSON, H. Dandelion Days [revised ed.]. *London, Faber & Faber*, 1930, 8 *in.* 'T. E. S.'

—— The Gold Falcon, or the Haggard of Love, dedicated to T. E. Lawrence. *N. pl., printed for the author*, 1933, 8 *in.* Parchment, gold lettering

—— The Labouring Life. *London, Cape*, 1932, 8 *in.* No covers, proof?

—— The Linhay on the Downs. *London, Cape*, 1934, 8 *in.* 'T. E. S.'

—— The Old Stag: stories. *London, Putnam's*, 1926, 7½ *in.* Copiously annotated author's copy presented to T. E. Shaw

—— The Pathway [4th imp.]. *London, Cape*, 1929, 7½ *in.* 'T. E. S.'

—— Tarka the Otter: his joyful water-life and death in the country of the two rivers, with an introduction by the Hon. Sir John Fortescue [lim. ed.]. *London, Putnam*, 1927, 9½ *in.* 'T. E. S.'

WILLIAMSON, H. The Village Book, illus., twice only, by sketches from the original MSS. *London, Cape*, 1930, 8 *in.* Paper covers. Proof?

—— The Wild Red Deer of Exmoor: a digression on the logic and ethics and economics of stag-hunting in England to-day [lim. ed., no. 52]. *London, privately printed*, 1931, 8 *in.* 'T. E. S.'

WOOLF, V. Mr. Bennett and Mrs. Brown. *London, Hogarth Press*, 1924, 8½ *in.*

—— The Waves. *London, Hogarth Press*, 1931, 7 *in.*

WOOLLEY, C. L. and LAWRENCE, T. E. Carchemish: report on the excavations at Djerabis by C. Leonard Woolley and T. E. Lawrence, part I. *London, British Museum*, 1914, 12½ *in.*

WOOLLEY, C. L. Dead Towns and Living Men. *London, Oxford University Press*, 1920, 8½ *in.* 'E. T. L. from C. L. W.']

—— Dead Towns and Living Men [Life and Letters, series no. 29]. *London, Cape*, 1932, 8 *in.*

WORDSWORTH, W. Poetical Works, ed. by Thomas Hutchinson [Oxford ed.]. *London, Oxford University Press*, 1917, 7 *in.* 'T. E. L.'

—— A Decade of Years: poems by William Wordsworth 1798–1807 [selected by T. J. Cobden-Sanderson, from the text of 1857, lim. ed.]. *Hammersmith, Doves Press*, 1911, 9½ *in.* Limp vellum. 'T. E. L.'

—— The Prelude: an autobiographical poem by William Wordsworth [lim. ed., of which 10 copies are printed on vellum]. *Hammersmith, The Doves Press*, 1915, 9½ *in.* Printed on vellum. Binding red tooled leather: The Doves Bindery, 19 C-S 19. 'T. E. L.'

WRENCH, SIR J. E. Uphill: the first stage in a strenuous life [1st ed.]. *London, Ivor Nicholson & Watson*, 1934, 8½ *in.* 'To T. E. Shaw with good wishes from Evelyn Wrench'

XENOPHON. Complete Works, trans. by Ashley, Spelman Smith, Fielding [new ed.]. *London, W. P. Nimmo*, 1877, 9 *in.*

YEATS, J. B. Sligo. *London, Wishart*, 1930, 7½ *in.*

YEATS, W. B. The Collected Poems of W. B. Yeats. *London, Macmillan*, 1923, 8 *in.*

—— The Hour-glass; Cathleen ni Houlihan; the Pot of Broth [vol. 2 of Plays for an Irish theatre]. *London, A. H. Bullen*, 1904, 7½ *in.*

—— Poems [reprint]. *London, Fisher Unwin*, 1913, 8 *in.* 'T. E. L.'

LITERATURE

YEATS, W. B. Poems: second series [new ed.]. London, A. H. Bullen, 1913. 7½ in. T.E.L.

—— The Tables of the Law, and the Adoration of the Magi. London, Elkin Mathews, 1904. 6½ in.

—— The Winding Stair [signed lim. ed., no. 367]. New York, Fountain Press, 1929. 9 in.

—— The Winding Stair, and other poems. London, Macmillan, 1933. 7½ in.

—— Words for Music Perhaps, and other poems [lim. ed.]. Dublin, Cuala Press, 1932. 8½ in.

YEATS-BROWN, F. Dogs of War! [1st ed.]. London, Darwin, 1934. 8 in. "For that sabre-rattling militarist, T. E. Shaw from Y. B. 2 July, 1934"

YEATS-BROWN, F. Golden Horn. London, Gollancz, 1932. 8½ in. "To Aircraftman T. E. Shaw with the best wishes of the author F. Yeats-Brown, July 15th, 1932'

YOUNG, F. BRETT. Marching on Tanga with General Smuts in East Africa [new and rev. ed., illus.]. London, Collins, 1919. 8½ in.

YOUNG, SIR H. The Independent Arab [1st ed.]. London, Murray, 1933. 8½ in.

ZINSSER, H. Rats, Lice and History: being a study in biography which deals with the life history of typhus fever. Boston, Little, Brown, 1935. 8½ in.

A Lawrence Bibliography

Books By Lawrence

The Seven Pillars of Wisdom, The Complete 1922 'Oxford' Text, J. and N. Wilson, 2004

The Seven Pillars of Wisdom, Jonathan Cape, 1935

The Seven Pillars of Wisdom, Penguin, 1986

Oriental Assembly, Edited by A. W. Lawrence, Imperial War Museum, 1939 & 1991

Crusader Castles, Michael Haag, 1986. Also Oxford, Clarendon Press, 1988, Intro. and notes by Denys Pringle

The Mint, Cape, 1955 & Penguin, 1978

The Letters, Edited by David Garnett, Cape, 1938

The Letters, Edited by Malcolm Brown, Dent, 1988

Selected Letters, Edited by David Garnett, The Reprint Society, 1941

The Home Letters of T. E. Lawrence and his Brothers, Oxford, Basil Blackwell, 1954

Minorities, Edited by J. M. Wilson, Doubleday and Co, 1972

The Odyssey, translated by T. E. Lawrence, Wordsworth Editions Ltd, 1992

Secret Despatches from Arabia and other writings by T. E. Lawrence, Edited by Malcolm Brown, Bellew Publishing Co, 1991

Revolt in the Desert, Century Hutchinson, 1986, Jonathan Cape, 1927

The Wilderness of Zin, C. L. Wooley and T. E. Lawrence, Cape, 1915

Books About Lawrence

Lawrence of Arabia – The Authorised Biography, Jeremy Wilson, Minerva Paperback, 1989

The Essential T. E. Lawrence, Selected by David Garnett, Oxford University Press, 1992 & Penguin, 1956

A Prince of Our Disorder, John E. Mack, O.U.P., 1990

T. E. Lawrence, Desmond Stewart, Paladin, 1997

Images of Lawrence, S. E. Tabachnick and C. Matheson, Cape, 1998

T. E. Lawrence by His Friends, Edited by A..W. Lawrence, Cape, 1937

The Journal of the T. E. Lawrence Society

Threnos for T. E. Lawrence and other writings, Henry Williamson, The Henry Williamson Society, 1994

Lawrence The Rebel, Edward Robinson, Lincolns-Prager, 1946

Letters to His Biographers, Robert Graves and Liddell Hart, Cassell, 1963

The Golden Reign, Clare Sydney Smith, Cassell, 1949

Lawrence of Arabia and his World, Richard Perceval Graves, Thames and Hudson, 1976

T. E. Lawrence, Jeremy Wilson, National Portrait Gallery Publications, 1988

A Touch of Genius – The Life of T. E. Lawrence, Malcolm Brown and Julia Cave, J. M. Dent, 1988

Backing into the Limelight, Michael Yard, Harrap, 1985

The Medievalism of Lawrence of Arabia, M. Allen, Pennsylvania State University Press, 1961

Solitary in the Ranks, H. Montgomery Hyde, Constable, 1987

The Secret Lives of Lawrence of Arabia, Philip Knightly and Colin Simpson, Thomas Nelson and Sons, 1969 & Panther, 1971

Lawrence of Arabia, Richard Aldington, Collins, 1955 & Pelican, 1971

Lawrence of Arabia, B. H. Liddell Hart, Halcyon House, 1935

Lawrence of Arabia in Dorset, Rodney Legg, Dorset Publishing Co., 1988,

With Lawrence in Arabia, Lowell Thomas, no date,

Lawrence and the Arabs, Robert Graves, Jonathan Cape, 1927

In the Steps of Lawrence of Arabia, Douglas Glenn, Rich and Cowan Ltd, no date

T. E. Lawrence, Vyvyan Richards, Duckworth, 1939

The Golden Warrior, Lawrence James, George Weidenfeld & Nicholson, 1990 & Abacus, 1995

Lawrence of Arabia, Zionism and Palestine, Sir Ronald Storrs, Penguin, 1940

Letters to T. E. Lawrence, Edited by A. W. Lawrence, Jonathan Cape, 1962

The Desert and the Stars, Flora Armitage, Faber, MCMLVI

T. E. Lawrence: The Enigma Explained, Andrew Norman, The History Press, 2008

T. E. Lawrence or the Search for the Absolute, Jean Beraud Villars, Duell, Sloan & Pearce Inc, 1959 (Translated from the French by Peter Dawney)

338171 T. E. [Lawrence of Arabia], Victoria Ocampo. Translated by David Garnett, Victor Gollancz, 1963

Orientations, Ronald Storrs, Readers Union Ltd. By arrangement with Ivor Nicholson & Watson
    Ltd, 1939
Desert Queen – The Extraordinary Life of Gertrude Bell, Janey Wallach, Phoenix, 1997
Gertrude Bell, H.V.F. Winstone, Cape, 1978
With Lawrence in the Royal Air Force, Paul Tunbridge, Buckland Publications, 2000
Lawrence of Arabia – The Life, The Legend, Malcolm Brown, Thames and Hudson with The Imperial
    War Museum, 2005
Hero – The Life and Legend of Lawrence of Arabia, Michael Korda, JR Books, 2001
Lawrence of Arabia – The Man and the Motive, Anthony Nutting, Trust Books, Louvain Landsborough
    Ltd, 1961,
Another Life: Lawrence After Arabia, Andrew R.B. Simpson, Spellmount, The History Press, 2008

Books about Chivalry
Chivalry, Maurice Keen, Yale, 1990
The Knight in History, Frances Gies, Robert Hale, 1986
The Knight and Chivalry, Richard Barber, Longman, 1970
The Book of the Ordre of Chyualry, Translated by William Caxton. Edited by Alfred T.P. Byles, Early
    English Text Society, 1926 & 1971
King Arthur in Legend and History, Richard Barber, Cardinal, 1973
Le Morte D'Arthur, Sir Thomas Malory, Penguin, 1969
Aspects of Malory, Edited by Takamiya & Brewer, Boydell & Brewer Ltd, 1986
The History of the Kings of Britain, Geoffrey of Monmouth. Translated by Lewis Thorpe, Penguin,
    1996
Chronicles, Froissart. Translated by Geoffrey Brereton, Penguin, 1978
The Waning of the Middle Ages, J. Huizinga, Penguin, 1972
Arthurian Romances, Chretian De Troyes, W.W. Kiber & W. Carroll [Trans.] Penguin, 1991
The Chevalier Bayard: A Study in Fading Chivalry, Samuel Shellabarger, Skeffington & Son Ltd,
    No date,
Malory – Works, Ed. Eugene Vinaver, O.U.P., 1977
The Song of Roland, Trans. Glyn Burgess, Penguin, 1990
The Quest of the Holy Grail, Trans. P.M. Matarasso, Penguin, 1969
The Trial of the Templars, Malcolm Barber, Cambridge, 1991
Idylls of the King, Tennyson, Penguin, 1983
Tirant Lo Blanc, Joanot Martorell & Marti Joan de Galba, Translated David H. Rosenthal,
    Macmillan, 1984
French Medieval Romances: From the Lays of Marie de France, Translated Eugene Mason, Dent, no date
Medieval Romance, John Stevens, Hutchinson, 1973
Pearl and Sir Gawain and the Green Knight, Dent, 1962
Chivalry, Michael Foss, Michael Joseph, 1975
Two Lives of Charlemagne, Einhard and Notker the Stammerer, Penguin, 1969
Lancelot of the Lake, Translated Corin Corley, O.U.P., 1989
A Knight's Life in the Days of Chivalry, Walter Clifford Meller, T. Werner Laurie, 1924
Aucassin and Nicolette, Christine de Pisan, Translated Andrew Lang, David Nutt, 1896
The World of the Troubadours, Linda M, Paterson, C.U.P., 1993
The Life and Death of Richard Yea and Nay, Maurice Hewlett, Macmillan, 1990
William Marshal: Knight-Errant, Baron, and Regent of England, Sidney Painter, John Hopkins Press,
    1933
The Knight in History, Frances Gies, Robert Hale, 1986
The Book of Chivalry of Geoffroi De Charny, University of Pennsylvania Press, 1996
The Last of the Templars, William Watson, Harvill Press, 1992 & 1999
The New Knighthood: A History of the Order of the Temple, Malcolm Barber, C.U.P., 1994 & 1995
The Monks of War: The Military Religious Orders, Desmond Seward, Penguin, 1995
Chivalry: A series of studies to illustrate its historical significance and civilizing influence, Ed. Edgar Presage,
    Kegan Paul, Trench and Trubner & Co. Ltd, 1928,
The Return to Camelot, Chivalry and the English Gentleman, Yale University Press, 1981
The Nine Famous Crusades of the Middle Ages, Anne E. Keeling, Robert Culley, No date

Jehan De Saintre, Antoine De La Sale, Edited by Jean Misrahi & Charles A Knudson, Libraire Droz, 1978
The Broadstone Of Honour, Kenelm Henry Digby. E. Lumley, 1844
The Boke of Duke Huon of Bordeux, done into English by Sir John Bourchier, Lord Berners, Early English Text Society, MDCCLXXXIV
Lord Berners: A selection from his works, Edited by Vivian De Sola Pinto, Sidgwick & Jackson, 1947
Kalevala, Translated by W.F. Kirby, J.M.Dent, 1956
The Storey of Sigurd The Volsung and the Fall of the Niblungs, William Morris, Reeves and Turner, MDCCCLXXXVII.
The Crusades through Arab Eyes, Amin Maalouf, Al Saqi Books, 1984
French Chivalry, Sidney Painter, Cornell University Press, 1965
Chronicle of the Abbey of Bury St. Edmunds, Jocelin of Brakelond, O.U.P., 1989

On Warfare
A History of Warfare, John Keegan, Random House/Pimlico, 1993
Combat Leader's Field Guide, James J, Gallaher, Stackpole Books, 1987
On War, Carl von Clausewitz, Edited and Translated by Michael Howard & Peter Paret, Everyman, 1993
On War, Clausewitz, Edited by Anatol Raport, Pengin, 1976
Clausewitz, Michael Howard, O.U.P., 1983
Clausewitz: Philosopher of War, Raymond Aron. Translated by Christine Booker and Norman Stone, Prentice-Hall, 1985
Clausewitz and the State: The Man his Theories and his Times, Peter Paret, Princeton University Press, 1985
A History of Military Thought: From the Enlightenment to the Cold War, Azar Gatt, O.U.P., 2001
Warriors' Words, Peter G, Tsouras, Cassell Arms & Armour, 1992
The Warrior Koans – Early Zen in Japan, Trevor Leggett, R.K.P./Akana, 1985
Chronicles of the Crusades, Joinville and Villehardouin, Translated by M.R.B.Shaw, Penguin, 1963
Giap: The Victor in Vietnam, Peter Macdonald, Warner Books, 1993
Plutarch on Sparta, Translated by R.J.A.Talbert, Penguin, 1988
The Spartans: An Epic History, Paul Cartledge, Channel Four Books, 2002
Spartan Reflections, Paul Cartledge, Duckworth, 2001
Gates of Fire, Stephen Pressfield, Bantam Books, 2000
Montrose, John Buchan, Hodder & Stoughton, 1928
The Life of Alexander the Great, Arrian. Translated by Aubrey De Selincourt, Penguin, 1958
A Distant Mirror, Barbara Tuchman, Penguin, 1978
Looking for Trouble, General Sir Peter De La Billiere, Harper Collins, 1984
What Were the Crusades? Jonathan Riley-Smith, Macmillan, 1997
A History of the Crusades, 3 Vols, Steven Runciman, Penguin and C.U.P., 1951
The Mask of Command, John Keegan, Penguin, 1988
The Art of War – Baron Antoine Henri de Jomini, Greenhill Books and Stackpole Books, 1992
Machiavelli – Discourses on Livy, Oxford World's Classics, Translated and Introduced by Julia Conaway Bondanella and Peter Bondanella, 1997
Machiavelli – The Art of War, Da Capo Press, 1965
The Storm of Steel, Ernst Jünger, Constable, 1929 & 1994 and Allen Lane, 2003
On Pain, Ernst Jünger. Translated by David C. Durst, Telos Press Publishing, 2008
Ernst Jünger and Germany: Into The Abyss, 1914-1945, Thomas Nevin, Constable, 1997
War in European History, Michael Howard, O.U.P., 1976
The Peloponnesian War, Donald Kagan, Harper Collins, 2003
The Templars: Knights of God, Edward Burman, Crucible, 1986
The Last of the Templars, William Watson, Harvil Press, 1999
Art of War, Jomini, Greenhill Books, 1996
The Crusades and the Holy Land, George Tate, Thames and Hudson, 1996
The Ghost of Napoleon, Liddell Hart, Faber
Combat Leader's Field Guide, CSM James J.Gallagher, Stackpole Books, 1987
Setting the Desert on Fire, James Barr, Bloomsbury, 2006

On Philosophy and Religion

After Virtue: A Study in Moral Theory, Alasdair MacIntyre, Duckworth, 1981 & 1985
The Cistercian World — Monastic Writings of the 12th Century, Translated and Edited by P.Matarasso, Penguin, 1993
The Bible and the Sword, Barbara Tuchman, Macmillan, 1982
The Imitation of Christ, Thomas A Kempis, Translated by Leo Sherley-Price, Penguin, 1982
Early Christian Writings, Translated by Maxwell Staniforth, Penguin, 1968
The Little Flowers of St. Francis, Translated by M. Staniforth, Penguin, 1959
Enfolded in Love — Daily readings with Julian of Norwich, Darton, Longman and Todd, 1980
The Frontiers of Paradise, Peter Levi, Collins Harvill, 1987
Celebration of Discipline: The Path of Spiritual Growth, Fichard J.Foster, Hodder & Stoughton, 1989
Ramon Lull and Lullism in 14th Century France, J.N.Hillgarth, Oxford, Clarendon Press, 1971
Letters from the Desert, Carlo Carreto, Dartman, Longman, and Todd, 1972
The Early Church, Henry Chadwick, Penguin, 1967
The Desert Fathers, Helen Waddell, Constable, 1936
The Wisdom of the Desert, Thomas Merton, Shambala, 1994
The Roots of Christian Mysticism, Oliver Clement, New City, 1993
Jesus, Michael Grant, Rigel Publications, 2004
The Mind of St.Bernard of Clairvaux, G.R.Evans, Clarendon Press, 1983
Western Society and the Church in the Middle Ages, R.W.Southern, Penguin, 1970
Freedom of Simplicity, Richard Foster, Triangle, S.P.C.K., 1981
A Time to Keep Silence, Patrick Leigh Fermor, Penguin, 1988
St.Bernard of Clairvaux: As Seen through His Letters, Translated and Introduced by Rev. Bruno Scott James, Heenry Regney, Chicago, 1953
Bernard of Clairvaux, Henri Daniel-Rops, Hawthorn Books, 1964
St. Anthony of the Desert, St.Athanasius, Tan Books and Publishers Inc., 1995
The Early Christian Fathers, Henry Bettenson, O.U.P., 1956
The Conflict of the Faculties, Immanuel Kant, University of Nabraska Press, Translated by Mary J, Gregor, 1979 & 1992
Constructions of Reason, Onora O'Neill, C.U.P., 1984 & 1989
The History of Sexuality, Three Volumes, Michel Foucault, Allen Lane, The Penguin Press, 1984
Philosophy as a Way of Life, Pierre Hadot, Blackwell, 1995
The Inner Citadel, Pierre Hadot, Harvard University Press, 2001
Cynics, William Desmond, Acumen, 2008
The Cynics, Ed. R. Bracht Branham and Marie-Odile Goulet Caze, University of California Press, 1996
Meditations, Marcus Aurelius, Penguin, 1964
Nietzsche, *The Will to Power*, Vintage Books, 1968
Nietzsche, *Human All Too Human*, C.U.P., 1986
Nietzsche, *Writings from the Late Notebooks*, Ed. Rüdiger Bittner, C.U.P., 2003
Asceticism in the Graeco-Roman World, Richard Finn Op, C.U.P., 2010
Jocelin of Brakelond: Chronicle of the Abbey of Bury St,Edmunds, O.U.P., 1989
St.Anthony of the Desert, [251-356], St.Athanasius, Tan Books and Publishers, 1995
Cynics, Paul and the Pauline Churches, F.Gerald Downing, Routledge, 1998
The Greeks on Pleasure, J.C.B. Gosling and C.C.W.Taylor, Clarendon Press, 1982/1984

On Psychology

Sacher-Masoch: An Interpretation, Gilles Deleuze, *With Venus in Furs*, Faber 1971
Masochism in Sex and Society, Theodore Reik, Grove Press, 1962

The Classics

Epictetus, *Discourses*, Two Vols., Loeb, 1928
Epictetus, *The Discourses: The Handbook and Fragments*, Everyman, Dent 1995
Xenophon, *Memorabilia, Oeconomicus, Symposium, Apology*, Loeb, Vol. 4, MCMLXXIX
Xenophon, *The Persian Expedition*, Penguin, 1949
Xenophon, *Conversations of Socrates*, Penguin, 1990

Xenophon, *A History of My Times*, Penguin, 1966
Xenophon, J.K. Anderson, Duckworth, 1974
Lucian, Selected Dialogues, O.U.P., 2005
Lucian, Vol. 1, Loeb, 1913
Lucian, *Satirical Sketches*, Penguin, 1961
Gertrude Bell, *Amurath to Amurath*, Gorgias Press, 2002
Philostratus, *The Life of Apollonius of Tyana*, Three Vols., Loeb, 1912
Philostratus, *Life of Apollonius*, Penguin, 1970
Plutarch On Sparta, Penguin, 1988
Marcus Aurelius Antoninus, George Long, George Bell & Sons, 1898
Marcus Aurelius, Loeb, 1916
Unruly Eloquence: Lucian and the Comedy of Traditions, R.Bracht Branham, Harvard University Press, 1989
The Sea! The Sea! Tim Rood, Duckworth, 2006
Dio Chrysostom – Politics, Letters, and Philosophy, Ed,Simon Swain, O,U,P, 2000
Xenophon, *Anabasis*, Loeb, 1989
Lucian, *Chattering Courtesans and Other Sardonic Sketches*, Penguin, 2004
Diogenes Laertius, *Lives of Eminent Philosophers*, Loeb, 1925/2006, 2 Vols.,
Courtesans and Fishcakes, James Davidson, Fontana, 1998

Miscellaneous
Gertrude Bell, H.V.F.Winstone, Cape, 1978
Catalogue of Rubbings of Brasses and Incised Slabs, Muriel Clayton, Victoria and Albert Museum, H.M.S.O., 1915/1979
The Greek Anthology and other Ancient Epigrams: A selection in modern verse translations, Peter Jay, Penguin, 1981
Amurath to Amurath: A Journey along the banks of the Euphrates, Gertrude Lowthian Bell, Gorgias Press, 2002
Reactionary Modernism: Technology, Culture, and Politics in Weimar and the Third Reich, Jeffery Herf, C.U.P.,1986
Steel Chariots in the Desert, S.C.Rolls, Rolls-Royce Enthusiasts' Club, 1988
Safety Last, Col. W.F.Stirling, Hollis and Carter,1954
Marguerite Yourcenar, Inventing a Life, Josyane Savigneau, University of Chicago Press, 1993
Greenmantle, John Buchan, O.U.P., 1993
Nomad, Ayaan Hirsi Ali, Simon and Shuster 2010

Index

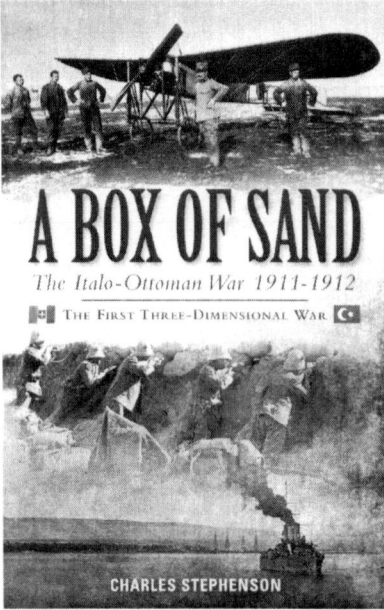

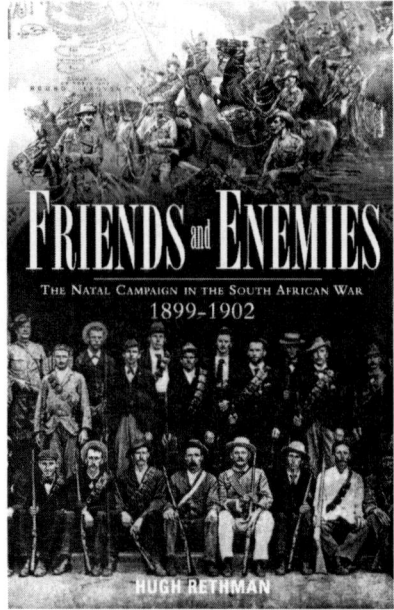

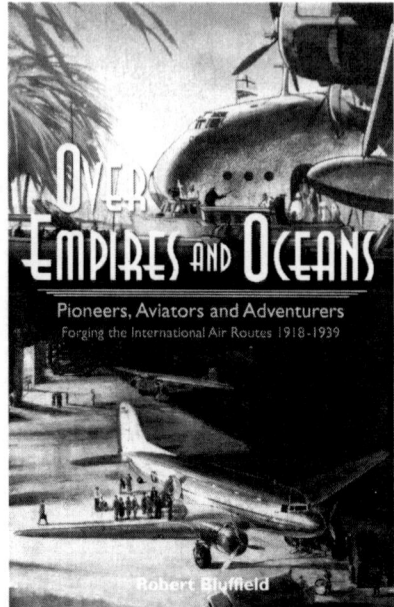